The Bataille Reader

Edited by

Fred Botting and Scott Wilson

BLACKWELL
Publishers

Copyright © Blackwell Publishers Ltd, 1997
Introduction, apparatus, selection and arrangement copyright © Fred Botting and Scott
  Wilson 1997

First published 1997

2 4 6 8 10 9 7 5 3 1

Blackwell Publishers Ltd
108 Cowley Road
Oxford OX4 1JF
UK

Blackwell Publishers Inc.
350 Main Street
Malden, MA 02148
USA

British Library Cataloguing in Publication Data

A CIP catalogue record for this book is available from the
British Library.

Library of Congress Cataloging in Publication Data
Bataille, Georges, 1897–1962.
   [Selections. English. 1997]
   The Bataille reader / edited by Fred Botting and Scott Wilson.
     p.   cm. — (Blackwell readers)
   Includes bibliographical references and index.
   ISBN 0-631-19958-6 (hc : alk. paper). — ISBN 0-631-19959-4 (pbk.
: alk. paper)
   1. Philosophy. 2. Criticism. I. Botting, Fred. II. Wilson,
Scott, 1962– . III. Title. IV. Series.
B2430.B3395B38213   1997
848′.91209—dc21   96-51520
                                                                 CIP

Typeset in 10 on 12 pt Plantin
by Best-set Typesetter Ltd., Hong Kong
Printed in Great Britain by TJ International Ltd, Padstow, Cornwall

This book is printed on acid-free paper

Contents

Acknowledgements

The editors and publishers wish to thank the following for permission to use copyright material:

Georges Borchardt, Inc. for Georges Bataille, 'On Nietzsche: The Will to Chance', v. 6, pp. 46–57; 'Program (Relative to *Acéphale*)', v. 2, p. 79; 'Un-knowing and its Consequences', v. 8, pp. 86–8; and 'Autobiographical Note', v. 8, pp. 107–10 from *October* 36 (1986); copyright © by Editions Gallimard. Marion Boyars Publishers Ltd. for Georges Bataille, '*Madame Edwarda*' from *My Mother, Madame Edwarda, The Dead Man*, trans. Austryn Wainhouse (1989) pp. 137–59, copyright © *Madame Edwarda* 1956 by Jean-Jacques Pauvert; translation copyright © 1989 Marion Boyars Publishers. City Lights Publishers for Georges Bataille, *The Impossible*, trans. Robert Hurley (1991) pp. 147–64, copyright © by Les Editions de Minuit; translation copyright © 1991 by City Lights Books. The Litho Shop, Inc. for Georges Bataille, *Guilty*, trans. Bruce Boone, intro. Denis Hollier (1988) The Lapis Press, pp. 69–86, 135–8, 139–41, copyright © 1961 Editions Gallimard; translation © 1988 by Bruce Boone. Paragon House for Georges Bataille, *On Nietzsche*, trans. Bruce Boone, intro. Sylvère Lotringer (1992) pp. 17–9, 68–71, 108–16, copyright © 1945 Editions Gallimard; translation copyright © 1992 by Paragon House. State University of New York Press and Editions Gallimard for Georges Bataille, 'The Torment' from *Inner Experience*, trans. and intro. Leslie Anne Boldt (1988) pp. 33–61, copyright © 1943 Editions Gallimard; translation © 1988 by State University of New York. Telos Press for Georges Bataille, 'The Psychological Structure of Fascism', trans. Carl R Lovett, *New German Critique*, 16 (1979) pp. 64–87. University of Minnesota Press for Georges Bataille, 'Base Materialism and Gnosticism', 'The Use-Value of D A F de Sade' and 'The Notion of Expenditure' from *Visions of Excess: Selected Writings 1927–39*, trans. Allan Stoekl, with Carl R Lovitt and Donald M Leslie, Jr. (1985), pp. 45–52, 91–102, 116–29, copyright © 1970 Editions Gallimard; translation copyright © 1993 by the University of Minnesota; and Georges Bataille, 'Letter to X' from *The College of Sociology 1937–39*, trans. Betsy Wing, intro. Denis Hollier (1988) pp. 89–93, copyright © 1979 by Editions Gallimard; translation copyright © by the University of Minnesota. Yale French Studies for Georges Bataille, 'Hegel, Death, and Sacrifice', trans. Jonathan Strauss, *Yale French Studies*, 78 (1990) pp. 9–28, copyright © 1990 Yale French Studies. Zone Books for Georges Bataille, *The Accursed Share*, vol. I, trans. Robert Hurley (1988), pp. 19–41, 63–77, copyright © 1988 by Urzone, Inc; Georges Bataille, *The Accursed Share*, vol. II, trans. Robert Hurley (1991) pp. 13–8, 79–86, 89–94, 95–101, 103–19, 187–91, copyright © 1991 by Urzone, Inc; Georges Bataille, *The Accursed Share*, vol. III, trans. Robert Hurley (1991) pp. 197–211, 213–23, copyright © 1991 by Urzone, Inc; and Georges Bataille, *The Theory of Religion*, trans. Robert Hurley (1989) pp. 43–61, 109–11, copyright © 1989 by Urzone, Inc.

Every effort has been made to trace the copyright holders, but if any have been inadvertently overlooked the publishers will be pleased to make the necessary arrangement at the first opportunity.

Introduction: From Experience to Economy

The Experience of Reading Bataille

'I read the first chapter and felt violently ill.' A colleague returns *On Nietzsche*. Unread, or read to the limit of tolerance, Bataille's text has nevertheless succeeded in throwing up a 'Bataillean' response. Experiences of nausea, sickness, pain, anguish are among the range of extreme states that concern Bataille precisely to the degree that they are uncontrollable, in so far as they shatter the composed rationality of the isolated individual. In this way, such experiences open on to a mode of communication that exceeds language. Communication, for Bataille, requires 'a being suspended in the beyond of oneself, at the limit of nothingness'.[1]

As reluctant and unappetizing as such an entry into communication with a text may be, the involuntary voidance of one reader amply testifies to the disruptive force of Bataille's writing. While the present reader may judge for him or herself, however, there would appear to be nothing in this chapter from *On Nietzsche*, notwithstanding the crucifixion of Christ, that is obviously disgusting at the level of objects represented. Rather, it is perhaps the way that Bataille's writing actively contests systematic codes of academic inscription and takes thought to the limits of comprehension. It is possible that this writing, which attempts to push understanding and empathy to a vertiginous summit, produces the reaction that bypasses or exceeds intellectual appraisal, leaping from reading to feeling in a violent movement that manifests an extreme subjective and corporeal disturbance.

The idea of someone throwing up all over one of Bataille's texts is also quite funny, of course. Laughter is frequently a response to repugnance, or to the discomfort of others. As Bataille notes in the Preface to *Madame Edwarda*, 'laughter is the sign of aversion, of horror' (p. 224). But equally frequently, laughter is a defence mechanism, warding off the horror: 'it is indeed in laughter that we find the justification for a form of castigation, of obloquy' (p. 224). It is quite possible that, in their subjective extremity and their intense seriousness about uncomfortable topics, Bataille's own texts may be subject to laughter, particularly to the derisory mirth of a comfortable Anglo-American pragmatic or utilitarian scepticism. But this would be to miss completely the importance of Bataille's thought – and Bataille's laughter:

> What the hearty laugh screens us from, what fetches up the bawdy jest, is the identity that exists between the utmost in pleasure and the utmost in pain: the identity between being and non-being, between the living and the death-stricken being, between the knowledge which brings one before this dazzling realization and definitive, concluding darkness . . . our laughter here is absolute, going far beyond scorning ridicule of something which may perhaps be repugnant, but disgust for which digs deep under our skin . . . the sight of blood, the odour of vomit, which arouse in us the dread of death, sometimes introduce us into a nauseous state ·which hurts more cruelly than pain. (p. 225)

That which is revolting, shocking, that which disarms predictable patterns of thinking and feeling, that which lies at the unhallowed extremes and unavowed interstices of social, philosophical or theoretical frameworks, are the objects of Bataille's fascination. Encounters with horror, violent disgust, that miraculously transform into experiences of laughter, intoxication, ecstasy, constitute, for Bataille, inner experiences that overwhelm any sense of the distinction between interiority or exteriority. At the limit of knowledge, un-knowing is activated, a process in which subjectivity is torn apart, unworked at the core of physical and mental being.

Bataille's writing strains to evoke such experiences, pushing language to its very limits, seeking the impossible in its refusal to remain contained within discourses predicated on sense, usefulness, responsibility, productivity and positivity. To feel violently ill at the encounter of such writing is perfectly natural in that the 'unnaturalness' of nature is disclosed as uncomfortable and horrifying in its negativity: the homogeneous subject of culture retches in a movement of negation that never quite expends or transcends the force of heterogeneity in which she or he must imminently dissolve. Reading exceeds the economy of ideas and meanings in which subject and addressee exchange sense and knowledge; the gift of writing cannot be returned or contained in such a restricted fashion: what arrives is a contestation of and challenge to modes of thinking, an expenditure of signification which consumes existing modes of commodification and exchange, laying waste to them in a wasteful presentation of the waste that is their own.

Bataille's Dés-oeuvre

To write about 'Bataille' presupposes an authorial presence at the origin of the numerous writings collected under that name. There is, however, a considerable problem in categorizing and classifying texts whose subject, in the dual sense of author and topic, is at once so diverse and singular. Bataille's texts could be subdivided under numerous disciplinary categories: literature, criticism, philosophy, art history, numismatics, history, anthropology, economy, sociology, eroticism, (a)theology among others. While contesting and transgressing the boundaries and styles of different disciplines, Bataille nonetheless addresses, with rigour and consistency, the sacred elementals of erotic, mystical and economic activity so that his writing has been said, by Jean Baudrillard, to constitute 'a single mythic thought'.[2] For Roland Barthes, Bataille exemplifies the excessive object called 'Text':

> the Text does not stop at (good) Literature; it cannot be contained in a hierarchy, even in a simple division of genres. What constitutes the Text is, on the contrary (or precisely), its subversive force in respect of the old classifications. How do you classify a writer like Georges Bataille? Novelist, poet, essayist, economist, philosopher, mystic? The answer is so difficult that the literary manuals generally prefer to forget about Bataille who, in fact, wrote texts, perhaps continuously one single text.[3]

A single text need not imply a single, or singular, author, or even that 'author-function' which establishes and engenders a new discursive practice.[4] Bataille corresponds to the model of neither the solitary Romantic visionary nor the father-founder of a tradition of thought like Freud or Marx. Evoking something irreducible to sense or meaning, Bataille's writing refuses the form and securities of discourse. Disavowing all privileges, all teleology, Bataille's writing 'maintains lack', producing 'a hole where totality becomes incomplete'; his writing marks 'the appearance in discourse form of that incompletion that form used to reject, the indestructible but always repressed bond of desire and of "its" dissatisfaction. Perhaps Bataille's work gets its greatest strength in this refusal of the temptation of form.'[5] To write *on* Bataille thus attempts to fill the hole and complete the incompletion, to arrest the movement of desire in the appropriation of the text.

The writing of Bataille must exceed or, as Jean-Luc Nancy puts it, 'exscribe' commentary:

> what matters, what thinks (at the very limit of thought if necessary) is what does not lend itself wholly to a univocal meaning and throws it off balance. Bataille never stops exposing this. Alongside all the themes he deals with, through all the questions and debates, 'Bataille' is *nothing but* a protest against the signification of his own discourse.

> If he is to be read, if reading rebels straight away against the commentary which it is, and against the understanding which it ought to be, we have to read in every line the work of the play of writing *against* meaning.[6]

Writing against meaning, the 'nothing but' of Bataille's protest discloses the movement of negativity and contestation. 'Bataille' thus paradoxically signifies authorial absence. The proper name appropriately discloses the combative 'variance' of the writing, but in a guise that refuses to deliver a retroactively imagined being behind the work, a phantasmatic past presence: it foregrounds instead the very movement of writing itself, fanning the flames of discourse, 'burning, consuming meaning'.[7]

Jacques Derrida locates two forms of writing in Bataille's texts, minor 'signicative discourse' and major sovereign expenditure. The latter '*exceeds* the *logos* of meaning, lordship, presence etc.', precipitating philosophical concepts towards ruin: 'Bataille's writing thus relates all semantemes, that is philosophemes, to the sovereign operation, to the consummation, without return, of meaning. It draws upon, in order to exhaust it, the resource of meaning. With minute audacity, it will acknowledge the rule which constitutes that which it efficaciously, economically, must deconstitute.'[8] By raising the stakes to the highest pitch, writing opens on to a general economy, exposing a communication that no longer informs, a communication attenuating a community whose existence and function bear little relation to the bounded circuits of linguistic and cultural exchange. The singular texts of Bataille, claims Maurice Blanchot, whose friendship with Bataille began in late 1940, were 'but the aborted prelude of the exigency of writing. It is diurnal communication: it doubles as nocturnal communication . . . or the notes of a tormented Journal.'[9] This is communication not in the daily sense of meaning's delivery, but one 'which does not avow itself, which antedates itself and its authority only from a non-existing author, [and thereby] opens up another form of community'.[10] For Blanchot this community is 'unavowable'; for Nancy, it is 'inoperative' [*désoeuvrée*]. In this light, it may be advisable to speak not of the work, or *oeuvre*, of Georges Bataille, but of the unworking performed by his writing in and against all discourse: it is not an *oeuvre* but a *désoeuvre*, in the sense that its negativity is unemployed, in the service of nothing and no one, inoperative in respect of specified and useful goals.

Communication and Community

In the years leading up to the Second World War, Bataille was involved in various mainstream political and cultural organizations as well as more unconventional groupings.[11] The commitment can be plotted by the journals and reviews he helped establish or to which he contributed. The range of essays produced by Bataille in the 1920s and 1930s display the active engagement of a medievalist librarian from the Bibliothèque Nationale in the currents of a volatile period of French intellectual and political life. An early involvement with surrealism in the 1920s led to its rejection and the pursuit of a different intellectual and critical course that took its bearings from Hegel, Marx and Nietzsche. Bataille's criticisms of surrealist idealism and hygienic rationalism provoked a virulent response by André Breton in the Second Surrealist Manifesto.[12] The 'mutual hostility', as Bataille describes it, earns him specific denunciation in the Manifesto's attack on ex-surrealists (p. 114).

In the essay 'The use-value of D. A. F. de Sade', Bataille addresses 'an open letter to my current comrades' in the surrealist movement only to sever Sade from his surrealist, literary admirers and reconceptualize a Marquis with implications for an understanding of social and political economy. Given the unlikelihood of this 'open letter', dating from the beginning of 1930, being received with much understanding or sympathy by either the surrealist or the anti-Stalinist Marxists of the review *La Critique sociale*, it is unsurprising that it remained unpublished in his lifetime. The essay, drawing from the sociology of Weber and Durkheim, provides a striking combination of religion and economy that overturns the assumptions of both.[13] Bataille's interest in the intimate connection between the sacred and profane, between waste and luxury, between filth, beauty and eroticism, the attraction of what Bataille calls 'heterology', placed him at odds with the political positions of the time and anticipates the innovative studies combining sociology, political economy and religious philosophy that Bataille continued to write throughout the 1930s.

After co-editing the *Documents* miscellany in the early 1930s, Bataille contributed to *La Critique sociale*, a journal associated with the Democratic Communist Circle. This was followed by the setting up of the anti-fascist *Contre Attaque* (Counterattack) group with Breton in 1935 (Breton departed in 1936, throwing accusations of 'sur-fascism'). This group gathered together politically committed intellectuals at the time of the Popular Front's socialist–communist alliance. *Acéphale* followed, a sporadic review and supposedly secret society that included, among others, Pierre Klossowski, Jean Wahl and André Masson. With these political groupings Marx cedes to Nietzsche in their interrogations of forms and practices of archaic, mythical and tribal models of community. *Acéphale* continued to appear until 1939, and in 1937 Bataille set up the Collège de sociologie, which embraced a wider, more prominent association of disaffected intellectuals including Michel Leiris, Roger Caillois, Pierre Klossowski and Alexandre Kojève. It was also attended by Claude Levi-Strauss, Jean-Paul Sartre and Walter Benjamin.

The College of Sociology extended the theoretical interests of *Acéphale*.

Denis Hollier describes the project of the College as one of 'depoliticizing collective experience', a critique of the 'monopolization of community by the political'.[14] Initially in texts by Bataille, Michel Leiris and Roger Caillois, the College addressed the question of the sacred and the totality of human existence, developing a notion of community that attempted to resist its co-option by various governments and social movements. The 1930s were supremely the time when certain notions of community based on some essence, idea or project, be it organic nature, racial purity, the Fatherland, the body of Christ or the dignity of labour, were being employed as the goal and guarantee of liberal democratic, socialist and national socialist repressions. Beyond the individuating and depersonalizing effects of the homogeneous social order lies the realm of ritual, festival and artistic, mystical and religious experience. Against democracy's limitations, the College's lectures, delivered in regular open sessions, raised the question of human wholeness and communal vitality, often in its darkest forms. The sociology of the College, as described in the note on its foundation which appeared in *Acéphale*, was concerned with sacred forms beyond the limits of scientific enquiry: 'sacred sociology', Bataille and Caillois state, investigates all human activities, the 'entire communifying movement of society'.[15]

The notion of community, the object of the College's lectures, corresponds to the modes of communication and community reached in the experience of the extreme states to which Bataille was already being drawn. In one of the pieces inaugurating the College, Bataille contrasts the determined action, servility and usefulness of democratic societies with the total movement in which life plays and risks itself. The movement of communication allies itself with the precipitation towards communitarian existence. It involves, however, an inapprehensible energy rather than a restricted, and thus servile, framework. Like the College itself, the community must serve no master, no minister, no Führer: it must be headless. As Hollier notes, the College had no single voice, topic or programme, but many, often conflicting voices: its 'structure', more like a 'collage', was acephalic, headless.

Bataille's earlier 'Programme (relative to *Acéphale*)' offers a glimpse of the impossible totality addressed by the sacred sociology of the community. The excessive and radical nature of Bataille's programme suggests why disagreements about its direction caused the subsequent disbanding of the group. Through proposing the 'decomposition' of all communities, the forms of community that arise within bourgeois economic and social systems, Bataille establishes an impossible goal, the affirmation of a non-realizable and distinctly non-utilitarian 'universal community'. The programme eviscerates the idea of community, in its everyday sense, and displays the crime, aggression and violence within communal structures, noting their importance as values within an acephalic universe of energies without direction, a play of forces in excess of bounded states or defined duty. The values that the programme advances are thus shown to be heterogeneous to community even as they provide points of cohesion as sacred, unifying principles. The acephalic affirmation of (impossible) community emanates from a Nietzschean current of thought in which value is transvalued, overcoming the subordination of the opposition between good and evil.

Bataille's movement beyond conventional ideas of good and evil does not, however, involve the sort of transvaluation that leads to a sur-value or surplus value, nor to a pristine, purely self-affirming value born of an absolute forgetting. Rather, Bataille's notion of value retains a fundamental ambivalence in which good and evil are inseparable, a value apprehended only in anguish. In *On Nietzsche*, for example, Bataille discusses the sublimity of the crucified Christ whose broken and tormented body occupies a place at the summit of morality. This summit, however, is heterogeneous. It does not disclose goodness, but an 'excess', an 'exuberance of forces', 'measureless expenditures of energy' and 'a violation of the integrity of individual beings': 'it is thus closer to evil than to good' (p. 92). The difference between good and evil is developed further in *Literature and Evil*: good is associated with rules, tied to the function of homogeneity; evil is a value that demands excess, of going 'as far as possible'.[16] Evil bursts out from the headless summit of morality, a volcanic eruption of energies without limit: the access to an 'acephalic universe'.

The force of expenditure associated with evil remains integral to the modes of communication and 'inner experience' developed in Bataille's *somme atheologique*, a radical inversion of St Thomas Aquinas's *Somme theologique*, in which the summit of religious experience is interrogated and evaporated. The prefix 'a', which evacuates theology while retaining something of religious, poetic or mystical experience, denotes the headlessness of both the summit and the subject of inner experience, and marks the place of loss, the enormity of which tears a hole that opens up being to the communication that unites beings. The texts published under the titles of *Guilty*, *Inner Experience* and *On Nietzsche*, produced during the Second World War, were written mainly in notebook form during Bataille's solitary wanderings in Vichy France after tuberculosis had caused him to leave his post at the Bibliothèque Nationale. They are difficult texts to categorize:

> *Guilty* isn't actually a book, and if it's a collection of notes jotted from day to day, it isn't what is conventionally known as a journal either. Rather, it's an experimental document: a record of involvement, or of meditation and illumination practices, as these devolved in the confines of non-religious mysticism, and of various meditation techniques

– a registering and rapid transcribing, while they are taking place, of experiences whose waves or turbulence Bataille felt in the course of the war years.[17]

The other two, one concerned with an experience the 'interior' nature of which becomes questionable, and the other 'on' Nietzsche in the loosest of senses, follow a similar pattern of intense fragmentary accounts of experience within an ongoing series of philosophical and quasi-mystical speculations.

Nietzsche's importance to these texts is evident in three main respects: in its contestation of religion and morality, in its articulation of an 'extreme, unconditional human yearning' independent of moral goals or of serving God (p. 331) and in its opening out of the 'inner world' of the subject. In these texts, the 'phenomenality of the inner world', as Nietzsche put it, 'is governed by just the same forms and procedures as the "outer world"', a world in which the causal relation between thoughts, feelings, desires and perceptions is both hidden and elusive, where boundaries between interior and external realms are ultimately indeterminate.[18] As Nietzsche writes in *Will to Power*, ' "Inner experience" enters our consciousness only after it has found a language the individual understands – i.e., a translation of a condition into conditions familiar to him.'[19] However, for Bataille, the 'inner experience' precisely denotes the *opening out* into an unbearably unfamiliar or foreign condition exterior to the comforts and defences of consciousness. The writing of 'inner experience' describes that movement beyond the attainment, in meditation or ecstasy, of a knowing summit of experience and into an abyss of un-knowing or non-knowledge. Inner experience describes an anguished tearing of individual experience and existence from within and without itself, an encounter with forces at the extreme limit of possibility.

Further, the torment that such an inner experience implies can become the impossible object of meditation effecting similar states in the subject, dissolving the distinctions between the two. For example, in *Inner Experience* Christ's torment is seen to surpass the very summit of religious order, God. The Christian's love for Christ as the 'totality of being' draws him or her towards an inescapable torment: 'this is the torment which exceeds him, which exceeds God himself – God, who is no less man and tormentable than him' (p. 81). In *On Nietzsche* it is Christ's agony on the Cross, the lacerating, wounding experience that establishes (Christian) fellowship under God, that leads to a different form of communication. Individual integrity is torn apart and, by means of guilt, humans communicate, discovering a bond that holds them together. In a line of argument which resembles the primordial act of crime that Freud describes in *Totem and Taboo*, the evil of crucifixion establishes community and communication, taking individual being, in the moment of risk, pain and shame, beyond itself.

Community is founded in the act of killing, in the rupturing of separate existence. But the rules and taboos that are established as a result reactivate the excessive impulse of evil to break all constraints: in the Preface to *On Nietzsche*, evil continually drives towards a completeness, a freedom beyond the limit imposed by taboos. Evil is tied to the question of the 'whole man', a reaching towards the totality of existence, the exuberance of life-forces in which 'consciousness requires my relation to the immense, comic, playful convulsion which is that of all men' (p. 338). Bataille notes the absurdity and frivolity of the project, but therein accedes to something other than sense, rationality, teleology or usefulness. With laughter, as in ecstasy or intoxication, the expenditure of energies, the affirmation of the value of evil, tends towards the inner experience at the silent, anguished heart of communication.

In later works like *Literature and Evil* and the posthumously published *The Impossible*, poetry comes close to communication in its relation to evil. Its proximity, however, is also a cause of hatred in that it only represents what is crucial in the experience of communication. Broaching a leap beyond the givens of law and nature, poetry involves 'the simple evocation through words of inaccessible possibilities', opening 'the night to desire's excess', revealing 'a power of the unknown'. Poetry is, then, a 'middle term', since it 'conceals the known within the unknown: it is the unknown painted in blinding colours, in the image of the sun' (p. 112). In a much earlier essay of the 1930s, Bataille had already linked the dark radiance of poetry to sacrificial forms of expenditure, 'creation by means of loss' (p. 171). It occupies the heterogeneous place once accorded religion, and also suffers the same fate. From being a mode of sacrificial expenditure, exposing the heterogeneous realm through the energy of loss, it becomes a form of appropriation, returning to the world with 'any one of a number of aesthetic homogeneities' (p. 153). Poetry's escape, its excess, follows an Icarian path: it drives upwards in a transgressive trajectory only to reach its limits and fall. Hence the ambivalent role of the arts in relation to 'extreme states of being':

> Literature (fiction) took the place of what had formerly been the spiritual life; poetry (the disorder of words) that of real states of trance. Art constituted a small free domain, outside action: to gain freedom it had to renounce the real world. This is a heavy price to pay, and most writers dream of recovering that lost reality. They must then pay in another sense, by renouncing freedom in the service of propaganda. The artist who restricts himself to fiction knows that he is not a whole man, but the same is true of the writer of propaganda.

The domain of the arts does, in a sense, embrace totality, which nevertheless escapes it. (p. 340)

Poetry thus oscillates between sovereignty and servility, between a heterogeneous position of excessive undirected activity and a slavish existence replicating and representing rather than contesting the order of things.

Poetry is still included by Bataille among the forms of communication and 'inner experience' that in the bourgeois world it has come to replace. In *Guilty*, poetry along with sacrifice and laughter are opposed to the closed intellectual, political and economic systems governing human activity in general (p. 56). Poetry is linked to laughter in a process of questioning that goes 'hand in hand with expenditure or a consumption of surplus energy'; along with ecstasy, poetry opens on to a field of 'negative thought' (p. 57). Like laughter, the ecstatic quality of poetry does not simply link discrete beings in a convulsive movement and momentary loss of consciousness; the 'poetry' of inner experience opens communication up to something entirely other as a

> communication, through death, with our beyond (essentially in sacrifice) – not with nothingness, still less with a supernatural being, but with an indefinite reality (which I sometimes call *the impossible*, that is: what can't be grasped in any way, what we can't reach without dissolving ourselves, what's slavishly called God). If we need to we can define this reality (provisionally associating it with a finite element) at a higher (higher than the individual on the scale of composition of beings) social level as the sacred, God or created reality. Or else it can remain in an undefined state (in ordinary laughter, infinite laughter, or ecstasy in which the divine form melts like sugar in water). (p. 59)

This form of communication has the rupturing intensity of flames, electrical discharge, lightning (p. 60). Inner experience, and the communication it involves, takes individuated being to 'the extreme limit of the possible'. At this limit 'everything gives way' (p. 70). Non-knowledge bursts forth with the intensity of anguished ecstasy: 'NON-KNOWLEDGE LAYS BARE.' Non-knowledge, or un-knowing, is described as 'the knowledge of the absence of knowledge' (p. 323). In communicating ecstasy, inner experience induces torment and anguish, revealing the 'yawning gap' in which subject and object are dissolved. Communication exposes what Blanchot describes as an 'unavowable' sense of community:

> 'The Inner Experience' says the opposite of what it seems to say: it is a movement of contestation that, coming from the subject, devastates

it, but has as a deeper origin the relationship with the other which is community itself, a community that would be nothing if it did not open the one who exposes himself to it to the infiniteness of alterity, while at the same time deciding its inexorable finitude.[20]

Being circulates around a void that lies at its heart and limit, while the insufficiency that marks all beings establishes the constitutive apprehension of alterity that shapes community.

Eroticism

For Bataille, it is 'the identity of these perfect contraries, divine ecstasy and its opposite, extreme horror' that blows identity apart, unleashes experience from the 'prison' of anguish and establishes continuity with alterity: communication. This statement comes as the 'inevitable conclusion to a history of eroticism'. It is with eroticism that 'the contraries seem visibly conjoined, where the religious horror disclosed in sacrifice becomes linked to the abyss of eroticism'.[21] Two texts written in 1941 exemplify the link between horror and eroticism. 'The torment' from *Inner Experience*, already cited, is the companion to another text written in a different register, though one concerned, essentially, with the same experience. 'I wrote this slim volume in September and October 1941, just before 'Le Supplice' ['The torment'], which makes up the second part of *L'Expérience intérieure*. To my mind the two texts are closely interdependent and one cannot be understood without the other . . . I could not have written 'Le Supplice' if I had not first provided its lewd key.'[22] *Madame Edwarda* has been called by Maurice Blanchot, one of the first persons to read it during the worst days of the Occupation in 1941,[23] 'the most beautiful narrative of our time'.[24] This narrative, like 'The torment', makes the atheological connection between inner experience and eroticism in a horrifyingly literal way:

> She was seated, she held one long leg stuck up in the air, to open her crack yet wider she used her fingers to draw the folds of skin apart . . . 'Why', I stammered in a subdued tone, 'why are you doing that?' 'You can see for yourself', she said, 'I'm GOD'. (p. 229)

As an account of a visit to a brothel, the story is quite banal. The intensity of the experience, however, invests the encounter with the mystico-philosophical significance of 'eroticism', reversing the veiled pornographic flickerings of *erotica*. The difference Bataille suggests, in his Preface on the intentions of 'Pierre Angélique', pseudonymous author of *Madame*

Edwarda, lies in the unusual 'gravity' with which the matter of sexual life is treated, as opposed to the customary 'making light' of it (p. 223). In eroticism the object of desire radiates with a nocturnal brilliance that reduces the subject to nothing but the infinite movement of desire itself. In the ecstatic movement beyond individual experience, a movement of consumption by an unattainable, impossible object of desire, the hero, as religious ingenu, comes to understand the truth of Madame Edwarda's revelation: she is God, but 'GOD figured as a public whore and gone crazy – that, viewed through the optic of "philosophy", makes no sense at all' (p. 233). The non-sense of the un-knowing that manifests itself in poetic intoxication, laughter's expenditure, or ecstasy's flight, also drives eroticism, dissociating it from the impulses of natural animality or sexuality. 'Eroticism, unlike simple sexual activity is a psychological quest independent of the natural goal.'[25] Located in a psychological or psychoanalytical domain, eroticism constitutes one of those experiences in which the fundamental form of the human is brought into question.

For Bataille, it is woman that occupies the place where the object of desire exceeds both objectivity and subjectivity with a glimpse of an unknown infinity. That this is so is no doubt an effect of a particular cultural conjuncture: 'a new representation of woman was emerging at the center of the intellectual epic of the interwar years', Elisabeth Roudinesco argues. This representation, for the surrealists, took the shape of the female criminal. For psychoanalysis it was the 'female ecstatic' (as represented in Bernini's statue of the *Ecstasy of Saint Teresa*), culminating with Madame Edwarda herself, 'a triumphant madwoman, capable of inscribing the name of God on the "rags" hanging from her scarlet sex'.[26] Woman, in godless modernity, assumes the intermediary function of a discredited priesthood, the impossible object between finite being and infinity that guarantees sacred excess. Woman's proximity to the divine is manifested in her *jouissance*:

> Edwarda's pleasure – fountain of boiling water, heartbursting furious tideflow – went on and on, weirdly, unendlingly; that stream of luxury, its strident inflexion, glorified her being unceasingly, made her nakedness unceasingly more naked, her lewdness ever more intimate. Her body, her face swept in ecstasy were abandoned to the unspeakbale coursing and ebbing, in her sweetness there hovered a crooked smile: she saw me to the bottom of my dryness, from the bottom of my desolation I sensed her joy's torrent run free. My anguish resisted the pleasure I ought to have sought. Edwarda's pain-wrung pleasure filled me with an exhausting impression of bearing witness to a miracle. (p. 235)

Eroticism describes the joys, anguish and pain of an encounter with divine totality, the eruptive, exuberant continuity of things. Woman embodies the very totality and surplus of existence; a fluid movement beyond bodily constraints peals with a joy repeating 'encore'; her god-like gaze penetrates the emptiness of male subjectivity immobilized, transfixed, torn apart in its own horrified encounter with a hole within and a joy beyond itself.[27] Eroticism, then, for both male and female subjects, but in different ways, connotes a tearing, an opening on to something entirely other, the abjection of being before an experience which appears sovereign.

In volume II of *The Accursed Share*, eroticism is discussed in relation to the central Bataillean notion of the 'general economy', given its emergence as an effect of cultural systems of rejection, prohibition and taboo. The 'inner experience' of eroticism is, of course, bound up with the transgression that defines both the limit of human systems of productivity and the place of the particular being in relation to them. Where culture recoils in horror from death, decay, filth and sexuality, it restores its homogeneous limits and binds individuals to its service. Eroticism's transgression of boundaries turns, thereby, on abjected forms of existence, animal, sexual and taboo, 'leaping into the unknown, with animality as its impetus' (p. 251). From such expenditure of natural energies, in its embrace of the rejected, profane world, eroticism paradoxically accedes to the sphere of the sacred, negating nature, precisely through its adoration of the base corporeality of the flesh. Hence the erotic attraction of limits and taboos, the dreadful apprehension of death, producing the 'inner experience' which 'places us before a nauseating void':

A void in the face of which our being is a plenum, threatened with losing its plenitude, both desiring and fearing to lose it. As if the consciousness of plenitude demanded a state of uncertainty, of suspension. As if being itself were this exploration of all possibility, always going to the extreme and always hazardous. And so, to such stubborn defiance of impossibility, to such full desire for emptiness, there is no end but the definitive emptiness of death. (p. 257)

Eroticism is thus a form of expenditure which goes beyond use-value: it does not conserve energy but discharges it, consuming it in the act of using it and thereby destroying it: 'erotic activity always takes place at the expense of the forces committed to their combat' (p. 273). It displays the accession to divine chance in that it risks everything. In eroticism the poles of life and death, being and nothingness, fullness and emptiness are one, dissolved like subject and object in the insensible totality of things. This is why desire exceeds any particular object: directed instead at the ungraspable, impossible reality of 'inner experience' and the 'totality of being', it moves exorbitantly in search of the desirable. Desire without object.

Negativity

Eroticism contests being, negates nature. As in other modes of inner experience, it manifests a particular kind of negativity, one intimately connected to death. *Madame Edwarda* is prefaced with a quotation from Hegel: 'Death is the most terrible of all things; and to maintain its works is what requires the greatest of all strength' (p. 223). The work of death is the unworking, the destruction of every human trace. But death remains integral to experience insofar as that experience is human. Death completes the work of negativity, but in life death only constitutes an imaginary limit: an absolute master before whom living beings remain servile, unless, of course, they live up to the (un)workings of death and look it, and thus their mortal selves, in the face.

Hegel's 'philosophy of death' is addressed in 'Hegel, death and sacrifice', where the human destruction of nature enables the production of consciousness and the world of things. Death is central to the emergence of spirit and the operations of the dialectic, the negation that is negated and conserved in the movement of transcendence. Bataille argues that, even as humanity cuts itself off from simple bodily existence, a sacrifice of corporeal being to cultural individuality, the very act of sacrifice enacts a transformation that retains the negativity of death. Sacrifice makes humans human, transforming existence from one subordinated to need, useful production and discursively determined ends to one that is sovereign, serving nothing. Bataille's reading of Hegel began, according to Raymond Queneau, in 1929, and takes its principal bearings from the influential lectures of Alexandre Kojève. These lectures provided a forum for the growth of interest in Hegel in France after the First World War.[28] Kojève's *Introduction to the Reading of Hegel*, assembled from his lectures by Queneau, develops an interpretation of the master–slave dialectic in terms of the class struggle and desire. Animal desire provides some of the conditions for self-consciousness: desire negates, consumes or destroys its object, transforming it in the process of assimilating it, as in eating. In contrast, human desire is directed towards other desires in a struggle in which animal life is risked: another human being is fought in order to seek 'recognition' of oneself as a purely human value. The positions of master and slave are determined when one of the combatants refuses to risk everything, succumbs to the other and is put into service. The master, although autonomous, is recognized as master, but only, it transpires, by a slave. The master, left unsatisfied by the quality of the recognition he receives, has nothing to do but consume things produced by the slave. It is the slave who works, and in working discovers the power to transform nature and the slavish condition: the negativity of death that has been embraced by the master is subsequently put productively to work by the slave.[29]

Kojève translates the Hegelian myth into a Marxian reading of world history, supposing a Marxist resolution of the dialectic in which the redundancy of the bourgeois masters becomes more and more evident with the rise of the proletariat, who overcome, through work and revolutionary action, the existing bourgeois totality. In this movement, the end of history is realized. Kojève seemed to think that, with the establishment and industrialization of the Soviet Union in the 1930s, that endpoint had already arrived. It is at this point, however, that Bataille's questions about the negativity of Hegel and Kojève are seriously raised.

Bataille's 'Letter to X' addresses his concerns directly to Kojève. Bataille suggests that putting negativity to work does not exhaust its power in the positive outcome of the 'negation of the negation', the resolution Kojève imagines as the coming of revolutionary communism: 'if action ("doing") is – as Hegel says – negativity, the question arises as to whether the negativity of one who has "nothing more to do" disappears or remains in a state of "unemployed negativity"' (p. 296). Bataille inclines towards the latter. Something may be left over, an energy to be expended or consumed, a negativity in excess of work and directed action. This constitutes the dialectic's 'blind spot'. As Bataille wrote in *Inner Experience*:

> Action introduces the known (the manufactured); then understanding, which is linked to it, relates the non-manufactured, unknown elements, one after the other, to the known. But desire, poetry, laughter, unceasingly cause life to slip in the opposite direction, moving from the known to the unknown. Existence in the end discloses the blind spot of understanding and right away becomes completely absorbed in it. It could not be otherwise unless a possibility for rest were to present itself at a certain point. But nothing of the kind takes place: what alone remains is circular agitation – which does not exhaust itself in ecstasy and begins again from it.[30]

The dynamic momentum of negativity is neither contained in a productive system of thought nor expended in exhaustion. It remains at play in the 'double movement' of action and questioning or contestation, in which the one is endlessly opposed to the other in a continual 'rupturing and disequilibrium of the system' (p. 57). Thus 'inner experience is the opposite of action. Nothing more' (p. 76). In action, dependent on project and teleology, discursive thought defers existence and is led by reason; in questioning reason is taken to its limit, undoing its work. The putting to work of reason thus exposes it to the negativity it would conserve: its 'use-value' encounters the impossible, its consumption and destruction in use.

Economy

Within the notion of 'general economy' there is no separation between Bataille's explorations of 'inner experience' and his discursive analyses of social and economic processes; both forms of writing deal with different yet related modes of expenditure. Bataille's consideration of the distribution and consumption of energy, his awareness of the need for the loss or discharge of energy includes individual organisms in the context of both the totality of natural being and the systems and subjects of diverse social, cultural and economic formations. Jürgen Habermas, in an essay critical of the so-called irrationalism of Bataille's writing, suggests he 'seeks an economics of the total social ecology of drives'. The phrase appreciates the extent of Bataille's writings and the way that they regularly invoke a notion of 'totality', but Habermas seems to think that the goal of Bataille's general economy is to render this 'totality' homogeneous, to seek 'the stabilization of boundaries'. This is implied in the use of 'ecology', and his assumption that Bataille's concern is to 'explain why modernity continues its life-endangering expulsions and exclusions, and why hope in a dialectic of enlightenment . . . is in vain'.[31] In this way Bataille is seen to attempt to outflank 'the dialectic of enlightenment' though retain, fundamentally, its project. For all the proximity Bataille occasionally shows to Critical Theory, there remains something fundamentally alien to, or at odds with, dialectical thinking: the disclosure of a negativity that is unemployed.

'Totality', however, is repeatedly invoked in Bataille's discussions of the human and non-human universe. Inner experience, as he argues in the Preface to *On Nietzsche*, draws subjectivity beyond servile existence to the extremes where 'my totality in consciousness requires my relation to the immense, comic, painful convulsion which is that of all men' (p. 338), and further, to the 'affirmation in which *all of life* is revealed in consciousness' (p. 339). The totality of the 'whole man' is separated from 'the living mass' by political, social and economic systems and requires the 'total liberation, as he [Nietzsche] defined it, of human possibility, of all possibility' (p. 332). In political terms, suggested in the critique of fascism, the liberation implies a sacred convulsion 'which continues to pursue the emancipation of human lives' (p. 145). In eroticism, the embrace with the fatal or luxurious object opens on to 'the totality of the real' (p. 264). While these statements seem to imply a desire to identify a complete human and natural system, the aspiration of an unashamed humanism bolstered by the holism of an ecological imperative, the totality proposed always seems to slip away, lost to that ungraspable, indefinite reality called 'the impossible'. In *Méthode de méditation*, the short volume appended to the publication of *Inner Experience* as a 'continuation' of it, the experience in which subjectivity exceeds itself and encounters the impossible occurs at the moment of the vanishing of discursive reality, the reality lived and shaped by systems of culture.[32] Bataille's 'economics of the total social ecology of drives' is predicated on loss, on the disequilibrium of any system by forces which, within it, remain surplus to it. Totality is an impossible term; it remains irreducible to any system of knowledge, absolute spirit or completion (the end of history); it is the occasion of unemployed negativity, of sovereign energies without purpose or limit which perpetually break any totality imagined in philosophical or theoretical terms.

Philippe Sollers discounts the idea that Bataille's position involves a return to a 'mystified and mystifying Hegelianism', arguing that, though 'untenable', it 'questions dialectical materialism in a decisive manner, and in such a way as to rule out any return of this later to a humanistic ideology (which would be a swing back into petit-bourgeois ideology, into the worldwide apotheosis of the so-called scientific, simple-minded, comfortable, docile, shallow, petit-bourgeoisie)'.[33] Bataille explodes the humanistic concept of a fully integrated, rounded, self-consciously autonomous individual and the idea of a benevolent, ideal universe that is its mirror and support. Hollier, too, discussing Bataille's 'dualist materialism', finds no place for any humanistic or anthropocentric attitude. Anthropocentrism 'represses dehumanising and decentring excesses' which break out in a blind 'Dionysian surpassing of the theoretical (Apollonian) attitude'.[34] Homogeneous systems, human architectures, have at their apex something other, something in excess of the whole, a point of absence, loss and expenditure. The excess of the summit is paralleled by the formlessness at the base of holistic architectural foundation: the whole that is imagined thus finds itself consumed by excess, by the unthinkable expenditures of energy within and without any system; it cedes, as Hollier notes, to the 'cosmic *hole*'.

The significance of 'Base materialism and Gnosticism', a relatively early essay in the context of Bataille's writings, lies in the way it articulates the more experientially orientated writings of *somme atheologique* with the general economic concerns of *The Accursed Share*.[35] The essay first appeared in *Documents* in 1929, the review formed around a number of ex-surrealists that was devoted mainly to cultural and aesthetic issues. Michel Leiris, who, along with Bataille, had an editorial role, subsequently described it as a magazine 'made in his [Bataille's] image': 'a Janus publication turning one of its faces toward the higher spheres of culture (of which Bataille was willy-nilly a native through his vocation as well as training) and the other toward a wild place into which one ventured without any sort of geographical map or passport'.[36] To interrogate the highest, sacred extremes of culture also invokes, without ever even seeming to turn one's head in an opposite direction, an encounter with that which is most inaccessible, an uncharted wildness associated with the most base or profane of elements. The two are joined in the monstrous figure of 'base materialism': 'The severed ass's head of the acephalic personification of the sun undoubtedly represents, even if imperfectly, one of materialism's most virulent manifestations' (p. 161). At the head of cultural aspiration there is only the headlessness of an ass that is hideous and comic, Bataille states, but an ass that is also 'the most humanly virile' of beasts. At the summit, baseness. Headlessness, however, does not simply disclose the absence of an apex: beyond the summit is the figure of exuberant expenditure, the sun blazing its energy with absolute generosity. Bataille's essay, a critique of both idealism *and* materialism in its ontological and dialectical senses, discloses another force beyond the dualities that sustain human systems of thought. It turns to the Gnostic conception of matter 'as an *active* principle having its own eternal autonomous existence as darkness (which would not simply be the absence of light, but the monstrous *archontes* revealed by this absence), and as evil (which would not be the absence of good, but a creative action)' (p. 162). This is neither presence nor absence, but something monstrous in excess of opposition; neither good nor evil, but something truly, creatively evil of the kind manifested by Christ's suffering and the evil at the core of communication. The matter which is active, dark and evil, formless and deforming all modes of systematic knowledge, constitutes the extreme limit which confounds idealism and materialism:

> base matter is external and foreign to ideal human aspirations, and it refuses to allow itself to be reduced to the great ontological machines resulting from these aspirations. But the psychological process brought to light by Gnosticism had the same impact: it was a question of disconcerting the human spirit and idealism before something base, to the extent that one recognised the helplessness of superior principles. (p. 163)

Base matter introduces something other below the foundations and in excess of the idealizing imaginings of materialist knowledge. Not a 'thing' in the sense of the object-world, base matter affects subjects with an alien, insubordinate and disconcerting force, an exuberant, irrepressible expenditure of energy.

'Base matter', articulating the unknown point of dissipation for philosophical, material and psychological systems, offers itself as one term among many in the attempt to address, as 'heterology', 'the science of what is completely other' (p. 159). Economically, otherness emerges as that part of human activity which remains irreducible to systems of production and use. While productive social activity absorbs the bulk of living energy, there remain certain aspects that escape useful work (pp. 167–9). In the religious domain, alterity becomes the 'accursed share', the sacred and cursed part, which articulates a sacred realm with the utterly profane world of filth, sexuality and crime. Attenuating the sacred realm in acts of sacrifice, the ritual destruction of objects transforms them into values, destroying goods and resources for no good reason other than the glory of it. The sacrificial act is also sovereign in that it respects nothing, insubordinate, like base matter, to a world of use and exchange, thus transforming existence from a servile dependence upon commodities and systems predicated on need, necessity and utility. This sort of loss exemplifies, for Bataille, the general principle of expenditure. It takes place at an organic, individual and universal level, and within societies and economic systems: 'the excess must be spent' for the organism or system to grow (pp. 183–4). Excess energy is discharged, waste is expelled; the sun radiates, organisms excrete. In the burst of laughter, the body convulses and sense evaporates, the loss akin to that of sacrifice: 'we laugh at ourselves as other and at the other as ourselves, in this suspended instant in which we are at once ourselves *and* the other. In short: in which we *are*, period, laughing, and laughing at being.'[37] We lose ourselves; we are cast beyond a restricted and homogeneous system.

The complex, dynamic relations that Bataille's writings trace between individual experiences and cultural and economic systems suggest that there is, ultimately, no such thing as a self-contained, self-regulating system in the human or natural world. Every system requires something outside of itself in order to function and maintain itself: plants draw energy from the sun and minerals from the soil; animals eat, shit, fuck in acts of absorption and expulsion by which objects are destroyed or transformed, and energy is consumed and discharged. Societies work by the exclusion of useless, destructive 'anti-social' elements as much as by the utilitarian production and assimilation of accepted bodies and goods. Factories spew out effluent as well as saleable commodities. Thought comprehends, grasps, assimilates or criticizes, rejects and denies, explaining or explaining away in the service of a system of rules and principles. Culture, too, which superstructurally serves to integrate economic, social and individual requirements according to work and exchange, also produces things in excess of commodities or goods: values, while organizing groups according to particular precepts, lie outside, heterogeneous to the very system they homogenize.

With 'use-value' the contradiction or antagonism between use and value is displayed: to use something is to contravene the principle of conservation by which value is sustained; once used, value is no more. 'The use-value of D. A. F. de Sade' begins to develop general economic questions of consumption and expenditure according to an axis of appropriation and excre-

tion. In this essay the assimilable and the excremental articulate the operations of homogeneous forms of existence in relation to the heterogeneous,
sacred or profane modes. The 'static equilibrium' of homogeneity, though
prevalent, is continually threatened by heterogeneous impulses: eating, for
example, serves to regulate the system, but in excess can produce the
'physiological tumult' of gluttony and the vomiting that returns the system
to equilibrium (p. 151). Heterology addresses the violence and agitation of
sacred and profane excesses, but not to integrate it usefully within a system:
concerned with what is 'resolutely placed outside the reach of scientific
knowledge', it stands opposed to the appropriations of science and philosophy. The aim is neither to limit nor to assimilate the character of heterogeneous elements, not to return the other to system or stasis, but to follow the
disequilibrating energies toward an expression of 'the urges that today
require worldwide society's fiery and bloody Revolution.' The essay was
written in 1933.

Gifts and Sacrifice

The energy that Bataille invokes as a challenge to bourgeois capitalism's
troubled drive towards the homogenization of modern life is manifested
quite differently in other epochs and societies. As a historian of modes of
expenditure, Bataille drew not only on his background as a medievalist
librarian, but also on the work of the renowned anthropologist Marcel
Mauss, in particular his essay on the gift. Mauss' text provides numerous examples of a phenomenon called *potlatch* that occurred among pre-
capitalist tribes.[38] Foreign to western assumptions about rational modes of
production and exchange, potlatch describes the rules of a type of gift
giving in which expenditure is privileged over acquisition. Gift exchange
often involved an escalating series of highly prized commodities, drawing
tribal chiefs into a form of rivalry that was ruinous in that the gifts could be
neither refused nor returned. Bound up with festivals, potlatch, Bataille
contends,

> excludes all bargaining and, in general, it is constituted by a consid-
> erable gift of riches, offered openly with the goal of humiliating,
> defying, and *obligating* a rival. The exchange-value of the gift results
> from the fact that the donee, in order to efface the humiliation and
> respond to the challenge, must satisfy the obligation (incurred by him
> at the time of acceptance) to respond later with a more valuable gift,
> in other words, to return with interest. (p. 172)

This profitable aspect of gift exchange is noted by Bataille and compared to
the operations of banking and investment in bourgeois economies. Bataille,

however, stresses the role of loss and risk in the determination and escalation of gift exchange: they entail the sacrifice of a thing for a value in a move destroying material constraints in the interests of symbolic benefit. It affirms, precisely, that a value is not a thing. In some ways the mode of expenditure is akin to the master–slave dialectic, since goods, often those which ensure physical survival, are risked not for material benefit, but, as Bataille puts it, to gain prestige: they are a 'sign of glory', and thus their significance is detached from materiality and usefulness (p. 203). Abandoning real, material wealth in the interests of glory and prestige, the rivalry discloses the symbolic value of expenditure: '*Glory*, the consequence of superiority, is itself something different from an ability to take another's place and seize his possessions: it expresses a movement of senseless frenzy, of measureless expenditure of energy, which the fervour of combat presupposes' (p. 204). The struggle for prestige has no useful, rational or economic end other than that determined by potlatch itself: it is a 'game' entirely opposed to 'the principle of conservation': 'it puts an end to the stability of fortunes within the totemic economy, where possession was hereditary. An activity of excessive exchange replaced heredity (as a source of possession) with a kind of deliriously formed ritual poker. But players can never retire from the game . . .' Instead, they, and their possessions, remain '*at the mercy of the need for limitless loss*' (p. 174). In other forms, in which the squandering of riches and resources involves the wholesale destruction of goods, the principle of the consumption of surpluses is also dominant. The sun, which 'dispenses energy – wealth – without any return', constitutes the paradigmatic form of the gift, an expenditure which avoids stagnation and stasis by enabling a general process of growth (p. 189).

The ritual destruction of goods is linked by Bataille to forms of religious sacrifice as a mode of consumption: 'to sacrifice is not to kill but to relinquish and to give' (p. 213). There is a difference, however, in the quality of goods that are sacrificed or given: 'in general, sacrifice withdraws useful products from profane circulation; in principle the gifts of potlatch liberate objects that are useless from the start' (p. 208). Luxurious objects like jewels, limited in their usefulness, are already signs of rank and prestige, charged with the heterogeneous part of existence. Sacrifice – 'the production of *sacred* things' (p. 170) – invests objects, and the community as a whole, with value by negating materiality and animality. Hence the importance of death and the identification between sacrificers, the community and sacrificial objects or beings. The real, material world 'rejects the affirmation of intimate life, whose measureless violence is a danger to the stability of things, an affirmation that is fully revealed only in death'. Death 'discloses the imposture of reality', the reality of systems and rules, and reveals the heterogeneous, sacred part: 'life's intimacy does not reveal its dazzling consumption until the moment it gives out', inducing a 'keen awareness of shared life grasped in its intimacy' (p. 212). The sacrifice, in its social as well as religious function as part of a festival, is a kind of collective inner experience, a mode of communication which, through the violent injection of absence and loss, establishes the heterogeneous, unifying movement of community. In experiencing sacrifice's moment of horror and death, the intimacy of life emerges; in festivals it is a 'prodigious effervescence' that comes to the fore with the threat of violent eruptions. Festival

> constantly threatens to break the dikes, to confront productive activity with the precipitate and contagious movement of a purely glorious consumption. The sacred is exactly comparable to the flame that destroys the wood by consuming it. It is that opposite of a thing which an unlimited fire is; it spreads, it radiates heat and light, it suddenly inflames and blinds in turn. Sacrifice burns like the sun that slowly dies of the prodigious radiation whose brilliance our eyes cannot bear, but it is never isolated and, in a world of individuals, it calls for a general negation of individuals as such. (p. 215).

The negation transforms separate entities from things determined by labour and animal existence into beings participating in a general movement beyond individuals. The festival is a moment of communal excess in which the fact or materiality of community is less important than the emergence of its sacred dimension. Ultimately the festival sustains group identity and coherence. Festival thus manifests the quasi-Hegelian modality of transgression in that it operates to negate and conserve.[39] Nonetheless, the heterogeneous energies it releases unleash the possibilities of communal experience beyond recuperation or containment.

Consumption, Expenditure, Sovereignty

Consumption, the unproductive expenditure of energy represented in cosmic terms by the burning sun, is released from within homogeneous society by sacrifice and festival. War, too, involves communities in non-productive expenditures of excess. In the twentieth century, the two world wars marked the explosive consumption of industrial and imperial development. Wars, as Bataille observes, 'organize the greatest orgies of wealth', involving the enormously wasteful destruction of goods, resources and lives. A 'catastrophic' mode of expenditure, the two world wars nonetheless led to an appreciable rise in economic output and standards of living (p. 197). War exemplifies the principle of general economy: 'if the system can no longer grow, or if the excess cannot be completely absorbed in its growth, it must necessarily be lost without profit; it must be spent, willingly or not, gloriously or catastrophically' (p. 184). The 'glory' of such war lies not so much in national prestige or the sacralizing commemoration of the heroic dead; 'glory' veils the fundamentally material aspect of the enterprise: like the warrior who survives the wager of death, the imagined nobility of catastrophic expenditure is belied by the truth of 'self-interest' (p. 218). War, in its modern form, has little to do with the glorious expenditure associated with the gift.

Indeed, glorious unproductive expenditure, whose residues may be seen in huge (but tax-free) charitable donations or the erection of vain monuments, is generally alien to modern bourgeois practices and values. Predicated on a hostility towards prodigality and luxury, features of the feudal and aristocratic societies from and against which bourgeois moral values and economic practices were developed, modern society generally suppresses modes of unproductive activity. Hence the opposition to sexual indulgence, gambling, drunkenness, all forms of waste. The emphasis on values of sobriety, hygiene, duty, useful activity constitutes the subordination and rationalization of all forms of human life to a homogenized moral economy. As Bataille notes, however, human activity is not reducible to production, morality or utility. A pint of beer after work may be explained as mere thirst, but the savouring of it remains a small token of useless, sovereign enjoyment, a moment outside the bounds of a regulated existence; an extramarital affair may be more pleasurable not because it satisfies a sexual urge, but because it constitutes an act charged with the erotic *frisson* of transgression as it crosses (transports and erases) and thereby highlights the limits of social taboos.[40] These exhibit little, however, of the heterogeneous force manifested in gift exchange or sacrifice. The market economy abandons agonistic expenditures in favour of an 'acquisitive sense' of exchange in interests of more stable forms of profiting (p. 174). Enormous losses and extravagant risks cede to cautious investment. Great discharges of wealth and energy are replaced by careful consumption. On a social level, bourgeois formations confine themselves to a mode of consumption that 'is represented by the use of the minimum necessary for the conservation of life and the continuation of individuals' productive activity in a given society', rather than the consumption 'represented by so-called unproductive expenditures: luxury, mourning, war, cults, the construction of sumptuary monuments, games, spectacles, arts, perverse sexual activity . . . which, at least in primitive circumstances, have no end beyond themselves' (p. 169). Bourgeois society, conforming to 'a reasoning that balances *accounts*', 'has only managed to develop a universal meanness'.

Sovereignty partakes of a second form of consumption in that it is opposed to all forms of servile existence determined by work, usefulness and ends prescribed by a system. Bataille's sense of the word is distinct from its usage to describe the 'sovereignty' of states (p. 301). The sovereign acts insubordinately and consumes with regard only to the moment of consumption, prepared to risk death if only to affirm a human status beyond that of a thing. In opposition to the labour and subordination of the worker, the sovereign is distinguished by the ability to consume wealth and energy without working for it, enjoying the surplus rather than reinvesting it in production. The sovereign's position is similar to that of Hegel's master and thus, via Kojève, to the bourgeoisie. Wealth is at the disposal of the bourgeoisie, though they consume it (or some of it) in what Bataille describes as a 'furtive manner' (p. 302). While visible expressions of lavish expenditure are frowned upon and wealth is restricted to display 'behind closed doors', the bourgeoisie accumulates in order to spend only on itself. Nonetheless, Bataille detects a form of potlatch, with other classes as one's rivals, that persists in the shape of the bourgeoisie's effort to rise above and distance itself from the degraded and slave-like condition of the proletariat. Within the supposedly rational system of economic and social organization there lies a destructive and irrational division. While workers work in order to live, bosses continue to degrade them as they try to elevate themselves above baseness. All efforts to ameliorate this antagonistic division are, Bataille contends, 'subterfuges' (p. 177). Framed by capitalism, the excesses of this limited form of sovereignty are still servile in respect of wealth and acquisition. Sovereignty broaches a sacred, impossible condition, 'there', Bataille writes, and 'at the same time removed from the world of practice (insofar as it might destroy it) and valorized as something that frees itself from the subordination characterizing the world' (p. 313). Sovereignty finds its condition and its momentary enjoyments of a non-alienated state in terms of, but outside, the alienation of the worker. The internally contradictory status of the sacred relation to death provides the impetus, the heterogeneous charge, that disrupts regulated, servile existence: 'familiar with death', the sovereign resists individual consciousness, the slavish subjectivity of individuated, separate being, to display 'a *playful* impulse' more intense 'than the considerations that govern *work*.' Sovereignty transgresses the limits, laws, prohibitions sustaining work, prohibitions enforced by the work of death: 'sovereignty is essentially the refusal to accept the limits that the fear of death would have us respect in order to ensure, in a general way, the laboriously peaceful life of individuals' (pp. 317–18).

The insubordination displayed by the sovereign figure need not pertain solely to the bourgeois master. On the contrary, heterogeneity embraces both the sacred and the profane objects and energies irreducible and unassimilable to the circuits of useful, productive systems: inaccessible, the sacred connotes the realm of values and spirits, while the profane describes the waste, detritus and abjectly human things expelled from the system. Along with the shit, bodily fluids and effluent discharged by the human and economic systems, there are numerous beings reduced to the condition of begging, crime and indolence: the lumpenproletariat, the unemployed, outcasts and rebels of all varieties, the bodies that are surplus to economic requirements. Violently ejected from the systems of production, their disconnectedness, though abject and profane, may furnish them with something of an insubordinate position in respect of the values and practices from which they are excluded. Assembled in mobs, they retain a violently negative charge; *en masse* they become indifferent to morality, their position affords greater licence for the expenditure of free energies against systems of taboo and prohibition. The evil presented by the thieving rabble, the squanderer or the depraved becomes *de facto* a defiant gesture 'of spitting on the good', of turning morality into nothing.[41] Moreover, an indifference to, or contempt for, wealth displays a fundamentally sovereign condition:

> present-day society is a huge counterfeit, where this *truth* of wealth has underhandedly slipped into *extreme poverty*. The true luxury and real potlatch of our times falls to the poverty-stricken, that is to the individual who lies down and scoffs. A genuine luxury requires the complete contempt for riches, the sombre indifference of the individual who refuses to work and makes his life on the one hand an infinitely ruined splendour, and on the other, a silent insult to the laborious lie of the rich. Beyond a military exploitation and a religious mystification and a capitalist misappropriation, henceforth no one can rediscover the meaning of wealth, the explosiveness that it heralds, unless it is in the splendour of rags and the sombre challenge of indifference. One might say, finally, that the lie destines life's exuberance to revolt. (p. 208)

Sovereignty, an effect of economic contradiction, is precipitated beyond organization and appropriation to a space outside of and indifferent to work.

Heterogeneous energies partially contained by military, religious or capitalist organization and structure can nonetheless throw up some disturbing forms of sovereignty in which sacred values and profane violence conjoin at economic and psychological levels. In the 1930s, when Bataille began his studies on heterology and general economy, the rise of fascism presented a fascinating instance of homogeneous bourgeois society convulsed by the internal contradictions it was unable to control. 'The psychological structure of fascism' deploys a revision of the Marxist theory of the relation between base and superstructure in order to investigate an unprecedented and irrational mutation in bourgeois social and economic organization based on the increasingly unstable configuration of capitalism, nation and state. The stability of social homogeneity depends on repressive 'imperative elements', socially heterogeneous institutions like the government, army and police, to maintain the order of what is a 'precarious form', continually threatened by 'unruly elements and internal dissent' (p. 124). Tensions emerged in Germany between the wars, between the state as the site of civic law, and the nation as supreme ideological form, and these tensions provided the sacred charge of communal identification. Beset by acute economic contradictions (mass unemployment, uncontrollable inflation), they led to a dissociation of German unity in the Weimar Republic and initiated a recharging of heterogeneous identifications. The resurgence of unassimilable or excluded elements reversed the usual polarities of attraction and repulsion sustaining the separation of homogeneous and heterogeneous forms, and provided the conditions for the elevation of a single figure to the sacred status of leader. The leader becomes the apex ·of the heterogeneous energy, invested with a general 'moral identification' that seeks its ascendancy in relation to the inept and decadent pragmatism of democratic government. Heterogeneous authority is consituted by the fascist 'appeal to sentiments traditionally defined as *exalted* and *noble*', 'an unconditional principle, situated above any utilitarian judgement' (p. 130). The leader is imagined as something quite 'other', no longer rational or ordinarily human, but someone who assumes a form of unquestioned authority that is associated with the sovereign roles of master, father, general and emperor.

The 'imperative character' of militaristic discipline, the way it transforms impoverished, abject and formless elements into a unified body, is akin to the fascist leader's sovereign function in turning the formless, lumpen mass of heterogeneous elements, both higher and lower, into a national body with noble purpose. Heterogeneity thus gives homogeneous social systems a reason for being, resolving the contradictions of homogeneous social decomposition and atrophying democracy from the bottom up. As a 'sovereign form of sovereignty', fascism presents a violent 'condensation of power' that negates the 'fundamentally revolutionary effervescence' tapped by the leader (p. 139). Symbolically uniting classes and joining heterogeneous and homogeneous elements, the fascist state emerges out of social decomposition to transform it, violently excluding all forms of subversion in the interests of capitalism. Instead, however, of remaining freely competing private enterprises, the interests become those of a group: the structure of capitalism is profoundly altered. The force of heterogeneity, condensed in the figure of the leader, puts its violence to work in a general unification predicated upon a vicious expulsion: as in military structures, where humans are incorporated in the army with a negating rage, so with the national body. This can be seen in a clear and more awful light in events that followed the appearance of Bataille's essay: the motto that hung over the gates of the labour camp, *Arbeit macht Frei* (work makes you free); that freedom, of course, meant death. With this motto the shocking and violent conjunction of fascist heterogeneity is displayed: the new subordination to work, to sacrifice oneself for the interests of the Reich, produces its truth in genocidal extermination.

Fascism harnessed heterogeneous energies latent in homogeneous structures. Fascism elevated work, whose morality and rationale is fascism itself, to a sacred status, thereby turning servility and abjection into imagined sovereignty within a framework of capitalism dominated by a (national) corporate rather than private structure. Heterogeneity is thus violently put to work in repairing and renewing the order of nation, state and capitalism. In Bataille's terms, however, there remains something beyond the energies redeployed in totalitarian, or communist, models, an imperative beyond the 'psychological structure' of fascism that discloses 'the deep subversion which continues to pursue the emancipation of human lives'. Heterogeneous energies are never fully appropriated; the sovereign moment is not the unifying apex, but a hole, the point of dissipation and expenditure of the summit, within and beyond it. Sovereignty involves the 'un-knowing' that leaves behind, in contempt, the system of value and all its commodified riches, an un-knowing linked to laughter as it detaches consciousness 'from the ground on which we are grovelling, in the concatenation of useful activity' (p. 305). Instead of being 'subordinated to some anticipated result, completely enslaved', thought reaches its limit. It accedes to un-knowing: 'only un-knowing is *sovereign*' (p. 308). The challenge that un-knowing throws in the face of thought is the excess with which energy and base matter confront and subvert systems: a violent and disruptive contestation rages from the impossible, the limit of thought. Sovereignty's object being impossible, or 'the impossible', it nevertheless produces an intense movement of expenditure that tears system and subjectivity apart: 'Sovereignty designates the movement of wrenching violence that animates the whole, dissolves into tears, into ecstasy and into bursts of laughter, and reveals the impossible in laughter, ecstasy, or tears. But the impossible thus revealed is not an equivocal position; it is the sovereign self-consciousness that, precisely, no longer turns away from itself' (pp. 277–8).

A strange ethics of horror, an insubordinate politics of total and permanent revolution, emerges from such an impossible encounter. Eschewing the securities and pleasures of knowing and serving, the writing of the impossible, Bataille's writing, addresses that which is least bearable, palatable or avowable in order not to turn away from itself, attending to his own call for 'a thinking that does not fall apart in the face of horror, a self-consciousness that does not steal away when it is time to explore possibility to the limit' (p. 238).

The rest is silence, but echoing, still, in the composed yet inane babble of servile thought.

Postscript

Georges Bataille died in 1962. A man who lived through one of the most turbulent and violent periods of modernity, his death precluded a rigorous encounter with the massive and rapid transformations of capitalism and global society that began in the postwar period. The revolutionary tones of his writing now appear as fleeting memories of a recent past, assured and optimistic about the possibilities of radical socialist change and imminent emancipation. The Revolution seems a long way off, far beyond any horizon of possibility. But Bataille's writing, his 'paradoxical philosophy' as he called it, never appears completely enamoured with or immersed in the parameters of any single position or system, whether emancipatory, rational or totalitarian. For Habermas this is the problem with Bataille, marking the irrationalism and anarchism that renders his work alien to the enlightenment project of Critical Theory. Jean Baudrillard, in contrast, draws on Bataille in his own critique of psychoanalysis and Marxism, but remains uncertain about the proposed destiny of capitalism and the 'solar economy'.

The relation of Bataille's general economy to postmodern forms of capitalism is explicitly addressed by Jean-Joseph Goux. To what extent, Goux asks, can one continue to consider capitalism as a restricted, utilitarian and morally guided economy, given the spectacular and unprecedented modes of waste, luxury and consumption it creates? Moreover, the very distinctions not only between the sacred and the profane, but also between use and uselessness, necessity and superfluity, the serious and the superficial have been erased in postwar society. As Goux writes: 'Is it useful or superfluous to manufacture microwave ovens, quartz watches, video games, or collectively, to travel to the moon and Mars, to photograph Saturn's rings etc.?'[42]

Reason itself, in the form of scientific inquiry, has gone into outer space, pitched its ruinous, imperial drive for knowledge of any kind, of anything, way beyond the terrestrial boundaries of need and utility, consuming billions of dollars. The economy itself, unbound by reason (by a reason that is itself unbound) or usefulness, has long since ceased to understand itself according to classical ideas of supply and demand. With the death of socialism, capitalism no longer has to justify itself along utilitarian, quasi-altruistic lines; it no longer needs to point to an 'invisible hand' that eventually enables wealth to trickle down to a general populace, enabling a greater good than that ever envisaged (never mind delivered) by socialist states. If it justifies itself at all, capitalism does so in a more robust, self-affirming mode. In the risks, gambles and chances by which entrepreneurs risk their fortunes on new ventures, capitalism enters a new heroic phase, without apology. Unimaginable fortunes can be made or lost on the throw of a die, a minor innovation in software, or the whim of consumer fashion. Continually, new objects of consumer desire are given, precisely as *gifts*, to a market that, sovereignly, will decide the success or failure of the venture.

Perhaps the era of modernity and capitalism that Bataille interrogates has passed. And yet, Bataille's terms and the very topics that his writing addresses have more than ever come to prominence.

Though capitalism, it seems, is no longer predicated on principles of conservation or an ethics of production, with the reverse being more evident, its modes of consumption and expenditure remain central issues. Thatcher's and Reagan's neo-libertarian 1980s, freeing markets from state restraint, also liberated a petit-bourgeois class from Protestant reserve. With the force of *ressentiment*, 'yuppies' manifested their enjoyment of loadsamoney in extravagant displays of wealth, claiming a 'higher' culture of art auctions, luxurious goods and expensive restaurants as their own by the sheer force of spending power. Wealth, neither acquired gradually nor passed on steadily, was grasped at the speed of a mortgage signature, a credit card swipe or an electronic impulse between stock exchanges. Fortunes, gathered the day before, disappeared overnight: entrepreneurs, self-made and unmade, became shooting stars. The volatility of the market, the speed of exchange, escalated within a consumptive culture of credit. No longer a matter of saving, conserving or producing in order to indulge in limited pleasures of expenditure, the imperative now became immediate consumption, apparently without limit. Buy now, pay later. And the sovereign market regularly demanded its dues: businesses collapsed by the thousand, insurance brokers crashed and banks were bankrupted. Not to mention the unemployment. Sovereign excess in one direction, abjection in the other.

None of these phenomena, it seems, is directly imaginable in the context of the development of the general economy, published in 1949, as *The Accursed Share*. The first volume, as it discusses the inability of capitalism and its state powers to expend their surplus other than through the catastrophic expenditure of war, proposes two options. Surplus production should be diverted 'either into the rational extension of a difficult industrial growth, or into unproductive works that will dissipate an energy that cannot be accumulated in any case' (p. 186). While neither the rational productive extension nor the monumental scale of public works manifested themselves in historically predictable ways, the terms of the general economy enable a Bataillean interrogation of subsequent events. Instead of rational development, the postwar political/economic blocs embarked on the enormous, escalating and ultimately ruinous expenditure of the arms race, a battle for superiority which inscribes potlatch on a global scale. But with a difference: the products of the military-industrial complex could be neither exchanged nor expended. The standoff, predicated on stability and the equivalence of destructive potential, was irrational, quite literally 'MAD' (the acronym for the superpowers' policy of Mutually Assured Destruction): it only accelerated the expensive production of increasingly powerful weapons, while at the same time, the logic of deterrence determined that the stockpile, an arsenal holding sun-like power, could never be used, but was (and is) endlessly held in reserve. Nuclear weapons constituted an 'accursed share', an unusable part of excessive cost that was sacred in the manner it guaranteed a way of life through its promise of its utter obliteration: material things would be completely sacrificed in the name of cultural values alone. The principle of conservation, rather than the destruction of surplus, determined the general, military economy to the extent that the reserves of the restricted, productive economy were exhausted, particularly in the case of the Soviet Union. The Soviet Bloc, economically ruined, lost this war of nuclear poker and, riven with internal contradictions, folded.

The Iron Curtain constituted a psychological as well as a political barrier that sustained the borders of a generally productive homogeneous 'West' by opposing it to the heterogeneity of the 'other', the 'Evil Empire' of 'the Eastern Bloc'. Within this wider oppositional framework, national and state interests were relatively secure, notwithstanding the perpetual promise of apocalypse. When the Berlin Wall came down, however, it did not signal the joyful reunion of East and West Germany, it radically placed the very notion of 'Germany' as a homogeneous nation-state in question. With the end of the Cold War, it is the concept of the nation-state itself that has come under stress and appears to be growing more and more redundant in the face of globalized corporatism, superstatism, and militant regionalism, ethnic conflict.

Beyond the crumbling Berlin Wall, the eruptive force of capitalist heterogeneity became evident in the uninhibited rush of consumer culture. Dissociated as a result of economic and state collapse, some eastern European nations have attempted to return to a past political agenda, sometimes with the justification of paying off old scores held suspended, left cryogenized in the Siberian winter of state communism. Spectres of fascism have begun to stalk the margins with violent renewal and ethnic cleansing.

But without the rationale of nation or the morality of production, there is only one cause to follow: the unrestrained consumption of transnational capitalism extending itself, not rationally but irrationally, or hyperrationally, as it expands into the unproductive terrain of consumption itself. The production of unlimited useless commodities situates pleasure and desire, rather than need and work, as the object of expenditure. Restricted, utilitarian production expands to encompass, assimilate, territorialize the general economy, rendering it, if not strictly speaking useful, then extremely saleable. Enjoy!

Bataille, a historian of different modes of non-productive expenditure, never insisted on a rigid or absolute separation between restricted and general economies. In the Preface to the second volume of *The Accursed Share*, he addressed the 'paradox' of showing the 'absurdity' of a completely servile system without any form of sovereignty: a world without some kind of sovereignty, he writes, 'is the most unfavourable one; but that is to say in sum that we need sovereign values, hence that it is useful to have useless values . . .' (p. 239). This is self-criticism. There is a similar problem concerning the mobile borders between restricted production and general consumption. Bataille observes that he 'could not prevent consumption from being seen as something useful, even to production itself'. The second volume, he continues, will be different in that, examining eroticism, its concerns lie among base consumption and sovereignty, *'which cannot serve any purpose'*.

And yet capitalism now appears to be engaged in a massive process of autoeroticization, turning itself into a single, global erogenous zone through its marketing of endless commodified thrills. No capital, no desire: a pure, total, desiring machine. The total eroticization of the economy has little to do with advertisers' perennial attempt to sell products by associating them with sex. The totally eroticized economy opens desire on to an unlimited terrain for the *ex nihilo* supply of ever more commodities whose saleability alone determines whether they will have become 'useful'. Desire, here, is predicated on the absence of any final object: the drive of eroticism, opening deep hollows of insufficiency within any subject or system, detaches desire from objects and redirects it nowhere, towards nothing. There is no 'other' enjoyment towards which desire can tend, no heterogeneous object, value, force which one can love or hate. The hyper-homogenization of economic systems consumes sovereign expenditure to the extent that acquisition, as an index of optimization, is the only, internally generated, rule. Beyond that, nothing.

Except unthinkable (non-commodifiable) modes of waste. The assimilation of a restricted, productive economy by generalized consumption, however, does not simply reduce, or expand, one into another, into a 'total ecology of the drives', notwithstanding the moral guarantee of the autoerotic economy, the ecological imperative to recycle everything. All sorts of waste, different excesses, are continually ejected. The contemporary incorporation of excess divides rich and poor countries to an extreme degree and continues to discharge enormous amounts of unassimilable material. While industrial and domestic wastage, like history, is recycled within the assimilative circuits of eco-friendly hyper-homogeneous systems, the excess being returned to useful ends, new forms of waste manifest themselves in spectacularly disturbing ways. The principal object of expulsion seems to be human beings themselves: mass starvation, global death, mass unemployment and homelessness. On a lesser but still disarming scale, and closer to the (western) home, appear the unproductive expenditures of violent crime, destitution and drug use. For those without the career necessary to support the security blankets of hyper-homogeneity, the insurance, health and pension policies that replace the social responsibilities now beyond the means of the atrophying state, there lies the baseness, the abjection of non-corporate existence. Human garbage.

Corporate existence, meanwhile, requires an adaptation to technological and performance imperatives that totally transform the notion of 'work'. No longer the productive transformation of nature, 'work' becomes the strictly meaningless human subordination to the autocratic functionality of corporate speed and efficiency, a machine 'ethic' that has no purpose, that bears no relation to any human end. Paul Virilio, in *The Art of the Motor*, comments on the race, dominating the twentieth century, for biological and technological supremacy.[43] Drawing a parallel between the eugenic goals of the Nazi mobilization machine and the sociopolitical implications of the techno-military cybernetics that defeated and succeeded it, Virilio comments on 'the subtle enslavement of the human being to "intelligent" machines, [the] programmed symbiosis of man and computer [which] scarcely conceal the premises: not of an avowed racial discrimination this time so much as of the total, unavowed disqualification of the human in favour of the definitive instrumental conditioning of the individual'.[44] Conditioned, perhaps, out of existence? *Arbeit macht Frei*. Exhausted and burnt out, humanity is consumed by the hyperefficient performance-imperative of the global corporate machine, endlessly turning in and around its vicious circuitry, purifying itself, spewing out its human residues in a trail of waste, of broken, malfunctioning, deformed bodies. The horror . . .

In Bataille, then, one might catch a glimpse of the possibility for thinking in the face of horrors, thinking with a rigour that refuses to avert its gaze into the comforting mists of nostalgia or to collapse in the face of collapsing states, nations, democracies and political possibilities.

Notes

1 p. 93. All references to Bataille's texts, unless otherwise noted, will be to this volume, with page numbers cited in brackets in the text.

2 Jean Baudrillard, 'When Bataille attacked the metaphysical principle of economy', tr. David James Miller, *Canadian Journal of Political and Social Theory*, 15 (1991), pp. 63–6. Reprinted in *Bataille: a critical reader*, eds Fred Botting and Scott Wilson (Blackwell, Oxford, 1997).

3 Roland Barthes, 'From work to text', in *Image Music Text*, tr. Stephen Heath (Fontana, London, 1977), p. 157.

4 Michel Foucault, 'What is an author?', in *Language, Counter-Memory, Practice*, ed. Donald F. Bouchard, tr. Donald F. Bouchard and Sherry Simon (Cornell University Press, Ithaca, NY, 1977), pp. 113–38.

5 Denis Hollier, *Against Architecture: the writings of Georges Bataille*, tr. Betsy Wing (MIT Press, London, 1989), p. 24.
6 Jean-Luc Nancy, 'Exscription', *Yale French Studies*, 79 (1991), p. 62. See also his *The Inoperative Community*, tr. Peter Connor, Lisa Garbus, Michael Holland and Simona Sawhney (University of Minnesota Press, Minneapolis, MN, 1991).
7 Jacques Ehrmann, 'The death of literature', *New Literary History*, 3 (1971), p. 45.
8 Jacques Derrida, 'From restricted and general economy: a Hegelianism without reserve', in *Writing and Difference*, tr. Alan Bass, Routledge and Kegan Paul, London, 1985, pp. 267 and 270. Reprinted in *Bataille: a critical reader*, eds Botting and Wilson.
9 Maurice Blanchot, 'The negative community', in *The Unavowable Community*, tr. Pierre Joris (Station Hill Press, Barrytown, NY, 1988), p. 20.
10 Ibid.
11 For further biographical information, please consult 'An autobiographical note', this volume, pp. 113–17.
12 A. Breton, *Second manifeste du surréalisme. Manifestes du surréalisme* (J. J. Pauvert, Paris, 1962). For further accounts of surrealism, see Bataille, *The Absence of Myth: writings on surrealism*, ed. and tr. Michael Richardson (Verso, London, 1994), and Michèle Richman, *Beyond the Gift: Reading Georges Bataille* (Johns Hopkins University Press, Baltimore, MD, 1982).
13 On the sociological context of Bataille's work, see Richman, *Beyond the Gift*, Annette Michelson, 'Heterology and the critique of instrumental reason', *October*, 36 (1986), pp. 111–27, and Jürgen Habermas, 'The French path to postmodernity: Bataille between eroticism and general economics', tr. Frederic Lawrence, *New German Critique*, 33 (1984), pp. 79–102. Reprinted in *Bataille: a critical reader*, eds Botting and Wilson.
14 Denis Hollier, Introduction, p. ix, in *The College of Sociology*, ed. D. Hollier, tr. Betsy Wing (University of Minnesota Press, Minneapolis, MN, 1988).
15 Georges Bataille and Roger Caillois, 'Sacred sociology', ibid., p. 74.
16 Georges Bataille, *Literature and Evil*, tr. Alastair Hamilton (Marion Boyars, London, 1985), p. 74.
17 Denis Hollier, Introduction, p. vii, Georges Bataille, *Guilty*, tr. Bruce Boone (The Lapis Press, San Francisco, CA, 1988).
18 Friedrich Nietzsche, *The Will to Power*, tr. Walter Kaufmann and R. J. Hollingdale, (Random House, New York, 1968), p. 477.
19 Ibid., p. 479.
20 Blanchot, 'The negative community', p. 16.
21 Georges Bataille, *The Tears of Eros*, tr. Peter Connor (City Lights, San Francisco, CA, 1989), p. 207.
22 Bataille, 'Notes to *Mme Edwarda*', *Georges Bataille: Oeuvres complètes*, III (Editions Gallimard, Paris, 1973), p. 491.
23 Maurice Blanchot, 'After the fact', in *Vicious Circles: two fictions and after the fact*, tr. Paul Auster (Station Hill Press, New York, 1985), p. 62.
24 Maurice Blanchot, *The Infinite Conversation*, tr. Susan Hanson (University of Minnesota Press, Minneapolis, MN, 1993), p. 202.
25 Georges Bataille, *Erotism: death and sensuality*, tr. Mary Dalwood (City Lights, San Francisco, CA, 1986), p. 11.
26 Elisabeth Roudinesco, *Jacques Lacan and Co.*, tr. Jeffrey Mehlman (Free Association Books, London, 1990), pp. 18–20.
27 A few copies of *Madame Edwarda* were published in 1941. Shortly before then, at the beginning of the Nazi occupation of Paris, Jacques Lacan moved into 5 rue de Lille, next door to Bataille, who lived at number 3. Lacan was already cohabiting with Bataille's wife Sylvia and would adopt his daughter Laurence. After the Liberation, Bataille moved out and Lacan took over 3 rue de Lille as well, conducting his first seminars in the living room

of number 3. Elizabeth Roudinesco notes that when Lacan came to theorize 'the *jouissance* of the (under erasure) woman' as an experience, essentially, of unknowing – 'there is a *jouissance* proper to her of which she herself may know nothing, except that she experiences it' – he turned his seminar into 'an act of homage to the Bataille of *Madame Edwarda*, to the absolute figure of the hatred and love of God' (Roudinesco, *Jacques Lacan and Co.*, p. 524). See also Jacques Lacan, 'God and the *jouissance* of the [under erasure] woman', in *Female Sexuality*, eds Juliet Mitchell and Jacqueline Rose, (Macmillan, Basingstoke and London, 1981), p. 145.

28 See Raymond Queneau, 'Premières confrontations avec Hegel', *Critique* 195/6 (1963), pp. 694–700.

29 See Alexandre Kojève, *Introduction to the Reading of Hegel*, tr. James Nichols, Jr (Basic Books, New York, 1969).

30 Georges Bataille, *Inner Experience*, tr. Leslie Anne Boldt (SUNY Press, New York, 1988), p. 111.

31 Habermas, 'The French path to Postmodernity', pp. 84–5.

32 Bataille, *Oeuvres complètes*, V, p. 231.

33 Philippe Sollers, 'The roof' from *Writing and the Experience of Limits* (Columbia University Press, New York, 1983), p. 115. Reprinted in *Bataille: a critical reader*, eds Botting and Wilson.

34 Denis Hollier, 'The dualist materialism of Georges Bataille', *Yale French Studies*, 78 (1990), pp. 124–39, at p. 135. Reprinted in *Bataille: a critical reader*, eds Botting and Wilson.

35 Ibid., p. 130.

36 Michel Leiris, 'From the impossible Bataille to the impossible *Documents*', in *Brisées*, tr. Lydia Davis (North Point Press, San Francisco, CA, 1989), pp. 237–47, at p. 241.

37 Mikkel Borch-Jacobsen, 'The laughter of being', *Modern Language Notes*, 102 (1987), pp. 737–60, at p. 758. Reprinted in *Bataille: a critical reader*, eds Botting and Wilson.

38 See Marcel Mauss, *The Gift*, tr. W. D. Halls (Routledge, London, 1990).

39 See Bataille, *Erotism*, pp. 63–70.

40 See Michel Foucault, 'Preface to Transgression', in *Language, Counter-Memory, Practice*, pp. 29–52. Reprinted in *Bataille: a critical reader*, eds Botting and Wilson.

41 Bataille, *Erotism*, pp. 138–9.

42 Jean-Joseph Goux, 'General economics and postmodern Capitalism', tr. Kathryn Ascheim and Rhonda Garelick, *Yale French Studies*, 78 (1990), pp. 206–24, at p. 220. Reprinted in *Bataille: a critical reader*, eds Botting and Wilson.

43 Paul Virilio, *The Art of the Motor*, tr. Julie Rose (University of Minnesota Press, Minneapolis, MN, 1995), p. 133.

44 Ibid., p. 135.

PART I

Inner Experience

1

Chance

Pain shaped my character. In school, with my frostbitten fingers – pain is the teacher. 'Without your pain, you're nothing!'

Tears in my eyes at this idea of being waste! I'm whining, ready to pray, but just can't make myself.

A moment later I'm clenching and unclenching my teeth, and drowsiness sets in.

A toothache strikes, my brain turns to mush.

I'm writing and appealing – but hoping for relief from the pain makes me feel that much worse.

Knowing nothing about the creature I am or what kind of thing I am – is there anything I do know? At night not being able to go on and banging my head against the wall, trying to find a way, not from self-confidence but because of being sentenced to search, bumping into things, bleeding, falling down, not getting up . . . Feeling I can't go on, aware of pincers torturing my fingers, of red-hot branding irons burning the soles of my feet. Where is the way out, except for pincers and branding irons! No compromise and no escape. In actuality I'm *safe* from them?! At least they'd confer legitimacy on my body. Which can't *in truth* be separated from them. Which can't be separated from them *in truth*. (You can't separate the body from the head either.)

What if this urgent pain finally didn't matter? At least I'd have some hope of rest. Thinking stops for me, I'm in sunlight, no more worry. How

The text is taken from the 'Games of chance' chapter of *Guilty*, tr. Bruce Boone (The Lapis Press, San Francisco, CA, 1988), pp. 69–86. Originally published in French by Editions Gallimard in 1944 as *Le Coupable*, the manuscript was produced between 1939 and 1944. Re-edited, it appeared in 1961 as the second volume to the *Somme athéologique*. See *Georges Bataille: Oeuvres complètes*, V (Editions Gallimard, Paris, 1973), pp. 310–29. Hereafter, this twelve-volume edition of Bataille's works, which was published between 1970 and 1988, will be cited in the text as *OC* followed by volume and page numbers.

is it possible that earlier I had moments of total well-being on the banks of rivers, in woods, gardens, cafés, in my room? (Leaving aside the darker joys.)

A slipping, glance down, the molar's extracted, but the anaesthetic isn't working? What an awful experience!

What would it be like, how big a coward would I have been, without the hope the cocaine gave? When I get home, I bleed profusely. I stick my tongue in the hole . . . there's a piece of meat there, a blood clot getting larger, starting to protrude. I spit it out – another follows. The clots have the consistency of snot, taste like food gone bad. They're plugging up my mouth. I decide that by falling asleep I'll get over my disgust, won't be tempted to fuss with them or spit them out. I drift off and wake up at the end of an hour . . . Blood streamed from my mouth in my sleep, stained the pillow and sheet, and there are clots stuck in the sheet-folds, almost dry, some black like snot. I'm still upset and exhausted. I'm picturing an incident of haemophilia, maybe followed by death (is that so impossible?). I don't want to die. Or maybe what I mean is – to hell with death. My disgust grows. I put a basin at the foot of the bed to avoid getting up during the night to spit in the toilet. In the coal stove, the fire's gone out and the thought of having to start it again depresses me. I can't get back to sleep . . . Time drags on. Sometimes I get drowsy. At 5 or 6 in the morning I decide to light the fire. I might as well make some use of this insomnia and get a thankless job out of the way. The ashes from the stove have to be taken out. I do the job badly, and soon the room's strewn with pieces of coal, clinkers and ashes. The enamel basin is filled with blood, it's dirty with it, and with clots, the blood has made puddles on my filthy sheets. Exhausted by insomnia, I'm still bleeding and the snotty taste of the clots gets more and more disgusting all the time. Finally the fire catches. My hands black with coal and dirty with blood. Blood-caked lips. A thick coal smoke fills the room; as usual, it takes a huge effort to get the resistant coal to catch fire. I'm not impatient, and no more anguished than other days. There's a nagging need in me . . . to rest.

Little by little the uproar, hearty laughter, and songs disappeared in the distance. The bow still drew out its dying note which continued with diminished strength and finally disappeared like an indistinct sound in the vastness of the atmosphere. At times a rhythmic shock was heard on the road, something that resembled the distant roar of the sea, then nothing, nothing but emptiness and silence.

And isn't it in some way like this that happiness – a guest as delightful as he is fickle – slips away from us, and then how vainly does isolated sound claim to express joy! For in its own echo it can't hear

anything but melancholy and loneliness, and how pointlessly we insist
on lending our ear to it.

Gogol, *Nights in the Ukraine*

We can't *know* if humanity is generally good luck or bad. The fact that
we confine ourselves to polemical truth shows ambiguous judgement, tying
good luck to what we are and bad luck to the curse embodied by the
wicked. In contrast, clear judgement welcomes the fact of evil and the
warfare of good against evil (the incurable wound of being). With ambiguous judgement, however, merit isn't conditional; and good (which we are)
isn't luck but a thing we deserve. It's being's answer to the necessity of
being, everything appearing planned out in advance, 'cooked up', arranged,
it seems, by a God whose ends we can't question.

The human mind is set up to take no account of chance, except insofar
as the calculations that eliminate chance allow you to forget it: that is, *not
take it into account*. But going as far as possible, reflection on chance strips
the world bare of the entirety of predictions in which reason encloses it.
Like human nakedness, the nakedness of chance – which in the last resort
is definitive – is obscene and disgusting: in short, *divine*. Since the course of
the things of the world hangs on chance, this course is as depressing for us
as a king's absolute power.

My reflections on chance are *in the margin of* thought's development.
All the same, we can't make them more radical (decisive). Descending as
far as possible, they pull the rug out from under us when we think that the
development of thought allows sitting down, allows rest.

A part of what applies to us can be – must be – reduced to reason or
(through knowledge or science) to systematic understanding. We can't
suppress the fact that at one point everything and every law was decided
according to the whims of chance – or *luck* – without reason entering the
picture, except when the calculation of probabilities allowed it to.

It's true, the omnipotence of reason limits luck's power. This limitation
in principle suffices, and in the long run the course of the world obeys law.
And since we're rational we see this; but the course of things escapes us at
the extremes.
At the extremes, there's freedom.

At the extremes, thought ceases to be!
At least within the limits of possibilities that pertain to us, thought can
only be present in two ways:

1 Thought is allowed to catch sight of and (in fascination) meditate on the open expanses of catastrophe. The calculus of probabilities limits the scope of this catastrophe, but as death makes us subjects of its empire, the meaning (or non-meaning) of catastrophe isn't to that extent 'humanly' cancelled.

2 Part of human life escapes from work and reaches freedom. This is the part of play that is controlled by reason, but, within reason's limits, determines the brief possibilities of a leap beyond those limits. Play, which is as fascinating as catastrophe, allows you to positively glimpse *the giddy seductiveness of chance*.

I grasp the object of my desire. I tie myself to this object, live in it. It's as sure as light, and like the first hesitant star in the night sky, it's a marvel. In order to know this object with me, someone would have to accommodate my darkness. This distant object is unfamiliar, but familiar too – every flowery exhalation of a young girl, the hectic flush of her cheeks touches it. And it's so transparent a breath will tarnish it, a word dissipate it.

A man betrays chance in a million ways, and in a million ways he betrays 'what he is'. Can you claim you'll never give in to repressive frowning rigidity? The mere fact of not giving in is itself a betrayal. In the fabric of chance, dark interlinks with light. It was only to pursue and mutilate me on a path to horror, depression and denial (as well as to licence and excess) that chance touched me in airy lightness, in utter weightlessness (slow down, dawdle, grow sluggish even for an instant, and chance will disappear). I'd have never found it by looking. Speaking, I've surely betrayed it already. Only if I don't care about betraying myself or about other people's betrayal of me do I escape treachery. I'm dedicated to chance with everything in me, my whole life, all my strength – and there's only absence and inanity in me . . . laughter, such *light* laughter! Chance: I imagine, in the gloom of night, a knife-tip entering my heart, a happiness beyond limits, unbearable happiness . . .

> *the light too much joy too much heaven too much*
> *the earth too vast a fast-moving horse*
> *I hear the waters I'm weeping for light*

> *the earth turns beneath my eyelids*
> *stones roll in my bones*
> *the anemone and glow-worm*
> *help me to unconsciousness*

in a shroud of roses
an incandescent teardrop
proclaims the day.

Two opposing impulses seek out chance. One of these is predatory, inducing dizziness; the other promotes harmony. One requires violent sexual union – bad luck sinks voraciously on luck, consumes it or at least abandons it and marks it with the sign of doom. There's a flaring up and bad luck takes its course, ending in death. The other is divination, the wish to read chance, be its reflection, be lost in its light. Mostly the opposing movements reach an understanding, each with the other. But if we seek the kind of harmony that's found in turning away from violence, chance is cancelled out as such, it's set on a regular and monotonous path. Chance arises from disorder, not regularity. It demands randomness – its light sparkles in dark obscurity. We fail it when we shield it from misfortune, and its sparkle abandons it when failed.

Chance is more than beauty, but beauty derives its sparkle from chance. The huge majority (bad luck) drags beauty down to prostitution.

All chance is sullied. Beauty can't exist without a flaw. Perfect, chance and beauty have stopped being what they are: they're the rule. The desire for chance is inside us like a sore tooth, and at the same time it's the opposite – it wants misfortune's unfocused cosiness.

The consummation of chance in a burst of lightning and the fall that follows the consummation can't be – painlessly – imagined by anyone.

The gossamer-like lacerating idea of chance!

Chance is hard to bear. Commonly it's destroyed and the bottom of things drops out. Chance wants to be *impersonal* (or it's vanity, a bird in a cage), hard to put your hands on, melancholy, slipping out into night like a song . . .

I can't imagine a *spiritual* way of life that isn't impersonal, dependent on chance, never on efforts of the will.

On a roof I saw large, sturdy hooks[1] placed halfway up. Suppose someone falls from a rooftop . . . couldn't he maybe *catch hold* of one of those hooks with an arm or leg? If I fell from a rooftop, I'd plummet to the ground. But if a hook was there, I'd come to a stop halfway down!

Just a little later I might say to myself: 'Once an architect planned this hook, and without it I'd be dead. I should be dead, but I'm not at all – in fact, I'm alive. A hook was put there.'

Let's say my presence, my life are inescapable. Something impossible and incomprehensible would still be its principle.

I understand now – picturing the momentum of falling – that there's nothing in this world unless it meets up with a *hook*.

Usually we avoid seeing a hook. We confer an aspect of necessity on ourselves, on the universe, on the earth, on people.

With a hook arranging the universe, I plunged into an infinite play of mirrors. This play had the same principle as a fall blocked by a hook. Can anyone get more into the core of things? I shook. I couldn't go on. Rapture within me, emotion welling up to the point of tears, rituals of darkness that defy description, every orgy in the world and all times blending in this light.

Do I have it in me to say it? It hardly matters. Since chance has again been given to me, so has rapture – to the point that in a sense it never stopped. Sometimes, though rarely, I feel a need to remind myself of the fact. But this is from weakness. Sometimes from the indifference that comes from utter impurity or in the expectation of death.

There was anguish in me because every value was chance, and its existence and my ability to find it depended on chance. A value was when X number of people agreed, and when chance was each person's motivation and when chance – the chance that existed in their affirmation – brought them to agree (this chance could only *after the fact* be called will or calculation). I pictured this chance not in mathematical form but as a key that could bring being into harmony with whatever surrounded it, since being is itself harmony, a harmony with what chance *is* in the first place. A light is destroyed in the depths of the possibility of being. Being is destroyed and breath is suspended; it's reduced to a feeling of silence, so that there's a harmony there which is completely improbable. Strokes of luck wager being, successively enrich (human) being with the potentiality to harmonize with luck, with the power of revealing or creating luck (since luck is the art of being, or beings is the art of welcoming and loving luck). There's no great distance from anguish to a feeling of bad luck to harmony. Anguish is necessary to harmony, bad luck to luck, a mother's insomnia to a child's laughter.

Value not based on chance would be arguable.

Ecstasy is linked to knowledge. I enter ecstasy looking for the manifest or obvious, for a value that isn't arguable and is given in advance, but which, from powerlessness and impotence, I couldn't ever find. What might finally be the object of my knowing answers the question of my anguish. Let me prophesy: in the end I will say and know 'what is'.

If the will to anguish can only *ask* questions, the answer, if it comes, wills that anguish be maintained. The answer is, anguish is your fate. How could a person like you know what you are or what is . . . or anything? Alone in escaping definitive checkmate are platitude, deception, and the trickery of those who are anguished.

In a certainty of impotence, anguish stops asking questions, or all its questions remain hopeless. Chance impulse never asks questions and to this end makes use of the opposite impulse, anguish, its accomplice, which it adopts and without which it would perish.

Chance is an effect of gambling. This effect can never come to rest. Wagered again and again, chance is a *misunderstanding* of anguish (to the extent that anguish is a desire for rest, for satisfaction). This impulse leads to the only real end of anguish – the absence of an answer. It's an impulse that can never overcome anguish, for in order to be chance and nothing other than chance, the movement of chance has to *desire* that anguish will subsist and chance remain wagered.

If it didn't stop along the way, art would exhaust the movement of chance. It would become something else and more.[2] Chance, though, isn't capable of dawdling, and its lightness of foot protects it from this 'more'. It wants to have its success incomplete and quickly emptied of meaning, one success is soon left behind for another. Hardly does the success appear than its light is extinguished, and another is called forth. Success wants to be gambled, gambled again, wagered endlessly whenever the cards are dealt in a new game.

Personal luck hasn't much to do with luck. Mostly it's a sorry blend of conceit and anguish. Chance is only chance provided that impersonality, or a game of communication that never ends, can be glimpsed.

The light of chance is dimmed by artistic success. As a matter of fact, chance is a woman who wants to be undressed.

Bad luck or anguish sustains the possibility of luck. The same cannot be said of vanity or reason (or, generally, of whatever impulses lead a person to give up playing – gambling, that is).

A fleeting, stifling beauty, embodying chance in a woman's body, is attained through love. But possession of chance requires fingers as light as chance itself. You have to have fingers that don't grasp. Nothing is more contrary to chance (to love) than endless questioning or anxious trembling or the need to exclude unfavourable chance developments; nothing is more pointless than exhausting reflection. I come to love with an enchanted lack of concern, which in its folly is the reverse of a lack of concern. Ponderousness excludes passion so thoroughly you might as well not consider it. In its singlemindedness, love is weakness, melodrama, a need to suffer. Chance summons a chaos through which its links are for ever and continuously forged. Affectation, a closed mind and conventional love feelings represent a negation *in spite of which* love is intense, passionate (but we reply to chance by *intentionally* setting the odds against ourselves).

– Even momentarily, ponderousness is a destruction of chance. – All philosophy (all of knowledge makes chance into an exception) is reflection on a lifeless residue, on a regular process that allows neither chance nor mischance. To recognize chance[3] is a suicide of knowledge, and chance, concealed in a philosopher's despair, bursts out in the frothings of the demented. – I base my conviction on the folly of my fellow human beings (or on the intensity of my pleasure). If I hadn't previously exhausted and measured the possibilities of the mind, turning them upside down, what would I have to say? One day I'll *try chance out*, and, moving across eggs like a sprite, I'll let it be understood I'm walking, and my wisdom will seem magical. Possibly this excludes other people – assuming that my attaining chance demands *knowing nothing about them*! Man reads the possible outline of chance in his 'customs', an outline that is himself, a state of grace, an arrow let fly. Animals were a wager, and so is man, we're an arrow released into air. Where it will fall, I can't say. Where I'll fall, I can't say.

What is more frightening for humankind than play?

Humanness can't stop halfway. But I'm wrong to say *humanness* . . . A human being is also the opposite of a human being – the endless questioning of what his name designates!

You can only oppose mischance's tumultuous act of consuming chance by yielding to the greed for chance. Greed is more opposed to chance – and ruins it more completely – than the tumultuous event of a storm. Tumult reveals chance's nature, showing it nakedly and breathing it out like fever. In the equivocal glare of tumult, the cruelty of chance, its impurity and the perverse meaning of chance appear as they are, adorned in sovereign magic.
	With women, chance can be seen in signs readable on the lips, kisses that recall moments of deadly tumultuousness.

In principle, death is opposed to chance. Still, chance is sometimes linked to its opposite: so death could be the mother of chance.

On the other hand, chance (which differs in this way from mathematical scarcity) is defined by the will it fulfils. Willpower can't be indifferent to the chance it summons up. We couldn't think of will without the chance that accomplishes it – nor of chance without the willpower that seeks it out.

Willpower negates death, it's even unconcerned with it. Only anguish produces concern for death, paralysing the will. The will relies on the certainty of chance and is the opposite of the fear of death. Will guesses what chance is and fixes it: it's an arrow that moves towards it. Chance and will unite in love. Love hasn't any object but chance, and only chance has the strength to love.

Chance is for ever at the mercy of itself. It's always at the mercy of play, always *in* play. If it was definitive, chance wouldn't be chance. And reciprocally, if there was definitive being in the world, there'd be no more chance (the chance in it would be dead).

Irrational faith and chance flare-ups attract chance. Chance is given in a living state of heat, not in an outside, objective randomness. Chance is a state of grace, a gift of heaven, permission to roll the dice without any possibility of repetition, without anguish.

The attractions of completion come from its inaccessible character. The habit of cheating adorns definitive being in chance apparel.

This morning a sentence of mine lacerated me, 'With women, chance can be seen . . .' Only the way mystics depict *their* condition can correspond to my laceration.

There's no room for doubt now: intelligence must apprehend chance if it's to limit itself to its own domain, that is action. Similarly, chance is an object of human ecstasy, because it's the opposite of a response to the desire to know.

THE OBJECT OF ECSTASY IS THE ABSENCE OF AN OUTSIDE ANSWER. THE INEXPLICABLE PRESENCE OF MAN IS THE ANSWER THE WILL GIVES ITSELF SUSPENDED IN THE VOID OF UNKNOWABLE NIGHT. THIS NIGHT, THROUGH AND THROUGH, HAS THE SHAMELESSNESS OF A ROOF-HOOK.

The will grasps the fact of its own conflagration, discerns within itself an aspect which is dream-like, a shooting star which night can't grasp.

From chance to poetry, the distance derives from the inanity of so-called poetry. A calculated use of words, the negation of poetry, destroys chance and reduces things to what they are. Using words poetically involves a perversion akin to the hellish beauty of faces or bodies – which death reduces to nothing.

The absence of poetry is the eclipse of chance.
Chance is like death: 'the harsh embrace of a lover, desired, feared'. Chance is the painful place of overlap of life and death – in sex and in ecstasy, in laughter and in tears.

Chance has the power to love death. But this desire destroys death too (less certainly than hatred of death or fear of it). The path to chance is hard to follow; it's threatened by, but also inseparable from, horror and death. Without horror and death or without the *risk* of them, where would the magic of chance be?

'Every flowery exhalation of a young girl, the hectic flush of her cheek touches it. And it's so transparent a breath will tarnish it, a word dissipate it.' To discern the audacity of play with each passing impulse – but I'm prevented from this by anguish. In anguish a flower withers . . . life reeks of death.

Life is the folly of rolling dice without another thought – the insistence on a state of grace, on lack of consequences. To worry about consequences is the beginning of greed and anguish. The latter comes from the former: it's the trembling produced by chance. Often anguish punishes greed in its initial stages, drawing it on to its more developed perversion, anguish.

In a general way, religion *questions everything*. And particular religions are structures that create the particular responses. Sheltered by these structures, unlimited questioning takes place. But the question to be answered subsists in its entirety, untouched by the history of the particular religions. The uneasiness, deep-seated, has remained while the answers have dissipated.

The answers are lucky or unlucky throws of the dice, and life has been wagered on these. It's even true the wagering of life has been so innocent that combinations of the dice can't be perceived as results of chance. But only wagering was the truth of the response. The response caused a renewal of the game, maintained the questioning, the wagering. Withdrawal of the response, though, is a second aspect of this.

But if a response is chance, the questioning won't stop and the stakes are still untouched: the response is the questioning itself.

Chance calls up *spiritual* life – the highest stakes. In traditional contacts with chance (from card playing to poetry), we only skim the surface. (As I write this, it happens that I feel chance's searing hand abruptly pulling me up – wrenching me out of the bed where I'm writing this – leaving me paralysed. I can't speak except of the necessity of loving chance to the point of giddiness, and of how far chance withdraws, in this understanding, from what my vulgarity took it to be!)

Nothing goes as violently beyond *understanding*'s limits. At a pinch we can imagine utmost intensity, beauty and nakedness. But not at all a being endowed with speech, not at all God, a sovereign lord . . .

Just a few minutes later my memory is already shaky. A vision like this can't be fitted into the world. It's related to this statement: 'What is present, but demented, all the same is *impossible*.' *What is present* is fragility itself (God is the foundation)! In any case it's what couldn't not have been.

Intellectual curiosity puts chance beyond my reach. I seek it and it escapes, as if I just missed it.

Though once again . . . This time I've seen it as *a light shining through*. As if nothing existed except in this clarity – suspended from a roof-hook. Nothing except what possibly might not have been, what possibly should not have been . . . nothing except what dies and is consumed and wagered. This *shining through* came to me in a new light – a precarious, questionable light that couldn't be, except *at that cost*.

A sunset sky dazzles me and fills me with wonder . . . but that doesn't make it a living being.

Imagine the incomparable beauty of a woman who happens to be dead. She's not a living being, there's nothing to be understood about her. No one's in the bedroom. God's not. The room's empty.

To be an arrow is the nature of chance. This particular arrow, one that's different from the rest, and only *my* heart is wounded. If I fall down and die and it's this arrow at last, it's this and not another. It is what it is, thanks to the power of my heart; it's stopped being distinct from me.

How can you *recognize* chance unless you're filled with secret love for it?

An insane love creates it, hurling itself at your face in silence. And chance fell on me from heaven's heights like a bolt from the blue – and chance was who I am! A tiny drop shattered by the bolt, a brief moment shines brighter than the sun.

In front of me and inside me there's no God, no separate being, but flickering *connections*.

Laughter on my lips, as I *recognize* chance on them. Chance!

'I'm probably doomed,' mused Thomas. 'I don't have the strength to wait any longer. Even if I thought I could overcome my weakness a little longer as long as I wasn't alone – now there's no reason to keep making efforts. It's obviously depressing to get so close to the goal and not be able to touch it. I'm sure if I reached those last steps I'd understand why I've struggled uselessly looking for something I haven't found. This is rotten luck, and I'm dying of it.'

'It's only in this last room, located at the top of the house, that night will completely unfold. Usually it's lovely and peaceful. It's a relief not to have to shut your eyes to get rid of daytime's insomnia. It's also rather seductive to find in outer darkness the same night that for such a long time struck your inner truth with death. This night has a very special nature. It's not accompanied either by dreams or by premonitory thoughts that are sometimes substituted for dreams. It's a vast dream itself which, if it covers you, you never attain. When at last it swathes your bed, we'll draw the curtains around you and the splendour of the objects revealed at that point will be worthy of consoling even those who are unhappiest. At that instant I'll become really beautiful myself. This false light makes me rather unattractive now, but at that auspicious moment I'll appear as I actually am. I'll look at you for a long time and I'll lie down close to you – and you won't need to ask about things, I'll answer all your questions. Also – and at the same time – the lamps whose inscriptions you wanted to read will be turned around so they face the right way, and wise sayings that allow everything to be understood will no longer be illegible. So don't be impatient. The night will render you justice, and you'll lose sight of all sorrow and fatigue.'

'One last question,' said Thomas after listening with lively interest. 'Will the lamps be lit?'

'Of course not,' the girl said. 'What a ridiculous question! Everything will be lost in the night.'

'The night,' Thomas said in a dreamy way. 'So I won't see you?'

'Most likely not,' said the girl. 'Did you think it would be different from this? It's precisely because you'll be lost for ever in darkness and you won't be able to perceive anything yourself that I'm telling you about it now. You can't expect to hear, see and be at rest all at one. So I'm letting you know what will happen when night reveals its truth to you while you're deeply at rest. Doesn't it please you to know that in a short time everything you've wanted to learn will be read in a few straightforward words on the walls, on my face and on my mouth? Now the fact that this revelation won't actually be disclosed to you, to be honest, is a drawback, but the main thing is to be sure you won't have struggled in vain. Picture for a minute how it will be. I'll take you in my arms and the words I'll murmur in your ear will have such incredible importance that, if you heard them, you'd be transformed. And my face! My deepest wish is for you to see it then, since at that moment – and not a minute sooner – you'll recognize me. And you'll know whether you've found the person you believe you've been searching for during your journeys, the person for whom miraculously you came to this house – miraculously, but pointlessly. Think of the joy it would be! More than anything, you've desired to see her again. Arriving at this place, which is so hard to enter, you thought at last the goal was near and that the worst was behind you. Oh how you stuck with memory! It was extraordinary, I admit. Others totally forget their former life when they arrive. But you've kept a small memory inside, a weakened signal you've not allowed to fail. Of course, since you've allowed many memories to become indistinct, for me it's as if thousands of miles separated us. I can hardly make you out. It's difficult for me to imagine that one day I'll know who you are. But soon, very soon we'll finally be united. I'll open my arms and throw them around you – and I'll move with you through deep secrets. We'll lose – then find – each other. Nothing will ever come between us again. It's sad you won't be present for this happiness!'

Maurice Blanchot, *Aminadab*

To wager or question 'self'.

When a person pursues a minor object he's not questioning *himself* (questioning 'self' would be suspended then). To love a minor object – even when the object is a concatenation of lacerating words – hinders laceration (unless the laceration is attained and your sentence, no longer an object but a transition, becomes the expression of *laceration*).

Insanely loving chance, you wager everything ... even reason itself. When the power of speech comes into the picture, the limit of possibility is the only limit.

Currently a human being's chance results from the play of natural or physiological factors (the lucky dimensions of humankind are intellectual, psychological or physical). Acquiring chance is what's at stake when constantly questioning yourself.

But chance is finally purified. It's freed from minor objects and is reduced to its own inner nature. Chance no longer is a solitary lucky response (among many) to the simple fact of risk. In the end the response is chance itself – gambling, endlessly putting questions. Finally chance is a wagering of all possibilities and it *depends* on that wagering (so it's not *distinct* from it any more).

If Good didn't question itself it would be the judge's power of execution. Take Good out of the picture, even for a minute, and you end up kissing the hem of the judge's robe.

Good and its retainers breathe the air exhaled by murderers – they kiss the muddy footprints of killers.

If I say Good risks anything, I'm giving dead stone a living heart.

In me, the living idea of *Good* has a function like 'a man holding onto a roof-hook'. It depends on some random 'hook'. Isolated from the pitch of the roof, from slipping, from tumbling down, the idea of Good is frozen. Everything's always moving. If I get an idea, I wager it – and motion's imparted.

God discloses the horror of a world where there is constant risk and nothing is protected. In fact, the opposite is true. The multitude of random beings corresponds with the possibility that things are always in play. If God existed (if he unchangeably was once and for all) the possibility of play would disappear at the pinnacle.

When I'm not my choice of love object any more, I love a grey cloud ... and grey heavens. In flight from me, chance is in free play in the heavens. The heavens – which obliquely link me even with beings of the future. How could the issue, or problem, of the multitude of individual beings be tolerable?

Haunted by the idea of knowing what the key to the mystery is, a man becomes a reader of detective novels. Still, could the universe resemble calculations worked out by writers to evoke recognizable worlds?

There's no explanation and *the mystery has no key*. There's nothing conceivable outside 'appearance', and the desire to escape appearance ends up switching appearances: we're in no way closer to the truth *that isn't*. Outside appearance, there's nothing. Or outside appearance, *there's night*. And: in the night there's only the night. If at night there was anything that could be expressed by using language, this would be night all the same. Being itself can be reduced to appearance or doesn't exist. Being is the absence that appearances conceal.

Night is richer, as a representation, than being is. Chance comes from night, returns to night – it is both daughter and mother of night. Night doesn't exist, and neither does chance. Chance, since it *is* what *isn't*, reduces being to the deposing of chance (chance, now removed from the game, searches for substance). Being, Hegel says, is the most impoverished notion. Chance, I say, is the richest. Chance – by which being is destroyed in its beyond.

What I call gambling is the world seen from the night of unknowing. Which is different from *laws* obeyed by the world as it's gambled.

Truths wagered like instances of chance, gambled on the lie of being – these truths are wagered and then wagered again. The truths that express being have a need *not* to change – to be changeless.

What does it mean if you say, 'I could have been him or her'? To put it less maniacally, 'What if I was God?' A definitive distribution of being – guaranteed by God who himself is distinct from other people – doesn't terrify me any less than emptiness as soon as I fall into it. God can't just forget or annihilate the differences we long for. It's obvious he's their negation! (God wouldn't be subject to distribution.) *God is not me*: that proposition makes me laugh until, all alone at night, I stop laughing, and, being alone, I'm lacerated by my unrestrained laughter. 'Why am I not God?' From my childishness comes the answer – 'I'm me.' But, 'Why am I who I am?' 'If I wasn't myself, would I be God?' The terror is rising in me, since – what do *I* know anyway? And catching hold of the drawer-handle I squeeze tight with my finger-bones. What if God started wondering, 'Why am I myself?' or 'Why not be this person who is writing?' Or . . . '*Somebody*, anyway!' Do I have to draw the conclusion that 'God's a person who doesn't question himself, a *self* who knows the reasons he is who he is'? When I act dumb, I resemble him. How true is this? I'd be terrified *to be him* right now. Only humility makes my powerlessness bearable. If I were all-powerful . . .

God is dead. He's so dead, in fact, that the only way to make this comprehensible is by killing myself.

The normal development of knowledge limits me to myself. It convinces me that the world ends with me. But I can't dwell on that connection. I stray, I evade and neglect myself, and I find it impossible to return to an attachment to self except through taking up a neglectful attitude. I live only by neglecting myself, I care about myself only provided I'm alive.

The beloved self! I see him now, devoted, familiar, romping around. No doubt about it – that's *him*! But the old dog doesn't care about being taken that seriously any more. Under certain circumstances and in a spirit of fun, he might opt for the somewhat eccentric doggy role that shows up in stories, or, when feeling down, be a doggy ghost.

Before I was born – you might ask – what were my chances of coming into this world? I'm alluding to times my family experienced. I'm imagining meetings without which I wouldn't be. The chances of their taking place were *that infinitely small*.

The big lie: existing in this world under these conditions and thinking up a God who's like us! A God who calls himself *me*!

Imagine a God – a being distinct from others – calling himself *I*, though this I never occurred and doesn't result from occurrence. This kind of nonsense transposes a notion we have of ourselves on to a scale of totality. God is the kind of impasse that happens when the world (which simultaneously destroys both us and whatever exists) surrounds our *self* to give it the illusion of possible salvation. Self then blends the giddy prospects of ceasing to exist with the dreams we have of escaping death.

Once we return to straightforwardness, the God of theology is only a response to a nagging urge of the self to be finally *taken out of play*.

Theology's God, reason's god, is never brought into play. The unbearable self we are comes into play endlessly. 'Communication' brings it into play endlessly.

Occurrence itself – or origin – is 'communication', sperm and egg slide into each other in the heart of the sexual storm.

Chance wagers people as they join – when two by two or in larger groupings they sometimes dream, act, make love, curse, dominate, and kill each other.

Before conjunction, a man forgets about himself – he's drawn to his beloved. Like rain raining or thunder thundering, in this tumultuous conjunction a child occurs.

In sacrifice, mischance 'tempestuously consumes chance', designating a priest 'with the sign of disaster' (making him sacred). Nonetheless, the priest is not chance, but uses mischance for the purposes of chance. In other words, chance, consumed by mischance, sometimes is chance in its origin and result. That, apparently, is the secret of chance; it can be discovered only when being gambled away. But the best way to gamble it away is to destroy it.

Prostitutes and organs of pleasure are marked with 'the sign of disaster'. Mischance is a drinking glass filled with horrible fluid – I have to put my finger inside. How otherwise could I receive chance's discharge? Laughter and thunder are wagered in me. But hardly do I withdraw, exhausted from the horrible game, than the storm (or a crash I dream about, or a heart attack) is replaced by a vulgar feeling of emptiness.

At a time of confusion and anxiety when I searched frantically for something to link me to chance, I still had to kill time. I didn't want to give in to the cold then. To keep from giving in, I intended to find consolation in a book. But available books were ponderous, hostile, too stilted – except for poems of Emily Brontë.

That inconceivable creature answered . . .

> *Heaven's great laughter bursts on our beads*
> *earth never misses Absence.*

She spoke of a time

> *when his fine golden hair*
> *would tangle roots of grass beneath the ground.*

Notes

1 [Hooks like these are used to hold poles on the roofs to prevent snow from sliding off in the winter. TR.]
2 In fact, art escapes. On principle artists mostly limit themselves to their specialty. If they

exceed it, it's sometimes to further a truth that's even more important in their eyes than art itself. Most artists refuse to see that art encourages them to create a god-like (in our times, a God-like) world.

3 This has nothing to do with a calculus of probabilities. [1959 note]

2

Guilt

I'm appealing to the friendship of human existence for itself – for what we are (at the moment) and what we'll be, for the fate that's ours, that we've willed, our loathing of natural givens, and goals outside us to which we submit in weariness (love or friendship implies this loathing).

Every 'response' is an outside order, a morality inscribing human existence in nature (as a creature). Submission makes man into a non-man, a natural being, but broken and humbled by *himself*, so as to no longer be the insubordination *he is* (in which asceticism is a *humanness* that remains in him and is insubordination reversing itself, turned back on itself).

Belief in poetry's (or inspiration's) omnipotence is upheld in Christianity, but the Christian world cheats at its madness, and what it calls inspiration is essentially a language of reason.

Human existence is guilty: it *is* this to the degree it opposes nature. A humility that makes humanity ask forgiveness (Christianity) overwhelms human existence without excusing it. Christianity's advantage is that it at least aggravates the guilt it proclaims . . .

The only way to reach innocence is to be rooted firmly in crime: man questions nature *physically* – in the dialectic of laughter, love, ecstasy (this last envisaged as a physical state).

In our time everything is simplified: mind no longer plays the part of opposition, it's finally no more than a servant, the servant of nature. And everything takes place at the same level. I can excuse laughter, love and ecstasy . . . though laughter, love and ecstasy . . . are sins against mind. They physically lacerate *physis* or nature, which mind sanctified as it incriminated mankind. Mind was the fear of nature. The autonomy of a man is physical.

Negativity is action, and action consists in taking possession of things.

Translated into English as 'Fragment on guilt', *Guilty*, tr. Bruce Boone (The Lapis Press, San Francisco, CA, 1988), pp. 135–8, the text was appended to the 1944 Gallimard edition of *Le Coupable*. See *OC*, V, pp. 383–7.

There is taking possession through work;
　　work is human activity in general,
　　intellectual,
　　political, or
　　economic;
　to which is opposed
　　sacrifice,
　　laughter,
　　poetry,
　　ecstasy, etc.,
which break closed systems as they *take* possession.

Negativity is this double movement of 'action' and 'questioning'.
Likewise, guilt is associated with this double movement.
Human existence *is* this double movement.

The freedom of the double movement is linked to absence of response.
Between each movement and the other, interaction is necessary and incessant.
Questioning develops action.
What's called mind, philosophy and religion[1] is founded on interferences.
Guilt arises in a zone of interference – on the way to an attempted accord with nature (human existence is guilty, it asks forgiveness).
The feeling of guilt is a *renunciation* by man (or rather, his attempt at renunciation) of a double movement (of negation of nature). Each interference is a middle term between man and nature – and a *response* to the mystery is both a brake on this double movement (a gentle and in fact *reactionary* interference) and a (practical) system of life founded on guilt.
Humanly speaking, stopping the interference is a lie (it's a response, it's guilt, it's the exploitation of guilt).

Intellectual 'givens' have meaning on the level of being action, and they respond to being questioned (they proceed from this) to the degree that interaction is possible, which is to say exclusively on the level of being action.
Still, an infinite questioning (pruning away mediocrity and interference) accords with an ultimate and systematic action (human existence defines itself as a negation of nature and renounces its guilty attitude). Hence a sort of non-religious sacrifice, laughter, poetry and ecstasy, partly released from forms of social truth.

Action and questioning are endlessly opposed. On the one hand as acquisition for the benefit of a closed system, and on the other, as a rupturing and disequilibrium of the system.

I can imagine an action so well conceived that the questioning of the system for whose benefit it took place would now be meaningless; in this case, precisely, the questioning could only be infinite. However, the limited system could still be questioned again: criticism would then bear on the absence of limits and the possibilities of *infinite* growth in acquisition. In a general way, insofar as questioning is laughter, poetry . . . it goes hand in hand with expenditure or a consumption of surplus energy. Now, the amount of energy produced (acquired) is always greater than the amount necessary for production (acquisition). Questioning introduces a general critical aspect that bears on the results of a successful action from a point of view no longer that of production, but its own (that of expenditure, sacrifice, celebration). Action from then on is likely to shore up any response at all, to escape questioning that challenges its possibilities of growth. In this case, it would be brought back to the confused level of interference – to the category of *guilty*. (Everything continually gets mixed up with everything else. Would I still be this implacable theoretician, if a *guilty* attitude didn't remain in me?)

What I propose isn't an equivalent of a *response*. The truth of my assertions is linked to my activity.

As assertion, the recognition of negativity only has meaning through its implications at the practical level (it's linked to my attitudes). My continual activity is linked first of all to ordinary activity. I live, I fulfil the usual functions that found great truths in us. And from there the opposite aspect commences: the method of questioning prolongs the establishing of original truths in me. I slip from the trap of responses and take the critical viewpoint of philosophies to its logical conclusion – as clearly as I distinguish objects among themselves. But bringing negative thought to action isn't limited to prolongations of general activity; on the other hand, this thought realizes its essence when it modifies life. It tends to undo ties – detaching the subject from the object brought into action. Moreover, this sort of activity, intimate and intense, possesses a field of development of basic importance. Beginning with intellectual operations, what's at issue is an infrequent, strange experience which is difficult to bring up here (but which isn't less decisive for that). But this – ecstatic – experience doesn't essentially have the nature of a monstrous exception which would first of all define it. Not only is it easy of access (a fact that religious traditions don't mind keeping hidden), but it obviously has the same nature as other common experiences. What distinguishes ecstasy is, rather, its relatively developed (at least in comparison with other forms) intellectual nature, *susceptible* in any case of infinite development. Sacrifice, laughter, eroticism, on the contrary, are naive forms that exclude clear awareness or receive it from the outside. Poetry, it's true, surrounds itself with various intellectual ambitions – sometimes even intentionally sows confusion between its procedures and 'mystical' exercises – but its nature returns it to naïveté (an *intellectual* poet is made restless by interference, by a submissive, *guilty* attitude to the point of logomachy. But poetry remains blind and deaf. Poetry is poetry, in spite of the majority of poets).

Neither poetry nor laughter nor ecstasy is a response; but the field of possibilities that belongs to them defines activity linked to assertions of negative thought. In this realm, the activity linked to questioning is no longer exterior to it (as it is with partial challenges, which are necessary to the progress of science and technology). Negative action is decided freely as such (consciously or not). However, in this positioning, agreement with pure practical activity is an accommodation with the fact of the abolition of interference. Thus man comes to the point of recognizing *what he was*. (It can't be said in advance, though, that he won't find his greatest danger in this fashion.) Maybe an agreement with self is a sort of death. What I've said would be annihilated as pure negativity. The very fact of success would remove the opposition, dissolve man in nature. Once history's finished, the existence of man would enter animal night. Nothing is more uncertain than this. But wouldn't the night need only this as its initial condition – that we remain unaware that it's night? Night that knows it's night wouldn't be night but would be the fall of day . . . (the human odyssey ending up like *Aminadab*).

Note

1 Religion in this sentence doesn't have the meaning of religion independent of given religions but of whatever religion is given, among other religions. [1960 note]

3

Laughter

1

We have to distinguish:

– Communication linking up *two* beings (laughter of a child to its mother, tickling, etc.)

– Communication, through death, with our beyond (essentially in sacrifice) – not with nothingness, still less with a supernatural being, but with an indefinite reality (which I sometimes call *the impossible*, that is: what can't be grasped [*begreift*] in any way, what we can't reach without dissolving ourselves, what's slavishly called God). If we need to we can define this reality (provisionally associating it with a finite element) at a higher (higher than the individual on the scale of composition of beings) social level as the sacred, God or created reality. Or else it can remain in an undefined state (in ordinary laughter, infinite laughter, or ecstasy in which the divine form melts like sugar in water).

This reality goes beyond (humanly definable) nature insofar as it's undefined, not insofar as it has supernatural determination.

Autonomy (with respect to nature), which is inaccessible in a finished state, functions when we renounce that state (without which it's not *conceivable*); that is, in the abolition of someone who wills it for himself or herself. It can't therefore be a state but a *moment* (a moment of infinite laughter or ecstasy . . .). The abolition takes place – provisionally – at a time of lightning-like communication.

2 Correlation of Rupture in Laughter with Communication and Knowledge (in Laughter, Sacrificial Anguish, Erotic Pleasure, Poetry and Ecstasy)

In laughter, in particular, there is a knowledge given of a common object (which varies according to the individuals in question, the times and races,

Translated into English as 'Two fragments on laughter', *Guilty*, tr. Bruce Boone (The Lapis Press, San Francisco, CA, 1988), pp. 139–43, the text was appended to the 1944 edition of *Le Coupable*. See *OC*, V, pp. 388–92.

but the differences aren't in degree, only in nature). This object is always known, but normally from the outside. A difficult analysis is required if an inner knowledge of it is attempted.

Given a relatively isolated system, perceived as an isolated system, and given that a circumstance occurs that makes me perceive it as linked with another (definable or non-definable) whole, this change makes me laugh under two conditions: 1) that it's sudden; 2) that no inhibition is involved.

I recognize a passer-by as a friend of mine . . .

Someone falls to the ground like a bag: he's isolated from the system of things by falling . . .

Perceiving its mother (or any other person), a child suddenly undergoes a contagion – it understands that *she* is like *it*, so that the child moves from a system outside it to one that is personal.

The laughter of tickling comes from the preceding, but it's the sharp *contact* – a rupture of a personal system (insofar as it's isolated within) – that's the underscored element.

In any kind of *joking*, a system that's given as isolate liquefies, falls suddenly into another.

Deterioration in the strict sense isn't necessary. But if the fall is accelerated, say, this works in the direction of suddenness; while the factor of the situation of the child, the suddenness of the change (the fall of the adult system – that of grown-ups – into an infantile one) is always found in laughter. Laughter is reducible, in general, to the laugh of recognition in the child – which the following line from Vergil calls to mind: *incipe, parve puer, risu cognoscere matrem.*[1] All of a sudden, *what controlled the child falls into its field.* This isn't an authorization but a fusion. It's not a question of welcoming the triumph of man over deteriorated forms, but of intimacy communicated thoughout. Essentially, the laugh comes from *communication*.

Conversely, intimate communication doesn't utilize exterior forms of language but sly glimmerings analogous to laughter (erotic raptures, sacrificial anguish, or – in poetry – evocation). The strict communication of language has as its object a concern for things (our relations with things), and the portion which it exteriorizes is exterior beforehand (unless language becomes perverse, comical, poetic, erotic . . . or unless it's accompanied by contagious procedures). Full communication resembles flames – the electrical discharge of lightning. Its attraction is the *rupturing* it is built on and which increases its intensity in proportion to its depth. The rupture which is *tickling* can appear to the will in an unattractive light – laceration and discomfort are more or less sharply felt according to the forms. In sacrifice, rupture is violent, and often violent in eroticism as well. You find it again in the laugh Vergil refers to: a mother provokes a child's laughter by making faces at it, leading to the disequilibrium of sensations. She brings her face suddenly near her child, engages in games of startling expressions or makes funny, little cries.

The main thing is the moment of violent contact, when life slips from one person to another in a feeling of magical subversion. You encounter this same feeling in tears. On another level, to look at each other and laugh can be a type of erotic relation (in this case, rupture has been produced by the development of intimacy in lovemaking). In a general way, what comes into play in physical or psychological eroticism is the same feeling of 'magical subversion' associated with one person slipping into another.

In the various forms whose foundation is the union of two beings, rupture can enter only at the beginning, and the contact afterwards remains set: then the intensity is less great. *Intensity of the contact* (and thereby the magical feeling) *is a function of resistance*. Sometimes removing an obstacle is felt as a delicious contact. From this there results a fundamental aspect – these contacts are *heterogeneous*. What fusion brings into me is *another* existence (it brings this *other* into me as *mine* but at the same time as *other*); and insofar as it's a transition (the contrary of a state) and in order to be actually produced, fusion requires heterogeneity. When the transition factor isn't involved (if the fusion's accomplished, it's only a state), only stagnant water subsists, instead of the waters of two torrents mixing together with a roar; the removal of resistance has changed fusion into inertia. Hence this principle: the comic (or erotic) elements are exhausted in the long run. At the moment the waters mix, the slipping of this into that is violent. Resistance (the same that an individual sets up in opposition to death) is violated. But two similar individuals can't endlessly laugh or make love in the same way.

Laughter, though, only infrequently corresponds to the outline of compenetration. Ordinarily what it puts into play is a comic object, facing which it's (theoretically) sufficient to have one person laughing, not two. As a general rule, two or several people laugh. The laugh reverberates, amplified from one person to another, but those laughing may be unaware – they may be – of their compenetration; they can treat it as a negligible element or have no awareness of it. It's not among those who laugh that the rupture takes place and otherness comes into the picture, but in the movement of the comic object.

The transition from two people laughing to several (or one person) brings into the interior of the realm of laughter the difference that generally separates the realm of eroticism from that of sacrifice.

The erotic struggle can *also* (in drama) be given as spectacle, and the immolation of a victim can *also* become a middle term between the believer and his or her god: lovemaking isn't less tied to compenetration (of two beings) than sacrifice is to *spectacle*. *Spectacle* and *compenetration* are two rudimentary forms. Their relationship is given in the formula: *contagion* (the intimate compenetration of two beings) is *contagious* (susceptible of indefinite reverberation). The development of the two forms in the interior of the realm of laughter contributes to its inextricable nature. It's easy to discern their articulation in another way: in the difference between love and sacrifice and in the fact that each can have the value of the other (lovemaking's interest as spectacle and the element of intimate compenetration in sacrifice).

If there's *contagious contagion*, it's because the element of spectacle is of the same nature as its reverberation. The spectacle is *for others* what the compenetration brought into play is for *the two individuals*. In the spectacle, and more generally in each theme brought *to the attention of others* (in puns, anecdotes, etc.), the compenetrating elements don't seek out their own interest. But those who suggest these themes pursue the interest of *others*. It's even unnecessary for two individuals to be involved. Most frequently compenetration (contagion) sets two worlds against each other and limits itself to a transition, to the fall of an individual of *one* of these worlds into the *other*. The most meaningful fall is death.

This movement is related to an intermediate figure, in which compenetration again involves two individuals; one of them, the one we look at (*the actor*), can die. It's the death of one of the terms that gives communication its human character. From that time on, it no longer unites one individual being to another, but an individual being to the beyond of beings.

In the laughter of tickling, the one who's tickled goes from a tranquil state to a convulsive state – it alienates him, he undergoes it and it reduces him to the impersonal state of living substance; he escapes from himself and so opens up to another (who tickles him). The one who's tickled is the spectacle, the one who tickles watches, but they communicate; the separation of spectacle from spectator isn't effectuated between them (the spectator is still an actor, isn't a 'viewer', etc.).

I'm bringing up the following supposition: that a tickled person, being intoxicated – just for fun and as a joke – might kill his tormentor. Not only does death inhibit the laughter, but it abolishes any possibility of communicating between the two. This rupture of communication isn't only negative: it is, from another view, analogous to ticklings. The dead person had been united with the tickled person through the repeated rupturings of tickling. Similarly murder unites the tickled person with death – or rather, since the dead person is dead, with the beyond of the dead person. On the other hand, from the very fact of death, the tickler is separated from the tickled person like the spectacle from the spectator.

Note

1 In a meeting of the College of Sociology, Roger Caillois, citing this line on the subject of laughter, remained reticent about the meaning. It is possible to translate 'Begin, young child, to recognize your mother by your laughter' also as 'by *her* laughter'. [1960 note]

4

The Torment

I

There is in divine things a transparency so great that one·slips into the illuminated depths of laughter beginning even with opaque intentions.

I live by tangible experience and not by logical explanation. I have of the divine an experience so mad that one will laugh at me if I speak of it.

I enter into a dead end. There all possibilities are exhausted; the 'possible' slips away and the impossible prevails. To face the impossible – exorbitant, indubitable – when nothing is possible any longer is in my eyes to have an experience of the divine; it is analogous to a torment.

There are hours when Ariadne's thread is broken: I am nothing but empty irritation; I no longer know what I am; I am hungry, cold and thirsty. At such moments, to resort to will would make no sense. What counts is the distaste for what I have been able to say, write, which could bind me: I feel my good faith to be insipid. There is no way out from the contradictory impulses which agitate men and it is in this that they satisfy me. I have doubts: I no longer see in me anything but cracks, impotence, useless agitation. I feel corrupt; everything that I touch is corrupt.

A singular courage is necessary in order not to succumb to depression and to continue – in the name of what ? Nevertheless I continue, in my darkness: man continues in me, goes through this. When I utter within myself: WHAT IS IT? When I am there without a conceivable reply, I believe that within me, at last, this *man* should kill what I am, become *himself* to that point that my stupidity ceases to make me laughable. As for . . . (rare and furtive witnesses will perhaps find me out) I ask them to hesitate: for condemned to becoming man (or more), it is necessary for me to die (in my

'The torment' is taken from *Inner Experience*, tr. Leslie Anne Boldt (SUNY Press, New York, 1988), pp. 33–61. Originally published in French as *Le Supplice*, part 2 of *L'Expérience intérieure* (Editions Gallimard, Paris, 1943), it became, in 1947, the first volume of the *Somme athéologique*. See *OC*, V, pp. 43–76.

own eyes), to give birth to myself. Things could no longer remain in their state; man's 'possible' could not limit itself to this constant distaste for himself, to the dying individual's repeated disavowal. We cannot be without end that which we are: words cancelling each other out, at the same time as resolute non-entities, believing ourselves to be the foundation of the world. Am I awake? I doubt it and I could weep. Would I be the first one in the world to feel human impotence make me mad?

Glances wherein I perceive the path travelled. Fifteen years ago (perhaps a bit more), I returned from I don't know where, late in the night. The rue de Rennes was deserted. Coming from Saint Germain, I crossed the rue du Four (the post office side). I held in my hand an open umbrella and I believe it wasn't raining. (But I hadn't drunk: I tell you, I'm sure of it.) I had this umbrella open without needing to (if not for what I speak of later). I was extremely young then, chaotic and full of empty intoxications: a round of unseemly, vertiginous ideas, but ideas already full of anxieties, rigorous and crucifying, ran through my mind. In this shipwreck of reason, anguish, the solitary fall from grace, cowardice, bad faith profited: the festivity started up again a little further on. What is certain is that this freedom, at the same time as the 'impossible' which I had run up against, burst in my head. A space constellated with laughter opened its dark abyss before me. At the crossing of the rue du Four, I became in this 'Nothingness' unknown – suddenly . . . I negated these grey walls which enclosed me, I rushed into a sort of rapture. I laughed divinely: the umbrella, having descended upon my head, covered me (I expressly covered myself with this black shroud). I laughed as perhaps one had never laughed; the extreme depth of each thing opened itself up – laid bare, as if I were dead.

I don't know if I stopped, in the middle of the street – concealing my transport under an umbrella. Perhaps I jumped (no doubt that's just an illusion): I was illuminated convulsively; I laughed, I imagine, while running.

Doubt fills me with anguish without respite. What does illumination mean? of whatever nature? even if the brilliance of the sun blinded me inwardly and set me ablaze? A bit more, a bit less light changes nothing; in any case, solar or not, man is only man: to be nothing but man, not to emerge from this – is suffocation, burdensome ignorance, the intolerable.

'I teach the art of turning anguish to delight', 'to glorify': the entire meaning of this book. The bitterness within me, the 'unhappiness' is only the condition. But anguish which turns to delight is still anguish: it is not delight, not hope – it is anguish, which is painful and perhaps decomposes. He who does not 'die' from being merely a man will never be other than a man.

Anguish, obviously, is not learned. One would provoke it? It is possible: I hardly believe so. One can stir up the dregs of it . . . If someone admits of having anguish, it is necessary to show the inexistence of his reasons. He imagines the way out for his torments: if he had more money, a woman, another life . . . The foolishness of his anguish is infinite. Instead of going to the depths of his anguish, the anxious one prattles, degrades himself and flees. Anguish however was his chance: he was *chosen* in accordance with his *forebodings*. But what a waste if he escapes: he suffers as much and humiliates himself, he becomes stupid, false, superficial. Anguish, once evaded, makes of a man an agitated Jesuit, but agitated to emptiness.

Trembling. To remain immobile, standing, in a solitary darkness, in an attitude without the gesture of a supplicant: supplication, but without gesture and above all without hope. Lost and pleading, blind, half dead. Like Job on the dung heap, in the darkness of night, but imagining nothing – defenceless, knowing that all is lost.

Meaning of supplication. I express it thus, in the form of a prayer: O God our father, You who, in a night of despair, crucified Your son, who, in this night of butchery, as agony became *impossible* – to the point of distraction – became the *Impossible* Yourself and felt *impossibility* right to the point of horror – God of despair, give me that heart, Your heart, which fails, which exceeds all limits and tolerates no longer that You should be!

One does not grasp the way in which one should speak of God. My despair is nothing, but that of God! I can live or know nothing without imagining it lived, known by God. We back away, from 'possible' to 'possible', in us everything begins again and is never *risked*, but in God: in this 'leap' of being which He is, in his 'once and for all'? No one would go to the end of supplication without placing himself within the exhausting solitude of God.

But in me everything begins again; nothing is ever risked. I destroy myself in the infinite possibility of my fellow beings: it annihilates the sense of this *self*. If I attain, an instant, the extreme limit of the 'possible', shortly thereafter, I will flee, I will be *elsewhere*. And what sense is there in the ultimate absurdity: to add to God the unlimited repetition of 'possibles' and this torment of being forsaken, drop by drop, within the multitude of man's misfortunes? Like a herd chased by an infinite shepherd, the bleating flock which we are would flee, would flee without end the horror of a reduction of Being to totality.

God speaks to me the idiot, face to face: a voice like fire comes from the darkness and speaks – cold flame, burning sadness – to . . . the man with the umbrella. When I collapse, God answers the supplication (what? At whom should I laugh in my room? . . .) *I, myself*, am standing on various summits, so sadly ascended; my different nights of terror collide – they multiply, they intertwine and these summits, these nights . . . unspeakable joy! . . . I stop. I am? a cry – thrown back, I collapse.

Philosophy is never supplication: but without supplication, there is no conceivable reply: no answer ever preceded the question: and what does the question without anguish, without torment mean? At the moment of going mad, the answer springs forth: how would one hear it without that?

The essential is the extreme limit of the 'possible', where God himself no longer knows, despairs and kills.

Forgetting of everything. Deep descent into the night of existence. Infinite ignorant pleading, to drown oneself in anguish. To slip over the abyss and in the completed darkness experience the horror of it. To tremble, to despair, in the cold of solitude, in the eternal silence of man (foolishness of all sentences, illusory answers for sentences, only the insane silence of night answers). The word *God*, to have used it in order to reach the depth of solitude, but to no longer know, hear his voice. To know nothing of him. God final word meaning that all words will fail further on: to perceive its own eloquence (it is not avoidable), to laugh at it to the point of unknowing stupor (laughter no longer needs to laugh, nor crying to cry, nor sobbing to sob). Further on one's head bursts: man is not contemplation (he only has peace by fleeing); he is supplication, war, anguish, madness.

The voice of the good apostles: they have an answer for everything; they indicate limits, discreetly, the steps to follow, as does, at burial, the master of ceremonies.

Feeling of complicity in: despair, madness, love, supplication. Inhuman, dishevelled joy of *communication* – for, despair, madness, love . . . not a point in empty space which is not despair, madness, love and even more: laughter, dizziness, vertigo, nausea, loss of self to the point of death.

II

Mockery! that one should call me pantheist, atheist, theist . . . But I cry out to the sky: 'I know nothing.' And I repeat in a *comical* voice (I cry out to the sky, at times, in this way): 'absolutely nothing'.

The extreme limit of the 'possible' – We are there in the end. But so late? . . . what, without knowing it we reached it? (in truth, nothing is changed) by a detour: one man bursts out laughing, the other is goaded and beats his wife, we become dead drunk, we make others perish in torture.

Absurdity of reading what should tear one apart to the point of dying and, to begin with, of preparing one's lamp, a drink, one's bed, of winding one's watch. I laugh at this, but what to say of 'poets' who imagine themselves above calculated attitudes, without admitting to themselves that like me their heads are empty: to show this one day, with discipline – cold – up to the moment where one is broken, pleading, where one ceases to dissimulate, to be absent. Is it a question of exercises? well thought-out? intended? It is a matter, in effect, of exercises, of *constraints*. The joke of wanting to be a man flowing with the current, without ever hemming oneself in, without ever leaving a leg to stand on – this is to become the accomplice of inertia. What is strange is that, in evading experience, one doesn't see the responsibility which one has assumed; none can overwhelm more: it is *inexpiable sin*, the possibility glimpsed for once of abandoning it for the grains of a life without distinction. The possibility is mute, it neither threatens nor condemns, but one who, fearing to die himself, lets it die, is like a cloud disappointing the anticipation of sunlight.

I no longer imagine man to be *laughing*, laughing at the ultimate possibility itself – laughing, turning his back, mute, in order to give himself to the enchantment of life, without ever, be it once, evading experience. But should failure one day take hold of him, should he refuse, in failure, to go to the end (through the route of failure – then the possibility itself claims him, lets him know that it waits for him), he evades the possibility and that's it for his innocence: in him begins the ungraspable play of sin, of remorse, of the pretence of remorse, then total forgetting and the pedestrian.

Should one look at last at the history of men – man by man; in the long run, it appears in its entirety as if it were a flight; at first in the face of life (this is sin), then in the face of sin (this is the long night traversed by foolish laughter), with anguish at an innermost depth only.

Every man, to conclude, has conquered the right to absence, to certainty; each street is the limited face of this conquest.

To experience the slow pleasure, the decisive rigour of firm despair, to be hard, and guarantor of death rather than victim. The difficulty, in despair, is to be whole: however, the words, as I write, fail me . . . Egotism inherent in despair: in it arises the indifference to communication. 'Arises' at the very least, for . . . I write. Moreover words designate poorly what the human being experiences; I say 'despair' – one must understand me: here I am defeated, in the depths of cold, inhaling an odour of death, at the same time lethargic, committed to my destiny, loving it – like an animal its little ones – no longer desiring anything. The summit of joy is not joy, for, in joy, I sense the moment coming when it will end, while, in despair, I sense only death coming: I have of it only an anguished desire, but a desire and no other desire. Despair is simple: it is the absence of hope, of all *enticement*. It is the state of deserted expanses and – I can imagine – of the sun.

I fail, no matter what I write, in this, that I should be linking the infinite – insane – richness of 'possibles' to the precision of meaning. To this fruitless task I am compelled – happily? Perhaps, for I can henceforth not conceive of my life, if not pinned to the *extreme limit of the 'possible'*. (This assumes, to begin with, a superhuman intelligence, while I have often had to resort to the more resourceful intelligence of others . . . But what to do? Forget? immediately, I sense, I would go *mad*: one still understands poorly the misery of a mind *divested*.) No doubt, it suffices that a single individual reach the extreme limit: for all that, between him and the others – who avoid him – he keeps a link. Without that he would only be an oddity, not the extreme limit of the 'possible'. Noises of all sorts, cries, chatter, laughter – it is necessary that everything be lost within him, become empty of meaning in his despair. Intelligence, communication, supplicating misery, *sacrifice* (the hardest no doubt is to *open oneself* to an infinite foolishness: in order to escape it – the extreme limit is the only point through which man escapes his limited stupidity – but at the same time in order to sink into it). There is nothing which mustn't go to the appointed place of meeting. The strangest is despair, which paralyses the rest and absorbs it into itself. And 'my everything'? 'My everything' is nothing but a naive being, hostile towards joking: when it is there, my night becomes colder, the desert in which I find myself more empty, there is not longer any limit: beyond known possibilities, an anguish so great inhabits the grey of the sky, in the same way that a monk inhabits the darkness of a tomb.

My effort will be in vain if it doesn't compel conviction. But it is dissipated within me every hour! from the *extreme limit* I descend to the most stupefied state – assuming that at rare moments I have touched the *extreme limit*. In these conditions, how does one believe that the *extreme limit* should one day be the *possibility* of man, that one day men (be it in an infinitesimal number) should have access to the extreme limit? And yet, without the extreme limit, life is only a long deception, a series of defeats without combat followed by impotent retreat – it is degradation.

By definition, the extreme limit of the 'possible' is that point where, despite the unintelligible position which it has for him in being, man, having stripped himself of enticement and fear, advances so far that one cannot conceive of the possibility of going further. Needless to say to what degree it is vain to imagine a pure play of intelligence without anguish (although philosophy closes itself in this impasse). Anguish is no less than intelligence the means for knowing, and the extreme limit of the 'possible', in other respects, is no less life than knowledge. Communication still is, like anguish, to live and to know. The extreme limit of the 'possible' assumes laughter, ecstasy, terrified approach towards death; assumes error, nausea, unceasing agitation of the 'possible' and the impossible and, to conclude – broken, nevertheless, by degrees, slowly desired – the state of supplication, its absorption into despair. Nothing of what man can *know*, to this end, could be evaded without degradation, without sin (I think, by taking a more negative view of the situation, the stakes being ultimate, of the worst of disgraces, of desertion: for one who has felt himself to be called once, there is no further reason, further excuse; he can only remain where he is). Every human being not going to the extreme limit is the *servant* or the *enemy* of man. To the extent that he does not attend, through some servile task, to communal subsistance, his desertion contributes to giving man a despicable destiny.

Common knowledge or knowledge found in laughter, anguish or all other analogous experience is subordinated – this arises from the rules which they follow – to the extreme limit of the 'possible'. Each bit of knowledge is worth something in its limits, although it is necessary to know what it is worth if the extreme limit is there – to know what an ultimate experience would add to it. At first, at the extreme limit of the 'possible', everything gives way: the edifice itself of reason – in an instant of insane courage, its majesty is dissipated; what subsists at the worst, like a piece of shaking wall, increases, does not calm the vertiginous feeling. Useless impudence of recriminations: it was necessary to experience this, nothing resists the necessity of going further. If it had been required, madness would have been the payment.

A despicable destiny . . . Everything has solidarity in man. There was always in some the bitter will – be it diffuse – to go to the furthest point that man could go. But if man ceased to *wish to be himself* with as much bitterness, that would only occur with the collapse of all desire – in whatever way that this desire is exerted (enchantment, combat, quest).

In order to proceed to the end of man, it is necessary, at a certain point, no longer to submit to, but to force destiny. What is contrary: poetic nonchalance, the passive attitude, the distaste for a virile reaction which is decisive – this is literary débâcle (beautiful pessimism). The downfall of Rimbaud who had to turn his back on the 'possible' which he attained, in order to find once again a decisive force intact within him. Access to the extreme limit has as a condition the hatred not of poetry, but of poetic femininity (the absence of decision; the poet is woman; invention, words rape him). I oppose to poetry the experience of the possible. It is less a matter of contemplation than of rupture. It is however of 'mystic experience' that I speak (Rimbaud practised it, but without the tenacity which he later exerted in trying his fortune. To his experience, he gave a poetic outlet; in general, he ignored the simplicity which affirms (inclinations not worth pursuing are mentioned in some of his letters). He chose feminine evasiveness; that which is aesthetic; uncertain, involuntary expression).

A feeling of impotence: to the apparent disorder of my ideas, I have the key, but I don't have the time to open. Closed-in, solitary distress, the ambition which I have conceived being so great that . . . I would like, as well, to go to bed, to cry, to fall asleep. I remain there, several moments longer, wanting to force destiny, *and broken.*

Last hope: to forget, to come back to innocence, to the playfulness of despair.

Prayer to put me to bed: 'God who sees my efforts, give me the night of your blind man's eyes.'

Provoked, God replies; I become strained to the point of collapse and *I see Him*; then I forget. As much disorder as in dreams.

III

Release of tension. Crossed the church of Saint-Roch. Before the giant, golden, hazy image of sun, a movement of gaity, of childish spirits and of rapture. Further on, I looked at a wooden balustrade and I saw that the housekeeping was shoddy. I touched, on a whim, one of the banisters: my finger left a mark in the dust.

Conclusion of a discussion on the train. – Those who don't know that the foundation is lacking, who are satisfied with wise maxims, while they would be reduced, if they suddenly knew, to the absurd, to pleading. I waste my time in wanting to warn. Tranquillity, good-naturedness, genteel discussion as if war . . . and when I say war. Decidedly, no one looks squarely at the sun, the human eye evades it . . . the skull of God bursts . . . and no one hears.

My friends avoid me. I frighten, not because of my cries, but because I cannot leave anyone in peace. I simplify: haven't I often given good pretexts?

To grasp the extent of knowledge, I go back to the source. First a small child, in every way similar to the madmen (the absent ones) I play with today. The miniature 'absent ones' are not in contact with the world, *if not through the channel of grown-ups*: the result of an intervention on the part of grown-ups is *childishness*, a fabrication. Grown-ups *clearly* reduce being coming into the world, which we are at first, to the level of trinkets. This seems to me to be important: that the passage to the state of nature (from birth) to our state of reason should necessarily take place through the route of *childishness*. It is strange on our part to attribute to the child itself the responsibility for childishness, which would be the character proper of children. Childishness is the state into which *we put* naive being, by virtue of the fact that, even without precisely willing this, we direct it towards the point at which we find ourselves. When we laugh at infantile absurdity, laughter disguises our shame, seeing to what we reduce life emerging from Nothingness.

Suppose that the universe engenders the stars, the stars the earth . . . the earth the animals and children, and children adults. The error of children: to derive truth from grown-ups. Each truth possesses a convincing force (and why put it into doubt?) but it has as a consequence its counterpart of errors. It is a fact that our truths, at first, introduce the child into a series of errors which constitute childishness. But one speaks of childishness when it is *visible* to all: no one laughs at a scholar, for to see in him childishness would demand that one surpass him, as much as the grown-up surpasses the child (this is never completely true – if he is not inherently ridiculous – and, in a word, it almost never happens).

My conduct with my friends is motivated: each being is, I believe, incapable on his own, of going to the end of being. If he tries, he is submerged within a 'private being' which has meaning only for himself. Now there is no meaning for a lone individual: being alone would of itself reject the 'private being' if it saw it as such (if I wish my life to have meaning for me, it is necessary that it have meaning *for others*: no one would dare give to life a meaning which he alone would perceive, from which life in its entirety would escape, except within himself). At the extreme limit of the 'possible', it is true, there is nonsense . . . but only of that which had a prior sense, for *supplication* – arising from the absence of sense – fixes, in short, a sense, a final sense: this is fulguration, even 'apotheosis' of nonsense. But I don't attain the extreme limit on my own and, in actual fact, I can't believe the extreme limit attained, for I never remain there. If I had to be the only one having attained it (assuming that I had . . .), it would be as though it hadn't occurred. For if there subsisted a satisfaction, as small as I imagine it to be, it would distance me as much from the extreme limit. I cannot for a moment cease to incite myself to attain the extreme limit, and cannot make a distinction between myself and those with whom I desire to communicate.

I can only, I suppose, reach the extreme limit in repetition, for this reason, that I am never sure of having attained it, that I will never be sure. And even supposing the extreme limit attained, it would still not be the extreme limit, if I 'fell asleep'. The extreme limit implies 'one mustn't sleep during that time' (right to the moment of dying), but Pascal accepted sleeplessness in view of the beatitude to come (at least he gave himself that reason). I refuse to be *happy* (to be saved).

What the desire to be happy means: suffering and the desire to escape. When I suffer (for example: yesterday, rheumatism, the cold and above all, anguish – having read passages from the *120 Days*), I become attached to little pleasures. The nostalgia for salvation responds perhaps to the increase of suffering (or rather to the incapacity to bear it). The idea of salvation comes, I believe, from one whom suffering *breaks apart*. He who masters it, on the contrary, needs to be broken, to proceed on the path towards rupture.

A comic little summary. Hegel, I imagine, touched upon the extreme limit. He was still young and believed himself to be going mad. I even imagine that he worked out the system in order to escape (each type of conquest is, no doubt, the deed of a man fleeing a threat). To conclude, Hegel attains *satisfaction*, turns his back on the extreme limit. *Supplication is dead within him.* Whether or not one seeks salvation, in any case, one continues to live, one can't be sure, one must continue to supplicate. While yet alive, Hegel won salvation, killed supplication, *mutilated himself*. Of him, only the handle of a shovel remained, a modern man. But before mutilating himself, no doubt he touched upon the extreme limit, knew supplication:

his memory brought him back to the perceived abyss, *in order to annul it!* The system is the annulment.

Conclusion of the summary. Modern man, the annulled one (but at no cost), took pleasure in salvation on earth. Kierkegaard is the extreme limit of the Christian. Dostoevsky (in the *Underground*) that of shame. In the *120 Days*, we attain the summit of voluptuous terror.

In Dostoevsky, the extreme limit is the effect of the breaking apart; but it is a breaking apart which is like a winter flood: it overflows. Nothing is more painful, more sickly, more like pale religious complication. The *Underground* attributes the extreme limit to misery. There is trickery, as in Hegel's writing, but Dostoevsky extricates himself differently. In Christianity it may not count to degrade supplication, to engulf man entirely in shame. One says: 'Never mind that . . .' but no, for (except for the ambiguity) it is a matter of humiliating, of depriving of value. All the same, I didn't moan: that the extreme limit should be attained through shame is not so bad, but to limit it to shame! Dazzled in the depths, to pass the extreme limit off to the demoniacal – at all costs – is to betray.

My means: expression, my awkwardness. The ordinary condition of life: rivalry between various individuals, striving to be the best. Caesar: '. . . rather than be second in Rome'. Men are such – so wretched – that everything seems worthless – unless it surpasses. Often I am so sad that to measure my insufficiency of means without despairing wears me out. The problems which are worth being considered have meaning only on the condition that, posing them, one attains the summit: mad pride necessary for being torn apart. And at times – our nature slips into dissolution for nothing – one tears oneself apart with the sole aim of satisfying this pride: everything is ruined in an all-absorbing vanity. It would be better to be nothing more than a village pedlar, to look at the sun with a sickly eye, rather than . . .

The linkage of the extreme limit to vanity, then of vanity to the extreme limit. Childishness, knowing itself to be such, is deliverance, but taking itself seriously, it is enmired. The search for the extreme limit can in its turn become a habit, dependent on childishness: one must laugh at it, unless, by chance, one has a heavy heart: then ecstasy and madness are within reach.

Once again, childishness recognized as such is the glory, not the shame of man. On the other hand, if one says, with Hobbes, that laughter degrades, one reaches the depths of degradation. Nothing is more childish, nor further from knowing itself to be so. All seriousness avoiding the extreme limit is the degradation of man: through this his slavish nature is rendered tangible. Once again, I call forth childishness, glory: the extreme limit is at the end, is only at the end, like death.

At the elusive extreme limit of my being, I am already dead, and *I* in this growing state of death speak to the living: of death, of the extreme limit. The most serious seem to me to be children, who don't know that they are children: they separate me from true children who know it and who laugh at being. But to be a child, one must know that the serious exists – elsewhere and mattering little – if not, the child could no longer laugh nor know anguish.

It is the extreme limit, mad tragedy, not the seriousness of the statistical, which children need in order to play and to become afraid.

The extreme limit is a window: fear of the extreme limit commits one to the darkness of a prison, with an empty will for 'penal administration'.

IV

In the infinite horror of war, man, en masse, has access to the extreme point which terrifies him. But man is far from wanting horror (and the extreme limit): his destiny is, in part, to try to avoid the unavoidable. His eyes, although eager for light, persistently avoid the sun, and the gentleness of his glance, in advance, betrays the quickly arrived darkness of sleep: if I envisage the human masses, in their opaque consistency, it is as if already asleep, fleeing and withdrawn in stupor. The fatality of a blind movement nevertheless throws them back towards the extreme limit to which, one day, they suddenly gain access.

The horror of war is greater than that of inner experience. The desolation of a battlefield, in principle, has something more grave about it than 'dark night'. But on the battlefield, one approaches horror with a movement which overcomes it: action, project linked to action, permits the *surpassing* of horror. This surpassing gives to action, to project, a captivating grandeur – but horror is in itself negated.

I have understood that I was avoiding the project of an inner experience, and I contented myself with being at its mercy. I have such an eager desire for it; its necessity imposes itself upon me, without my having *decided* anything. In truth, no one can – the nature of experience is, apart from derision, not to be able to exist as project.

I live, and everything becomes as though life without the extreme limit were conceivable. And what is more, desire persists in me, but it is weak. Still yet, the dark perspectives of the extreme limit are inscribed within my memory, but I no longer dread them, and I remain an imbecile, concerned about laughable miseries, about cold, about the sentence which I shall write, about my projects: the 'night' into which I know I am thrown, into which I fall during this time, and with me everything that is – this truth that I am aware of, that I can have no doubts about – I am like a child before it, it escapes from me, I remain blind. I belong, for the moment, to the realm of objects which I use, and I remain unconnected to what I write. To be in night, to sink into night, without even having enough strength to *see it*, to know oneself to be in this closed darkness, and despite it, to *see clearly* – I can still bear this trial while laughing, my eyes closed, at my 'childishness'.

I come to this position: inner experience is the opposite of action. Nothing more.

'Action' is utterly dependent upon project. And what is serious, is that discursive thought is itself engaged in the mode of existence of project. Discursive thought is evinced by an individual engaged in action: it takes place within him beginning with his projects, on the level of reflection upon projects. Project is not only the mode of existence implied by action, necessary to action – it is a way of being in paradoxical time: *it is the putting off of existence to a later point.*

One who, now, discovers pity for multitudes wasting their lives (to the extent that projects dominate them), could have the simplicity of the Gospel: anguish, the beauty of tears, would together introduce transparency into his words. I say this as simply as I can (although a ruthless irony provokes me): impossible for me to meet others and their concerns. Moreover, the news is not good. And this is not a bit of 'news'; in a sense, it is a secret.

Therefore, to speak, to think, short of joking or . . . is to dodge existence: it is not to die but to be dead. It is to enter the extinguished and calm world in which we usually linger: there everything is suspended, life is put off until later, from postponement to postponement . . . The slight displacement of projects suffices – the flame is extinguished; after the tempest of passions there follows a period of calm. What is strangest is that, on its own, the exercise of thought introduces in the mind the same suspension, the same peace, as activity in the place of work. Descartes' small affirmation is the most subtle of escapes. (Descartes' motto: '*Larvatus prodeo*'; what proceeds, though hidden: I am in anguish and I think; thought in me *suspends* anguish;

I am the being gifted with the power to *suspend* within him being itself. Following Descartes: the world of 'progress', in other words, of project, is the world in which we find ourselves. War disturbs it, it is true: the world of project remains, but in doubt and anguish.)

Principle of inner experience: to emerge through project from the realm of project.

Inner experience is led by discursive reason. Reason alone has the power to undo its work, to hurl down what it has built up. Madness has no effect, allowing debris to subsist, disturbing along with reason the faculty for communicating (perhaps, above all, it is rupture of inner communication). Natural exaltation or intoxication have a certain 'flash in the pan' quality. Without the support of reason, we don't reach 'dark incandescence'.

Up until now, almost all inner experience depended upon the obsession for salvation. Salvation is the summit of all possible project and the height of matters relating to projects. Moreover, by virtue of the very fact that salvation is a summit, it is negation of projects of momentary interest. At the extreme limit, the desire for salvation turns into the hatred of all project (of the putting off of existence until later): of salvation itself, suspected of having a commonplace motive. If I, in anguish, exhaust remote prospects and inner depths, I see this: salvation *was* the sole means of dissociating eroticism (the Bacchic consummation of bodies) from the nostalgia for existing without delay. A commonplace means, no doubt, but eroticism . . .

Against pride. My privilege is to be humiliated by my profound stupidity and, no doubt, through others, I perceive a greater stupidity. It is vain to linger over differences at this degree of thickness. What I am able to do more than others: to see within me immense storage closets, dressing-rooms; I have not succumbed to the dread which ordinarily averts one's glances; during the feeling that I had of an inner collapse, I didn't flee – I tried only feebly to mislead myself and above all, I didn't succeed. What I perceive is the complete destitution of man, his thickness thrown in – the condition for his complacency.

The imitation of Jesus: according to Saint John of the Cross, we must imitate in God (Jesus) the fall from grace, the agony, the moment of 'non-knowledge' of the *'lamma sabachtani'*; drunk to the lees, Christianity is absence of salvation, the despair of God. It fails, in that it attains its goals out of breath. The agony of God in the person of man is fatal – it is the abyss into which vertigo tempted him to fall. In the agony of a God, the confession of sin is irrelevant. This agony justifies not only heaven (the dark incandescence of the heart), but hell (childishness, flowers, Aphrodite, laughter).

Despite appearances to the contrary, the concern for misfortune is the dead part of Christianity. It is anguish reducible to project: indefinitely workable formula, each day a bit more thickness, an increased state of death. Existence and death losing themselves, on the scale of the human masses, in project – life put off infinitely. Of course, ambiguity plays a part in this: life is condemned in Christianity, and the men of progress sanctify it; Christians have limited it to ecstasy and to sin (this was a positive attitude); progress negates ecstasy, sin – equates life with project, sanctifies project (work): in the world of progress, once project is recognized as the serious side of existence, life is nothing but permissible childishness (anguish, to which misery gives substance, is necessary for authority, but project occupies the mind).

Where the intimate character of project is revealed: its mode of existence transposed into the idleness of rich women and, in general, of the worldly. If the polite, calmed manners and the emptiness of project prevail, life no longer puts up with idleness. In a similar way, consider the boulevards on a Sunday afternoon. The worldly life and bourgeois Sundays bring out the character of ancient festivals, the forgetting of all project, consummation beyond measure.

And above all, 'nothing', I know 'nothing' – I moan this like a sick child, whose attentive mother holds his forehead (mouth open over the basin). But I don't have a mother, the basin is the starry sky (in my poor nausea, it is thus).

Several lines read in a recent brochure:[1]

'I have often thought of the day when the birth of a man who would have his eyes very genuinely *on the inside* would at last be consecrated. His life would be like a long tunnel of phosphorescent furs and he would only have to stretch out in order to plunge into everything which he has in common with the rest of the world and which is atrociously incommunicable to us. At the thought that the birth of such a man were to be rendered possible, tomorrow, by a common accord with his fellow beings and his world, I would like everyone to be able to shed tears of joy.' This is accompanied by four pages in which an intention principally turned towards the outside is expressed. The possibility of the envisaged birth leaves me, hélas! with my eyes dry: I have *fever* and no longer any tears.

What can they mean, this 'Golden Age', this vain concern for the 'best possible conditions' and the sick will of a mankind in complete accord? In truth, the will for an *exhausting* experience always begins in euphoria. Impossible to grasp what one is engaging oneself in, to guess the price that one will pay – but later, one will pay *without getting one's fill of paying*; no one felt the extent to which he would be ruined or the shame he would have at not being ruined enough. This said, if I see that one cannot bear to *live*, that one is suffocating, that in any case one flees from anguish and resorts to project, my anguish grows from the anguish which turbulence evades.

Poetic idleness, poetry put into the form of a project – that which an André Breton could not tolerate laid bare, which the intended abandon of his sentences was to conceal. And for me, anguish without escape, the feeling of complicity, of being harassed, hunted. Never, however, more complete! one can't offend me: it is the desert which I wanted, the site (the condition) which was necessary for a clear and interminable death.

What I see: poetic facility, diffuse style, verbal project, ostentation and the fall into the worst: commonness, literature. One trumpets that one is going to revive man: one commits him a bit more to the old rut. Vanity! This is quickly said (vanity is not what it appears; it is only the condition for a project, for a putting off of existence until later). One has egotistical satisfaction only in projects; the satisfaction escapes as soon as one accomplishes; one returns quickly to the plan of the project – one falls in this way into flight, like an animal into an endless trap; on one day or another, one dies an idiot. In the anguish enclosing me, my gaiety justifies, as much as it can, human vanity, the immense desert of vanities, its dark horizon where pain and night are hiding – a dead and divine gaiety.

> *And vanity within me!*
> *Undoubtedly.*

'That which I write: an appeal! the most insane, the best destined for the deaf. I address a prayer to my fellow beings (at least to some of them): vanity of this cry of the desert man! You are such that if you perceived yourselves as I do, you could no longer be so. For (here I fall to the ground) have pity on me! I have seen what you are.'

Man and his 'possible'. Sordid being, stupid (to the point of crying out in the cold), has laid down his *possible*. The gentle (flattering) idea occurs: he follows it, catches it. But, this *possible* placed, for a moment, on the ground?
He forgets it!

Decidedly, he forgets!
That's it: it has left.

Speaking here or there of the extreme limit attained, I have spoken of writers, even of a 'man of letters' (Dostoevsky). At the thought that confusion might arise easily, I will be more precise. One can know nothing of man which has not taken the form of a sentence, and the infatuation for poetry, on the other hand, makes of untranslatable strings of words a summit. The extreme limit is elsewhere. It is only completely reached if communicated (man is several – solitude is the void, nothingness, lies). Should some sort of expression give evidence of it: the extreme limit is distinct from it. It is never literature. If poetry expresses it, the extreme limit is distinct from it: to the point of not being poetic, for if poetry has it as an object, it doesn't reach it. When the extreme limit is there, the means which serve to attain it are no longer there.

The last known poem of Rimbaud is not the extreme limit. If Rimbaud reached the extreme limit, he only attained the communication of it by means of his despair: he suppressed possible communication, he no longer wrote poems.

The refusal to communicate is a more hostile means of communication, but the most powerful; if it was possible, it is because Rimbaud turned his back on it. In order not to communicate any longer, he gave up. If not, it was in order to have given up that he ceased to communicate. No one will know if horror (weakness) or modesty was responsible for Rimbaud's giving up. It is possible that the limits of horror have been extended (no more God). In any case, to speak of weakness makes little sense: Rimbaud maintained his will for the extreme limit on other levels (that above all of giving up). It is possible that he gave up, failing having attained it (the extreme limit is not disorder or luxuriance) being too demanding to bear it, too lucid not to see. It is even possible that after having attained it, but doubting that this should have a meaning or even that this should take place – as the state of one who attains it does not last – he couldn't bear doubt. A longer search would be useless, although the will for the extreme limit stops at nothing (we can't really attain it).

The self in no way matters. For a reader, I am any individual: name, identity, the historical don't change anything. He (the reader) is any one and I (the author) am also any one. He and I, having emerged without name from . . . without name, are for this . . . without name, just as two grains of sand are for the desert, or rather two waves losing themselves in two adjacent waves are for a sea. The . . . without name to which the 'known personality' of the world of etc. belongs, to which it belongs so totally that it is not aware of it. O death infinitely blessed without which a 'personality' would belong to the world of etc. Misery of living men, disputing to the death the possibilities of the world of etc. Joy of the dying man, wave among waves. Inert joy of the dying, of the desert, fall into the impossible, cry without resonance, silence of a fatal accident.

The Christian easily dramatizes life: he lives in the presence of Christ and this takes him outside of himself. Christ is the totality of being, and yet he is, like the 'lover', personal, like the 'lover', desirable: and suddenly – torment, agony, death. The follower of Christ is led to torment. Has led himself to torment: not to some insignificant torment, but to divine agony. Not only has he the means of attaining torment, but he could not avoid it, and this is the torment which exceeds him, which exceeds God himself – God, who is no less man and tormentable than him.

It does not suffice to recognize – this only puts the mind into play; it is also necessary that the recognition take place in the heart (intimate, half-blind movements . . .). This is no longer philosophy, but sacrifice (communication). Strange coincidence between the naive philosophy of sacrifice (in ancient India) and the pleading philosophy of non-knowledge: sacrifice, the movement of the heart, transposed into knowledge (there is an inversion from the origin to the present moment – the old path leading from the heart to the intelligence, the present one in the opposite direction).

What is strangest is that non-knowledge should have the ability to sanction. As if, from the outside, it had been said to us: 'Here you are at last.' The path of non-knowledge is the emptiest of nonsense. I could say: 'Everything has been attained.' No. For supposing that I say it, immediately thereafter I perceive the same closed horizon as the instant before. The more I advance into knowledge, be it through the path of non-knowledge, and the more ultimate non-knowledge becomes heavy with import, anguishing. In point of fact, I give myself to non-knowledge (this is communication), and as there is communication with the darkened world, rendered unfathomable by non-knowledge, dare I say God: and it is thus that there is once again (mystical) knowledge, but I can't stop (I can't – but I must regain my breath): 'God if he knew.' And further on, always further on. God as the lamb substituted for Isaac. This is no longer sacrifice. Further on there is naked sacrifice, without Isaac. The sacrifice is madness, the renunciation of all knowledge, the fall into the void, and nothing, neither in the fall nor in the void, is revealed, for the revelation of the void is but a means of falling further into absence.

NON-KNOWLEDGE LAYS BARE.

This proposition is the summit, but must be understood in this way: lays bare, therefore *I see* what knowledge was hiding up to that point, but if I see, *I know*. Indeed, I know, but non-knowledge again lays bare what I have known. If nonsense is sense, the sense which is nonsense is lost, becomes nonsense once again (without possible end).

If the proposition (non-knowledge lays bare) possesses a sense – appearing, then disappearing immediately thereafter – this is because it has the meaning: NON-KNOWLEDGE COMMUNICATES ECSTASY. Non-knowledge is ANGUISH before all else. In anguish, there appears a nudity which puts one into ecstasy. But ecstasy itself (nudity, communication) is elusive if anguish is elusive. Thus ecstasy only remains possible in the anguish of ecstasy, in this sense, that it cannot be satisfaction, *grasped knowledge*. Obviously, ecstasy is *grasped knowledge* above all else, in particular in the extreme surrender [*dénuement*]² and the extreme construction of the surrender which I, my life and my written work represent (this I know: no one has ever taken knowledge as far, no one has been able to do so; but for me, it was easy – obligatory). But when the extreme limit of knowledge is there (and the extreme limit of knowledge which I have just proposed is beyond absolute knowledge), it is the same as with absolute knowledge – everything is upset. Barely have I known – entirely known – then surrender in the realm of knowledge (where knowledge leaves me) is revealed, and anguish begins again. But anguish is the horror of surrender and the moment comes when, in audacity, surrender is loved, when I give myself to surrender: it is therefore the nudity which puts one into ecstasy. Then knowledge returns, satisfaction, once again anguish, I begin again, more quickly, right up to exhaustion (just as, in mad laughter, anguish arising from the fact that it is misplaced to laugh increases the laughter).

In ecstasy, one can *let oneself go* – this is satisfaction, happiness, platitude. Saint John of the Cross contests rapture and the seductive image, but calms himself in the theopathic state. I have followed right to the very end his method of hardening the heart.

Suppression of the subject and of the object: the only means of not resulting in the possession of the object by the subject, that is to say in avoiding the absurd rush of *ipse* wanting to become everything.

Conversation with Blanchot. I say to him: inner experience has neither goal, nor authority, which justify it. If I destroy, burst the concern for a goal, at the very least, a void subsists. Blanchot reminds me that goal, authority are the requirements of discursive thought; I insist, describing experience in its extreme form, asking him how he believes this to be possible without authority or anything. On the subject of this authority he adds that it must be expiated.

I want to provide once again the schema of the experience which I call pure experience. I reach first of all the extreme limit of knowledge (for example, I mimic absolute knowledge, in whatever way, but that assumes an infinite effort of the mind wanting knowledge). I know then that I know nothing. As *ipse* I wanted to be everything (through knowledge) and I fall into anguish: the occasion of this anguish is my non-knowledge, nonsense beyond hope (here non-knowledge does not abolish particular knowledge, but its sense – removes from it all sense). I can know after the fact what constitutes the anguish of which I speak. Anguish assumes the desire to communicate – that is, to lose myself – but not complete resolve: anguish is evidence of my fear of communicating, of losing myself. Anguish is given in the theme of knowledge itself: as *ipse*, through knowledge, I would like to be everything, therefore to communicate, to lose myself, however to remain *ipse*. The subject (me, *ipse*) and the object (in part undefined, as long as it is not entirely grasped) are presented for communication, before it takes place. The subject wants to take hold of the object in order to possess it (this will results from being engaged in the play of compositions), but the subject can only lose itself: the nonsense of the will to know appears, nonsense of all possible, making *ipse* know that it is going to lose itself and knowledge with it. As long as *ipse* perseveres in its will to know and to be *ipse*, anguish lasts, but if *ipse* abandons itself and knowledge with it, if it gives itself up to non-knowledge in this abandon, then rapture begins. In rapture, my existence finds a sense once again, but the sense is referred immediately to *ipse*; it becomes *my* rapture, a rapture which I *ipse* possess, giving satisfaction to my will to be everything. As soon as I emerge from it, communication, the loss of myself cease; I have ceased to abandon myself – I remain there, but with a new knowledge.

The movement begins again starting from there: I can formulate new knowledge (I have just done so). I arrive at this notion: that subject, object, are perspectives of being at the moment of inertia, that the intended object is the projection of the subject *ipse* wanting to become everything, that all representation of the object is phantasmagoria resulting from this foolish and necessary will (that one postulates the object as thing or as existing matters little), that one necessarily ends up speaking of communication by grasping that communication pulls the rug out from under the object as well as from under the subject (this is what becomes clear at the summit of communication, when there is communication between subject and object of the same type, between two cells, between two individuals). I can formulate this representation of the world and regard it at first as the solution of all puzzles. Suddenly I perceive the same thing as with the first form of knowledge, that this supreme knowledge leaves one as night leaves a child, naked in the depths of the woods. This time, what is more serious is that the sense of communication is at stake. But when communication itself – at a moment when, inaccessible, it had disappeared – appears to me as nonsense, I attain the height of anguish; in a surge of despair, I abandon myself and communication is once again given to me – rapture and joy.

At this moment, the formulation is no longer necessary – it is done: it is immediately thereafter and from rapture itself that I enter once again into the night of the bewildered child, into anguish, in order at a later point to return to rapture – and this without other end than exhaustion, without possibility of stopping other than a collapse.

This is supplicating joy.

The maladies of inner experience. In it the mystic has the power to animate what pleases him; the intensity suffocates, eliminates doubt and one perceives what one was expecting. As if we disposed of a powerful breath of life: each presupposition of the mind is animated. Rapture is not a window looking out on the outside, on the beyond, but a mirror. This is the first malady. The second is the putting into project of experience. No one can lucidly have an experience without having had the project for it. This less serious malady is not avoidable: project must even be maintained. Now experience is the opposite of project: I attain experience contrary to the project I had of having it. There is established between experience and project the link which exists between pain and the voice of reason: reason represents the inanity of a moral pain (saying: time will erase pain – as when we must give up a loved one). The wound is there, present, dreadful and contesting reason, recognizing its own solid grounds, but only seeing in this one more horror. I don't suffer any less from a wound, if I sense that it will soon be healed. It is necessary to *make use of* project as of the assurance of an imminent healing. Project can, like the assurance, be a mocking servant, aware of everything, sceptical and knowing itself to be a servant, withdrawing as soon as experience, once it takes place, demands solitude, as do pain (and torment), and cries bitterly: 'Leave me alone.'

The servant, if everything takes place as he intends it, must make himself be forgotten. But he can trick. The first malady, the mirror, is evidence of a crude servant, whose ties to a profound servitude escape him.

The servant of experience is discursive thought. Here, the nobility of the servant rests upon the discipline of the servitude.

Non-knowledge attained, absolute knowledge is no longer anything but one knowledge among others.

V

One must. Is this to moan? I no longer know. Where am I going? Where is this insipid cloud of thoughts headed – this cloud which I imagine to be similar to the sudden blood in a wounded throat? Insipid, in no way bitter (even in the lowest disarray I remain gay, open, generous. And rich, too rich, this throat rich with blood . . .).

My difficulty: total loss of certainty, the difference between a sculpted object and fog (usually we imagine that it is dreadful). If I expressed joy, I would be off the mark: the joy which I have differs from other joys. I am accurate in speaking of fiascos, of collapses without end, of absence of hope. Yet . . . fiasco, collapse, despair are, in my eyes, light, laying bare, glory. One the other hand: deadly indifference – towards what is important to me; incoherent succession of characters, dissonance, chaos. If I still speak of equilibrium, of euphoria, of power, one will only grasp this on the condition that one resemble me (already). To be less obscure: I crucify myself on my own time, drag my feet on the question, but without any right (without the authority to do so). If I had authority at my disposal, everything within me would be servitude, I would admit to being 'guilty'. This is not the case: I have no bitterness. Here a deceptive inconsistency is unveiled, inescapable *sovereign*.

The concern for harmony is a great servitude. We can't escape by refusal: in wanting to avoid the false window, we introduce an aggravated lie: the *false* at least admitted itself to be so!

Harmony is the means of 'realizing' project. Harmony (measure) leads project to a good end: passion, childish desire prevent one from waiting. Harmony is made manifest by the man engaged in project; he has found calm, has eliminated the impatience of desire.

The harmony of the fine arts realizes project in another sense. In the fine arts, man makes 'real' the harmonious mode of existence inherent in project. Art creates a world in the image of the man of project, reflecting this image in all its forms. Yet art is less harmony than the passage (or the return) of harmony to dissonance (in its history and in each work).

Harmony, like project, throws time back into the outside; its principle is the repetition through which all that is 'possible' is made eternal. The ideal is architecture, or sculpture, immobilizing harmony, guaranteeing the duration of motifs whose essence is the annulment of time. Art has moreover borrowed repetition – the tranquil investment of time through a renewed theme – from project.

In art, desire returns, but it is, at first, the desire to annul time (to annul desire) while in project, there was simply rejection of desire. Project is expressly made manifest by the slave; it is work and work executed by one who does not enjoy its fruits. In art, man returns to sovereignty (to the expiration of desire) and – if it is at first the desire to annul desire – barely has it arrived at its goals, than it is the desire to rekindle desire.

Of the successive characters that I am, I do not speak. They are not of interest or I must silence them. I am my words – evoking an inner experience – without having to challenge them. These characters, in principle, are neutral, a bit comical (in my eyes). With respect to the inner experience of which I speak, they are deprived of meaning, except in this respect: that they complete my disharmony.

> *I can't go on, I moan,*
> *I can no longer bear*
> *my prison.*
> *I say this*
> *bitterly:*
> *words which stifle me –*
> *leave me,*
> *release me,*
> *I thirst*
> *for something else.*
> *I want death*
> *and not to admit of*
> *this reign of words,*
> *continuity*
> *without dread,*
> *such that dread*
> *be desirable;*
> *it is nothing*
> *this self which I am,*
> *if not*
> *cowardly acceptance*
> *of what is.*
> *I hate*
> *this life of instrument,*
> *I search for a fissure,*
> *my fissure,*
> *in order to be broken.*

I love rain,
lightning,
mud,
a vast expanse of water,
the depths of the earth,
but not me.
In the depths of the earth,
O my tomb,
deliver me from myself,
I no longer want to be.

Almost every time, if I tried to write a book, fatigue would come before the end. I slowly became a stranger to the project which I had formulated. I would forget what enflamed me the day before, changing from one hour to the next with a drowsy slowness. I escape from myself and my book escapes from me; it becomes almost completely like a forgotten name: I am too lazy to look for it but the obscure feeling of forget fills me with anguish.

And if this book resembles me? If the conclusion escapes from the beginning; is unaware of it or keeps it in indifference? Strange rhetoric! Strange way of invading the impossible! Denial, forgetting, existence without form, ambiguous weapons ... Laziness itself used as unbreakable energy.

At nightfall, on the street, suddenly I remembered, Quarr Abbey, a French monastery on the Isle of Wight, where in 1920 I spent two or three days – remembered as a house surrounded by pines, beneath a moonlit softness, at the seashore; the moonlight linked to the medieval beauty of the service – everything which made me hostile towards a monastic life disappeared – in this place I only experienced the exclusion of the rest of \the world. I imagined myself within the walls of the cloister, removed from agitation, for an instant imagining myself a monk and saved from jagged, discursive life: in the street itself, with the help of darkness, my heart streaming with blood became inflamed – I knew a sudden rapture. With the help as well of my indifference to logic, to the spirit of consequence.

Within the walls, the sky a ghostly grey, dusk, the damp uncertainty of space at that precise time; divinity had then a mad, deaf presence, illuminating up to intoxication. My body hadn't interrupted its rapid step, but ecstasy slightly wrenched its muscles. No uncertainty this time, but an indifference towards certainty. I write divinity, not wanting to know anything, not knowing anything. At other times, my ignorance was the abyss over which I was suspended.

What I must *execrate* today: voluntary ignorance, methodical ignorance by which I have come to search for ecstasy. Not that ignorance opens, in fact, the heart to rapture. But I put the *impossible* to the bitter test. All profound life is heavy with the *impossible*. Intention, project together destroy. Yet *I have known* that I knew nothing and this, my secret: 'non-knowledge communicates ecstasy'. Existence has since begun again, banal, and based on the appearance of a knowledge. I wanted to escape it, to say to myself: this knowledge is false. I know nothing, absolutely nothing. But I know: 'non-knowledge communicates ecstasy'. I no longer had any *anguish*. I lived enclosed (miserably). At the beginning of this night, the precise image within me of monastic harmony communicated ecstasy to me: no doubt through the foolishness to which I abandoned myself in this way. Unworkability, the impossible! within the disharmony to which *I must* honestly adhere, harmony alone, by virtue of the *I must*, represents a possibility of disharmony: necessary dishonesty, but one cannot become dishonest through a concern for honesty.

And ecstasy is the way out! Harmony! Perhaps, but heart-rending. The way out? It suffices that I look for it: I fall back again, inert, pitiful: the way out from project, from the will for a way out! For project is the prison from which I wish to escape (project, discursive experience): I formed the project to escape from project! And I know that it suffices to break discourse in me; from that moment on, ecstasy is there, from which only discourse distances me – the ecstasy which discursive thought betrays by proposing it as a way out, and betrays by proposing it as absence of a way out. Impotence cries out within me – (I remember) a long, inner, anguished cry: to have known, to know no longer.

That through which discourse is nonsense in its rage as well, but (I moan) not *enough* (within me *not enough*).

Not enough! not enough anguish, suffering . . . I say it, I, child of joy, whom a wild, happy laugh – never ceased to carry (it released me at times: its infinite *distant* levity remained temptation in collapse, in tears and even in the blows which I made with my head against walls). But . . . to maintain a finger in boiling water . . . and I cry out 'not enough'!

I forget – one more time: suffering, laughter, that finger. Infinite surpassing in oblivion, ecstasy, indifference, towards myself, towards this book: I see – that which discourse never managed to attain. I am *open*, yawning gap, to the unintelligible sky and everything in me rushes forth, is reconciled in a final irreconciliation. Rupture of all 'possible', violent kiss, abduction, loss in the entire absence of all 'possible', in opaque and dead night which is nonetheless light – no less unknowable, no less blinding than the depth of the heart.

And above all *no more object*. Ecstasy is not love: love is possession for which the object is necessary, and at the same time possession of the subject, possessed by it. There is no longer subject–object, but a 'yawning gap' between the one and the other and, in the gap, the subject, the object are dissolved; there is passage, communication, but not from one to the other: *the one* and *the other* have lost their separate existence. The questions of the subject, its will to know are suppressed: the subject is no longer there; its interrogation no longer has either meaning or a principle which introduces it. In the same way no answer remains possible. The answer should be 'such is the object', when there is no longer a distinct object.

The subject preserves on the fringes of its ecstasy the role of a child in a drama: surpassed, its presence persists, incapable of more than vaguely and distractedly sensing – presence profoundly absent, it remains off in the wings, occupied as with toys. Ecstasy has no meaning for it, if not that it captivates, *being new*; but should it remain and the subject become bored: ecstasy decidedly no longer has meaning. And as there is in it no desire to persevere in being (this desire belongs to distinct beings), it has no consistency and is dissipated. As if foreign to *man*, ecstasy arises from him, ignorant of the concern of which it was the object, as it is of the intellectual scaffolding dependent upon it (which it allows to collapse): for concern, it is nonsense; for the eagerness to know, it is non-knowledge.

The subject – weariness of itself, necessity of proceeding to the extreme limit – seeks ecstasy, it is true: never does it have *the will* for its ecstasy. There exists an irreducible discord between the subject seeking ecstasy and the ecstasy itself. However, the subject knows ecstasy and senses it: not as a voluntary direction coming from itself, but like the sensation of an effect coming from the outside. I can go before it, instinctively, driven by the distaste for being enmired: then ecstasy arises from a lack of equilibrium. I attain it better by external means, by virtue of the fact that a necessary predisposition cannot exist within me. The spot where I have earlier known ecstasy, memory bewitched by physical sensations, the banal ambiance of which I have kept an exact memory, together have an evocative power greater than the voluntary repetition of a describable movement of the mind.

I carry within me the concern for writing this book like a burden. In reality, I am *acted upon*. Even if nothing, absolutely, responded to the idea which I have of necessary interlocutors (or of necessary readers), the idea alone would act in me. I create with it to such a point that one would more easily remove from me one of my limbs.

The *third*, the companion, the reader who acts upon me is discourse. Or yet still: the reader is discourse – it is he who speaks in me, who maintains in me the discourse intended for him. And no doubt, discourse is project, but even more than this it is that *other*, the reader, who loves me and who already forgets me (kills me), without whose present insistence I could do nothing, would have no inner experience. Not that in moments of violence – of misfortune – I don't forget him, as he himself forgets me – but I tolerate in me the action of project in that it is a link with this obscure *other* sharing my anguish, my torment, desiring my torment as much as I desire his.

Blanchot asked me: why not pursue my inner experience as if I were the *last man*? In a certain sense . . . However, I know myself to be the reflection of the multitude and the sum of its anguish. On the other hand, if I were the last man, the anguish would be the most insane imaginable! I could in no way escape, I would remain before infinite annihilation thrown back into myself or yet still: empty, indifferent. But inner experience is conquest and as such *for others*! The subject in experience loses its way, it loses itself in the object, which itself is dissolved. It could not, however, become dissolved to this point, if its nature didn't allow it this change; the subject in experience in spite of everything remains: to the extent that it is not a child in the drama, a fly on one's nose, it is *consciousness of others* (I had neglected this the other time). Being the fly, the child, it is no longer exactly the subject (it is laughable, in its own eyes laughable); making itself *consciousness of others* and, as the ancient chorus, the witness, the popularizer of the drama, it loses itself in human communication; as subject, it is thrown outside of itself, beyond itself; it ruins itself in an undefined throng of possible exist-ences. But if this throng were to be absent, if the possible were dead, if I were . . . the last one? Would I have to renounce leaving myself, would I remain enclosed in this self as in the depth of a tomb? Would I from today onward have to moan at the idea of not being, of not being able to hope to be the last one; from today onward a monster, to weep for the *misfortune* which overcomes me? For it is possible that *the last one* without chorus, as I want to imagine him, would die, dead to himself, at the infinite twilight that he would be, would sense the walls (even the depth) of the tomb open . . . I can still imagine . . . (I only do it for others!): it is possible that already alive, I am enshrouded in his tomb – that of the *last one*, of this being in distress, unleashing being within him. Laughter, dream and, in sleep, the rooftops fall in a rain of gravel . . . to know nothing, to this point (not of ecstasy, but of sleep): to strangle myself thus, unsolvable puzzle, to accept sleep, the starry universe my tomb, glorified, glory constelled with deaf stars, unintelligible and further than death, terrifying (nonsense: the taste of garlic which the roasted lamb had).

Notes

1 *La Transfusion du Verbe*, in *Naissance de l'homme – object*, by J.-F. Chabrun.
2 [For the term *dénuement*, I have chosen the English word 'surrender'. I would like this word to suggest the state of 'being entirely without means'. The English 'destitution' and 'penury' seemed to be too closely tied to material loss to be satisfactory. TR.]

5

Christ

> The crucified Christ is the most sublime of all symbols – even at
> present.
>
> Friedrich Nietzsche, 1885–6

I now want to contrast, not good and evil, but the 'moral summit', which is
different from the good, and the 'decline', which has nothing to do with evil
and whose necessity determines, on the contrary, modalities of the good.

The summit corresponds to excess, to an exuberance of forces. It brings
about a maximum of tragic intensity. It relates to measureless expenditures
of energy and is a violation of the integrity of individual beings. It is thus
closer to evil than to good.

The decline – corresponding to moments of exhaustion and fatigue –
gives all value to concerns for preserving and enriching the individual. From
it come rules of morality.

To begin with, I will show how the summit of Christ on the cross is an
extremely equivocal expression of evil.

The killing of Jesus Christ is held by Christians as a group to be evil.

It is the greatest sin ever committed.

It even possesses an unlimited nature. Criminals are not the only actors
in this drama, since the fault devolves on all humans. Insofar as someone
does evil (every one of us being *required* to do evil), that person puts Christ
on the cross.

Pilate's executioners crucified Jesus, though the God they nailed to the
cross was put to death as a sacrifice. Crime is the agent of this sacrifice, a
crime that sinners since Adam have infinitely committed. The loathsome-
ness concealed in human life (everything tainted and impossible carried in
its secret places, whit its evil condensed in its stench) has so successfully
violated good that nothing close to it can be imagined.

The text is from chapter 1 of *On Nietzsche*, tr. Bruce Boone (Paragon House, New York,
1992), pp. 17–19. Projected as the third volume of the *Somme athéologique*, the text appeared
in French as part of *Sur Nietzsche: volonté de chance* (Editions Gallimard, Paris, 1945). See *OC*,
VI, pp. 42–4.

The killing of Christ injures the being of God.

It looks as if creatures couldn't communicate with their Creator except through a wound that lacerates integrity.

The wound is intended and desired by God.

The humans who did this are not less guilty.

On the other hand – and this is not the least strange – the guilt is a wound lacerating the integrity of every guilty being.

In this way God (wounded by human guilt) and human beings (wounded by their own guilt with respect to God) find, if painfully, a unity that seems to be their purpose.

If human beings had kept their own integrity and hadn't sinned, God on one hand and human beings on the other would have persevered in their respective isolation. A night of death wherein Creator and creatures bled together and lacerated each other and on all sides, were challenged at the extreme limits of shame: that is what was required for their communion.

Thus 'communication', without which nothing exists for us, is guaranteed by crime. 'Communication' is love, and love taints those whom it unites.

In the elevation upon a cross, humankind attains a summit of evil. But it's exactly from having attained it that humanity ceases being separate from God. So clearly the 'communication' of human beings is guaranteed by evil. Without evil, human existence would turn in upon itself, would be enclosed as a zone of independence: And indeed an absence of 'communication' – empty loneliness – would certainly be the greater evil.

The position of human beings evokes sympathy.

They're driven to 'communicate' (with both indefinite existence and themselves): the absence of 'communication' (an egotistic folding back into self) clearly evokes the greatest condemnation. But since 'communication' can't take place without wounding or tainting our humanity, 'communication' itself is guilty. However the good is construed, it's the good of individuals – but by wanting to attain it (at night and through evil) we are impelled to question the very individuals in relation to whom we had sought it .

A fundamental principle is expressed as follows:

'Communication' cannot proceed from one full and intact individual to another. It requires individuals whose separate existence in themselves is *risked*, placed at the limit of death and nothingness; the moral summit is the moment of risk taking, it is a being suspended in the beyond of oneself, at the limit of nothingness.

6

Love

When all is said and done, I have more than one face. I don't know which is laughing at which.

Love is so excessive a feeling that I prop my head up in my hands. Arising from the passions, this realm of dreams isn't fundamentally a domain of lies. In the end the face is dispersed. In the place where the fabric of things rips open – in the lacerating rip – nothing remains but a person introduced into the fabric's texture.

Layers of dead leaves aren't steps ascending to a throne, and tugboat hoots disperse illusions of enchantment.

Though still, what would correspond to the magnificence of the world if no one spoke to us and communicated a (no doubt indecipherable) message: 'As to this fate that befalls you, this fate you consider yours (the fate of the human being you are) or that you consider the destiny of existence generally (of the immensity you form part of), nothing allows you to reduce it to the poverty of things that remain only what they are. On the contrary, whenever a casual lie happens, or whenever something is transfigured, don't you hear an appeal which must be answered? You can't claim you wished for the journey, only that you are it. And who would challenge the utter distance, the extremity, the desirability of the way? Desirability?! Am I the measure of mysteries? If, perceiving me, you hadn't chosen an unreachable goal, you wouldn't even have approached the mystery!'

Of course night falls, but only to exasperate this desire.

I hate lies (poetic nonsense). But the desire within us has never lied. There's a sickness in desire that often makes us perceive some gap between the object imagined and the real object. It's true, the beloved individual

The text appeared in translation as chapter 5 of the 'February–April 1944' section of *On Nietzsche*, tr. Bruce Boone (Paragon House, New York, 1992), pp. 68–71. Projected as the third volume of the *Somme athéologique*, the text appeared in French as part of *Sur Nietzsche: volonté de chance* (Editions Gallimard, Paris, 1945). See *OC*, VI, pp. 83–6.

differs from the conception I have of that individual. What's worse: to identify the real with the object of desire, it seems, presupposes extraordinary luck.

Contrary to which is the obvious splendour of a universe that reverses the idea we have of this chance. *If nothing in us veils the celestial glories, we are worthy of infinite love.* The beloved doesn't emerge from prosaic reality like a miracle from a series of defined facts. The chance transfiguring this beloved is only the absence of unhappiness. The universe acting within us denies itself in commonly occurring unhappiness (a dreary existence), but affirms itself with the chosen few.

Compared to the person I love, the universe seems poor and empty. This universe isn't 'risked' since it's not 'perishable'.

But the beloved is the 'beloved' for only a single person.

Carnal love, because not 'sheltered from thieves' or vicissitudes, is greater than divine love.

It 'risks' me and the one I love.

God by definition isn't risked.

However far the lovers of God go with their passion, they conceive of it as outside the play of risk, as beyond grace (in the happiness of the elect).

And it's true of course that a woman's lover can't give up (he's compelled to abolish tormenting absence) till at last he has her beneath his roof in this possession. The truth is that, for the most part, love is extinguished in attempts to elude its nature: which has to risk love again and again . . .

Is there anyone who can't comprehend the fact that happiness is the most demanding test of all for lovers? All the same, voluntarily renouncing it would be an artifice, would make love overly sophisticated, something intended, cunning, contrived (I think of lovers as wilfully maintaining their difficult conditions). There remains, however small it be, a chance of going beyond, of exhausting happiness.

Chance, in French, has the same origin (*cadentia* in Latin) as *échéance* ('deadline'). Chance *échoit*, that is, it turns out to be the case. Or it just falls, *tombe* (like good luck or bad, originally). It is the randomness of dice as they fall.

Hence the whimsical idea that I am suggesting Hyperchristianity!

In that popular notion, it isn't humanity that falls and becomes separated from God – though God himself does (or to put it differently, the totality).

God here does not involve 'less than his idea implies'. In fact the opposite, more. But the 'more' is cancelled out insofar as it is God – because God's essence is to be continuously 'risked', or be 'put into risk situations'. In the end humankind remains alone.

To put this in a joking way – humankind is *generalized incarnation*!

Still, in the fall of universality into humankind, certain obnoxious pretences at risk taking, such as with Jesus, no longer apply. (God only seems to relinquish Jesus.) The surrender involved in risk taking is total.

What I love in the person I love – to the point of wanting to die from this love – isn't some individuated existence but the universal aspect of that person. Although this aspect is what risks itself, risks me.

At the popular level of these ideas, God himself is an individual and not a totality (God isn't me), although risk taking isn't applicable to the animals (they are by themselves).

How ponderous and grandiloquent that being is – compared to *beings that fall* (into the 'teacup') of a human being.

Ponderousness is the price paid by impatience, by a search for security.

To speak about the absolute: an ignoble phrase, an inhuman term! Something you would imagine ghosts longing for.

I don't intend to make a deity out of anyone. And I laugh when God falls from banality into the precariousness of incomprehensibility.

A woman has her handkerchiefs, her bed, her stockings. She thinks of going back to the house or to the woods for a moment. Nothing changes if I perceive her existence as transparency, as a gamble, or in fact as chance. Her truth isn't above her. But like the 'teacup', I reach her only in the few moments of chance. She is a voice in which the world answers me. Although – unless I'm infinitely attentive, and unless there's a transparence associated with the excesses that drain off suffering – I wouldn't understand a thing.

In carnal love we ought to love excesses of suffering. Without them no risk would exist. In divine love the limitation of suffering is given in divine perfection.

I love irreligiousness, the disrespect involved in risk taking and gambling.

In risk taking, I sometimes push my luck so far that I lose even anguish as a possibility. Anguish in this case would be withdrawal from risk. Love is my necessity. I'm impelled to drift into happiness, sensing chance there. First rapturously to win – then laceratingly to let go of the winnings – in a game that exhausts me.

To encourage bitterness in those last words – words of renewed anguish – would be to avoid taking risks.

I can't take risks without this anguish of feeling suspended. But to take risks means to overcome anguish.

I'm afraid this apology will only encourage foolishness and banal rhetoric. Love is simple, uncomplicated.

My wish is that in any love of the unknown (and no matter what its personal sources in me may be, it arises from mystical traditions) we can, by ousting transcendence, attain such great simplicity as to relate that love to an earthly love, echoing it to infinity.

7

Life

Learned about the landing. The news didn't penetrate – it slowly sank in.
Went back to my room.
A hymn to life.

Would I have felt like laughing yesterday?
A toothache (over with now, it seems).
This morning. Still some fatigue. My mind a blank. The last of the fever.
Feelings of impotence. Afraid of the possibility of no more news.
I'm calm, emptied. Hope in important events keeps me even-keeled and
steady.
All the same, taken aback in this solitude. Resigned. Relative indiffer-
ence to my personal life.
Ten days ago, on the contrary, returning from Paris, I was
surprised . . . I've got to the egotistic stage of wanting stability right now!
No, just the opposite. I'm ruling out even the thought of rest today –
though, even so, that's what's probable.

Sounds from distant bombs (these becoming commonplace). No option
for me but to spend twelve uninterrupted days, alone and without friends,
staying in my room, depressed and vulnerable to gnawing anguish.
What about connecting with someone? Finding my life again? My shame
about anguish related to the idea of chance. To be honest: under present
conditions connecting up would be the only authentic chance, the full 'state
of grace' that is chance.
For a man, loving a woman (or some other kind of passion) is the sole
means of not being God. The priest adorned in arbitrary ornamentation
isn't God either – something in him pukes out logic, vomits out God's
necessity. An officer, a bellboy, etc. submits to the arbitrary.
I suffer – because happiness might be taken away tomorrow. Whatever
life remained in me would then seem empty (empty, truly empty). Should

The text is chapter 10 of the 'April–June 1944' section of *On Nietzsche*, tr. Bruce Boone
(Paragon House, New York, 1992), pp. 108–16. Projected as the third volume of the *Somme
athéologique*, the text appeared in French as part of *Sur Nietzsche: volonté de chance* (Editions
Gallimard, Paris, 1945). See *OC*, VI, pp. 128–36.

I attempt to fill this void? With another woman? A sickening thought. With a human task? I would be God! Or . . . I'd attempt to be him. As soon as you lose what you love, you're told – work! Submit to this or that reality, live for it (or live for the interest you have in such reality)! But if reality seems empty – what then?

Never before (I'm really reaching the limit of the possible, after so many excesses) have I ever felt myself so intensely under a necessity that compels me to love the essentially perishable and to live under the possibility of losing it.

I am aware of deep moral urgencies.

Today I suffer acutely – knowing that the only way to be God is to be untrue to myself.

Eleven more days of solitude . . . (given that nothing untoward develops). Yesterday afternoon, started on an article I am taking a break from – to emphasize its intent. The light of my life is missing, and I'm desperately working, I'm studying the unity of humanness and the world, I'm making interconnected outlines of knowledge, political action and unlimited contemplation.

Impossible not to yield to this truth, that my life implies a beyond of light, a beyond of the chance I love.

Still – insanity or utter wisdom demonstrates that the beyond of chance, a beyond that supports me if some immediate chance (someone I love) fails, itself has characteristics of chance.

Normally we deny those characteristics. We can only deny them if we seek some ground or stable foundation so as to endure contingency – a contingency that then becomes reduced to the subordinate role. We track down this 'beyond' principally when we suffer. Hence Christianity's superficiality (with attitudes of piety built in from the outset). Hence the necessity of a reduction to reason, of an infinite confidence in systems that eliminate chance (probability theories succeed in doing this apparently).

Utter fatigue.

My life no longer a welling up – without which non-meaning is present.

A basic difficulty: if welling up is necessary for chance, the light (or chance) fails on that on which the welling up depended . . .

The irreducible feature is found in this welling up, which didn't wait for light to occur but stimulated it. Random welling up defines the essence of and beginning of chance. Chance is defined in relation to desire, which itself either gives up in desperation, or 'wells up'.

Deciding to make use of fictions, I dramatize being, I lacerate its solitude, and in this laceration I communicate.

Or once again: mischance is only humanly viable when dramatized. Drama accentuates a mischance factor in chance, which persists in chance, or proceeds from it. The essence of the dramatic hero is a welling up, a rising to chance (dramatic situations require an elevation, from which to fall) . . .

Once again I'm breaking off the article I began. Confusion as a method. In Café du Taureau I'm drinking too many aperitifs. My neighbour, an old man, wheezing softly like a fly. A family drinks beer around a girl dressed for her first communion. German soldiers in the street pass by quickly. A hooker sits between two workers. ('You both could fool around with me . . .') The (inconspicuous) old man goes on wheezing. Sun, clouds. Women all dressed up, looking like a grey day. The sun naked under the clouds.

Exasperation. Depressed and then excited.
Regaining calm. A little firmness is all it takes.
My life (or rather my lack of one) is my method.
Less and less do I question to know. That's something that pretty much leaves me indifferent. And I live. And I question in order to live. I live out my quest, enduring relatively harsh ordeals (harsh because of the jangled state of my nerves). I see no escape at this point. I'm alone with myself, lacking the previous means of escape (pleasure, excitement). I have to get a grip. If I don't, is there any alternative?

Getting a grip? Easy!
Though . . . I myself in control of myself could scare me.
Shifting to decisiveness, I quickly return to a friendship with myself, gentleness. Hence, the necessity for endless chance.
At this point I can only look for chance and attempt to catch it as I laugh.
Taking risks, going looking for chance – this requires patience, love and total letting go.

A truly isolated period (ten days left, I'm shut up in my room) starts out this morning for me. (I went out yesterday, the day before.)

Yesterday. Kids following behind, running. One behind a street-car, the other trailing a bus. What's in their small heads? The same thing as is in my own. A basic difference – a decisiveness on my part (I can't depend on others). Here I am, a *self*: awakening, emerging, from a long period of human infancy, in which people relied on each other for everything. But essentially, this dawn of knowledge and this full possession of self is only night, only powerlessness (impotence).

A short phrase will excessively suggest chance – 'Could freedom some-how not be powerless?'

Any activity whose object is simply what can be wholly measured is powerful but slavish. Freedom derives from hazard. If we adapt the sum of energy produced to the amount necessary to be produced, human potency leaves nothing to desire, in that it suffices and represents the satisfaction of needs. However, that sort of adaptation would be characterized by con-straints, since the distribution of energy to different sectors of production would be stabilized once and for all. But if the amount produced exceeds the necessary, the object of impotent activity is a production that can't be measured.

This morning resigned myself to waiting.

Without fussing, and gently, I came to a decision . . .

Obviously this wasn't reasonable. Still, I left, buoyed up by feelings of chance.

After being encouraged, chance responded to me. Much beyond my hopes.

The horizon clears up (a portion dark).

The wait reduced – from ten to six days.

The game changes. Possibly . . . I knew how to play it today.

Anguish and anxiety preoccupy me and gnaw at me.

Anguish is present and hovering over possible depths . . . I hoist myself up to my summit and see the grounding of things opening up.

Like an unwelcome knock at the door, anguish is present.

Which is the sign of risk and chance.

In its demented voice – chance urging me.

I 'well up' out of myself, flames 'welling up', right in front of me!

There's no getting around it. My life (under current conditions?), a nightmare, a moral agony.

Which isn't of any account, obviously!

Endlessly, we 'annihilate' ourselves – thought and life falling into the void where they dissipate.

To call this void God – this void at which I have aimed, at which my thought aims!

In the prisonhouse of the body what can we do, other than provoke glimpses of something beginning beyond the walls?

My life, strange and exhausting, tonight weighed down with grief.
Spent an hour waiting, suspecting the worst.
Then finally – chance. Though my situation remains implacable.

At midnight opening my window on to the black street, black sky: street,
sky and shadows are crystal clear.
Beyond darkness I easily attain purity, laughter, freedom.

My life recommences.
The lighthearted, familiar shock of it as it hits me.
Dazed, drifting downstream.
K tells me that on the third, after drinking, she went looking for the key
to the reservoir, without luck; discovered herself at about four in the
morning sleeping in the woods, damp.

Unpleasant effects from drinking today.
I'd like (and everything urges me toward this) the course of my life to be
definitively playful, vivacious. Demanding of it a miraculous gentleness, an
atmospheric clarity such as the summit would have. Transfiguring things
around me. In the spirit of play, I imagine to myself making a pact with K:
the lightheartedness of it, the void itself, transparent (because aimless)
emptiness, at some impossible altitude.
Again to make demands, to act, to realize chance in some specific way:
this corresponds to the 'welling up' of desire.
Acting, not with narrow ends but with unlimited ones, glimpsing chance
beyond all my ends as a surpassing of willpower: the practice of free activity.

Going back over the course of my life.
I see myself slowly reaching a limit.
With anguish waiting for me on all sides, walking a narrow tightrope,
raising my eyes heavenward, I perceive a tiny and dazzling bright light – a
star – consuming this anguish of mine. My anguish waits for me, no matter
where I turn.
I possess a power to attract, an infinite power.

This morning I doubted my chance.
As the moment went on and on, in interminable waiting, there came the
dawn of a thought, 'All is lost.' At the time, it was logical.
I reasoned like this. 'My life is a leap, an impulse, whose strength is
chance. At this stage – at the level at which I presently gamble my life – if
I lack chance, I collapse. What am I but a man setting chance possibilities
for himself? Didn't I give myself that power – myself? But if misfortune, or
mischance, begins for me, the chance giving me that impetus turns out to

be merely illusion! I lived believing I had the capacity to fascinate chance, but that wasn't the case.' (I had not finished my complaints). 'My lightness and distracted victory over anguish were wrongly conceived. I gambled away desire and the will to act (I didn't choose this game) on my chance. Today mischance answers me. I despise ideas dismissed by life itself when these ideas suggest chance as a prominent value . . .'

At the time, I was in a bad way. And a special kind of despair only added (comic) bitterness to my despondency. Is there anything more depressing than waiting? It's an emptiness opening up before you along a path.

As K walked along and spoke with me, my awareness of my misfortune persisted. K was present – I behaved awkwardly. I could hardly believe she was there. And it was hard to think that 'my chance lives . . .'

Within me, anguish contests possibility.

My anguish considers vague impossibility to be at odds with my vague desire.

Within me, now, chance and a possibility of chance contest anguish.

Anguish says 'impossible', and impossibility depends on whims of chance.

Chance is defined by desire, though not necessarily every response to desire is a chance.

Anguish alone completely defines chance, and chance is what anguish in me regards as impossible.

Anguish can be defined as contesting chance.

Still, I grasp anguish as dependent on whims of chance, which contests, and alone contests, the right of anguish to define us.

After this morning's laceration, my nerves were shattered again (yet again).

Interminable waiting, lighthearted gambling, suspended above the worst eventualities, wracking my nerves, until an interruption makes it even worse . . . There is no helping it, I am compelled to moan in one long groan, 'This ode to life and to its glassy transparency!'

Whether despite herself K isn't perhaps manipulating this instability, I can't tell. The confusion she keeps me in seems to stem from her nature.

It's said, 'Instead of God there is the impossible – not God.' It should be added, 'The impossible, which depends on the whims of chance.'

Why complain about K?

Chance is endlessly contested, endlessly gambled.

If K had decided to embody chance right down to the last molecule in her, she couldn't have done beter. Appearing – although when anguish . . . Then disappearing so suddenly that anguish . . . As if night alone could precede her, as if only night would follow her. But each time without intending it. Appropriately (if she is chance).

'Instead of God, chance.' This means nature insofar as it occurs, though not as occurring once and for all but as surpassing itself in infinite occurrences, excluding any possible limits. In this infinite representation (a representation that quite likely is the boldest and most deranged ever tried out by humankind) the idea of God explodes like a bombshell – divine impoverishment and impotence clashing with human chance!

God, a cure applied to anguish (though the anguish can't be healed).
Beyond anguish, dependent on it, defined by it, is chance.
Without anguish – utter anguish – chance wouldn't even be perceived.

'Simply out of appropriateness, if God in fact did exist, he would only be revealed to the world in a human form.' (*The Will to Power*)
Being human/human being: to have impossibility opposite you like a wall . . . a wall that chance and only chance could . . .

This morning. Depressed following a night of ungrounded fears, insomnia – sounds of massed planes filling her with dread – K started softly shaking. Frail, despite her appearance of being spirited, playful and full of zip. Generally, anxiety prevents me from noticing an unfounded distress like this. Empathizing with my woes and hardships – ruts that turn into a way forward for me – she laughed with me good-naturedly. Surprised suddenly to think of her – against the odds – as friend, sister even . . . But had things been otherwise, we would be strangers.

8

Poetry

The night is my nudity
the stars are my teeth
I throw myself among the dead
dressed in white sunlight

Death dwells in my heart
like a little widow
she sobs she is a coward
I'm afraid
I could vomit

the widow laughs to the skies
and rips the birds to pieces

At my death
the horse teeth of the stars
whinny with laughter I death

blank death
moist grave
one-armed sun
the death-toothed gravedigger
effaces me

The excerpts are from 'I throw myself among the dead' and 'To be Orestes' in part 3 of *The Impossible*, tr. Robert Hurley (City Lights, San Francisco, CA, 1991), pp. 147–64. *L'Impossible* was published in France in 1947 by Editions de Minuit under the title of *La Haine de la poésie*. See *OC*, III, pp. 211–23.

the raven-winged angel
cries
    glory to thee

I am the emptiness of caskets
and the absence of myself
in the whole universe

the horns of joy
trumpet madly
and the sun's bull's-eye
explodes

death's thunder
fills the universe

too much joy
turns back the fingernails.

I imagine
in the infinite depth
the deserted expanse
different from the sky that I see
no longer containing
those glittering points of light
but sheets of flame
greater than a sky
dazzling like the daybreak

formless abstraction striated with fractures
heap of inanities
of things forgotten
here the subject I
there the object universe littered with dead notions
where I throw out the rubbish
the impotent gestures
the gasps
the shrill cock-crows of ideas

o manufactured nothingness
in the factory of infinite vanity
like a trunk full of false teeth

I leaning on the trunk
I feel
my desire to vomit desire

o collapse
ecstasy from which I fall
asleep
when I cry out
you who are and will be
when I will be no more
deaf X
giant mallet
crushing my head

The sparkle
the top of the sky
the earth
and me.

My heart spits you out star

incomparable anguish

I laugh but I'm cold.

The gaming table is the starry night where I fall, cast like the die on a field of fleeting possibilities.

I see no reason to 'find fault' with it.

Being a blind fall in the night, I exceed my will in spite of myself (which is only the *given* within me); and my fear is the cry of an infinite freedom.

If I did not exceed nature, in a leap beyond 'the static and the given', I would be defined by laws. But nature *plays me*, casting me further than herself, beyond the laws, the limits that make *humble people* love her.

I am the outcome of a game, that which if I were not, would not be, might not be.

Within an immensity, I am a *more* exceeding that immensity. My happiness and my very being stem from that excessiveness.

My stupidity gave its blessing to succouring nature, on her knees before God.

What I am (my drunken laughter and happiness) is nonetheless at stake, handed over to chance, thrown out into the night, chased away like a dog.

The wind of truth responded like a slap to piety's extended cheek.

The heart is human to the extent that it rebels (this means: to be a man is 'not to bow down before the law').

A poet doesn't justify – he doesn't accept – nature completely. True poetry is outside laws. But poetry ultimately accepts poetry.

When to accept poetry changes it into its opposite (it becomes the mediator of an acceptance)! I hold back the leap in which I would exceed the universe, I justify the given world, I content myself with it.

Fit myself into what surrounds me, explain myself, or see only a children's fable in my unfathomable night (give myself a physical or mythological image of myself)? No! . . .

I would drop out of the game . . .

I refuse, rebel, but why lose my way. Were I to rave, I would be *merely natural*.

Poetic delirium has its place *in nature*. It justifies nature, consents to embellish it. The refusal belongs to clear consciousness, evaluating what-ever occurs to it.

Clear discrimination of the various possibles, the gift for going to the end of the most distant one, are the province of clear attention. The irrevocable venturing of oneself, the one-way voyage beyond every given require not only that infinite laughter, but also that slow meditation (senseless but through excess).

It is penumbra and uncertainty. Poetry removes one from the night and the day at the same time. It can neither bring into question nor bring into action this world that binds me.

The menace of it is maintained: nature can annihilate me – reduce me to that which she is, cancel the game that I play further than she – which demands my infinite madness, my infinite gaiety, my infinite alertness.

Relaxation withdraws one from the game – as does an excess of atten-tion. Enthusiasm, the heedless plunge, and calm lucidity are required of the player, until the day when chance releases him – or life does.

I approach poetry: but only to miss it.

In nature's excessive game it makes no difference whether I exceed her or *she* exceeds herself in me (she is perhaps entirely excess of herself), but, in time, the excess will finally take its place in the order of things (I will die at that moment).

It was necessary, in order to grasp a possible within an evident impossibility, for me to imagine the opposite situation first.

Supposing I wish to reduce myself to the lawful order, I have little chance of succeeding completely: I will err through inconsequence – through defective rigour . . .

In extreme rigour, the exigency of order holds such a great power that it cannot turn back against itself. In the experience of it which devout worshipers (mystics) have, the person of God is placed at the apex of an immoral absurdity: the devout worshiper's love *realizes* in God – with whom he identifies himself – an excess which if he were to assume it personally would bring him to his knees, demoralized.

The reduction to order fails in any case: formal devotion (devotion without excess) leads to inconsequence. The opposite endeavour has chances, then. It has to use bypaths (laughs, incessant nauseas). There where things are ventured, each element ceaselessly changes into its contrary. God suddenly takes on a 'horrible grandeur'. Or poetry slips into embellishment. With each effort that I make to grasp it, the object of my anticipation changes into a contrary.

Poetry's lustre reveals itself outside the moments which it reaches in a deathlike disorder.

(A common agreement makes an exception of the two authors who added the lustre of a failure to that of poetry. Misunderstanding is linked to their names, but both exhausted the sense of poetry that culminates in its opposite, in a feeling of hatred for poetry. Poetry that does not rise to the non-sense of poetry is only the hollowness of poetry, is only beautiful poetry.)

For whom are these serpents . . . ?

The unknown and death . . . without bovine silence, the only kind strong enough on such paths. In that unknown, blind, I succumb (I renounce the reasoned exhaustion of possibles).

Poetry is not a knowledge of oneself, and even less the experience of a remote possible (of that which, before, was not) but rather the simple evocation through words of inaccessible possibilities.

Evocation has the advantage over experience of richness and an endless facility but it distances one from experience (which is essentially paralysed).

Without the exuberance of evocation, experience would be rational. It begins to emanate from my madness, if the impotence of evocation disgusts me.

Poetry opens the night to desire's excess. In me the night abandoned by the ravages of poetry is the measure of a refusal – of my mad will to exceed the world. – Poetry also exceeded this world, but it could not *change me*.

My fictitious freedom tightened the constraints of the natural given more than it weakened them. If I had been content with it, in the end I would have yielded to the limit of that given.

I continued to question the world's limit, seeing the wretchedness of anyone who is content with it, and I couldn't bear the facility of fiction for long: I demanded its reality, I became mad.

If I was untruthful I remained in the domain of poetry, of a verbal transcendence of the world. If I persevered in a blind disparagement of the world, my disparagement was false (like the transcendence). In a sense, my accord with the world deepened. But being unable to lie knowingly, I became mad (capable of ignoring the truth). Or no longer knowing how, for myself alone, to act out the farce of a delirium, I became mad again, but inwardly: I experienced the night.

Poetry was simply a detour: through it I escaped the world of discourse, which had become the natural world for me; with poetry I entered a kind of grave where the infinity of the possible was born from the death of the logical world.

Logic on its death bed gave birth to mad riches. But the possible that's evoked is only unreal, the death of the logical world is unreal, everything is shady and fleeting in that relative darkness. I can make light of myself and of others in that darkness: all the real is valueless, every value unreal! Whence that facility and that fatality of equivocations, where I don't know if I am lying or if I am mad. Night's necessity springs from that unhappy situation.

The night could only proceed by way of a detour.
The questioning of all things resulted from the exasperation of a desire, which could not come to bear on the void!

The object of my desire was illusion first of all and could be the *void of disillusion* only in the second instance.

Questioning without desire is formal, immaterial. About it we cannot say, 'It's the same thing as man.'

Poetry reveals a power of the unknown. But the unknown is only an insignificant void if it is not the object of a desire. Poetry is a middle term, it conceals the known within the unknown: it is the unknown painted in blinding colors, in the image of a sun.

Dazzled by a thousand figures composed of worry, impatience, and love. Now my desire has just one object: the beyond of those thousand figures, and the night.
But in the night, desire tells lies and in this way night ceases to be its object. This existence led by me 'in the night' resembles that of the lover at the death of his beloved, of Orestes learning of Hermione's suicide. In the form that night takes, existence cannot recognize 'what it anticipated'.

9

Autobiographical Note

Born, Billom (Puy-le-Dôme), 10 September 1897. Family of peasant stock for two or three generations, originally from the Ariège, Puy-le-Dôme and the Cantal. Father blind (prior to birth) and paralytic (1900).

Schooling at Reims lycée, very bad student, almost expelled in January 1913, refuses to continue schooling and stays idle at home until October, but agrees to enter Epernay secondary school as a boarder. Now becomes a good student. Brought up with no religious instruction, now leans toward Catholicism, and is formally converted in August 1914.

Having fled to safety with his mother's family in the Cantal, is called up for service in January 1916. Falls gravely ill, is discharged in 1917. Briefly considers becoming a priest, or rather a monk. Enters the School of Paleography and Library Science in November 1918, is regularly at the head of his class, but graduates second.

Two months in England in 1920. Following a stay with the Benedictines of Quarr Abbey on the Isle of Wight, suddenly loses his faith because his Catholicism has caused a woman he has loved to shed tears.

Upon graduation from the School of Paleography is named fellow of the school of Advanced Hispanic Studies in Madrid (later the Casa Velásquez). Enthusiasm for bullfights; witnesses death of Granero, one of Spain's most popular matadors (certainly the most popular after Belmonte) in the Madrid arena.

Enters the Bibliothèque nationale as a librarian in July 1922.

Is convinced, from 1914 on, that his concern in this world is with writing and, in particular, with the formulation of a paradoxical philosophy. Reading of Nietzsche in 1923 is decisive. Resolving to travel, begins study of

The text was first translated in *October*, 36 (1986), pp. 107–10. It is dated '1958?' and is among the papers collected in *OC*, VII, pp. 459–62.

Russian, Chinese, and even of Tibetan, which he quickly abandons. Translates, with collaborator, book by Leon Chestov from the Russian (1924).

Forms friendship with Michel Leiris, then with André Masson, Théodore Fraenkel. Enters into contact with the surrealists, but the result is mutual hostility between himself and André Breton. In 1926, writes a short book entitled *W.-C.* (this book, of violent opposition to any form of dignity, will not be published and is finally destroyed by its author), then, in 1927, *The Solar Anus* (published, with Masson's etchings, by the Galerie Simon in 1931). The virulently obsessive character of his writing troubles one of his friends, Dr Dausse, who has him undergo psychoanalysis with Dr Borel. The psychoanalysis has a decisive result; by August 1927 it put an end to the series of dreary mishaps and failures in which he had been floundering, but not to the state of intellectual intensity, which still persists.

Marriage in 1928. Meeting at that time with Georges Henri Rivière through the publication, in 1929, of *Documents*, an art magazine containing a miscellaneous section edited by Bataille under the somewhat remote supervision of Carl Einstein. Bataille publishes a certain number of articles in this journal, his earliest published writings, of which the first is a text on Gallic coins admired by him. (Breton will, following a misunderstanding, come to see this article as an attack on Gallic art.) The mutual hostility of Bataille and Breton at that time brings Bataille into closer relation with ex-members of the surrealist group; in addition to friends such as Leiris and Masson, Jacques Baron, Jacques-André Boiffard, Robert Desnos, Georges Limbour, Max Morise, Jacques Prévert, Raymond Queneau, Georges Ribemont-Dessaignes, Roger Vitrac. These are largely the names listed at the end of the Second Surrealist Manifesto (published in *La Révolution surréaliste*, 1929), in which they are subjected to a violent attack, ending with the denunciation of Georges Bataille, considered to be planning the formation of an anti-surrealist group. This group never existed; nevertheless those singled out by the Second Manifesto were agreed upon the publication of *Un Cadavre* (a title already used by the future surrealists on the death of Anatole France), a blistering indictment of Breton (which in no way prevented most of them, including Bataille himself, from later reconciliation).

Documents, the journal which had been at the origin of these polemics owing to its publication of numerous articles by the authors of *Un Cadavre*, ceased to exist in 1931. Shortly afterward, Bataille entered the Democratic Communist Circle, which published *La Critique sociale* (from 1931 to 1934) under the editorship of Boris Souvarine. Bataille published several long studies, including 'The notion of expenditure', 'The psychological structure of fascism' and, in collaboration with Raymond Queneau, 'Critique of the foundations of the Hegelian dialectic'. Bataille was then a close friend of Queneau, who worked daily at the Bibliothèque nationale, gathering documentation for a book on 'literary madmen' (which, some years later, ended in the publication of *Enfants du Limon*).

The Democratic Communist Circle went out of existence in 1934. At that time Bataille, after several months of illness, underwent a serious psychological crisis. He separated from his wife. He then wrote *Blue of Noon*, which is in no way the narrative of this crisis, but which can be considered as reflecting it.

Bataille personally took the initiative in 1935 to found a small political group which, under the name of Counterattack, united some former members of the Communist Circle and, following a definite reconciliation with André Breton, the whole of the surrealist group. Some meetings of Counterattack took place in the 'Grenier des Augustine' (now Picasso's studio), with the last, on 21 January 1936, dedicated to the death of Louis XVI. Breton, Maurice Heine and Bataille took the floor.

Counterattack was dissolved at the end of the winter. (The supposed pro-fascist tendency on the part of certain of Bataille's friends, and, to a lesser degree, of Bataille himself. For an understanding of the element of truth in this paradoxical fascist tendency, despite its radically contrary intention, one should read Elio Vittorini's *The Red Carnation*, together with its strange postface. There is no doubt that the bourgeois world as it exists constitutes a provocation to violence and that, in that world, the exterior forms of violence hold a fascination. Be that as it may, Bataille considers, at least since Counterattack, that this fascination can lead to the worst.)

With Counterattack dissolved, Bataille immediately resolved to form, together with those of his friends who were former members (these included Georges Ambrosino, Pierre Klossowski, Patrick Waldberg), a 'secret society' which, turning its back on politics, would pursue goals that would be solely religious (but anti-Christian, essentially Nietzschean). This society was formed. Its intentions are in part expressed in the journal *Acéphale*, published in four issues between 1936 and 1939. The *Collège de sociologie*, founded in March 1936, represented, as it were, the outside activity of this 'secret society'; this 'college', whose domain was not all of sociology, but rather the 'sacred', expressed itself publicly through a series of lectures. The founding members were, in addition to Bataille, Roger Caillois and Michel Leiris. Lewitsky, Jean Paulhan and Georges Duthuit lectured there.

Of the 'secret society' properly so-called it is difficult to talk, but certain of its members have apparently retained the impression of a 'voyage out of the world'. Temporary, surely, obviously unendurable; in September 1939, all of its members withdrew. Disagreement arose between Bataille and the membership, more deeply absorbed than Bataille by immediate concern with the war. Bataille, in fact, had begun in 1938 to practise yoga, but really without close adherence to the precepts of the traditional discipline, in considerable chaos and in a state of mental turmoil pushed to the extreme. A death occurring in 1938 had torn him apart. It was in complete solitude that he began, in the opening days of the war, to write *Le Coupable*, in which he describes a mystical experience of a heterodoxical nature in the course of development and, at the same time, some of his reactions to the events then taking place. At the end of 1940 he meets Maurice Blanchot, with whom links of admiration and agreement are immediately formed. Toward the end of 1941, before *Le Coupable* has been completed. Bataille begins to write *L'Expérience intérieure*, completed before the end of the following year.

Owing to an infected lung, he is forced to leave the Bibliothèque nationale in April 1942. In 1943 he settles in Vézelay; there he remains until 1949. (*On Nietzsche, Memorandum.*) While living in Vézelay he founds a monthly review, *Critique*, in 1946. By dint of frequent trips to Paris he succeeds, in collaboration with Eric Weil and then with Jean Piel, in endowing this publication, in which he publishes many studies, with a definite authority.

If thought and its expression have become his main area of activity, this has not been without repeated attempts, within the limits of his means, at experiences lacking apparent coherence, but whose very incoherence signifies an effort to comprehend the totality of possibility, or to put it more precisely, to reject, untiringly, any possibility exclusive of others. Bataille's aspiration is that of a sovereign existence, free of all limitations of interest. He is, indeed, concerned with *being*, and being as *sovereignty*, with transcending the development of means. At issue is the attainment of an end over and above means – at the price, if necessary, of an impious disturbance. Philosophy, for example, for Bataille comes down to acrobatics – in the worst sense of the word. The issue is not that of attainment of a goal, but rather of escape from those traps which goals represent.

We must not elude the task incumbent upon all men, but reserve a share of sovereignty, a share that is irreducible. On this level it is an attitude which follows in the wake of religious experience, but the religious experience freed from the quest for means, that religious experience which must be an end if it is anything at all. There is work on Bataille's part, but it is an effort to escape, an effort of release toward a freedom that is direct.

PART II

Heterology

10

Programme (Relative to *Acéphale*)

1 Form a community creative of values, values creative of cohesion.
2 Lift the curse, the feeling of guilt which strikes men, sending them to wars they do not want, forcing them to a labour whose fruits escape them.
3 Assume the function of destruction and decomposition, but as accomplishment and not as negation of being.
4 Realize the personal accomplishment of being and of its tension through concentration, through a positive asceticism and through positive individual discipline.
5 Realize the universal accomplishment of personal being in the irony of the animal world and through the revelation of an acephalic universe, one of play, not of state or duty.
6 Take upon oneself perversion and crime, not as exclusive values, but as integrated within the human totality.
7 Fight for the decomposition and exclusion of all communities national, socialist, communist or churchly – other than universal community.
8 Affirm the reality of values, the resulting inequality of men, and acknowledge the organic character of society.
9 Take part in the destruction of the existing world, with eyes open to the world to come.
10 Consider the world to come in the sense of reality contained as of now, and not in the sense of a permanent happiness which is not only inaccessible, but hateful.
11 Affirm the value of violence and the will to aggression insofar as they are the foundation of all power.

The text appeared in English in *October*, 36 (1986), p. 79. Dated 4 April 1936, the French version is among the papers collected in *OC*, II, p. 273.

11

The Psychological Structure
of Fascism

Having affirmed that the infrastructure of a society ultimately determines or conditions the superstructure, Marxism did not undertake any general elucidation of the modalities peculiar to the formation of religious and political society. While Marxism did acknowledge possible responses by the superstructure it has not gone from mere assertion to scientific analysis. This essay attempts a rigorous (if not comprehensive) representation of the social superstructure and its relations to the economic infrastructure in the light of fascism. The fact that this is but a fragment of a relatively substantial whole explains a great number of lacunae, notably the absence of any methodological considerations;[1] it was even necessary to forgo justifying the novelty of my point of view, and to limit myself to the presentation of my basic position. However, the simple presentation of the structure of fascism had to be preceded by a description of the social structure as a whole.

It goes without saying that a study of the superstructure presupposes the development of a Marxist analysis of the infrastructure.

1 The Homogeneous Part of Society

A psychological description of society must begin with that segment which is most accessible to understanding – and apparently the most fundamental – whose significant trait is tendential homogeneity.[2] *Homogeneity* signifies here the commensurability of elements and the awareness of this commensurability: human relations are sustained by a reduction to fixed rules based on the consciousness of the possible identity of delineable persons and situations; in principle, all violence is excluded from this course of existence.

Production is the basis of social *homogeneity*.[3] *Homogeneous* society is productive society, namely useful society. Every useless element is ex-

'The psychological structure of fascism', tr. Carl R. Lovitt, was published in English translation in *New German Critique*, 16 (1979), pp. 64–87. 'La structure psychologique du fascisme' appeared, in two parts, in *La Critique sociale*, 10 (November 1933) and 11 (March 1934). See *OC*, I, pp. 339–71.

cluded, not from all of society, but from its *homogeneous* part. In this part, each element must be useful to another without the homogeneous activity ever being able to attain the form of activity *valid in itself*. A useful activity has a common measure with another useful activity, but not with activity *for itself*.

The common measure, the foundation of social *homogeneity* and of the activity arising from it, is money, namely the calculable equivalent of the different products of collective activity. Money serves to measure all work, and makes man a function of measurable products. According to the judgment of *homogeneous* society, each man is worth what he produces; in other words, he stops being an existence *for itself*: he is no more than a function, arranged within measurable limits, of collective production (which makes him an existence *for something other than itself*).

But the *homogeneous* individual is truly a function of his personal products only in artisanal production, where the means of production are relatively inexpensive and can be owned by the artisan. In industrial civilization, the producer is distinguished from the owner of the means of production, and it is the latter who appropriates the products for himself: consequently, it is he who, in modern society, is the function of the products; it is he – and not the producer – who founds social *homogeneity*.

Thus in the present order of things, the *homogeneous* part of society is made up of those men who own the means of production or the money *destined for their upkeep or purchase*. It is exactly in the middle segment of the so-called capitalist or bourgeois class that the tendential reduction of human character takes place, making it an abstract and interchangeable entity: a reflection of the *homogeneous things* the individual owns.

This reduction is then extended as much as possible to the so-called middle classes that variously benefit from realized profit. But the industrial proletariat remains for the most part irreducible. It maintains a double relation to homogeneous activity: the latter excludes it – not from work but from profit. As agents of production, the workers fall within the framework of the social organization, but the homogeneous reduction as a rule only affects their wage-earning activity; they are integrated into the psychological *homogeneity* in terms of their behaviour on the job, but not generally as men. Outside of the factory, and even beyond its technical operations, a labourer is, with regard to a *homogeneous* person (boss, bureaucrat, etc.), a stranger, a man of another nature, of a non-reduced, non-subjugated nature.

2 The State

In the contemporary period, social *homogeneity* is linked to the bourgeois class by essential ties: thus the Marxist conception is justified whenever the state is shown to be at the service of a threatened homogeneity.

As a rule, social *homogeneity* is a precarious form, at the mercy of violence and even of internal dissent. It forms spontaneously in the play of productive organization but must constantly be protected from the various unruly elements that do not benefit from production, or not enough to suit them, or simply, that cannot tolerate the checks that homogeneity imposes on unrest. In such conditions, the protection of *homogeneity* lies in its recourse to imperative elements which are capable of obliterating the various unruly forces or bringing them under the control of order.

The state is not itself one of these imperative elements; it is distinct from kings, heads of the army, or of nations, but it is the result of the modifications undergone by a part of homogeneous society as it comes into contact with such elements. This part is an intermediary formation between the homogeneous classes and the sovereign agencies from which it must borrow its obligatory character, but whose exercise of sovereignty must rely upon it as an intermediary. It is only with reference to these sovereign agencies that it will be possible to envision the way in which this obligatory character is transferred to a formation that nevertheless does not constitute an existence valid in itself (*heterogeneous*), but simply an activity whose usefulness with regard to another part is manifest.

In practical terms, the function of the state consists of an interplay of authority and adaptation. The reduction of differences through compromise in parliamentary practice indicates all the possible complexity of the internal activity of adaptation required by homogeneity. But against forces that cannot be assimilated, the state cuts matters short with strict authority.

Depending on whether the state is democratic or despotic, the prevailing tendency will be either adaptation or authority. In a democracy, the state derives most of its strength from spontaneous homogeneity, which it fixes and constitutes as the rule. The principle of its sovereignty – the nation – providing both its end and its strength, is thus diminished by the fact that isolated individuals increasingly consider themselves as ends with regard to the state, which would thus exist *for them* before existing *for the nation*. And, in this case, personal life distinguishes itself from homogeneous existence as a value which presents itself as incomparable.

3 Dissociations, Critiques of Social Homogeneity and the State

Even in difficult circumstances, the state is able to neutralize those *heterogeneous* forces that will yield only to its constraints. But it can succumb to the internal dissociation of that segment of society of which it is but the constrictive form.

Social *homogeneity* fundamentally depends upon the homogeneity (in the general sense of the word) of the productive system. Every contradiction arising from the development of economic life thus entails a tendential dissociation of *homogeneous* social existence. This tendency towards dissociation exerts itself in the most complex manner, on all levels and in every direction. But it only reaches acute and dangerous forms to the extent than an appreciable segment of the mass of *homogeneous* individuals ceases to have an interest in the conservation of the existing form of homogeneity (not because it is homogeneous, but on the contrary, because it is in the process of losing that character). This fraction of society then spontaneously affiliates itself with the previously constituted *heterogeneous* forces and becomes indistinguishable from them.

Thus, economic circumstances act directly upon homogeneous elements and promote their disintegration. But this disintegration only represents the negative form of social effervescence: the dissociated elements do not act before having undergone the complete alteration that characterizes the positive form of this effervescence. From the moment that they rejoin the *heterogeneous* formations that already exist in either a diffuse or an organized state, they acquire from the latter a new character: the general positive character of heterogeneity. Furthermore, social *heterogeneity* does not exist in a formless and disoriented state: on the contrary, it constantly tends to a split-off structure; and *when social elements pass over to the* heterogeneous *side, their action still finds itself conditioned by the actual structure of that side.*

Thus, the mode of resolving acute economic contradictions depends upon both the historical state and the general laws of the *heterogeneous* social region in which the effervescence acquires its positive form; it depends in particular upon the relations established between the various formations of this region when *homogeneous* society finds itself materially dissociated.

The study of *homogeneity* and of the conditions of its existence thus necessarily leads to the essential study of *heterogeneity*. In fact, it constitutes the first phase of such a study in the sense that the primary determination of *heterogeneity* defined as non-*homogeneous* supposes a knowledge of the *homogeneity* which delineates it by exclusion.

4 Heterogeneous Social Existence

The entire problem of social psychology rests precisely upon the fact that it must be brought to bear on a form which is not only difficult to study but whose existence has not yet been the object of a precise definition.

The very term *heterogeneous* indicates that it concerns elements which are impossible to assimilate; this impossibility which has a fundamental impact on social assimilation, likewise has an impact on scientific assimilation. These two types of assimilation have a single structure: the object of science is to establish the *homogeneity* of phenomena; that is, in a sense, one of the eminent functions of *homogeneity*. Thus, the *heterogeneous* elements excluded from the latter are excluded as well from the field of scientific consideration: as a rule, science cannot know *heterogeneous* elements as such. Compelled to note the existence of irreducible facts – of a nature as incompatible with its own homogeneity as are, for example, born criminals with the social order – science finds itself *deprived of any functional satisfaction* (exploited in the same manner as a labourer in a capitalist factory, used without sharing in the profits). Indeed, science is not an abstract entity: it is constantly reducible to a group of men living the aspirations inherent to the scientific process.

In such conditions, the heterogeneous elements, at least as such, find themselves subjected to a de facto censorship: each time that they could be the object of a methodical observation, functional satisfaction is lacking; and without some exceptional circumstance – like the intrusion of a satisfaction with a completely different origin – they cannot be kept within the field of consideration.

The exclusion of *heterogeneous* elements from the *homogeneous* realm of consciousness formally recalls the exclusion of the elements, described (by psychoanalysis) as *unconscious*, which censorship excludes from the conscious ego. The difficulties opposing the revelation of *unconscious* forms of existence are of the same order as those opposing the knowledge of *heterogeneous* forms. As will subsequently be made clear, these two kinds of form have certain properties in common and, without being able to elaborate immediately upon this point, it would seem that the *unconscious* must be considered as one of the aspects of the *heterogeneous*. If this conception is granted, given what we know about repression, it is that much easier to understand the incursions occasionally made into the *heterogeneous* realm have not been sufficiently co-ordinated to yield even the simple revelation of its positive and clearly separate existence.

It is of secondary importance to indicate here that, in order to avoid the internal difficulties that have just been foreseen, it is necessary to posit the limits of science's inherent tendencies, and to constitute a knowledge of the *non-explainable difference*, which supposes the immediate access of the intellect to a body of material, prior to any intellectual reduction. Tentatively, it is enough to present the facts according to their nature and, with a view to defining the term *heterogeneous*, to introduce the following considerations:

1 Just as, in religious sociology, *mana* and *taboo* designate forms restricted to the particular applications of a more general form, the *sacred*, so may the *sacred* itself be considered as a restricted form of the *heterogeneous*.

Mana designates the mysterious and impersonal force possessed by individuals such as kings and witch doctors. *Taboo* indicates the social prohibition of contact pertaining, for example, to cadavers and menstruating women. Given the precise and limited facts to which they refer, these aspects of *heterogeneous* life are easy to define. However, an explicit understanding of the *sacred*, whose field of application is relatively vast, presents considerable difficulties. Durkheim faced the impossibility of providing it with a positive scientific definition: he settled for characterizing the sacred world negatively as being absolutely heterogeneous compared to the profane.[4] It is nevertheless possible to admit that the *sacred* is known positively, at least implicitly (since the word is commonly used in every language, that usage supposes a signification perceived by the whole of mankind). This implicit knowledge of a heterogeneous value permits a vague but positve character to be communicated to its description. Yet, it can be said that the heterogeneous world is largely comprised of the sacred world, and that reactions analogous to those generated by sacred things are provoked by heterogeneous things that are not, strictly speaking, considered to be sacred. These reactions are such that the heterogeneous thing is assumed to be charged with an unknown and dangerous force (recalling the Polynesian mana) and that a certain social prohibition of contact (*taboo*) separates it from the *homogeneous* or ordinary world (which corresponds to the profane world in the strictly religious opposition).

2 Beyond the properly sacred things that constitute the common realm of religion or magic, the *heterogeneous* world includes everything resulting from *unproductive* expenditure[5] (sacred things themselves form part of this whole). This consists of everything rejected by *homogeneous* society as waste or as superior transcendent value. Included are the waste products of the human body and certain analogous matter (trash, vermin, etc.); the parts of the body; persons, words, or acts having a suggestive erotic value; the various unconscious processes such as dreams or neuroses; the numerous elements or social forms that *homogeneous* society is powerless to assimilate: mobs, the warrior, aristocratic and impoverished classes, different types of violent individual or at least those who refuse the rule (madmen, leaders, poets, etc.).

3 Depending upon the person, *heterogeneous* elements will provoke affective reactions of varying intensity, and it is possible to assume that the object of any affective reaction is necessarily *heterogeneous* (if not generally, at least with regard to the subject). There is sometimes attraction, sometimes repulsion, and in certain circumstance, any object of repulsion can become an object of attraction and vice versa.

4 *Violence, excess, delirium, madness* characterize heterogeneous elements to varying degrees: active, as persons or mobs, they result from breaking the laws of social *homogeneity*. This characteristic does not appropriately apply

to inert objects, yet the latter do present a certain conformity with extreme emotions (if it is possible to speak of the violent and excessive nature of a decomposing body).

5 The reality of *heterogeneous* elements is not of the same order as that of *homogeneous* elements. *Homogeneous* reality presents itself with the abstract and neutral aspect of strictly defined and identified objects (basically, it is the specific reality of solid objects). *Heterogeneous* reality is that of a force or shock. It presents itself as a charge, as a value, passing from one object to another in a more or less abstract fashion, almost as if the change were taking place not in the world of objects but only in the judgements of the subject. The preceding aspect nevertheless does not signify that the observed facts are to be considered as subjective: thus, the ·action of the objects of erotic activity is manifestly rooted in their objective nature. Nonetheless, in a disconcerting way, the subject does have the capacity to displace the exciting value of one element on to an analogous or neighbouring one.[6] In heterogeneous reality, the symbols charged with affective value thus have the same importance as the fundamental elements, and the part can have the same value as the whole. It is easy to note that, since the structure of knowledge for a homogeneous reality is that of science, the knowledge of a heterogeneous reality as such is to be found in the mystical thinking of primitives and in dreams: it is identical to the structure of the unconsious.[7]

6 In summary, compared to everyday life, heterogeneous existence can be represented as something other, as incommensurate, by charging these words with the positive value they have in affective experience.

Examples of heterogeneous elements

If these suggestions are now brought to bear upon actual elements, the fascist leaders are incontestably part of heterogeneous existence. Opposed to democratic politicians, who represent in different countries the platitude inherent to homogeneous society, Mussolini and Hitler immediately stand out as something other. Whatever emotions their actual existence as political agents of evolution provokes, it is impossible to ignore the force that situates them above men, parties and even laws: a force that disrupts the regular course of things, the peaceful but fastidious homogeneity powerless to maintain itself (the fact that laws are broken is only the most obvious sign of the transcendent, heterogeneous nature of fascist action). Considered not with regard to its external action but with regard to its source, the force of a leader is analogous to that exerted in hypnosis.[8] The affective flow that unites him with his followers – which takes the form of a moral identification[9] of the latter with the one they follow (and reciprocally) – is a function of the common consciousness of increasingly violent and excessive energies and powers that accumulate in the person of the leader and through him become widely available. (But this concentration in a single person intervenes as an element that sets the fascist formation apart within the heterogeneous realm: by the very fact that the affective effervescence leads to unity, it constitutes, as *authority*, an agency directed *against* men; this agency is an existence *for itself* before being useful; an existence for itself distinct from that of a formless uprising where *for itself* signifies 'for the men in revolt'.) This *monarchy*, this absence of all democracy, of all fraternity in the exercise of power – forms that do not exist only in Italy or Germany – indicates that the immediate natural needs of men must be renounced, under constraint, in favour of a transcendent principle that cannot be the object of an exact explanation.

In a quite different sense, the lowest strata of society can equally be described as heterogeneous, those who generally provoke repulsion and can in no case be assimilated by the whole of mankind. In India, these impoverished classes are considered untouchable, meaning that they are characterized by the prohibition of contact analogous to that applied to sacred things. It is true that the custom of countries in advanced civilizations is less ritualistic and that the quality of being untouchable is not necessarily hereditary; nevertheless, being destitute is all it takes in these countries to create between the self and others – who consider themselves the expression of normal man – a nearly insuperable gap. The nauseating forms of dejection provoke a feeling of disgust so unbearable that it is improper to express or even to make allusion to it. By all indications, in the psychological order of disfiguration, the material poverty of man has *excessive* consequences. And, in the event that *fortunate* men have not undergone *homogeneous* reduction (which opposes a legal justification to poverty), if we except those shameless attempts at evasion such as charitable pity, the hopeless violence of the reactions immediately takes on the form of a challenge to reason.

5 The Fundamental Dualism of the Heterogeneous World

The two preceding examples, taken from the broader domain of *heterogeneity*, and not from the sacred domain proper, nevertheless do present the specific traits of the latter. This is readily apparent with reference to the leaders, who are manifestly treated by their followers as sacred persons. It is much less evident with reference to forms of poverty which are not the object of any cult.

But the revelation that such vile forms are compatible with the sacred character precisely marks the decisive headway made in the knowledge of the sacred as well as in that of the *heterogeneous* realm. The notion of the

duality of sacred forms is one of the conclusive findings of social anthropology: these forms must be distributed among two opposing classes: *pure*
and *impure* (in primitive religions certain impure things – menstrual blood,
for example – are no less sacred than the divine nature; the awareness of this
fundamental duality has persisted until relatively recent times: in the Middle Ages, the word *sacer* was used to designate a shameful illness – syphillis
– and the deeper meaning of this usage was still intelligible. The theme of
sacred poverty – impure and untouchable – constitutes precisely the negative pole of a region characterized by the opposition of two extreme forms:
in a certain sense, there is an identity of opposites between glory and
dejection, between exalted and imperative (higher) forms and impoverished
(lower) forms. This opposition splits the whole of the *heterogeneous* world
and joins the already defined characteristics of *heterogeneity* as a fundamental element. (Undifferentiated *heterogeneous* forms are, in fact, relatively
rare – at least in developed societies – and the analysis of the internal
heterogeneous social structure is almost entirely reduced to that of the
opposition between two contrary terms.)

6 The Imperative Form of Heterogeneous
Existence: Sovereignty

Heterogeneous fascist action belongs to the entire set of higher forms. It
makes an appeal to sentiments traditionally defined as *exalted* and *noble* and
tends to constitute authority as an unconditional principle, situated above
any utilitarian judgement.

Obviously, the use of the words *higher, noble, exalted* does not imply
endorsement. Here these qualities simply designate that something belongs
to a category *historically* defined as *higher, noble* or *exalted*: such particu-
larized or novel conceptions can only be considered in relation to the
traditional conceptions from which they derive; they are, furthermore,
necessarily hybrid, without any far-reaching effect, and it is doubtless
preferable, if possible, to abandon any representation of this order (for what
admissible reasons would a man want to be noble, similar to a representative of the medieval, military caste and absolutely not ignoble, that is to
say similar, in accordance with the judgement of history, to a man whose
material destitution would have altered his human character, made him
something other?).

Having formulated this reservation, the meaning of higher values must
be clarified with the help of traditional qualifiers. *Superiority* (imperative
sovereignty)[10] designates the entire set of striking aspects – affectively
determining attraction or repulsion – characteristic of different human
situations in which it is possible to dominate and even to oppress one's

fellows by reason of their age, physical weakness, legal status or simply of their necessity to place themselves under the control of one person: specific situations correspond to diverse circumstances, that of the father with regard to his children, that of the military leader with regard to the army and the civilian population, that of the master with regard to the slave, that of the king with regard to his subjects. To these real situations must be added mythological situations whose exclusively fictitious nature facilitates a condensation of the aspects characteristic of superiority.

The simple fact of dominating one's fellows implies the *heterogeneity* of the master, insofar as he is the master: to the extent that he refers to his nature, to his personal quality, as the justification of his authority, he designates his nature as *something other*, without being able to account for it rationally. But not only as *something other* with regard to the rational domain of the common measure and the equivalent: the *heterogeneity* of the master is no less opposed to that of the slave. If the heterogeneous nature of the slave is akin to that of the filth to which his material situation condemns him to live, that of the master is formed by an act excluding all filth: an act pure in direction but sadistic in form.

In human terms, the ultimate imperative value presents itself in the form of royal or imperial authority in which cruel tendencies and the need, characterisitic of all domination, to realize and idealize order are manifest in the highest degree. This double character is not less present in fascist authority, but it is only one of the numerous forms of royal authority, the description of which constitutes the foundation of any coherent description of fascism.

In opposition to the impoverished existence of the oppressed, political sovereignty initially presents itself as a clearly differentiated sadistic activity. In individual psychology, it is rare for the sadistic tendency not to be associated with a more or less manifest masochistic tendency. But as each tendency is normally represented in society by a distinct agency, the sadistic attitude can be manifested by an imperative person to the exclusion of any corresponding masochistic attitudes. In this case, the exclusion of the filthy forms that serve as the object of the cruel act is not accompanied by the positioning of these forms as a value and, consequently, no erotic activity can be associated with the cruelty. The erotic elements themselves are rejected at the same time as every filthy object and, as in a great number of religious attitudes, sadism attains a brilliant purity. This differentiation can be more or less complete – individually, sovereigns have been able to live power in part as an orgy of blood – but, on the whole, within the *heterogeneous* domain, the imperative royal form has historically effected an exclusion of impoverished and filthy forms sufficient to permit a connection with *homogeneous* forms at a certain level.

In fact, as a rule, *homogeneous* society excludes every *heterogeneous* element, whether filthy or noble; the modalities of the operation vary as much as the nature of each excluded element. For homogeneous society, only the rejection of impoverished forms has a constant fundamental value (such that the least recourse to the reserves of energy represented by these forms requires an operation as dangerous as *subversion*); but, given that the act of excluding impoverished forms necessarily associates *homogeneous* forms with imperative forms, the latter can no longer be purely and simply rejected. To combat the elements most incompatible with it, *homogeneous* society uses free-floating imperative forces; and, when it must choose the very object of its activity (the existence *for itself* in the service of which it must necessarily place itself) from the domain that it has excluded, the choice inevitably falls on those forces which have already proved most effective.

The inability of *homogeneous* society to find in itself a reason for being and acting is what makes it dependent upon imperative forces, just as the sadistic hostility of sovereigns towards the impoverished population is what allies them with any formation seeking to maintain the latter in a state of oppression.

A complex situation results from the royal person's modalities of exclusion: since the king is the object in which homogeneous society has found its reason for being, maintaining this relationship demands that he conduct himself in such a way that the *homogeneous* society can exist *for him*. In the first place, this requirement bears upon the fundamental *heterogeneity* of the king, guaranteed by numerous prohibitions of contact (taboos); this heterogeneity, however, is impossible to keep in a free state. In no case may *heterogeneity* receive its law from without, but its spontaneous movement can be fixed, at least tendentially, once and for all. Thus, the destructive passion (sadism) of the imperative agency is as a rule exclusively directed either toward foreign societies or towards the impoverished classes, towards all those external or internal elements hostile to *homogeneity*.

Historically, royal power is the form that results from such a situation. As for its positive function, a determining role is reserved for the very principle of unification, actually carried out in a group of individuals whose affective choice bears upon a single *heterogeneous* object. A shared orientation has, in itself, a constitutive value: it presupposes – vaguely, it is true – the imperative character of the object. Unification, the principle of *homogeneity*, is only a tendential fact, incapable of finding in itself a motive for requiring and imposing its existence; and, in most circumstances, the recourse to an external requirement has the value of a primary necessity. Yet the pure *having to be*, the moral imperative, requires being *for itself*, namely the specific mode of *heterogeneous* existence. But this existence precisely escapes the principle of having to be and can in no case be subordinated to it: it immediately accedes to *Being* (in other words it produces itself as a value *being or not being*) and never as a value that has to be. The complex form in which the resolution of this incompatibility culminates poses the *having to be* of *homogeneous* existence in *heterogeneous* existences. Thus, imperative *heterogeneity* not only represents a differentiated form with regard to vague *heterogeneity*: it additionally supposes the structural modification of the two parts, *homogeneous* and *heterogeneous*, in contact with one another. On the one hand, the *homogeneous* formation akin to the royal agency, the state, derives its imperative character from this agency and seems to attain existence *for itself* by bringing about the barren and cold *having to be* of the whole of homogeneous society. But the state is in reality only the abstract, degraded form of the living *having to be* required, at the top, as an affective attraction and royal agency: it is simply vague *homogeneity* become a constraint. On the other hand, this mode of intermediary formation which characterizes the state penetrates imperative existence through reaction; but, in the course of this introjection, the proper form of homogeneity becomes – this time for real – existence *for itself* by denying itself: it becomes absorbed by *heterogeneity* and destroys itself as strictly *homogeneous* from the fact that, having become the negation of the principle of utility, it refuses all subordination. Although profoundly penetrated by the *reason of state*, the king nevertheless does not identify with the latter: he wholly maintains the separate character of divine supremacy. He is exempt fom the specific principle of homogeneity, the compensation of rights and duties constituting the formal law of the state: the king's rights are unconditional.

There is hardly any need to suggest at this point that the possibility of such affective formations has brought about the infinite subjugation that degrades most forms of human life (much more so than abuses of power which, furthermore, are themselves reducible – insofar as the force in play is necessarily social – to imperative formations). If sovereignty is now considered in its tendential form – such as it has been lived historically by the subject to whom it owes its attractive value – yet independently of any particular reality, its nature appears, in human terms, to be the noblest – exalted to majesty – pure in the midst of the orgy, beyond the reach of human infirmities. It constitutes the region formally exempt from self-interested intrigues to which the oppressed subject refers as to an empty but pure satisfaction. (In this sense the constitution of royal nature above an inadmissible reality recalls the fictions justifying eternal life.) As a tendential form, it fulfils the *ideal* of society and the course of things (in the subject's mind, this function is expressed naively: *if the king only knew . . .*). At the same time it is strict authority. Situated above *homogeneous* society, as well as above the impoverished populace or the aristocratic hierarchy that emanates from it, it requires the bloody repression of what is contrary to it and becomes synonymous in its split-off form with the heterogeneous foundations of the law: it is thus both the possibility of and the requirement for collective unity; it is in the royal orbit that the state and its functions of coercion and adaptation are elaborated; the homogeneous reduction develops, both as destruction and foundation, to the benefit of royal greatness.

Posing itself as the principle for the association of innumerable elements, royal power develops spontaneously as an imperative and destructive force against every other imperative form that could be opposed to it. It thereby manifests, at the top, the fundamental tendency and principle of all authority: the reduction to a personal entity, the individualization of power. While impoverished existence is necessarily produced as a multitude and homogeneous society as a reduction to the common measure, the imperative agency – the foundation of oppression – necessarily develops along the lines of a reduction to a unit in the form of a human being excluding the very possibility of a peer, in other words as a radical form of exclusion requiring avidity.

7 Tendential Concentration

This tendency toward concentration appears to be in contradiction, it is true, with the coexistence of distinct domains of power: the domain of royal sovereignty is different from military power and from the domain of religious authority. But taking note of this coexistence is precisely what draws attention to the composite character of royal power, in which it is easy to find the constitutive elements of the other two powers, the religious and the military.[11]

It thus becomes apparent that royal sovereignty should not be considered as a simple element having its own autonomous source, such as the army or the religious organization: it is exactly (and furthermore uniquely) the actualized concentration of these two elements formed in two different directions. The constant rebirth of military and religious powers in a pure state has never modified the principle of their tendential concentration in the form of a single sovereignty: even the formal refusal of Christianity has not prevented – to use vulgar symbolic terminology – the cross from lying on the steps of the throne with the sabre.

Considered historically, this concentration can be achieved spontaneously: the head of the army succeeds in having himself crowned *king* through the use of force, or the established *king* takes hold of military power (in Japan, the emperor recently actualized this form, without, it is true, his own initiative having played a determining role). But each time, even in the case where royalty is *usurped*, the possibility of the uniting of powers depended upon their fundamental affinities and especially upon their tendential concentration.

The consideration of the principles governing these facts obviously becomes crucial from the moment that fascism renews their historical existence, that is, once again unites military and religious authority to effect a total oppression. (In this regard, it can be stated – without prejudicing any other political judgement – that any unlimited actualization of imperative forms amounts to a negation of humanity as a value which depends upon the play of internal oppositions.) Like Bonapartism, fascism (which etymologically signifies *uniting, concentration*) is no more than an acute reactivation of the latent sovereign agency, but with a character in a sense purified by the fact that paramilitary groups substituted for the army in the constitution of power immediately have that power as an object.

8 The Army and the Heads of the Army

As a rule, the army exists functionally because of war, and its psychological structure is entirely reducible to the exercise of that function. Thus its imperative character does not directly result from the social importance linked to the material power of controlling weapons: its internal organization – discipline and hierarchy – is what makes it pre-eminently a noble society.

Obviously, the *nobility of arms* initially supposes an intense *heterogeneity*: discipline and hierarchy are themselves but forms and not the foundations of *heterogeneity*; bloodshed, carnage and death, exclusively, are commensurate with the fundamental nature of weapons. But the ambiguous horror of war still has only a vulgar *heterogeneity* (at best undifferentiated). The exalted, exalting control of weapons supposes the affective unification necessary to their cohesion, i.e., to their effective value.

The affective character of this unification is manifest in the form of the soldier's attachment to the head of the army: it implies that each soldier equates the latter's glory with his own. This process is the intermediary through which disgusting slaughter is radically transformed into its opposite, glory, namely into a pure and intense attraction. The glory of the chief essentially constitutes a sort of affective pole opposed to the nature of the soldiers. Even independently of their horrible occupation, the soldiers belong *as a rule* to a vile segment of the population; divested of its uniforms and wearing ordinary clothing, a professional army of the eighteenth century would have looked like a wretched populace. But even the elimination of enlistments from the lower classes would fail to change the deeper structure of the army; this structure would continue to base affective organization upon the social infamy of the soldiers. *Human beings* incorporated into the army are but negated elements, negated with a kind of rage (a sadism) manifest in the tone of each command, negated by the parade, by the uniform and by the *geometric* regularity of cadenced

Heterology

movements. The chief, insofar as he is imperative, is the incarnation of this violent negation. His intimate nature, the nature of his glory, is constituted by an imperative act that annuls the wretched populace (which constitutes the army) as such (in the same way that the slaughter is annulled as such).

In social psychology, this imperative negation generally appears as the characteristic of *action*; in other words, every affirmed social *action* necessarily takes the unified psychological form of *sovereignty*; every lower form, every ignominy, being by definition passive, is transformed into its opposite by the simple fact of a transition to action. Slaughter, as an inert result, is ignoble; but, shifted on to the social action that caused it, the ignoble heterogeneous value thus established becomes noble (the action of killing and nobility are associated by indefectible historical ties): all it takes is for the action to effectively affirm itself as such, to freely assume the imperative form that constitutes it.

This operation – the fact of assuming *in complete freedom* the imperative character of action – is precisely what characterizes the chief. It becomes possible to grasp here in an explicit form the role played by unification (individualization) in the structural modifications that characterize superior *heterogeneity*. Starting with formless and impoverished elements, the army, under the imperative impulse, becomes organized and internally achieves a *homogeneous* form on account of the negation directed at the disordered character of its elements: in fact, the mass that constitutes the army passes from a depleted and ruined existence to a purified geometric order, from formlessness to aggressive rigidity. In actuality, this negated mass has ceased to be itself in order to become affectively ('affectively' refers here to simple psychological behaviours, such as *standing at attention* or *marching double-time*) the chief's thing and like a part of the chief himself. A troop *at attention* is in a sense absorbed by the existence of the command and, thus, absorbed by the negation of itself. *Standing at attention* can be analogically considered as a figurative movement (a kind of geometrical negative) elevating not only the chief but all who follow his orders to the (geometrically) regular form of imperative sovereignty. Thus the implied infamy of the soldiers is only a basic infamy which, in uniform, is transformed into its opposite: order and glamour. The mode of *heterogeneity* explicitly undergoes a thorough alteration, completing the realization of intense *homogeneity* without a decrease of the fundamental *heterogeneity*. In the midst of the population, the army retains the distinction of being *wholly other*, but with a sovereignty linked to domination, to the imperative and separate character which the chief transmits to his soldiers.

Thus the dominant direction of the army, detached from its affective foundations (infamy and slaughter), depends upon the contrary *heterogeneity* of *honour* and *duty* incarnated in the person of the chief. (If the chief is not subordinate to a real agency or to an idea, duty is incarnated in his person in the same way as in that of the king.) Honour and duty, symbolically expressed by the geometry of the parades, are the tendential forms that situate military existence above homogeneous existence as imperative and as a pure reason for being. Having a limited bearing on certain levels of action, these forms, in their properly military aspect, are compatible with infinitely craven crimes, but they suffice to affirm the exalted value of the army and to make the internal domination characterizing its structure one of the fundamental elements of a supreme psychological authority instituted above the subjugated society.

Nevertheless, the immediate result of the power of the head of the army is only an internal homogeneity independent of social *homogeneity*, whereas specific royal power exists only in relation to homogeneous society. The integration of military power into social power therefore supposes a structural change: it supposes the acquisition of modalities characteristic of royal power in relation to the administration of the state, as they were described in relation to this power.

9 Religious Power

It is granted in an implicit and vague manner that holding military power has been sufficient to exert a general domination. Nevertheless, with the exception of colonizations, which extend a pre-established power, examples of long-lasting, exclusively military dominations are hard to find. In fact, simple material armed force is incapable of founding any power: in the first place, such force depends on the internal attraction exerted by the chief (money is insufficient to constitute an army). And when the chief wants to use the force at his disposal to dominate society, he must further acquire the elements of an external attraction (of a *religious* attraction valid for the entire population).

It is true that the latter elements are sometimes at the disposal of force, yet, as the origin of royal power, military attraction probably has no primacy over religious attraction. To the extent that it is possible to formulate a valid judgement about the distant past of mankind, it seems fairly clear that religion – not the army – is the source of social authority. Furthermore, the introduction of heredity regularly marks the predominance of a religious form of power: it can rely upon its blood lines, whereas military power depends first of all on personal value.

Unfortunately, it is difficult to ascribe a specific meaning to that which, in the blood or in the aspects of royalty, is characteristically religious: here one essentially confronts the bare and unlimited form of undifferentiated *heterogeneity*, before any of its perceptible elements (ones that can be made explicit) has been fixed by a still vague direction. This direction does exist nonetheless, but, in every causal state, the structural modifications that it introduces leave the field to free projection of general affective forms, such as anxiety or sacred attraction. Furthermore, structural modifications are not what are immediately transmitted through physiological contact in heredity or by sacred rites, but rather a fundamental *heterogeneity*.

The (implicit) signification of the purely religious royal character can only be attained to the extent that its origin and structure appear to be shared with those of a divine nature. Though it is impossible, in such a cursory presentation, to present all of the affective movements involved in the establishment of mythical authorities (culminating in the positioning of a fictitious supreme authority), a simple juxtaposition is amply revealing. Unequivocal facts (identifications with the divine, mythical genealogies, the Roman or Shintoist imperial cults, the Christian theory of divine right) correspond to the shared structure of the two formations. On the whole, the king is considered in one form or another to be an emanation of a divine nature, along with everything that the principle of emanation entails in the way of identity when dealing with heterogeneous elements.

The notable structural modifications that characterize the evolution of the representation of the divine – starting with free and irresponsible violence – simply make explicit those characterizing the formation of the royal nature. In both cases, the position of the sovereign is what directs the alteration of the heterogeneous structure. In both cases, we witness a concentration of attributes and forces; but, in the case of God, since the forces that he represents are only composed in a fictitious being (not subject to the limitation of having to be realized), it was possible to yield more perfect forms, more purely logical schemata.

The supreme being of theologians and philosophers represents the most profound introjection of the structure characteristic of *homogeneity* into *heterogeneous* existence: in his theological aspect, God pre-eminently fulfils the sovereign form. However, the counterpart to this possibility is implied by the fictitious character of divine existence, whose *heterogeneous* nature, lacking the limitative value of reality, can be overlooked in a philosophical conception (reduced to a formal affirmation that is in no way lived). In the order of free intellectual speculation, the idea can be substituted for God as supreme existence and power; this implies the admittedly partial revelation of a relative *heterogeneity* of the Idea (such as occurred when Hegel raised the Idea above the simple *having to be*).

10 Fascism as the Sovereign Form of Sovereignty

Stirring up such apparently anachronistic phantoms would surely be senseless if fascism had not, before our very eyes, reappropriated and reconstituted from the bottom up – starting, as it were, with nothing – the very process described above for the establishment of power. Until our times, there had only been a single historical example of the sudden formation of a total power, namely the Islamic Khalifat. While both military and religious, it was principally royal, relying upon no prior foundation. Islam, a form comparable to fascism in its meagre human wealth, did not even have recourse to an established nation, much less a constituted state. But it must be recognized that, for fascist movements, the existing state has first been something to conquer, then a means or a frame,[12] and that the integration of the nation does not change the schema of their formation. Just like early Islam, fascism represents the constitution of a total heterogeneous power whose manifest origin is to be found in the prevailing effervescence.

In the first place, fascist power is characterized by a foundation that is both religious and military, in which these two habitually distinct elements cannot be separated: it thus presents itself from the outset as an accomplished concentration.

It is true, however, that the military aspect is the predominant one. The affective relations that closely associate (identify) the leader to the member of the party (as they have already been described) are generally analogous to those uniting a chief to his soldiers. The imperative presence of the leader amounts to a negation of the fundamental revolutionary effervescence that he taps; the revolution, which is affirmed as a foundation, is, at the same time, fundamentally negated from the moment that internal domination is militarily exerted on the militia. But this internal domination is not directly subordinated to real or possible acts of war: it essentially poses itself as the middle term of an external domination of society and of state, as the middle term of a total imperative value. Thus, qualities characteristic of the two dominations (internal and external, military and religious) are simultaneously implied: qualities derived from the introjected *homogeneity*, such as duty, discipline and obedience, and qualities derived from the essential heterogeneity: imperative violence and the positioning of the chief as the transcendent object of collective affectivity. But the religious value of the chief is really the fundamental (if not formal) value of fascism, giving the activity of the militiamen its characteristic affective tonality, distinct from that of the soldier in general. The chief as such is in fact only the emanation of a principle which is none other than that of the glorious existence of a nation raised to the value of a divine force (which, superseding every other conceivable consideration, demands not only passion but ecstasy from its participants). Incarnated in the person of the chief (in Germany, the properly religious term, prophet, has sometimes been used), the nation thus plays the same role that Allah, incarnated in the person of Mahomet or the Khalif,[13] plays for Islam.

Fascism therefore appears first of all as a concentration and so to speak condensation of power[14] (a meaning actually indicated in the etymological value of the term). This general signification must furthermore be accepted in several ways. The accomplished uniting of imperative forces takes place at the top, but the process leaves no social fraction inactive. In fundamental opposition to socialism, fascism is characterized by the uniting of classes. Not that classes conscious of their unity have adhered to the regime, but because expressive elements of each class have been represented in the deep movements of adherence that led to the seizing of power. Here the specific type of unification is actually derived from properly military effectivity, which is to say that the representative elements of the exploited classes have been included in the affective process only through the negation of their own nature (just as the social nature of a recruit is negated by means of uniforms and parades). This process which *blends* the different social formations from the bottom up must be understood as a fundamental process whose scheme is necessarily given in the very formation of the chief, who derives his profound meaning from the fact of having shared the dejected and impoverished life of the proletariat. But, as in the case of military organization, the affective value characteristic of impoverished existence is only displaced and transformed into its opposite; and it is its inordinate scope that gives the chief and the whole of the formation the accent of violence without which no army or fascism could be possible.

11 The Fascist State

Fascism's close ties with the impoverished classes profoundly distinguish this formation from classical royal society, which is characterized by a more or less decisive loss of contact with the lower classes. But, forming in opposition to the established royal unification (the forms of which dominate society from too far above), the fascist unification is not simply a uniting of powers from different origins and a symbolic uniting of classes: it is also the accomplished uniting of the *heterogeneous* elements with the *homogeneous* elements, of sovereignty in the strictest sense with the state.

As a uniting, fascism is actually opposed as much to Islam as it is to traditional monarchy. In fact Islam created from nothing, and that is why a form such as the state, which can only be the result of a long historical process, played no role in its immediate constitution; on the contrary, the existing state served from the outset as a frame for the entire fascist process of organic organization. This characteristic aspect of fascism permitted Mussolini to write that 'everything is in the state', that 'nothing human or spiritual exists nor *a fortiori* does it have any existence outside of the state'.[15]

But this does not necessarily imply an identity of the state and the imperative force that dominates the whole of society. Mussolini himself, who leaned toward a kind of Hegelian divinization of the state, acknowledges in wilfully obscure terms a distinct principle of sovereignty that he alternately designates as *the people, the nation* and *the superior personality,* but which must be identified with the fascist formation itself and its leader: 'if the people . . . signifies the idea . . . that is incarnated in the people as the will of a few or even of a single person . . . It has to do', he writes, 'neither with race nor with a determined geographical region, but with a grouping that is historically perpetuated, of a multitude unified by an idea that is a will to existence and to power: it is a self-consciousness, a personality.'[16] The term *personality* must be understood as *individualization,* a process leading to Mussolini himself, and when he adds that 'this superior personality is the nation as state. It is not the nation that creates the state . . .'[17] it must be understood that he has: 1) substituted the principle of the sovereignty of the individualized fascist formation for the old democratic principle of the sovereignty of the nation; 2) laid the groundwork for a conclusive interpretation of the sovereign agency and the state.

Nationalist-Socialist Germany – which, unlike Italy (under the patronage of Gentile), has not officially adopted Hegelianism and the theory of the state as soul of the world – has not been afflicted with the theoretical difficulties resulting from the necessity of officially articulating a principle of authority: the mystical idea of race immediately affirmed itself as the imperative aim of the new fascist society; at the same time it appeared to be incarnated in the person of the Führer and his followers. Even though the conception of race lacks an objective base, it is nonetheless subjectively grounded, and the necessity of maintaining the racial value above all others obviated the need for a theory that made the state the principle of all value. The example of Germany thus demonstrates that the identity established by Mussolini between the state and the sovereign form of value is not necessary to a theory of fascism.

The fact that Mussolini did not formally distinguish the *heterogeneous* agency, the action of which he caused to penetrate deeply into the state, can equally be interpreted as an absolute seizure of the state, and as a strained adaptation of the sovereign agency to the necessities of a regime of *homogeneous* production. It is in the development of these two reciprocal processes that fascism and the reason of state came to appear identical. Nevertheless, the forms of life rigorously conserve a fundamental opposition when they maintain a radical duality of principles in the very person of the one holding power: the president of the Italian council and the German chancellor represent forms of activity radically distinct from those of the Duce or the Führer. Further, these two figures derive their fundamental power not from their official function in the state, like other prime ministers, but from the existence of a fascist party and from their personal position at the head of that party. In conjunction with the duality of *heterogeneous* and *homogeneous* forms, this evidence of the deep roots of power precisely maintains the unconditional supremacy of the *heterogeneous* form from the standpoint of the principle of sovereignty.

12 The Fundamental Conditions of Fascism

As has already been indicated, *heterogeneous* processes as a whole can only enter into play once the fundamental *homogeneity* of society (the apparatus of production) has become dissociated because of its internal contradictions. Further, it can be stated that, even though it generally occurs in the blindest fashion, the development of heterogeneous forces necessarily comes to signify a solution to the problem posed by the contradictions of *homogeneity*. Once in power, developed *heterogeneous* forces dispose of the means of coercion necessary to resolve the differences that had arisen between previously irreconcilable elements. But it goes without saying that, at the end of a movement that excludes all subversion, the thrust of these resolutions will have been consistent with the general direction of the existing homogeneity, namely, with the interests of the capitalists.

The change resides in the fact that, having had recourse to fascist *heterogeneity*, these interests, from the moment of crisis on, are those of a group opposed to privately owned enterprises. As a result, the very structure of capitalism – the principle of which had been that of a spontaneous *homogeneity* of production based on competition, a de facto coincidence of the interests of the group of producers with the absolute freedom of each enterprise – finds itself profoundly altered. The awareness, developed in some German capitalists, of the peril to which this freedom subjected them in a critical period, must naturally be placed at the origin of the effervescence and triumph of National-Socialism. However, it is evident that this awareness did not yet exist for Italian capitalists who, from the moment of the march on Rome, were exclusively preoccupied with the irresolvability of their conflicts with the workers. It thus appears that the unity of fascism is located in its actual psychological structure and not in the economic conditions that serves as its base. (This does not contradict the fact that a general logical development of the economy retroactively provides the different fascisms with a common economic signification that they share, to be sure, with the political activity – absolutely foreign to fascism in the strictest sense – of the current government of the United States.)

Whatever the economic danger to which fascism responded, the awareness of this danger and the need to avoid it actually represent an as yet empty desire, which could be propped up by money. The realization of the force able to respond to the desire and to utilize the available monies takes place only in the heterogeneous region, and its possibility depends upon the actual structure of that region: on the whole, it is possible to consider this structure as variable depending on whether the society is democratic or monarchical.

Truly monarchical societies (as distinct from the adapted or bastardized political forms represented by England today or pre-fascist Italy) are characterized by the fact that a sovereign agency, having an ancient origin and an absolute form, is connected to the existing *homogeneity*. The constant evolution of the constitutive elements of this *homogeneity* can necessitate fundamental changes, but the need for change can become represented internally only in an alerted minority: the whole of the homogeneous elements and the immediate principle of *homogeneity* remain committed to upholding the juridical forms and the existing administrative framework guaranteed by the authority of the king; the authority of the king coincides reciprocally with the upholding of these forms and this framework. Thus the upper part of the *heterogeneous* region is both immobilized and immobilizing, and only the lower part formed by the impoverished and oppressed classes is capable of entering into movement. But, for the latter, passive and oppressed by definition, the fact of entering into movement represents a profound alteration of their nature: in order to take part in a struggle against the sovereign agency and the legal homogeneity oppressing them, the lower classes must pass from a passive and diffuse state to a form of conscious activity; in Marxist terms, these classes must become aware of themselves as a revolutionary proletariat. This proletariat cannot actually be limited to itself: it is in fact only a point of concentration for every dissociated social element that has been banished to *heterogeneity*. It is even possible to say that such a point of concentration exists in a sense prior to the formation of what must be called the 'conscious proletariat': the general description of the heterogeneous region actually implies that it be posited as a constitutive element of the structure of a whole that includes not only imperative forms and impoverished forms but also *subversive forms*. These subversive forms are none other than the lower forms transformed with a view to the struggle against the sovereign forms. The necessity inherent to subversive forms requires that what is low become high, that what is high become low; this is the requirement in which the nature of subversion is expressed. In the case where the sovereign forms of a society are immobilized and bound, the diverse elements that have been banished to *heterogeneity* as a result of social decomposition can only ally themselves with the formations which result when the oppressed class become active: they are necessarily dedicated to subversion. The fraction of the bourgeoisie that has become aware of the incompatibility with established social frameworks becomes united against figures of authority and blends in with the effervescent masses in revolt; and even in the period immediately following the destruction of the monarchy, social movements continued to be governed by the initial anti-authoritarian character of the revolution.

But in a democratic society (at least when such a society is not galvanized by the necessity of going to war) the *heterogeneous* imperative agency (nation in republican forms, king in constitutional monarchies) is reduced to an atrophied existence, so that its destruction no longer appears to be a necessary condition of change. In such a situation, the imperative forms can even be considered as a free field, open to all possibilities of effervescence and movement, just as subversive forms are in a democracy. And when homogeneous society undergoes a critical disintegration, the dissociated elements no longer necessarily enter the orbit of subversive attraction: in addition there forms at the top an imperative attraction that no longer immobilizes those who are subjected to it. As a rule, until just recently, this imperative attraction only exerted itself in the direction of restoration. It was thus limited before hand by the prior nature of the disappeared sovereignty which most often implied a prohibitive loss of contact between the sovereign agency and the lower classes (the only spontaneous historical restoration, that of Bonapartism, must be put into relation with the manifest popular sources of Bonapartist power). In France, it is true, some of the constitutive forms of fascism were able to be elaborated in the formation – but especially in the difficulties of the formation – of an imperative attraction aimed at a dynastic restoration. The possibility of fascism nonetheless depended upon the fact that a reversion to vanished sovereign forms was out of the question in Italy, where the monarchy subsisted in a reduced state. Added to this subsistence, it was precisely the insufficiency of the royal formation that necessitated the formation of – and left the field open for – an entirely renewed imperative attraction with a popular base. Under these new conditions (with regard to the classical revolutionary dissociations in monarchical societies) the lower classes no longer exclusively experience the attraction represented by socialist subversion, and a military type of organization has in part begun to draw them into the orbit of sovereignty. Likewise, the dissociated elements (belonging to the middle or dominating classes) have found a new outlet for their effervescence, and it is not surprising that, given the choice between subversive or imperative solutions, the majority opted for the imperative.

An unprecedented situation results from the possibility of this dual effervescence. During the same period and in the same society, two competing revolutions, hostile to one another and to the established order, are being formed. There develop at the same time two segments that share a common opposition to the general dissociation of *homogeneous* society; this explains the numerous connections between them and even a kind of profound complicity. Furthermore, independently of their common origin, the success of one of the fractions implies that of the opposing fraction through a certain play of balance: it can cause it to occur (in particular, to the extent that fascism is an imperative response to the growing threat of a working-class movement), and should be considered in most cases as the sign of that occurrence. But, unless it is possible to re-establish the disrupted *homogeneity*, it is evident that the simple formation of a situation of this order dictates its own outcome in advance: an increase in this effervescence is accompanied by a proportionate increase in the importance of the *dissociated elements* (bourgeois and petty bourgeois) as compared to that of the elements that had never been integrated (pro-letariat). Thus the chances for a working-class revolution, a liberating subversion of society disappear to the extent that revolutionary possibilities are affirmed.

As a rule, it seems therefore that revolutionary movements that develop in a democracy are hopeless, at least so long as the memory of the earlier struggles against the royal authority has been attenuated and no longer necessarily sets *heterogeneous* reactions in opposition to imperative forms. In fact, it is evident that the situation of the major democratic powers, where the fate of the Revolution is being played out, does not warrant the slightest confidence: it is only the very nearly indifferent attitude of the proletariat that has permitted these countries to avoid fascist formations. Yet it would be puerile to presume to enclose the world in such a neat construction: from the outset, the mere consideration of affective social formations reveals the immense resources, the inexhaustible wealth of the forms par-ticular to affective life. Not only are the psychological situations of the democratic collectivities, like any human situation, transitory, but it re-mains possible to envision, at least as a yet imprecise representation, forms of attraction that differ from those already in existence, as different from present or even past communism as fascism is from dynastic claims. A system of knowledge that permits the anticipation of the affective social reactions that traverse the superstructure and perhaps even, to a certain extent, do away with it, must be developed from one of these possibilities. The fact of fascism, which has thrown the very existence of a workers' movement into question, clearly demonstrates what can be expected from a timely recourse to reawakened affective forces. Unlike the situation during the period of utopian socialism, morality and idealism are no more the questions today than they are in fascist forms. Rather, an organized understanding of the movements in society, of attraction and repulsion, starkly presents itself as a weapon at this moment when a vast convulsion opposes, not so much fascism to communism, but radical imperative forms to the deep subversion which continues to pursue the emancipation of human lives.

Notes

1 This is obviously the principal shortcoming of an essay that will not fail to astonish and shock those who are familiar with French sociology, modern German philosophy (phenomenology) and psychoanalysis. As a piece of information, it can nevertheless be insisted upon that the following descriptions refer to *actual experiences* and that the psychological method used excludes any recourse to abstraction.

2 The words *homogeneous, heterogeneous* and terms derived from them are stressed each time they are taken in a sense particular to this essay.

3 The most accomplished and expressive forms of social *homogeneity* are the sciences and the technics. The laws founded by the sciences establish relations of identity between the different elements of an elaborated and measurable world. As for the technics – that serve as a transition between production and the science – it is because of the very homogeneity of products and means that they are opposed, in underdeveloped civilizations, to religion and magic (cf. Hubert and Mauss, *Esquisse d'une théorie générale de la magie*, in *Année sociologique*, VII, 1902–3, p. 15).

4 *Formes élémentaires de la vie religieuse*, 1912, p. 53. Following his analysis, Durkheim comes to identify the *sacred* and the *social*, but this identification necessitates the introduction of a hypothesis and, whatever its scope, does not have the value of an immediately significant definition (it actually represents the tendency of science to posit a *homogeneous* representation in order to avoid the discernible presence of fundamentally *heterogeneous* elements).

5 Cf. G. Bataille, 'The notion of expenditure', this volume.

6 It appears that the displacements are produced under the same conditions as are Pavlov's conditioned reflexes.

7 On the primitive mind, cf. Lévy-Bruhl, *La Mentalité primitive*; Cassirier, *Das mythische Denken*; on the unconscious, cf. Freud, *The Interpretation of Dreams*.

8 On the affective relations of the followers to the leader and on the analogy with hypnosis, cf. Freud, *Group Psychology and the Analysis of the 'Ego'*; (reprinted in *Essais de psychanalyse*, 1929).

9 Cf. W. Robertson Smith, *Lectures on the Religion of the Semites*, First Series, *The Fundamental Institutions* (Edinburgh, 1889).

10 The word *sovereign* comes from the lower Latin adjective *superaneus* meaning *superior*.

11 Freud, in *Group Psychology and the Analysis of the 'Ego'*, studied precisely the two functions, military (army) and religious (church), in relation to the imperative form (unconscious) of individual psychology which he called the *Ego Ideal* or the *superego*. If one refers to the whole of the elements brought together in the present study, that work, published in German in 1921, appears as an essential introduction to the understanding of fascism.

12 The modern Italian state is to a great extent a creation of fascism.

13 *Khalif* etymologically signifies *lieutenant* (standing in for [tenant lieu]); the full title is 'lieutenant of the emissary of God'.

14 Condensation of *superiority*, evidently related to a latent inferiority complex: such a complex has equally strong roots in both Italy and Germany; this is why, even if fascism develops subsequently in regions having attained a complete sovereignty and the awareness of the sovereignty, it is inconceivable that it could ever have been the autochthonous and specific product of such countries.

15 Mussolini, *Enciclopedia italiana*, article *Fascismo*.

16 Ibid.

17 Ibid.

12

The Use-Value of D. A. F. de Sade (An Open Letter to My Current Comrades)

If I think it good to address this letter to my comrades, it is not because the propositions that it contains concern them. It will probably even appear to them that such propositions do not concern anyone in particular at all. But in this case I need to have at least a few people as witnesses to establish so complete a defection. There are, perhaps, declarations which, for lack of anything better, ridiculously need an Attic chorus, because they suppose, as their effect, in spite of everything, a minimum of astonishment, of misunderstanding or of repugnance. But one does not address a chorus in order to convince it or rally it, and certainly one does not submit to the judgement of destiny without revolting, when it condemns the declarant to the saddest isolation.

This isolation, as far as I am concerned, is moreover in part voluntary, since I would agree to come out of it only on certain hard-to-meet conditions.

In fact even the gesture of writing, which alone permits one to envisage slightly less conventional human relations, a little less crafty than those of so-called intimate friendships – even this gesture of writing does not leave me with an appreciable hope. I doubt that it is possible to reach the few people to whom this letter is no doubt intended, over the heads of my present comrades. For – my resolution is all the more intransigent in that it is absurd to defend – it would have been necessary to deal not with individuals like those I already know, but only with men (and above all with masses) who are comparatively decomposed, amorphous and even violently expelled from every form. But it is likely that such men do not yet exist (and the masses certainly do not exist).

The text is taken from the collection entitled *Visions of Excess: selected writings, 1927–1939*, ed. Allan Stoekl, tr. Allan Stoekl with Carl R. Lovitt and Donald M. Leslie, Jr (University of Minnesota Press, Minneapolis, MN, 1985), pp. 91–102. 'La valeur d'usage de Sade' was among the manuscripts written between 1925 and 1930, the period leading up to Bataille's involvement with *La Critique sociale*. It was first published in *OC*, II, pp. 54–6.

All I can state is that, one day or another, they certainly will not fail to exist, given that current social bonds will inevitably be undone, and that these bonds cannot much longer maintain the habitual enslavement of people and customs. The masses will in turn be decomposed as soon as they see the prestige of industrial reality, to which they find themselves attached, disappear; in other words, when the process of material progress and rapid transformation in which they have had to participate (docile as well as in revolt) leads to a disagreeable and terminal stagnation.

My resolution thus cannot be defended only in that it eliminates – not without bitterness – every immediate satisfaction.

Outside of propositions that can only take on meaning through very general consequences, it so happens that it is high time for me to quell – at little cost – a part of this bitterness: it is possible at the very least to clear the narrow terrain – where from now on the debate will be carried out – of the intellectual bartering that usually goes on there. In fact it is obvious that if men incapable of histrionics succeed those of today, they will not be able to better represent the tacky phraseology now in circulation than by recalling the fate reserved, by a certain number of writers, for the memory of D. A. F. de Sade (moreover it will, perhaps, appear fairly quickly, in a very general way, that the fact of needlessly resorting to literary or poetic verbiage, the inability to express oneself in a simple and categorical way, not only are the result of a vulgar impotence, but always betray a pretentious hypocrisy).

Of course, I do not allude in this way to the various people who are scandalized by the writings of Sade, but only to his most open apologists. It has seemed fitting today to place these writings (and with them the figure of their author) above everything (or almost everything) that can be opposed to them, but it is out of the question to allow them the least place in private or public life, in theory or in practice. The behavior of Sade's admirers resembles that of primitive subjects in relation to their king, whom they adore and loathe, and whom they cover with honours and narrowly confine. In the most favourable cases, the author of *Justine* is in fact thus treated as any given *foreign body*; in other words, he is only an object of transports of exaltation to the extent that these transports facilitate his excretion (his peremptory expulsion).

The life and works of D. A. F. de Sade would thus have no other use-value than the common use value of excrement; in other words, for the most part, one most often only loves the rapid (and violent) pleasure of voiding this matter and no longer seeing it.

I am thus led to indicate how, in a way completely different from this usage, the sadism which is not *completely different* from that which existed before Sade appears positively, on the one hand, as an irruption of excremental forces (the excessive violation of modesty, positive algolagnia, the violent excretion of the sexual object coinciding with a powerful or tortured ejaculation, the libidinal interest in cadavers, vomiting, defecation . . .) and on the other as a corresponding limitation, a narrow enslavement of everything that is opposed to this irruption. It is only in these concrete conditions that sad social necessity, human dignity, fatherland and family, as well as poetic sentiments, appear without a mask and without any play of light and shadow; it is finally impossible to see in those things anything other than subordinate forces: so many slaves working like cowards to prepare the beautiful blustering eruptions that alone are capable of answering the needs that torment the bowels of most men.

But, given that Sade revealed his conception of terrestrial life in the most outrageous form (even given that it is not possible to reveal immediately such a conception other than in a terrifying and inadmissible form), it is perhaps not surprising that people have believed it possible to get beyond its reach. Literary men apparently have the best reason for not confirming a brilliant verbal and low-cost apology through practice. They could even pretend that Sade was the first to take the trouble to situate the domain he described outside of and above all reality. They could easily affirm that the brilliant and suffocating value he wanted to give human existence is inconceivable outside of fiction, that only poetry, exempt from all practical applications, permits one to have at his disposal, to a certain extent, the brilliance and suffocation that the Marquis de Sade tried so indecently to provoke.

It is right to recognize that, even practised in the extremely implicit form it has retained up to this point, such a diversion discredits its authors (at the very least among those – even if, moreover, they are horrified by sadism – who refuse to become interested, for bad as well as for good reasons, in simple verbal prestidigitation).

The fact remains, unfortunately, that this diversion has been practised for so long without denunciation, under cover of a fairly poor phraseology, simply because it takes place in an area where, it seems, everything slips away . . . It is no doubt almost useless at the present time to set forth rational propositions, since they could only be taken up for the profit of some convenient and – even in an apocalyptic guise – thoroughly literary enterprise: in other words, on the condition that they be useful for ambitions calculated by the impotence of present-day man. The slightest hope, in fact, involves the destruction (the disappearance) of a society that has so ridiculously allowed the one who conceives that hope to exist.

The time has no less come, it seems to me – under the indifferent eyes of my comrades – to bet on a future that has, it is true, only an unfortunate, hallucinatory existence. At the very least the plan I think possible to sketch *intellectually* today of what will really exist later is the only thing that links the various preliminary propositions that follow to a still sickly will to *agitation*.

For the moment, an abrupt statement not followed by explanations seems to me to respond sufficiently to the intellectual disorientation of those who could have the opportunity to become aware of it. And (even though I am capable to a large extent of doing it now) I put off until later difficult and interminable explications, analogous to those of any other elaborated theory. At this point then I will set forth the propositions that, among other things, allow one to introduce the values established by the Marquis de Sade, obviously not in the domain of gratuitous impertinence, but rather directly in the very market in which, each day, the credit that individuals and even communities can give to their own lives is, in a way, registered.

Appropriation and Excretion

1 The division of social facts into religious facts (prohibitions, obligations, and the realization of sacred action) on the one hand and profane facts (civil, political, juridical, industrial and commercial organization) on the other, even though it is not easily applied to primitive societies and lends itself in general to a certain number of confusions, can nevertheless serve as the basis for the determination of two polarized human impulses: EXCRETION and APPROPRIATION. In other words, during a period in which the religious organization of a given country *is developing*, this organization represents the freest opening for excremental collective impulses (orgiastic impulses) established in opposition to political, juridical and economic institutions.

2 Sexual activity, whether perverted or not; the behaviour of one sex before the other; defecation; urination; death and the cult of cadavers (above all, insofar as it involves the stinking decomposition of bodies); the different taboos; ritual cannibalism; the sacrifice of animal-gods; omophagia; the laughter of exclusion; sobbing (which in general has death as its object); religious ecstasy; the identical attitude toward shit, gods and cadavers; the terror that so often accompanies involuntary defecation; the custom of making women both brilliant and lubricious with make-up, gems and gleaming jewels; gambling; heedless expenditure and certain fanciful uses of money, etc. together present a common character in that the object of the activity (excrement, shameful parts, cadavers, etc.) is found each time treated as a foreign body (*das ganz Anderes*); in other words, it can just as well be expelled following a brutal rupture as reabsorbed through the desire to put one's body and mind entirely in a more or less violent state of expulsion (or projection). The notion of the (heterogeneous) *foreign body*

permits one to note the elementary *subjective* identity between types of excrement (sperm, menstrual blood, urine, faecal matter) and everything that can be seen as sacred, divine or marvellous: a half-decomposed cadaver fleeing through the night in a luminous shroud can be seen as characteristic of this unity.[1]

3 The process of simple appropriation is normally presented within the process of composite excretion, insofar as it is necessary for the production of an alternating rhythm, for example, in the following passage from Sade:

> Verneuil makes someone shit, he eats the turd, and then he demands that someone eat his. The one who eats his shit vomits; he devours her puke.

The elementary form of appropriation is oral consumption, considered as communion (participation, identification, incorporation or assimilation). Consumption is either sacramental (sacrificial) or not depending on whether the heterogeneous character of food is heightened or conventionally destroyed. In the latter case, the identification takes place first in the preparation of foods, which must be given an appearance of striking homogeneity, based on strict conventions. Eating as such then intervenes in the process as a complex phenomenon in that the very fact of swallowing presents itself as a partial rupture of physical equilibrium and is accompanied by, among other things, a sudden liberation of great quantities of saliva. Nevertheless, the element of appropriation, in moderate and rational form, in fact dominates, because cases in which eating's principal goal is physiological tumult (gluttony or drunkenness followed by vomiting) are no doubt unusual.

The process of appropriation is thus characterized by a homogeneity (static equilibrium) of the author of the appropriation, and of objects as final result, whereas excretion presents itself as the result of a heterogeneity, and can move in the direction of an ever greater heterogeneity, liberating impulses whose ambivalence is more and more pronounced. The latter case is represented by, for example, sacrificial consumption in the elementary form of the orgy, which has no other goal than the incorporation in the person of irreducibly heterogeneous elements, insofar as such elements risk provoking an increase of force (or more exactly an increase of *mana*).

4 Man does not only appropriate his food, but also the different products of his activity: clothes, furniture, dwellings and instruments of production. Finally, he appropriates land divided into parcels. Such appropriations take place by means of a more or less conventional homogeneity (identity) established between the possessor and the object possessed. It involves sometimes a personal homogeneity that in primitive times could only be solemnly destroyed with the aid of an excretory rite, and sometimes

a general homogeneity, such as that established by the architect between a city and its inhabitants.

In this respect, production can be seen as the excretory phase of a process of appropriation, and the same is true of selling.

5 The homogeneity of the kind realized in cities between men and that which surrounds them is only a subsidiary form of a much more consistent homogeneity, which man has established throughout the external world by everywhere replacing a priori inconceivable objects with classified series of conceptions or ideas. The identification of all the elements of which the world is composed has been pursued with a constant obstinacy, so that scientific conceptions, as well as the popular conceptions of the world, seem to have voluntarily led to a representation as different from what could have been imagined a priori as the public square of a capital is from a region of high mountains.

This last appropriation – the work of philosophy as well as of science or common sense – has included phases of revolt and scandal, but it has always had as its goal the establishment of the homogeneity of the world, and it will only be able to lead to a terminal phase in the sense of excretion when the irreducible waste products of the operation are determined.

Philosophy, Religion and Poetry in Relation to Heterology

6 The interest of philosophy resides in the fact that, in opposition to science or common sense, it must positively envisage the waste products of intellectual appropriation. Nevertheless, it most often envisages these waste products only in abstract forms of totality (nothingness, infinity, the absolute), to which it itself cannot give a positive content; it can thus freely proceed in speculations that more or less have as a goal, all things considered, the *sufficient* identification of an endless world with a finite world, an unknowable (noumenal) world with the known (phenomenal) world.

Only an intellectual elaboration in a religious form can, in its periods of autonomous development, put forward the waste products of appropriative thought as the definitively heterogeneous (sacred) object of speculation. But in general one must take into account the fact that religions bring about a profound separation within the sacred domain, dividing it into a superior world (celestial and divine) and an inferior world (demoniacal, a world of decomposition); now such a division necessarily leads to a progressive homogeneity of the entire superior domain (only the inferior domain resists all efforts at appropriation). God rapidly and almost entirely loses his terrifying features, his appearance as a decomposing cadaver, in order to become, at the final stage of degradation, the simple (paternal) sign of universal homogeneity.

7 In practice, one must understand by religion not really that which answers the need for the unlimited projection (expulsion or excretion) of human nature, but the totality of prohibitions, obligations and partial freedom that socially channel and regularize this projection. Religion thus differs from a practical and theoretical *heterology*[2] (even though both are equally concerned with sacred or excremental facts), not only in that the former excludes the scientific rigour proper to the latter (which generally appears as different from religion as chemistry is from alchemy), but also in that, under normal conditions, it betrays the needs that it was not only supposed to regulate, but satisfy.

8 Poetry at first glance seems to remain valuable as a method of mental projection (in that it permits one to accede to an entirely heterogeneous world). But it is only too easy to see that it is hardly less debased than religion. It has almost always been at the mercy of the great historical systems of appropriation. And insofar as it can be developed autonomously, this autonomy leads it on to the path of a total poetic conception of the world, which ends at any one of a number of aesthetic homogeneities. The practical unreality of the heterogeneous elements it sets in motion is, in fact, an indispensable condition for the continuation of heterogeneity: starting from the moment when this unreality immediately constitutes itself as a superior reality, whose mission is to eliminate (or degrade) inferior vulgar reality, poetry is reduced to playing the role of the standard of things, and, in opposition, the worst vulgarity takes on an ever stronger excremental value.

The Heterological Theory of Knowledge

9 When one says that heterology scientifically considers questions of heterogeneity, one does not mean that heterology is, in the usual sense of such a formula, the science of the heterogeneous. The heterogeneous is even resolutely placed outside the reach of scientific knowledge, which by definition is only applicable to homogeneous elements. Above all, heterology is opposed to any homogeneous representation of the world, in other words, to any philosophical system. The goal of such representations is always the deprivation of our universe's sources of excitation and the development of a servile human species, fit only for the fabrication, rational consumption and conservation of products. But the intellectual process automatically limits itself by producing of its own accord its own waste products, thus liberating in a disordered way the heterogeneous excremental element. Heterology is restricted to taking up again, consciously and resolutely, this terminal process which up until now has been seen as the abortion and the shame of human thought.

*In that way it [heterology] leads to the complete reversal of the philoso-
phical process, which ceases to be the instrument of appropriation, and now
serves excretion; it introduces the demand for the violent gratifications implied
by social life.*

10 Only, on the one hand, the process of limitation and, on the other,
the study of the violently alternating reactions of antagonism (expulsion)
and love (reabsorption) obtained by positing the heterogeneous element, lie
within the province of heterology as science. This element itself remains
indefinable and can only be determined through negation. The specific
character of faecal matter or of the spectre, as well as of unlimited time
or space, can only be the object of a series of negations, such as the absence
of any possible common denominator, irrationality, etc. It must even be
added that there is no way of placing such elements in the immediate
objective human domain, in the sense that the pure and simple objectification of their specific character would lead to their incorporation in a
homogeneous intellectual system, in other words, to a hypocritical cancellation of their excremental character.

The objectivity of heterogeneous elements thus is of only purely theoretical interest, since one can only attain it on the condition that one envisage
waste products in the total form of the infinite obtained by negation (in other
words, objective heterogeneity's shortcoming is that it can only be envisaged in an abstract form, whereas the subjective heterogeneity of particular
elements is, in practice, alone concrete).

11 Scientific data – in other words, the result of appropriation –
alone retains an immediate and appreciable objective character, since
immediate objectivity is defined by the possibilities of intellectual
appropriation. If one defines real exterior objects it is necessary to introduce at the same time the possibility of a relation of scientific appropriation.
And if such a relation is impossible, the element envisaged remains in
practice unreal, and can only abstractly be made objective. All questions
posed beyond this represent the persistence of a dominant need for
appropriation, the sickly obstinacy of a will seeking to represent, in spite
of everything, and through simple cowardice, a homogeneous and servile
world.

12 It is useless to try to deny that one finds there – much more than in
the difficulty (less embarrassing than facility) met with in the analysis of the
process of excretion and appropriation – the weak point (in practice) of
these conceptions, for one must generally take into account the unconscious obstinacy furnished by defections and complacency. It would be too
easy to find in objective nature a large number of phenomena that in a
crude way correspond to the human model of excretion and appropriation,
in order to attain *once again* the notion of the unity of being, for example,
in a dialectical form. One can attain it more generally through animals,

plants, matter, nature and being, without meeting really consistent obstacles. Nevertheless, it can already be indicated that as one moves away from man, the opposition loses its importance to the point where it is only a superimposed form that one obviously could not have discovered in the facts considered if it had not been borrowed from a different order of facts. The only way to resist this dilution lies in the practical part of heterology, which leads to an action that resolutely goes against this regression to homogeneous nature.

As soon as the effort at rational comprehension ends in contradiction, the practice of intellectual scatology requires the excretion of unassimilable elements, which is another way of stating vulgarly that a burst of laughter is the only imaginable and definitively terminal result – and not the means – of philosophical speculation. And then one must indicate that a reaction as *insignificant* as a burst of laughter derives from the extremely vague and distant character of the intellectual domain, and that it suffices to go from a speculation resting on abstract facts to a practice whose mechanism is not different, but which immediately reaches concrete heterogeneity, in order to arrive at ecstatic trances and orgasm.

Principles of Practical Heterology

13 Excretion is not simply a middle term between two appropriations, just as decay is not simply a middle term between the grain and the ear of wheat. The inability to consider in this latter case decay as an end in itself is the result not precisely of the human viewpoint but of the specifically intellectual viewpoint (to the extent that this viewpoint is in practice subordinate to a process of appropriation). The human viewpoint, independent of official declarations, in other words as it results from, among other things, the analysis of dreams, on the contrary represents appropriation as a means of excretion. In the final analysis it is clear that a worker works in order to obtain the violent pleasures of coitus (in other words, he accumulates in order to spend). On the other hand, the conception according to which the worker must have coitus in order to provide for the future necessities of work is linked to the unconscious identification of the worker with the slave. In fact, to the extent that the various functions are distributed among the various social categories, appropriation in its most overwhelming form historically devolves on slaves: thus in the past serfs had to accumulate products for knights and clerks, who barely took part in the labour of appropriation, and then only through the establishment of a morality that regularized for their own profit the circulation of goods. But as soon as one attacks the accursed exploitation of man by man, it becomes time to leave to the exploiters this abominable appropriative

morality, which for such a long time has permitted their own orgies of wealth. To the extent that man no longer thinks of crushing his comrades under the yoke of morality, he acquires the capacity to link overtly not only his intellect and his virtue but his *raison d'être* to the violence and incongruity of his excretory organs, as well as to his ability to become excited and entranced by heterogeneous elements, commonly starting in debauchery.

14 The need – before being able to go on to radical demands and to the violent practice of a rigorous moral liberty – to abolish all exploitation of man by man is not the only motive that links the practical development of heterology to the overturning of the established order.

In that they are manifested in a social milieu, the urges that heterology identifies *in practice* with the *raison d'être* of man can be seen in a certain sense as anti-social (to the same degree that sexual corruption or even pleasure is seen by certain individuals as a waste of strength, like, for example, the great ritual destructions of goods in British Columbia, or, among civilized peoples, the pleasure of crowds watching great fires at night). Nevertheless, the impulses that go against the interests of a society in a state of stagnation (during a phase of appropriation) have, on the contrary, social revolution (the phase of excretion) as their end: thus they can find, through the historical movements by means of which humanity spends its own strength freely and limitlessly, both total gratification and use in the very sense of general conscious benefit. Besides, whatever the reality of this ulterior benefit might be, it is no less true that if one considers the submerged masses, doomed to an obscure and impotent life, the revolution by which these masses liberate force with a long-restrained violence is as much the practical *raison d'être* of societies as it is their means of development.

15 Of course the term *excretion* applied to the Revolution must first be understood in the strictly mechanical – and moreover etymological – sense of the word. The first phase of a revolution is *separation*, in other words, a process leading to the position of two groups of forces, each one characterized by the necessity of excluding the other. The second phase is the violent *expulsion* of the group that has possessed power by the revolutionary group.

But one also notes that each of the groups, by its very constitution, gives the opposing group an almost exclusively negative excremental character, and it is only because of this negativity that the sacrificial character of a revolution remains profoundly unconscious. The revolutionary impulse of the proletarian masses is, moreover, sometimes implicitly and sometimes openly treated as sacred, and that is why it is possible to use the word *Revolution* entirely stripped of its utilitarian meaning without, however, giving it an idealist meaning.

16 *Participation* – in the purely psychological sense as well as in the active sense of the word – does not only commit revolutionaries to a particular politics, for example, to the establishment of socialism through-out the world. It is also – and necessarily – presented as moral participation: immediate participation in the destructive action of the revolution (expulsion realized through the total shattering of the equilibrium of the social edifice), indirect participation in all equivalent destructive action. It is the very character of the revolutionary will to link such actions – not, as in the Christian apocalypse, to punishment – but to the enjoyment or the utility of human beings, and it is obvious that all destruction that is neither useful nor inevitable can only be the achievement of an exploiter and, consequently, of morality as the principle of all exploitation.[3] But then it is easy to ascertain that the reality of such *participation* is at the very basis of the separation of the socialist parties, divided into reformists and revolutionaries.

Without a profound complicity with natural forces such as violent death, gushing blood, sudden catastrophes and the horrible cries of pain that accompany them, terrifying ruptures of what had seemed to be immu-table, the fall into stinking filth of what had been elevated – without a sadistic understanding of an incontestably thundering and torrential na-ture, there could be no revolutionaries, there could only be a revolting utopian sentimentality.

17 The *participation* in everything that, among men, is horrible and allegedly sacred can take place in a limited and unconscious form, but this limitation and this unconsciousness obviously have only a provisional value, and nothing can stop the movement that leads human beings toward an ever more shameless awareness of the erotic bond that links them to death, to cadavers, and to horrible physical pain. It is high time that human nature cease being subjected to the autocrat's vile repression and to the morality that authorizes exploitation. Since it is true that one of a man's attributes is the derivation of pleasure from the suffering of others, and that erotic pleasure is not only the negation of an agony that takes place at the same instant, but also a lubricious participation in that agony, it is time to choose between the conduct of cowards afraid of their own joyful excesses, and the conduct of those who judge that any given man need not cower like a hunted animal, but instead can see all the moralistic buffoons as so many dogs.

18 As a result of these elementary considerations, it is necessary from now on to envisage two distinct phases in human emancipation, as under-taken successively by the different revolutionary surges, from Jacobinism to Bolshevism.

During the revolutionary phase, the current phase that will only end with the world triumph of socialism, only the social Revolution can serve as an outlet for collective impulses, and no other activity can be envisaged in practice.

But the post-revolutionary phase implies the necessity of a division between the economic and political organization of society on one hand, and on the other, an anti-religious and asocial organization having as its goal orgiastic participation in different forms of destruction, in other words, the collective satisfaction of needs that correspond to the necessity of provoking the violent excitation that results from the expulsion of heterogeneous elements.

Such an organization can have no other conception of morality than the one scandalously affirmed for the first time by the Marquis de Sade.

19 When it is a question of the means of realizing this orgiastic participation, [such] an organization will find itself as close to religions anterior *to the formations of autocratic states* as it is distant from religions such as Christianity or Buddhism.

One must broadly take into account, in such a forecast, the probable intervention of blacks in the general culture. To the extent that blacks participate in revolutionary emancipation, the attainment of socialism will bring them the possibility of all kinds of exchange with white people, but in conditions radically different from those currently experienced by the civilized blacks of America. Now black communities, once liberated from all superstition as from all oppression, represent in relation to heterology not only the possibility but the necessity of an adequate organization. All organizations that have ecstasy and frenzy as their goal (the spectacular death of animals, partial tortures, orgiastic dances, etc.) will have no reason to disappear when a heterological conception of human life is substituted for the primitive conception; they can only transform themselves while they spread, under the violent impetus of a moral doctrine of white origin, taught to blacks by all those whites who have become aware of the abominable inhibitions paralysing their race's communities. It is only starting from this collusion of European scientific theory with black practice that institutions can develop which will serve as the final outlets (with no other limitations than those of human strength) for the urges that today require worldwide society's fiery and bloody Revolution.

Notes

1 The identical nature, from the psychological point of view, of God and excrement should not shock the intellect of anyone familiar with the problems posed by the history of religions. The cadaver is not much more repugnant than shit, and the spectre that projects its horror is *sacred* even in the eyes of modern theologians. The following passage from Frazer very nearly sums up the basic historical aspect of the question: 'These different categories of people differ, in our eyes, by virtue of their character and their condition: we should say that

one group is sacred, the other filthy or impure. This is not the case for the savage, for his mind is much too crude to understand clearly what a sacred being is, and what an impure being is.'

2 The science of what is completely other. The term *agiology* would perhaps be more precise, but one would have to catch the double meaning of *agio* (analogous to the double meaning of *sacer*), *soiled* as well as *holy*. But it is above all the term *scatology* (the science of excrement) that retains in the present circumstances (the specialization of the sacred) an incontestable expressive value as the doublet of an abstract term such as *heterology*.

3 For example, imperialist war.

13

Base Materialism and Gnosticism

If one thinks of a particular object, it is easy to distinguish matter from form, and an analogous distinction can be made with regard to organic beings, with form taking on the value of the unity of being and of its individual existence. But if things as a whole are taken into account, transposed distinctions of this kind become arbitrary and even unintelligible. Two verbal entities are thus formed, explicable only through their constructive value in the social order: an abstract God (or simply the idea), and abstract matter; the chief guard and the prison walls. The variants of this metaphysical scaffolding are of no more interest than are the different styles of architecture. People become excited trying to know if the prison came from the guard or if the guard came from the prison; even though this agitation has had a primordial historical importance, today it risks provoking a delayed astonishment, if only because of the disproportion between the consequences of the debate and its radical insignificance.

It is nevertheless very remarkable that the only kind of materialism that up to now in its development has escaped systematic abstraction, namely dialectical materialism, had as its starting point, at least as much as ontological materialism, absolute idealism in its Hegelian form. (There is no need to go back on this method: materialism, whatever its scope in the positive order, necessarily is above all the obstinate negation of idealism, which amounts to saying, finally, of the very basis of *all* philosophy.) Now Hegelianism, no less than the classical philosophy of Hegel's period, apparently proceeded from very ancient metaphysical conceptions, conceptions developed by, among others, the Gnostics, in an epoch when metaphysics could still be associated with the most monstrous *dualistic* and therefore strangely abased cosmogonies.[1]

I admit that I have, in respect to mystical philosophies, only an unambiguous interest, analogous in practice to that of an uninfatuated psychiatrist toward his patients; it seems to me rather pointless to put one's

The text is from *Visions of Excess: selected writings, 1927–1939*, ed. Allan Stoekl, tr. Allan Stoekl with Carl R. Lovitt and Donald M. Leslie, Jr (University of Minnesota Press, Minneapolis, MN, 1985), pp. 45–8. 'Le bas matérialisme et la gnose' was published in *Documents*, second year, 1 (1930). See *OC*, I, pp. 220–6.

trust in tendencies that, without meeting resistance, lead to the most pitiful dishonesty and bankruptcy. But it is difficult today to remain indifferent even to partly falsified solutions brought, at the beginning of the Christian era, to problems that do not appear noticeably different from our own (which are those of a society whose original principles have become, in a very precise sense, the *dead letter* of a society that must put itself in question and overturn itself in order to rediscover motives of force and violent agitation). Thus the adoration of an ass-headed god (the ass being the most hideously comic animal, and at the same time the most humanly virile) seems to me capable of taking on even today a crucial value: the severed ass's head of the acephalic personification of the sun undoubtedly represents, even if imperfectly, one of materialism's most virulent manifestations.

I will leave it to Henry-Charles Puech to explain here, in future articles,[2] the development of such myths, so suspect in this period, hideous as chancres and carrying the germs of a bizarre but mortal subversion of the ideal and of the order expressed today be the words 'classical antiquity'. Yet I think it would be neither vain nor impossible to simplify things extremely, first of all, and indicate the meaning that must be given to the mythological and philosophical disorders which at that time affected the representation of the world. Gnosticism, in fact, before and after the preachings of Christianity, and in an almost bestial way, no matter what were its metaphysical developments, introduced a most impure fermentation into Graeco-Roman ideology, borrowed from everywhere, from the Egyptian tradition, from Persian dualism, from eastern Jewish heterodoxy, elements that conformed the least to the established intellectual order; it added its own dreams, heedlessly expressing a few monstrous obsessions; it was not revolted, in its religious practices, by the basest (and thus most upsetting) forms of Greek or Chaldeo-Assyrian magic and astrology; and at the same time it utilized, but perhaps more exactly it compromised, newborn Christian theology and Hellenistic metaphysics.

It is not surprising that the protean character of this agitation has given rise to contradictory interpretations. It has even been possible to represent Gnosticism as a strongly Hellenized intellectual form of a primitive Christianity too popular and indifferent to metaphysical developments, a kind of superior Christianity elaborated by philosophers who had broken with Hellenistic speculation, and rejected by the uncultivated Christian masses.[3] Thus the principal protagonists of Gnosticism – Basilides, Valentinus, Bardesanes, Marcion – appeared to be great religious humanists and, from the point of view of traditional Protestantism, great Christians. Their bad name and the more or less suspect character of their theories were supposedly explained by the fact that they were only known through the polemics of the church fathers, their violent enemies and obligatory slanderers.

The writings of the Gnostic theologians were systematically destroyed by the orthodox Christians (with few exceptions, nothing remains today of a considerable literature). Only the stones on which they engraved the figures of a provocative and especially indecent Pantheon permit one to comment at length on something other than diatribes: but they precisely confirm the bad opinion of the heresiologists. The most consistent modern exegesis admits, moreover, that the abstract forms of Gnostic entities evolved out of very crude myths, which correspond to the crudity of the images represented on the stones.[4] It establishes above all that Neoplatonism or Christianity must not be sought as the origin of Gnosticism, whose real foundation is Zoroastrian dualism.[5] A sometimes disfigured dualism, doubtless following Christian or philosophical influences, but a profound dualism and, at least in its specific development, not emasculated by an adaptation to social necessities, as in the case of the Iranian religion (on this subject, it is essential to observe that Gnosticism, and to the same degree Manicheanism, which in a way derived from it, never served any social organizations, never assumed the role of state religion).

In practice, it is possible to see as a *leitmotiv* of Gnosticism the conception of matter as an *active* principle having its own eternal autonomous existence as darkness (which would not be simply the absence of light, but the monstrous *archontes* revealed by this absence), and as evil (which would not be the absence of good, but a creative action). This conception was perfectly incompatible with the very principle of the profoundly monistic Hellenistic spirit, whose dominant tendency saw matter and evil as degradations of superior principles. Attributing the creation of the earth, where our repugnant and derisory agitation takes place, to a horrible and *perfectly illegitimate* principle evidently implies, from the point of view of the Greek intellectual construction, a nauseating, inadmissible pessimism, the exact opposite of what had to be established at all costs and made universally manifest. In fact the opposed existence of an excellent divinity, worthy of the absolute confidence of the human spirit, matters little if the baneful and odious divinity of this dualism is under no circumstances reducible to it, without any possibility of hope. It is true that even within Gnosticism things were not always so clear-cut. The fairly widespread doctrine of *emanation* (according to which the ignoble creator god, in other words the *cursed god* – sometimes associated with Jehovah of the Bible – emanated from the Supreme God) responded to a need for a palliative. But if we confine ourselves to the specific meaning of Gnosticism, indicated both by heresiological controversies and by carvings on stones, the despotic and bestial obsession with outlawed and evil forces seems irrefutable, as much in its metaphysical speculation as in its mythological nightmare.

It is difficult to believe that on the whole Gnosticism does not manifest above all a sinister love of darkness, a monstrous taste for obscene and lawless *archontes*, for the head of the solar ass (whose comic and desperate braying would be the signal for a shameless revolt against idealism in power). The existence of a sect of *licentious Gnostics* and of certain sexual rites fulfils this obscure demand for a baseness that would not be reducible, which would be owed the most indecent respect: black magic has continued this tradition to the present day.

It is true that the supreme object of the spiritual activity of the Manicheans, as of the Gnostics, was constantly the good and perfection: that was the way in which their conceptions in themselves had a pessimistic meaning. But it is more or less useless to take these appearances into account, and only the troubled concession to evil can in the end determine the meaning of these aspirations. If today we overtly abandon the idealistic point of view, as the Gnostics and Manicheans implicitly abandoned it, the attitude of those who see in their own lives an effect of the creative action of evil appears even radically optimistic. It is possible in all freedom to be a plaything of evil if evil itself does not have to answer before God. Having had recourse to *archontes*, it does not appear that one has deeply desired the submission of things that belong to a higher authority, to an authority the *archontes* stun with an eternal bestiality.

Thus it appears – all things considered – that Gnosticism, in its psychological process, is not so different from present-day materialism, I mean a materialism not implying an ontology, not implying that matter is the thing-in-itself. For it is a question above all of not submitting oneself, and with oneself one's reason, to whatever is more elevated, to whatever can give a borrowed authority to the being that I am, and to the reason that arms this being. This being and its reason can in fact only submit to what is lower, to what can never serve in any case to ape a given authority. Also I submit entirely to what must be called matter, since *that* exists outside of myself and the idea, and I do not admit that my reason becomes the limit of what I have said, for if I proceeded in that way matter limited by my reason would soon take on the value of a superior principle (which this *servile* reason would be only too happy to establish above itself, in order to speak like an authorized functionary). Base matter is external and foreign to ideal human aspirations, and it refuses to allow itself to be reduced to the great ontological machines resulting from these aspirations. But the psychological process brought to light by Gnosticism had the same impact: it was a question of disconcerting the human spirit and idealism before something base, to the extent that one recognized the helplessness of superior principles.

The interest of this juxtaposition is augmented by the fact that the specific reactions of Gnosticism led to the representation of forms radically contrary to the ancient academic style, to the representation of forms in which it is possible to see the image of this base matter that alone, by its incongruity and by an overwhelming lack of respect, permits the intellect to escape from the constraints of idealism. In the same way today certain plastic representations are the expression of an intransigent materialism, of a recourse to everything that compromises the powers that be in matters of form, ridiculing the traditional entities, naively rivalling stupefying scarecrows. This is no less important than general analytic interpretation, in the sense that only forms specific and meaningful to the same degree as language can give concrete and immediately perceptible expression to the psychological developments determined through analysis.

Notes

1 Since the Hegelian doctrine is above all an extraordinary and very perfect system of reduction, it is evident that it is only in a reduced and emasculated state that one finds there the *base elements* that are essential in Gnosticism.

   However, in Hegel the role of these elements in thought remains one of destruction, just as destruction is given as necessary for the constitution of thought. This is why, when dialectical materialism was substituted for Hegelian idealism (through a complete overthrow of values, giving matter the role that thought had had), matter was no longer an abstraction but a source of contradiction; moreover, it was no longer a question of the providential character of contradiction, which became simply one of the properties of the development of material facts.

2 [See H.-C. Puech's 'Le Dieu Besa et la magie hellénistique', in *Documents*, 7 (1930), pp. 415–25. TR.]

3 This interpretation has been developed in France by Eugène de Faye (cf. *Introduction à l'étude du gnosticisme* (Paris, 1903), taken from *Revue de l'histoire des religions*, vols 45 and 46, and *Gnostiques et gnosticisme. Etude critique des documents du gnosticisme chrétien aux IIe et IIIe siècles* (Paris, 1913), in *Bibliothèque de l'Ecole des Hautes Etudes, Sciences religieuses*, vol. 27).

4 Wilhelm Bousset, *Hauptprobleme der Gnosis* (Göttingen, 1907).

5 Ibid., ch. 3, 'Der Dualismus der Gnosis'.

PART III

General Economy

14

The Notion of Expenditure

1 The Insufficiency of the Principle of Classical Utility

Every time the meaning of a discussion depends on the fundamental value of the word *useful* – in other words, every time the essential question touching on the life of human societies is raised, no matter who intervenes and what opinions are expressed – it is possible to affirm that the debate is necessarily warped and that the fundamental question is eluded. In fact, given the more or less divergent collection of present ideas, there is nothing that permits one to define what is useful to man. This lacuna is made fairly prominent by the fact that it is constantly necessary to return, in the most unjustifiable way, to principles that one would like to situate beyond utility and pleasure: *honour* and *duty* are hypocritically employed in schemes of pecuniary interest and, without speaking of God, *Spirit* serves to mask the intellectual disarray of the few people who refuse to accept a closed system.

Current practice, however, is not deterred by these elementary difficulties, and common awareness at first seems able to raise only verbal objections to the principles of classical utility – in other words, to supposedly material utility. The goal of the latter is, theoretically, pleasure – but only in a moderate form, since violent pleasure is seen as *pathological*. On the one hand, this material utility is limited to acquisition (in practice, to production) and to the conservation of goods; on the other, it is limited to reproduction and to the conservation of human life (to which is added, it is true, the struggle against pain, whose importance itself suffices to indicate the negative character of the pleasure principle instituted, in theory, as the basis of utility). In the series of quantitative representations linked to this flat and untenable conception of existence only the question of reproduction seriously lends itself to controversy, because an exaggerated increase in the number of the living threatens to diminish the individual share. But on

Originally published in English in 1984, the text is from *Visions of Excess: selected writings, 1927–1939*, ed. Allan Stoekl, tr. Allan Stoekl with Carl R. Lovitt and Donald M. Leslie, Jr (University of Minnesota Press, Minneapolis, MN, 1985), pp. 116–29. 'La notion de dépense' appeared first in *La Critique sociale*, 7 (1933). See *OC*, I, pp. 302–20.

the whole, any general judgement of social activity implies the principle that all individual effort, in order to be valid, must be reducible to the fundamental necessities of production and conservation. Pleasure, whether art, permissible debauchery, or play, is definitively reduced, in the intellectual representations *in circulation*, to a concession; in other words it is reduced to a diversion whose role is subsidiary. The most appreciable share of life is given as the condition – sometimes even as the regrettable condition – of productive social activity.

It is true that personal experience – if it is a question of a youthful man, capable of wasting and destroying without reason – each time gives the lie to this miserable conception. But even when he does not spare himself and destroys himself while making allowance for nothing, the most lucid man will understand nothing, or imagine himself sick; he is incapable of a *utilitarian* justification for his actions, and it does not occur to him that a human society can have, just as he does, an *interest* in considerable losses, in catastrophes that, *while conforming to well-defined needs*, provoke tumultuous depressions, crises of dread and, in the final analysis, a certain orgiastic state.

In the most crushing way, the contradiction between current social conceptions and the real needs of society recalls the narrowness of judgement that puts the father in opposition to the satisfaction of his son's needs. This narrowness is such that it is impossible for the son to express his will. The father's partially malevolent solicitude is manifested in the things he provides for his son: lodgings, clothes, food and, when absolutely necessary, a little harmless recreation. But the son does not even have the right to speak about what really gives him a fever; he is obliged to give people the impression that for him no *horror* can enter into consideration. In this respect, it is sad to say that *conscious humanity has remained a minor*; humanity recognizes the right to acquire, to conserve and to consume rationally, but it excludes in principle *non-productive expenditure*.

It is true that this exclusion is superficial and that it no more modifies practical activities than prohibitions limit the son, who indulges in his unavowed pleasures as soon as he is no longer in his father's presence. Humanity can allow itself the pleasure of expressing, in the father's interest, conceptions marked with flat paternal sufficiency and blindness. In the practice of life, however, humanity acts in a way that allows for the satisfaction of disarmingly savage needs, and it seems able to subsist only at the limits of horror. Moreover, to the small extent that a man is incapable of yielding to considerations that either are official or are susceptible of becoming so, to the small extent that he is inclined to feel the attraction of a life devoted to the destruction of established authority, it is difficult to believe that a peaceful world, conforming to his interests, could be for him anything other than a convenient illusion.

The difficulties met with in the development of a conception that is not guided by the servile mode of father–son relations are thus not insurmountable. It is possible to admit the historical necessity of vague and disappointing images, used by a majority of people, who do not act without a minimum of error (which they use as if it were a drug) – and who, moreover, in all circumstances refuse to find their way in a labyrinth resulting from human inconsistencies. An extreme simplification represents, for the uncultivated or barely cultivated segments of the population, the only chance to avoid a diminution of aggressive force. But it would be cowardly to accept, as a limit to understanding, the conditions of poverty and necessity in which such simplified images are formed. And if a less arbitrary conception is condemned to remain esoteric, and if as such, in the present circumstances, it comes into conflict with an unhealthy repulsion, then one must stress that this repulsion is precisely the shame of a generation whose rebels are afraid of the noise of their own words. Thus one cannot take it into account.

2 The Principle of Loss

Human activity is not entirely reducible to processes of production and conservation, and consumption must be divided into two distinct parts. The first, reducible part is represented by the use of the minimum necessary for the conservation of life and the continuation of individuals' productive activity in a given society; it is therefore a question simply of the fundamental condition of productive activity. The second part is represented by so-called unproductive expenditures: luxury, mourning, war, cults, the construction of sumptuary monuments, games, spectacles, arts, perverse sexual activity (i.e., deflected from genital finality) – all these represent activities which, at least in primitive circumstances, have no end beyond themselves. Now it is necessary to reserve the use of the word *expenditure* for the designation of these unproductive forms, and not for the designation of all the modes of consumption that serve as a means to the end of production. Even though it is always possible to set the various forms of expenditure in opposition to each other, they constitute a group characterized by the fact that in each case the accent is placed on a *loss* that must be as great as possible in order for that activity to take on its true meaning.

This principle of loss, in other words, of unconditional expenditure, no matter how contrary it might be to the economic principle of balanced accounts (expenditure regularly compensated for by acquisition), only *rational* in the narrow sense of the word, can be illustrated through a small number of examples taken from common experience.

1 Jewels must not only be beautiful and dazzling (which would make the substitution of imitations possible): one sacrifices a fortune, preferring a diamond necklace; such a sacrifice is necessary for the constitution of this necklace's fascinating character. This fact must be seen in relation to the symbolic value of jewels, universal in psychoanalysis. When in a dream a diamond signifies excrement, it is not only a question of association by contrast; in the unconscious, jewels, like excrement, are cursed matter that flows from a wound: they are a part of oneself destined for open sacrifice (they serve, in fact, as sumptuous gifts charged with sexual love). The functional character of jewels requires their immense material value and alone explains the inconsequence of the most beautiful imitations, which are very nearly useless.

2 Cults require a bloody wasting of men and animals in *sacrifice*. In the etymological sense of the word, sacrifice is nothing other than the production of *sacred* things.

From the very first, it appears that sacred things are constituted by an operation of loss: in particular, the success of Christianity must be explained by the value of the theme of the Son of God's ignominious crucifixion, which carries human dread to a representation of loss and limitless degradation.

3 In various competitive games, loss in general is produced under complex conditions. Considerable sums of money are spent for the maintenance of quarters, animals, equipment or men. As much energy as possible is squandered in order to produce a feeling of stupefaction – in any case with an intensity infinitely greater than in productive enterprises. The danger of death is not avoided; on the contrary, it is the object of a strong unconscious attraction. Besides, competitions are sometimes the occasion for the public distribution of prizes. Immense crowds are present; their passions most often burst forth beyond any restraint, and the loss of insane sums of money is set in motion in the form of wagers. It is true that this circulation of money profits a small number of professional betters, but it is no less true that this circulation can be considered to be a real *charge* of the passions unleashed by competition and that, among a large number of betters, it leads to losses disproportionate to their means; these even attain such a level of madness that often the only way out for gamblers is prison or death. Beyond this, various modes of unproductive expenditure can be linked, depending on the circumstances, to great competitive spectacles, just as elements moving separately are caught up in a mightier whirlwind. Thus horse races are associated with a sumptuary process of social classification (the existence of Jockey Clubs need only be mentioned) and the ostentatious display of the latest luxurious fashions. It is necessary in any case to observe that the complex of expenditure represented by present-day racing is insignificant when compared to the extravagance of the

Byzantines, who tied the totality of their public activity to equestrian competition.

4 From the point of view of expenditure, artistic productions must be divided into two main categories, the first constituted by architectural construction, music and dance. This category is comprised of *real* expenditures. Nevertheless, sculpture and painting, not to mention the use of sites for ceremonies and spectacles, introduces even into architecture the principle of the second category, that of *symbolic* expenditure. For their part, music and dance can easily be charged with external significations.

In their major form, literature and theatre, which constitute the second category, provoke dread and horror through symbolic representations of tragic loss (degradation or death); in their minor form, they provoke laughter through representations which, though analogously structured, exclude certain seductive elements. The term poetry, applied to the least degraded and least intellectualized forms of the expression of a state of loss, can be considered synonymous with expenditure; it in fact signifies, in the most precise way, creation by means of loss. Its meaning is therefore close to that of *sacrifice*. It is true that the word 'poetry' can only be appropriately applied to an extremely rare residue of what it commonly signifies and that, without a preliminary reduction, the worst confusions could result; it is, however, impossible in a first, rapid exposition to speak of the infinitely variable limits separating subsidiary formations from the residual element of poetry. It is easier to indicate that, for the rare human beings who have this element at their disposal, poetic expenditure ceases to be symbolic in its consequences; thus, to a certain extent, the function of representation engages the very life of the one who assumes it. It condemns him to the most disappointing forms of activity, to misery, to despair, to the pursuit of inconsistent shadows that provide nothing but vertigo or rage. The poet frequently can use words only for his own loss; he is often forced to choose between the destiny of a reprobate, who is as profoundly separated from society as dejecta are from apparent life, and a renunciation whose price is a mediocre activity, subordinated to vulgar and superficial needs.

3 Production, Exchange and Unproductive Activity

Once the existence of expenditure as a social function has been established, it is then necessary to consider the relations between this function and those of production and acquisition that are opposed to it. These relations immediately present themselves as those of an *end* with *utility*. And if it is true that production and acquisition in their development and changes of form introduce a variable that must be understood in order to comprehend historical processes, they are, however, still only means subordinated to expenditure. As dreadful as it is, human poverty has never had a strong enough hold on societies to cause the concern for conservation – which gives production the appearance of an end – to dominate the concern for unproductive expenditure. In order to maintain this pre-eminence, since power is exercised by the classes that expend, poverty was excluded from all social activity. And the poor have no other way of re-entering the circle of power than through the revolutionary destruction of the classes occupying that circle – in other words, through a bloody and in no way limited social expenditure.

The secondary character of production and acquisition in relation to expenditure appears most clearly in primitive economic institutions, since exchange is still treated as a sumptuary loss of ceded objects: thus at its *base* exchange presents itself as a process of expenditure, over which a process of acquisition has developed. Classical economics imagined that primitive exchange occurred in the form of barter; it had no reason to assume, in fact, that a means of acquisition such as exchange might have as its origin not the need to acquire that it satisfies today, but the contrary need, the need to destroy and to lose. The traditional conceptions of the origins of economy have only recently been disproved – even so recently that a great number of economists continue arbitrarily to represent barter as the ancestor of commerce.

In opposition to the artificial notion of barter, the archaic form of exchange has been identified by Mauss under the name *potlatch*,[1] borrowed from the north-western American Indians who provided such a remarkable example of it. Institutions analogous to the Indian *potlatch*, or their traces, have been very widely found.

The *potlatch* of the Tlingit, the Haida, the Tsimshian and the Kwakiutl of the north-western coast has been studied in detail since the end of the nineteenth century (but at that time it was not compared with the archaic forms of exchange of other countries). The least advanced of these American tribes practise *potlatch* on the occasion of a person's change in situation – initiations, marriages, funerals – and, even in a more evolved form, it can never be separated from a festival; whether it provides the occasion for this festival, or whether it takes place on the festival's occasion. *Potlatch* excludes all bargaining and, in general, it is constituted by a considerable gift of riches, offered openly and with the goal of humiliating, defying and *obligating* a rival. The exchange value of the gift results from the fact that the donee, in order to efface the humiliation and respond to the challenge, must satisfy the obligation (incurred by him at the time of acceptance) to respond later with a more valuable gift, in other words, to return with interest.

But the gift is not the only form of *potlatch*; it is equally possible to defy rivals through the spectacular destruction of wealth. It is through the intermediary of this last form that *potlatch* is reunited with religious sacrifice, since what is destroyed is theoretically offered to the mythical ancestors of the donees. Relatively recently a Tlingit chief appeared before his rival to slash the throats of some of his own slaves. This destruction was repaid at a given date by the slaughter of a greater number of slaves. The Tchoukchi of far north-western Siberia, who have institutions analogous to *potlatch*, slaughter dog teams in order to stifle and humiliate another group. In north-western America, destruction goes as far as the burning of villages and the smashing of flotillas of canoes. Emblazoned copper ingots, a kind of money on which the fictive value of an immense fortune is sometimes placed, are broken or thrown into the sea. The delirium of the festival can be associated equally with hecatombs of property and with gifts accumulated with the intention of stunning and humiliating.

Usury, which regularly appears in these operations as obligatory surplus at the time of the returned *potlatch*, gives rise to the observation that the loan with interest must be substituted for barter in the history of the origins of exchange. It must be recognized, in fact, that wealth is multiplied in *potlatch* civilizations in a way that recalls the inflation of credit in banking civilizations; in other words, it would be impossible to realize at once all the wealth possessed by the total number of donors resulting from the obligations contracted by the total number of donees. But this comparison applies only to a secondary characteristic of *potlatch*.

It is the constitution of a positive property of loss – from which spring nobility, honour and rank in a hierarchy – that gives the institution its significant value. The gift must be considered as a loss and thus as a partial destruction, since the desire to destroy is in part transferred on to the recipient. In unconscious forms, such as those described by psychoanalysis, it symbolizes excretion, which itself is linked to death, in conformity with the fundamental connection between anal eroticism and sadism. The excremental symbolism of emblazoned coppers, which on the north-west coast are the gift objects *par excellence*, is based on a very rich mythology. In Melanesia, the donor designates as his excrement magnificent gifts, which he deposits at the feet of the rival chief.

The consequences in the realm of acquisition are only the unwanted result – at least to the extent that the drives that govern the operation have remained primitive – of a process oriented in the opposite direction. 'The ideal', indicates Mauss, 'would be to give a *potlatch* and not have it returned.' This ideal is realized in certain forms of destruction to which custom allows no possible response. Moreover, since the yields of *potlatch* are in some ways pledged in advance in a new *potlatch*, the archaic principle of wealth is displayed with none of the attenuations that result from the avarice developed at later stages; wealth appears as an acquisition to the extent that power is acquired by a rich man, but it is entirely directed toward loss in the sense that this power is characterized as power to lose. It is only through loss that glory and honour are linked to wealth.

As a game, *potlatch* is the opposite of a principle of conservation: it puts an end to the stability of fortunes as it existed within the totemic economy, where possession was hereditary. An activity of excessive exchange replaced heredity (as source of possession) with a kind of deliriously formed ritual poker. But the players can never retire from the game, their fortunes made; they remain at the mercy of provocation. At no time does a fortune serve to *shelter its owner from need*. On the contrary, it functionally remains – as does its possessor – *at the mercy of a need for limitless loss*, which exists endemically in a social group.

The non-sumptuary production and consumption upon which wealth depends thus appear as relative utility.

4 The Functional Expenditure of the Wealthy Classes

The notion of *potlatch*, strictly speaking, should be reserved for expenditures of an agonistic type, which are instigated by challenges and which lead to reponses. More precisely, it should be reserved for forms which, for archaic societies, are not distinguishable from *exchange*.

It is important to know that exchange, at its origin, was *immediately* subordinated to a human *end*; nevertheless it is evident that its development, linked to progress in the modes of production, only started at the stage at which this subordination ceased to be immediate. The very principle of the function of production requires that products be exempt from loss, at least provisionally.

In the market economy, the processes of exchange have an acquisitive sense. Fortunes are no longer placed on a gambling table; they have become relatively stable. It is only to the extent that stability is assured and can no longer be compromised by even considerable losses that these losses are submitted to the regime of unproductive expenditure. Under these new conditions, the elementary components of *potlatch* are found in forms that are no longer as directly agonistic.[2] Expenditure is still destined to acquire or maintain rank, but in principle it no longer has the goal of causing another to lose his rank.

In spite of these attenuations, ostentatious loss remains universally linked to wealth, as its ultimate function.

More or less narrowly, social rank is linked to the possession of a fortune, but only on the condition that the fortune be partially sacrificed in unproductive social expenditures such as festivals, spectacles and games. One notes that in primitive societies, where the exploitation of man by man is still fairly weak, the products of human activity not only flow in great quantities to rich men because of the protection or social leadership services these men supposedly provide, but also because of the spectacular collective expenditures for which they must pay. In so-called civilized societies, the fundamental *obligation* of wealth disappeared only in a fairly recent period. The decline of paganism led to a decline of the games and cults for which wealthy Romans were obliged to pay; thus it has been said that Christianity individualized property, giving its possessor total control over his products and abrogating his social function. It abrogated at least the obligation of this expenditure, for Christianity replaced pagan expenditure prescribed by custom with voluntary alms, either in the form of distributions from the rich to the poor, or (and above all) in the form of extremely significant contributions to churches and later to monasteries. And these churches and monasteries precisely assumed, in the Middle Ages, the major part of the spectacular function.

Today the great and free forms of unproductive social expenditure have disappeared. One must not conclude from this, however, that the very principle of expenditure is no longer the end of economic activity.

A certain evolution of wealth, whose symptoms indicate sickness and exhaustion, leads to shame in oneself accompanied by petty hypocrisy. Everything that was generous, orgiastic and excessive has disappeared; the themes of rivalry upon which individual activity still depends develop in obscurity, and are as shameful as belching. The representatives of the bourgeoisie have adopted an effaced manner; wealth is now displayed behind closed doors, in accordance with depressing and boring conventions. In addition, people in the middle class – employees and small shopkeepers – having attained mediocre or minute fortunes, have managed to debase and subdivide ostentatious expenditure, of which nothing remains but vain efforts tied to tiresome rancour.

Such trickery has become the principal reason for living, working and suffering for those who lack the courage to condemn this mouldy society to revolutionary destruction. Around modern banks, as around the totem poles of the Kwakiutl, the same desire to dazzle animates individuals and leads them into a system of petty displays that blinds them to each other, as if they were staring into a blinding light. A few steps from the bank, jewels, dresses and cars wait behind shop windows for the day when they will serve to establish the augmented splendour of a sinister industrialist and his even more sinister old wife. At a lower level, gilded clocks, dining room buffets and artificial flowers render equally shameful service to a grocer and his wife. Jealousy arises between human beings, as it does among the savages, and with an equivalent brutality; only generosity and nobility have disappeared, and with them the dazzling contrast that the rich provided to the poor.

As the class that possesses the wealth – having received with wealth the obligation of functional expenditure – the modern bourgeoisie is characterized by the refusal in principle of this obligation. It has distinguished itself from the aristocracy through the fact that it has consented only to *spend for itself*, and within itself – in other words, by hiding its expenditures as much as possible from the eyes of the other classes. This particular form was originally due to the development of its wealth in the shadow of a more powerful noble class. The rationalist conceptions developed by the bourgeoisie, starting in the seventeenth century, were a response to these humiliating conceptions of restrained expenditure; this rationalism meant nothing other than the strictly economic representation of the world – economic in the vulgar sense, the bourgeois sense, of the word. The hatred of expenditure is the *raison d'être* of and the justification for the bourgeoisie; it is at the same time the principle of its horrifying hypocrisy. A fundamental grievance of the bourgeois was the prodigality of feudal society and, after coming to power, they believed that, because of their habits of accumulation, they were capable of acceptably dominating the poorer classes. And it is right to recognized that the people are incapable of hating them as much as their former masters, to the extend that they are incapable of loving them, for the bourgeois are incapable of concealing a sordid face, a face so rapacious and lacking in nobility, so frighteningly small, that all human life, upon seeing it, seems degraded.

In opposition, the people's consciousness is reduced to maintaining profoundly the principle of expenditure by representing bourgeois existence as the shame of man and as a sinister cancellation.

5 Class Struggle

In trying to maintain sterility in regard to expenditure, in conformity with a reasoning that balances *accounts*, bourgeois society has only managed to develop a universal meanness. Human life only rediscovers agitation on the scale of irreducible needs through the efforts of those who push the consequences of current rationalist conceptions as far as they will go. What remains of the traditional modes of expenditure has become atrophied, and living sumptuary tumult has been lost in the unprecedented explosion of *class struggle*.

The components of *class struggle* are seen in the process of expenditure, dating back to the archaic period. In *potlatch*, the rich man distributes products furnished him by other, impoverished, men. He tries to rise above a rival who is rich like himself, but the ultimate stage of his foreseen elevation has no more necessary a goal than his further separation from the nature of destitute men. Thus expenditure, even though it might be a social function, immediately leads to an agonistic and apparently anti-social act of separation. The rich man consumes the poor man's losses, creating for him a category of degradation and abjection that leads to slavery. Now it is evident that, from the endlessly transmitted heritage of the sumptuary world, the modern world has received slavery, and has reserved it for the proletariat. Without a doubt bourgeois society, which pretends to govern according to rational principles, and which, through its own actions, moreover, tends to realize a certain human homogeneity, does not accept without protest a division that seems destructive to man himself; it is incapable, however, of pushing this resistance further than theoretical negation. It gives the workers rights equal to those of the masters, and it announces this *equality* by inscribing that word on walls. But the masters, who act as if they were the expression of society itself, are preoccupied – more seriously than with any other concern – with showing that they do not in any way share the abjection of the men they employ. *The end of the workers' activity is to produce in order to live, but the bosses' activity is to produce in order to condemn the working producers to a hideous degradation* – for there is no disjunction possible between, on the one hand, the characterization the bosses seek through their modes of expenditure, which tend to elevate them high above human baseness, and on the other hand this baseness itself, of which this characterization is a function.

In opposition to this conception of agonistic social expenditure, there is the representation of numerous bourgeois efforts to ameliorate the lot of the workers – but this representation is only the expression of the cowardice of the modern upper classes, who no longer have the force to recognize the results of their own destructive acts. The expenditures taken on by the capitalists in order to aid the proletarians and give them a chance to pull themselves up on the social ladder only bear witness to their inability (due to exhaustion) to carry out thoroughly a sumptuary process. Once the loss of the poor man is accomplished, little by little the pleasure of the rich man is emptied and neutralized; it gives way to a kind of apathetic indifference. Under these conditions, in order to maintain a neutral state rendered relatively agreeable by apathy (and which exists in spite of troublesome elements such as sadism and pity), it can be useful to compensate for the expenditure that engenders abjection with a new expenditure, which tends to attenuate it. The bosses' political sense, together with certain partial developments of prosperity, has allowed this process of compensation to be, at times, quite extensive. Thus in the Anglo-Saxon countries, and in particular in the United Sates of America, the primary process takes place at the expense of only a relatively small portion of the population: to a certain extent, the working class itself has been led to participate in it (above all when this was facilitated by the preliminary existence of a class held to be abject by common accord, as in the case of the blacks). But these subterfuges, whose importance is in any case strictly limited, do not modify in any way the fundamental division between noble and ignoble men. The cruel game of social life does not vary among the different civilized countries, where the insulting splendour of the rich loses and degrades the human nature of the lower class.

It must be added that the attenuation of the masters' brutality – which in any case has less to do with destruction itself than with the psychological tendencies to destroy – corresponds to the general atrophy of the ancient sumptuary processes that characterizes the modern era.

Class struggle, on the contrary, becomes the grandest form of social expenditure when it is taken up again and developed, this time on the part of the workers, and on such a scale that it threatens the very existence of the masters.

6 Christianity and Revolution

Short of revolt, it has been possible for the provoked poor to refuse all moral participation in a system in which men oppress men; in certain historical circumstances, they succeeded, through the use of symbols even more striking than reality, in lowering all of 'human nature' to such a horrifying ignominy that the pleasure found by the rich in measuring the poverty of others suddenly became too acute to be endured without vertigo. Thus, independently of all ritual forms, an exchange of exasperated challenges was established, exacerbated above all by the poor, a *potlatch* in which real refuse and revealed moral filth entered into a rivalry of horrible grandeur with everything in the world that was rich, pure and brilliant; and an exceptional outlet was found for this form of spasmodic convulsion in religious despair, which was its unreserved exploitation.

In Christianity, the alternations between the exaltation and dread, tortures and orgies constituting religious life were conjoined in a more tragic way and were merged with a sick social structure, which was tearing itself apart with the dirtiest cruelty. The triumphal song of the Christians glorifies God because he has entered into the bloody game of social war, and because he has 'hurled the powerful from the heights of their grandeur and has exalted the miserably poor'. Their myths associate social ignominy and the cadaverous degradation of the torture victim with divine splendour. In this way religion assumes the total oppositional function manifested by contrary forces, which up to this point had been divided between the rich and the poor, with the one group condemning the other to ruin. It is closely tied to terrestrial despair, since it itself is only an epiphenomenon of the measureless hate that divides men – but an epiphenomenon that tends to substitute itself for the totality of divergent processes it summarizes. In conformity with the words attributed to Christ, who said he came to divide and not to reign, religion thus does not at all try to do away with what others consider the scourge of man. On the contrary, in its immediate form, it wallows in a revolting impurity that is indispensable to its ecstatic torment.

The meaning of Christianity is given in the development of the delirious consequences of the expenditure of classes, in a mental agonistic orgy practised at the expense of the real struggle.

However, in spite of the importance that it has had in human activity, Christian *humiliation* is only an episode in the historic struggle of the ignoble against the noble, of the impure against the pure. It is as if society, conscious of its own intolerable splitting, had become for a time dead drunk in order to enjoy it sadistically. But the heaviest drunkenness has not done away with the consequences of human poverty, and, with the exploited classes opposing the superior classes with greater lucidity, no conceivable limit can be assigned to hatred. In historical agitation, only the word Revolution dominates the customary confusion and carries with it the promise that answers the unlimited demands of the masses. As for the masters and the exploiters, whose function is to create the contemptuous forms that exclude human nature – causing this nature to exist at the limits of the earth, in other words in mud – a simple law of reciprocity requires that they be condemned to fear, to the *great night* when their beautiful phrases will be drowned out by death screams in riots. That is the bloody hope which, each day, is one with the existence of the people, and which sums up the insubordinate content of the class struggle.

Class struggle has only one possible end: the loss of those who have worked to lose 'human nature'.

But whatever form of development is foreseen, be it revolutionary or servile, the general convulsions constituted eighteen hundred years ago by the religious ecstasy of the Christians, and today by the workers' movement, must equally be represented as a decisive impulse *constraining* society to use the exclusion of one class by another to realize a mode of expenditure as tragic and as free as possible, and at the same time *constraining* it to introduce sacred forms so human that the traditional forms become relatively contemptible. It is the tropic character of such movements that accounts for the total human value of the workers' Revolution, a Revolution capable of exerting a force of attraction as strong as the force that directs simple organisms toward the sun.

7 The Insubordination of Material Facts

Human life, distinct from juridical existence, existing as it does on a globe isolated in celestial space, from night to day and from one country to another – human life cannot in any way be limited to the closed systems assigned to it by reasonable conceptions. The immense travail of reckless-ness, discharge and upheaval that constitutes life could be expressed by stating that life starts only with the deficit of these systems; at least what it allows in the way of order and reserve has meaning only from the moment when the ordered and reserved forces liberate and lose themselves for ends that cannot be subordinated to anything one can account for. It is only by such insubordination – even if it is impoverished – that the human race ceases to be isolated in the unconditional splendour of material things.

In fact, in the most universal way, isolated or in groups, men find themselves constantly engaged in processes of expenditure. Variations in form do not in any way alter the fundamental characteristics of these processes, whose principle is loss. A certain excitation, whose sum total is maintained at a noticeably constant level, animates collectivities and indi-viduals. In their intensified form, the *states of excitation*, which are compa-rable to toxic states, can be defined as the illogical and irresistible impulse to reject material or moral goods that it would have been possible to utilize rationally (in conformity with the balancing of accounts). Connected to the losses that are realized in this way – in the case of the 'lost woman' as well as in the case of military expenditure – is the creation of unproductive values; the most absurd of these values, and the one that makes people the most rapacious, is *glory*. Made complete through degradation, glory, ap-pearing in a sometimes sinister and sometimes brilliant form, has never ceased to dominate social existence; it is impossible to attempt to do anything without it when it is dependent on the blind practice of personal or social loss.

In this way the boundless refuse of activity pushes human plans – including those associated with economic operations – into the game of characterizing universal matter; matter, in fact, can only be defined as the *non-logical difference* that represents in relation to the *economy* of the universe what *crime* represents in relation to the law. The glory that sums up or symbolizes (without exhausting) the object of free expenditure, while it can never exclude crime, cannot be distinguished – at least if one takes into account the only characterization that has a value comparable to matter – from the *insubordinate characterization*, which is not the condition for any-thing else.

If in addition one demonstrates the interest, concurrent with glory (as well as with degradation), which the human community necessarily sees in the qualitative change constantly realized by the movement of history, and if, finally, one demonstrates that this movement is impossible to contain or direct toward a limited end, it becomes possible, having abandoned all reserves, to assign a *relative* value to utility. Men assure their own subsist-ence or avoid suffering, not because these functions themselves lead to a sufficient result, but in order to accede to the insubordinate function of free expenditure.

Notes

1 On *potlatch*, see above all Marcel Mauss, 'Essai sur le don, forme archaïque de l'échange', in *Année sociologique*, 1925. [Translated as *The Gift: forms and functions of exchange in archaic societies*, tr. I. Cunnison (Norton, New York, 1967). TR.]
2 In other words: involving rivalry and struggle.

15

The Meaning of General Economy

The Dependence of the Economy on the Circulation of Energy on the Earth

When it is necessary to change an automobile tyre, open an abscess or plough a vineyard, it is easy to manage a quite limited operation. The elements on which the action is brought to bear are not completely isolated from the rest of the world, but it is possible to act on them as if they were: one can complete the operation without once needing to consider the whole, of which the tyre, the abscess or the vineyard is nevertheless an integral part. The changes brought about do not perceptibly alter the other things, nor does the ceaseless action from without have an appreciable effect on the conduct of the operation. But things are different when we consider a substantial economic activity such as the production of automobiles in the United States, or, *a fortiori*, when it is a question of economic activity in general.

Between the production of automobiles and the *general* movement of the economy, the interdependence is rather clear, but the economy taken as a whole is usually studied as if it were a matter of an isolatable system of operation. Production and consumption are linked together, but, considered jointly, it does not seem difficult to study them as one might study an elementary operation relatively independent of that which it is not.

This method is legitimate, and science never proceeds differently. However, economic science does not give results of the same order as physics studying, first, a precise phenomenon, then all studiable phenomena as a co-ordinated whole. Economic phenomena are not easy to isolate, and their general co-ordination is not easy to establish. So it is possible to raise this question concerning them: shouldn't productive activity as a whole be considered in terms of the modifications it receives from its surroundings or brings about in its surroundings? In other words, isn't there a need to study

The text is from *The Accursed Share*, vol. I, Consumption, tr. Robert Hurley (Zone Books, New York, 1988), pp. 19–26. *La Part maudite, I: La Consommation* was first published by Editions de Minuit in 1949, and re-edited in a 1967 edition. See *OC*, 7, pp. 27–33.

the system of human production and consumption within a much larger framework?

In the sciences such problems ordinarily have an academic character, but economic activity is so far reaching that no one will be surprised if a first question is followed by other, less abstract ones: In overall industrial development, are there not social conflicts and planetary wars? In the global activity of men, in short, are there not causes and effects that will appear only provided that *the general data of the economy* are studied? Will we be able to make ourselves the masters of such a dangerous activity (and one that we could not abandon in any case) without having grasped its *general* consequences? Should we not, given the constant development of economic forces, pose the *general* problems that are linked to the movement of energy on the globe?

These questions allow one to glimpse both the theoretical meaning and the practical importance of the principles they introduce.

The Necessity of Losing the Excess Energy that Cannot be Used for a System's Growth

At first sight, it is easy to recognize in the economy – *in the production and use of wealth* – a particular aspect of terrestrial activity regarded as a cosmic phenomenon. A movement is produced on the surface of the globe that results from the circulation of energy at this point in the universe. The economic activity of men appropriates this movement, making use of the resulting possibilities for certain ends. But this movement has a pattern and laws with which, as a rule, those who use them and depend on them are unacquainted. Thus the question arises: is the general determination of energy circulating in the biosphere altered by man's activity? Or rather, isn't the latter's intention vitiated by a determination of which it is ignorant, which it overlooks and cannot change?

Without waiting, I will give an inescapable answer.

Man's disregard for the material basis of his life still causes him to err in a serious way. Humanity exploits given material resources, but by restricting them as it does to a resolution of the immediate difficulties it encounters (a resolution which it has hastily had to define as an ideal), it assigns to the forces it employs an end which they cannot have. Beyond our immediate ends, man's activity in fact pursues the useless and infinite fulfilment of the universe.[1]

Of course, the error that results from so complete a disregard does not just concern man's claim to lucidity. It is not easy to realize one's own ends if one must, in trying to do so, carry out a movement that surpasses them. No doubt these ends and this movement may not be entirely irreconcilable;

but if these two terms are to be reconciled we must cease to ignore one of
them; otherwise, our works quickly turn to catastrophe.

I will begin with a basic fact: the living organism, in a situation determined by the play of energy on the surface of the globe, ordinarily receives
more energy than is necessary for maintaining life; the excess energy
(wealth) can be used for the growth of a system (e.g., an organism); if the
system can no longer grow, or if the excess cannot be completely absorbed
in its growth, it must necessarily be lost without profit; it must be spent,
willingly or not, gloriously or catastrophically.

The Poverty of Organisms or Limited Systems and
the Excess Wealth of Living Nature

Minds accustomed to seeing the development of productive forces as the
ideal end of activity refuse to recognize that energy, which constitutes
wealth, must ultimately be spent lavishly (without return), and that a series
of profitable operations has absolutely no other effect than the squandering
of profits. To affirm that it is necessary to dissipate a substantial portion of
energy produced, sending it up in smoke, is to go against judgements that
form the basis of a rational economy. We know cases where wealth has had
to be destroyed (coffee thrown into the sea), but these scandals cannot
reasonably be offered as examples to follow. They are the acknowledge-
ment of an impotence, and no one could find in them the image and
essence of wealth. Indeed, involuntary destruction (such as the disposal
of coffee overboard) has in every case the meaning of failure; it is experienced as a misfortune; in no way can it be presented as desirable. And yet
it is the type of operation without which there is no solution. When one
considers the *totality* of productive wealth on the surface of the globe, it is
evident that the products of this wealth can be employed for productive
ends only insofar as the living organism that is economic mankind can
increase its equipment. This is not entirely – neither always nor indefinitely
– possible. A surplus must be dissipated through deficit operations: the final
dissipation cannot fail to carry out the movement that animates terrestrial
energy.

The contrary usually appears for the reason that the economy is never
considered *in general*. The human mind reduces operations, in science as in
life, to an entity based on typical *particular* systems (organisms or enterprises). Economic activity, considered as a whole, is conceived in terms of
particular operations with limited ends. The mind generalizes by compos-
ing the aggregate of these operations. Economic science merely generalizes
the isolated situation; it restricts its object to operations carried out with a
view to a limited end, that of economic man. It does not take into consid-

eration a play of energy that no particular end limits: the play of *living matter in general*, involved in the movement of light of which it is the result. On the surface of the globe, for *living matter in general*, energy is always in excess; the question is always posed in terms of extravagance. The choice is limited to how the wealth is to be squandered. It is to the *particular* living being, or to limited populations of living beings, that the problem of necessity presents itself. But man is not just the separate being that contends with the living world and with other men for his share of resources. The general movement of exudation (of waste) of living matter impels him, and he cannot stop it; moreover, being at the summit, his sovereignty in the living world identifies him with this movement; it destines him, in a privileged way, to that glorious operation, to useless consumption. If he denies this, as he is constantly urged to do by the consciousness of a *necessity*, of an indigence inherent in separate beings (which are constantly short of resources, which are nothing but eternally *needy* individuals), his denial does not alter the global movement of energy in the least: the latter cannot accumulate limitlessly in the productive forces; eventually, like a river into the sea, it is bound to escape us and be lost to us.

War Considered as a Catastrophic Expenditure of Excess Energy

Incomprehension does not change the final outcome in the slightest. We can ignore or forget the fact that the ground we live on is little other than a field of multiple destructions. Our ignorance only has this incontestable effect: It causes us to *undergo* what we could *bring about* in our own way, if we understood. It deprives us of the choice of an exudation that might suit us. Above all, it consigns men and their works to catastrophic destructions. For if we do not have the force to destroy the surplus energy ourselves, it cannot be used, and, like an unbroken animal that cannot be trained, it is this energy that destroys us; it is we who pay the price of the inevitable explosion.

These excesses of life force, which locally block the poorest economies, are in fact the most dangerous factors of ruination. Hence relieving the blockage was always, if only in the darkest region of consciousness, the object of a feverish pursuit. Ancient societies found relief in festivals; some erected admirable monuments that had no useful purpose; we use the excess to multiply 'services' that make life smoother,[2] and we are led to reabsorb part of it by increasing leisure time. But these diversions have always been inadequate: their existence *in excess* nevertheless (in certain respects) has perpetually doomed multitudes of human beings and great quantities of useful goods to the destruction of wars. In our time, the relative importance of armed conflicts has even increased; it has taken on the disastrous proportions of which we are aware.

Recent history is the result of the soaring growth of industrial activity. At first this prolific movement restrained martial activity by absorbing the main part of the excess: the development of modern industry yielded the period of relative peace from 1815 to 1914.[3] Developing in this way, increasing the resources, the productive forces made possible in the same period the rapid demographic expansion of the advanced countries (this is the fleshly aspect of the bony proliferation of the factories). But in the long run the growth that the technical changes made possible became difficult to sustain. It became productive of an increased surplus itself. The First World War broke out before its limits were really reached, even locally. The Second did not itself signify that the system could not develop further (either extensively or in any case intensively). But it weighed the possibilities of a halt in development and ceased to enjoy the opportunities of a growth that nothing opposed. It is sometimes denied that the industrial plethora was at the origin of these recent wars, particularly the first. Yet it was this plethora that both wars exuded; its size was what gave them their extraordinary intensity. Consequently, the general principle of an excess of energy to be expended, considered (beyond the too narrow scope of the economy) as the effect of a movement that surpasses it, tragically illuminates a set of facts; moreover, it takes on a significance that no one can deny. We can express the hope of avoiding a war that already threatens. But in order to do so we must divert the surplus production, either into the rational extension of a difficult industrial growth, or into unproductive works that will dissipate an energy that cannot be accumulated in any case. This raises numerous problems, which are exhaustingly complex.[4] One can be sceptical of arriving easily at the practical solutions they demand, but the interest they hold is unquestionable.

I will simply state, without waiting further, that the extension of economic growth itself requires the overturning of economic principles – the overturning of the ethics that grounds them. Changing from the perspectives of *restrictive* economy to those of *general* economy actually accomplishes a Copernican transformation: a reversal of thinking – and of ethics. If a part of wealth (subject to a rough estimate) is doomed to destruction or at least to unproductive use without any possible profit, it is logical, even *inescapable*, to surrender commodities without return. Henceforth, leaving aside pure and simple dissipation, analogous to the construction of the Pyramids, the possibility of pursuing growth is itself subordinated to giving: the industrial development of the entire world demands of Americans that they lucidly grasp the necessity, for an economy such as theirs, of having a margin of profitless operations. An immense industrial network cannot be managed in the same way that one changes a tyre . . . It expresses a circuit of cosmic energy on which it depends, which it cannot limit, and whose laws it cannot ignore without consequences. Woe to those who, to the very end, insist on regulating the movement that exceeds them with the narrow mind of the mechanic who changes a tyre.

Notes

1 Of the materiality of the universe, which doubtless, in its proximate and remote aspects, is never anything but a beyond of thought. *Fulfilment* designates that which *fulfils itself*, not that which *is fulfilled*. *Infinite* is in opposition both to the limited determination and to the assigned *end*.
2 It is assumed that if industry cannot have an indefinite development, the same is not true of the 'services' constituting what is called the tertiary sector of the economy (the primary being agriculture and the secondary, industry), which includes specialized insurance organizations as well as the work of artists.
3 See this volume, pp. 194–5.
4 Unfortunately, it is not possible to discuss all these problems within the framework of a first – theoretical and historical – essay.

16

Laws of General Economy

The Superabundance of Biochemical Energy and Growth

That as a rule an organism has at its disposal greater energy resources than are necessary for the operations that sustain life (functional activities and, in animals, essential muscular exercises, the search for food) is evident from functions like growth and reproduction. Neither growth nor reproduction would be possible if plants and animals did not normally dispose of an excess. The very principle of living matter requires that the chemical operations of life, which demand an expenditure of energy, be gainful, productive of surpluses.

Let us consider a domestic animal, a calf. (In order not to go too deeply into the matter, I will first leave aside the different contributions of animal or human energy that enable its food to be produced; every organism depends on the contribution of others, and if this contribution is favourable, it extracts the necessary energy from it, but without it the organism would soon die.) Functional activity utilizes part of the available energy, but the animal commands an excess that ensures its growth. Under normal conditions, a part of this excess is lost in comings and goings, but if the stock grower manages to keep it inactive, the volume of the calf benefits; the saving appears in the form of fat. If the calf is not killed the moment comes when the reduced growth no longer consumes all of an increased excess; the calf then reaches sexual maturity; its vital forces are devoted mainly to the turbulence of the bull in the case of a male, or to pregnancy and the production of milk in the case of a female. In a sense, reproduction signifies a passage from individual growth to that of a group. If the male is castrated, its individual volume again increases for a time and a considerable amount of work is extracted from it.

In nature there is no artificial fattening of the newborn, nor is there castration. It was convenient for me to choose a domestic animal as an

The Accursed Share, vol. I, Consumption, tr. Robert Hurley (Zone Books, New York, 1988), pp. 27–41. *La Part maudite, I: La Consommation* was first published by Editions de Minuit in 1949, and re-edited in a 1967 edition. See *OC*, 7, pp. 34–47.

example, but the movements of animal matter are basically the same in all cases. On the whole, the excess energy provides for the growth or the turbulence of individuals. The calf and the cow, the bull and the ox merely add a richer and more familiar illustration of this great movement.

Plants manifest the same excess, but it is much more pronounced in their case. They are nothing but growth and reproduction (the energy necessary for their functional activity is neglible). But this indefinite exuberance must be considered in relation to the conditions that make it possible – and that limit it.

The Limits of Growth

I will speak briefly about the most general conditions of life, dwelling on one crucially important fact: solar energy is the source of life's exuberant development. The origin and essence of our wealth are given in the radiation of the sun, which dispenses energy – wealth – without any return. The sun gives without ever receiving. Men were conscious of this long before astrophysics measured that ceaseless prodigality; they saw it ripen the harvests and they associated its splendour with the act of someone who gives without receiving. It is necessary at this point to note a dual origin of moral judgements. In former times value was given to unproductive glory, whereas in our day it is measured in terms of production: precedence is given to energy acquisition over energy expenditure. Glory itself is justified by the consequences of a glorious deed in the sphere of utility. But, dominated though it is by practical judgement and Christian morality, the archaic sensibility is still alive: in particular it reappears in the romantic protest against the bourgeois world; only in the classical conceptions of the economy does it lose its rights entirely.

Solar radiation results in a superabundance of energy on the surface of the globe. But, first, living matter receives this energy and accumulates it within the limits given by the space that is available to it. It then radiates or squanders it, but before devoting an appreciable share to this radiation it makes maximum use of it for growth. Only the impossibility of continuing growth makes way for squander. Hence the real excess does not begin until the growth of the individual or group has reached its limits.

The immediate limitation, for each individual or each group, is given by the other individuals or other groups. But the terrestrial sphere (to be exact, the *biosphere*),[1] which corresponds to the space available to life, is the only real limit. The *individual* or group can be reduced by another individual or another group, but the total volume of living nature is not changed; in short, it is the size of the terrestrial space that limits overall growth.

Pressure

As a rule the surface of the globe is invested by life to the extent possible. By and large the myriad forms of life adapt it to the available resources, so that space is its basic limit. Certain disadvantaged areas, where the chemical operations essential to life cannot take place, seem to have no real existence. But taking into account a constant relation of the biomass to the local climatic and geological conditions, life occupies all the available space. These local conditions determine the intensity of the *pressure* exerted in all directions by life. But one can speak of pressure in this sense only if, by some means, the available space is increased; this space will be immediately occupied in the same way as the adjoining space. Moreover, the same is true every time life is destroyed at some point on the globe, by a forest fire, by a volcanic phenomenon or by the hand of man. The most familiar example is that of a path that a gardener clears and maintains. Once abandoned, the pressure of the surrounding life soon covers it over again with weeds and bushes swarming with animal life.

If the path is paved with asphalt, it is for a long time sheltered from the pressure. This means that the volume of life possible, assuming that the path were abandoned instead of being covered with asphalt, will not be realized, that the additional energy corresponding to this volume is lost, is dissipated in some way. This pressure cannot be compared to that of a closed boiler. If the space is completely occupied, if there is no outlet anywhere, nothing bursts; but the pressure is there. In a sense, life suffocates within limits that are too close; it aspires in manifold ways to an impossible growth; it releases a steady flow of excess resources, possibly involving large squanderings of energy. The limit of growth being reached, life, without being in a closed container, at least enters into ebullition: without exploding, its extreme exuberance pours out in a movement always bordering on explosion.

The consequences of this situation do not easily enter into our calculations. We calculate our interests, but this situation baffles us: the very word *interest* is contradictory with the *desire* at stake under these conditions. As soon as we want to act reasonably we have to consider the *utility* of our actions; utility implies an advantage, a maintenance or growth. Now, if it is necessary to respond to exuberance, it is no doubt possible to *use* it for growth. But the problem raised precludes this. Supposing there is no longer any growth possible, what is to be done with the seething energy that remains? To waste it is obviously not to use it. And yet, what we have is a draining-away, a pure and simple loss, *which occurs in any case*: from the first, the excess energy, if it cannot be used for growth, is lost. Moreover, in no way can this inevitable loss be accounted useful. It is only a matter of an acceptable loss, preferable to another that is regarded as unacceptable:

a question of *acceptability*, not utility. Its consequences are decisive, however.

The First Effect of Pressure: Extension

It is hard to define and precisely represent the pressure thus exerted. It is both complex and elusive, but one can describe its effects. An image comes to mind, then, but I must say in offering it that it illustrates the consequences yet does not give a concrete idea of the cause.

Imagine an immense crowd assembled in the expectation of witnessing a bullfight that will take place in a bullring that is too small. The crowd wants badly to enter but cannot be entirely accommodated: many people must wait outside. Similarly, the possibilities of life cannot be realized indefinitely; they are limited by the space, just as the entry of the crowd is limited by the number of seats in the bullring.

A first effect of the pressure will be to increase the number of seats in the bullring.

If the security service is well organized, this number is limited precisely. But outside there may be trees and lampposts from the top of which the arena is visible. If there is no regulation against it, there will be people who will climb these trees and lampposts. Similarly, the earth first opens to life the primary space of the waters and the surface of the ground. But life quickly takes possession of the air. To start with, it was important to enlarge the surface of the green substance of plants, which absorbs the radiant energy of light. The superposition of leaves in the air extends the volume of this substance considerably: in particular, the structure of trees develops this possibility well beyond the level of the grasses. For their part the winged insects and the birds, in the wake of the pollens, invade the air.

The Second Effect of Pressure: Squander or Luxury

But the lack of room can have another effect: a fight may break out at the entrance. If lives are lost the excess of individuals over the number of seats will decrease. This effect works in a sense contrary to the first one. Sometimes the pressure results in the clearing of a new space, other times in the erasing of possibilities in excess of the available room. This last effect operates in nature in the most varied forms.

The most remarkable is death. As we know, death is not necessary. The simple forms of life are immortal: the birth of an organism reproduced through scissiparity is lost in the mists of time. Indeed, it cannot be said to have had parents. Take for example the doubles A' and A", resulting from the splitting in two of A; A has not ceased living with the coming into being of A'; A' is still A (and the same is true of A"). But let us suppose (this is purely theoretical, for the purpose of demonstration) that in the beginning of life there was just one of these infinitesimal creatures: it would nonetheless have quickly populated the earth with its species. After a short time, in theory, reproduction would have become impossible for lack of room, and the energy it utilizes would have dissipated, e.g., in the form of heat. Moreover, this is what happens to one of these micro-organisms, duckweed, which covers a pond with a green film, after which it remains in equilibrium. For the duckweed, space is given within the narrowly determined limits of a pond. But the stagnation of the duckweed is not conceivable on the scale of the entire globe, where in any case ·the necessary equilibrium is lacking. It can be granted (theoretically) that a pressure everywhere equal to itself would result in a state of rest, in a general substitution of heat loss for reproduction. But real pressure has different results: it puts unequal organisms in competition with one another, and although we cannot say how the species take part in the dance, we can say what the dance is.

Besides the external action of life (climatic or volcanic phenomena), the unevenness of pressure in living matter continually makes available to growth the place left vacant by death. It is not a new space, and if one considers life as a whole, there is not really growth but a maintenance of volume in general. In other words, the possible growth is reduced to a compensation for the destructions that are brought about.

I insist on the fact that there is generally no growth but only a luxurious squandering of energy in every form! The history of life on earth is mainly the effect of a wild exuberance; the dominant event is the development of luxury, the production of increasingly burdensome forms of life.

The Three Luxuries of Nature: Eating, Death and Sexual Reproduction

The eating of one species by another is the simplest form of luxury. The populations that were trapped by the German army acquired, thanks to the food shortage, a vulgarized knowledge of this burdensome character of the indirect development of living matter. If one cultivates potatoes or wheat, the land's yield in consumable calories is much greater than that of livestock in milk and meat for an equivalent acreage of pasture. The least burdensome form of life is that of a green micro-organism (absorbing the sun's energy through the action of chlorophyll), but generally vegetation is less burdensome than animal life. Vegetation quickly occupies the available space. Animals make it a field of slaughter and extend its possibilities in this way; they themselves develop more slowly. In this respect, the wild beast is at the summit: its continual depredations of depredators represent an immense squandering of energy. William Blake asked the tiger: 'In what distant deeps or skies burned the fire of thine eyes?' What struck him in this way was the cruel pressure, at the limits of possibility, the tiger's immense power of consumption of life. In the general effervescence of life, the tiger is a point of extreme incandescence. And this incandescence did in fact burn first in the remote depths of the sky, in the sun's consumption.

Eating brings death, but in an accidental form. *Of all conceivable luxuries, death, in its fatal and inexorable form, is undoubtedly the most costly.* The fragility, the complexity, of the animal body already exhibits its luxurious quality, but this fragility and luxury culminate in death. Just as in space the trunks and branches of the tree raise the superimposed stages of the foliage to the light, death distributes the passage of the generations over time. It constantly leaves the necessary room for the coming of the newborn, and we are wrong to curse *the one without whom we would not exist.*

In reality, when we curse death we only fear ourselves: the severity of *our will* is what makes us tremble. We lie to ourselves when we dream of escaping the movement of luxurious exuberance of which we are only the most intense form. Or perhaps we only lie to ourselves in the beginning the better to experience the severity of this will afterward, carrying it to the rigorous extreme of consciousness.

In this respect, the luxury of death is regarded by us in the same way as that of sexuality, first as a negation of ourselves, then – in a sudden reversal – as the profound truth of that movement of which life is the manifestation.

Under the present conditions, independently of our consciousness, sexual reproduction is, together with eating and death, one of the great luxurious detours that ensure the intense consumption of energy. To begin with, it accentuates that which scissiparity announced: the division by which the individual being forgoes growth for himself and, through the multiplication of individuals, transfers it to the impersonality of life. This is because, from the first, sexuality differs from miserly growth: if, with regard to the species, sexuality appears as a growth, in principle it is nevertheless the luxury of individuals. This characteristic is more accentuated in sexual reproduction, where the individuals engendered are clearly separate from those that engender them and *give* them life as one *gives to others.* But without renouncing a subsequent return to the principle of growth for the period of nutrition, the reproduction of the higher animals has not ceased to deepen the fault that separates it from the simple tendency to eat in order to increase volume and power. For these animals sexual reproduction is the occasion of a sudden and frantic squandering of energy resources, carried in a moment to the limit of possibility (in time what the tiger is in space). This squandering goes far beyond what would be sufficient for the growth of the species. It appears to be the most that an individual has the strength to accomplish in a given moment. It leads to the wholesale destruction of property – in spirit, the destruction of bodies as well – and ultimately connects up with the senseless luxury and excess of death.

Extension Through Labour and Technology, and the Luxury of Man

Man's activity is basically conditioned by this general movement of life. In a sense, *in extension*, his activity opens up a new possibility to life, a new space (as did tree branches and bird wings in nature). The space that labour and technical know-how open to the increased reproduction of men is not, in the proper sense, one that life has not yet populated. But human activity transforming the world augments the mass of living matter with supplementary apparatuses, composed of an immense quantity of inert matter, which considerably increases the resources of available energy. From the first, man has the option of utilizing part of the available energy for the growth (not biological but technical) of his energy wealth. The techniques have in short made it possible to extend – to develop – the elementary movement of growth that life realizes within the limits of the possible. Of course, this development is neither continuous nor boundless. Sometimes the cessation of development corresponds to a stagnation of techniques; other times, the invention of new techniques leads to a resurgence. The growth of energy resources can itself serve as the basis of a resumption of biological (demographic) growth. The history of Europe in the nineteenth century is the best (and best known) illustration of these vast living proliferations of which technical equipment is the ossature: we are aware of the extent of the population growth linked at first to the rise of industry.

In actual fact the quantitative relations of population and tool-making – and, in general, the conditions of economic development in history – are subject to so many interferences that it is always difficult to determine their exact distribution. In any case, I cannot incorporate detailed analyses into an overall survey that seems the only way of outlining the vast movement which animates the earth. But the recent decline in demographic growth by itself reveals the complexity of the effects. The fact is that the revivals of development that are due to human activity, that are made possible or maintained by new techniques, always have a double effect: initially, they use a portion of the surplus energy, but then they produce a larger and larger surplus. This surplus eventually contributes to making growth more difficult, for growth no longer suffices to use it up. At a certain point the advantage of extension is neutralized by the contrary advantage, that of luxury; the former remains operative, but in a disappointing – uncertain, often powerless – way. The drop in the demographic curves is perhaps the first indicator of the change of sign that has occurred: henceforth what matters *primarily* is no longer to develop the productive forces but to spend their products sumptuously.

At this point, immense squanderings are about to take place: after a century of populating and of industrial peace, the temporary limit of development being encountered, the two world wars organized the greatest orgies of wealth – and of human beings – that history has recorded. Yet these orgies coincide with an appreciable rise in the general standard of living: the majority of the population benefits from more and more unproductive services; work is reduced and wages are increased overall.

Thus, man is only a roundabout, subsidiary response to the problem of growth. Doubtless, through labour and technique, he has made possible an extension of growth beyond the given limits. But just as the herbivore relative to the plant, and the carnivore relative to the herbivore, is a luxury, man is the most suited of all living beings to consume intensely, sumptuously, the excess energy offered up by the pressure of life to conflagrations befitting the solar origins of its movement.

The Accursed Share

This truth is paradoxical, to the extent of being exactly contrary to the usual perception.

This paradoxical character is underscored by the fact that, even at the highest point of exuberance, its significance is still veiled. Under present conditions, everything conspires to obscure the basic movement that tends to restore wealth to its function, to gift-giving, to squandering without reciprocation. On the one hand, mechanized warfare, producing its ravages, characterizes this movement as something alien, hostile to human will. On the other hand, the raising of the standard of living is in no way represented as a requirement of luxury. The movement that demands it is even a protest against the luxury of the great fortunes: hence the demand made in the name of *justice*. Without having anything against justice, obviously, one may be allowed to point out that here the word conceals the profound truth of its contrary, which is precisely *freedom*. Under the mask of justice, it is true that general *freedom* takes on the lacklustre and neutral appearance of existence subjected to the necessities: if anything, it is a narrowing of limits *to what is most just*; it is not a dangerous breaking-loose, a meaning that the word has lost. It is a guarantee against the risk of servitude, not a will to assume those risks without which there is no freedom.

Opposition of the 'General' Viewpoint to the 'Particular' Viewpoint

Of course, the fact of being afraid, of turning away from a movement of dilapidation, which impels us and even *defines* us, is not surprising. The consequences of this movement are distressing from the start. The image of the tiger reveals the truth of eating. Death has become our horror, and though in a sense the fact of being carnivorous and of facing death bravely answers to the demand of virility (but that is a different matter!); sexuality is linked to the scandals of death and the eating of meat.[2]

But this atmosphere of malediction presupposes anguish, and anguish for its part signifies the absence (or weakness) of the pressure exerted by the exuberance of life. Anguish arises when the anxious individual is not himself stretched tight by the feeling of superabundance. This is precisely what evinces the isolated, individual character of anguish. There can be anguish only from a personal, *particular* point of view that is radically opposed to the *general* point of view based on the exuberance of living matter as a whole. Anguish is meaningless for someone who overflows with life, and for life as a whole, which is an overflowing by its very nature.

As for the present historical situation, it is characterized by the fact that judgements concerning the *general* situation proceed from a *particular* point of view. As a rule, *particular* existence always risks succumbing for lack of resources. It contrasts with *general* existence whose resources are in excess and for which death has no meaning. From the *particular* point of view, the problems are posed *in the first instance* by a deficiency of resources. They are posed *in the first instance* by an excess of resources if one starts from the *general* point of view. Doubtless the problem of extreme poverty remains in any case. Moreover, it should be understood that *general economy* must also, whenever possible and first of all, envisage the development of growth. But if it considers poverty or growth, it takes into account the limits that the one and the other cannot fail to encounter and the dominant (decisive) character of the problems that follow from the existence of surpluses.

Briefly considering an example, the problem of extreme poverty in India cannot immediately be dissociated from the demographic growth of that country, or from the lack of proportion with its industrial development. India's possibilities of industrial growth cannot themselves be dissociated from the excesses of American resources. A typical problem of *general economy* emerges from this situation. On the one hand, there appears the need for an exudation; on the other hand, the need for a growth. The present state of the world is defined by the unevenness of the (quantitative or qualitative) pressure exerted by human life. General economy suggests, therefore, as a correct operation, a transfer of American wealth to India without reciprocation. This proposal takes into account the threat to

America that would result from the pressure – and the imbalances of pressure – exerted in the world by the developments of Hindu life.

These considerations necessarily give first priority to the problem of war, which can be clearly regarded only in the light of a fundamental ebullition. The only solution is in raising the global standard of living under the current moral conditions, the only means of absorbing the American surplus, thereby reducing the pressure to below the danger point.

This theoretical conception differs little from the empirical views that have recently appeared concerning the subject, but it is more radical, and it is interesting to note that these views have agreed with the above ideas, which were conceived earlier: this confirmation gives added strength, it seems, to both contradictions.

The Solutions of General Economy and 'Self-Consciousness'

But it has to be added at once that, however well defined the solutions, their implementation on the required scale is so difficult that from the outset the undertaking hardly looks encouraging. The theoretical solution exists; indeed, its necessity is far from escaping the notice of those on whom the decision seems to depend. Nevertheless, and even more clearly, what *general economy* defines first is the explosive character of this world, carried to the extreme degree of explosive tension in the present time. A curse obviously weighs on human life insofar as it does not have the strength to control a vertiginous movement. It must be stated as a principle, without hesitation, that the lifting of such a curse depends on man and *only on man*. But it cannot be lifted if the movement from which it emanates does not appear clearly *in consciousness*. In this regard it seems rather disappointing to have nothing more to propose, as a remedy for the catastrophe that threatens, than the 'raising of the living standard'. This recourse, as I have said, is linked to a *refusal to see*, in its *truth*, the exigency to which the recourse is intended to respond.

Yet if one considers at the same time the weakness and the virtue of this solution, two things become immediately apparent: that it is the only one capable of rather wide acceptance; and that, due to its equivocal nature, it provokes and stimulates an effort of lucidity all the greater for seeming to be far removed from such an effort. In this way the avoidance of the truth ensures, in reciprocal fashion, a recognition of the truth. In any case, the mind of contemporary man would be reluctant to embrace solutions that, not being negative, were emphatic and arbitrary; it prefers that exemplary rigour of consciousness which alone may slowly make human life commensurate with its truth. The exposition of a *general economy* implies intervention in public affairs, certainly; but first of all and more profoundly, what it aims at is consciousness, what it looks to from the outset is the *self-consciousness* that man would finally achieve in the lucid vision of its linked historical forms.

Thus, *general economy* begins with an account of the historical data, relating their meaning to the *present data*.

Notes

1 See W. Vernadsky, *La Biosphère* (Paris, 1929), where some of the considerations that follow are outlined (from a different viewpoint).
2 The association is apparently implied in the expression, 'the sin of the *flesh*'.

17

The Gift of Rivalry: 'Potlatch'

The General Importance of Ostentatious Gifts
in Mexican Society

Human sacrifices were only an extreme moment in the cycle of prodigalities. The passion that made the blood stream from the pyramids generally led the Aztec world to make unproductive use of a substantial portion of the resources it commanded.

One of the functions of the sovereign, of the 'chief of men', who had immense riches at his disposal, was to indulge in ostentatious squander. Apparently, he himself was supposed to have been, in more ancient times, the culmination of the cycle of sacrifices: his immolation – consented to by the people he embodied, if not by him – could have given the rising tide of killings the value of an unlimited consumption. His power must have saved him in the end. But he was so clearly the man of prodigality that he gave his wealth in place of his life. He was obliged to *give* and to *play*. Sahagún writes:

> The kings looked for opportunities to show their generosity and to achieve a reputation in that regard. This is why they would contribute large sums for war or for the *areitos* [dances preceding or following sacrifices]. They would pledge very precious things in the games and, when one of the commoners, man or woman, ventured to greet them and speak a few words that pleased them, they would give food and drink, along with fabrics for wearing and sleeping. If someone else composed songs that were agreeable to them, they would give gifts that were in keeping with his merit and with the pleasure he had caused them.[1]

The sovereign was merely the richest, but everyone according to his worth and his image – the rich, the nobles, the 'merchants' – had to answer

The Accursed Share, vol. I, Consumption, tr. Robert Hurley (Zone Books, New York, 1988), pp. 63–77. *La Part maudite, I: La Consummation* was first published by Editions de Minuit in 1949, and again in 1967. See *OC*, 7, pp. 66–79.

to the same expectation. The festivals were an outpouring not only of blood but also of wealth in general. Each one contributed in proportion to his power and each one was offered the occasion to display his power. Through capture (in warfare) or through purchase, the warriors and the merchants obtained the victims of the sacrifices. The Mexicans built stone temples embellished with divine statues, and the ritual service multiplied the expensive offerings. The officiants and the victims were richly adorned; the ritual feasts entailed considerable expenditures.

Public festivals were given personally by the wealthy, the 'merchants' in particular.[2]

The Wealthy and Ritual Prodigality

The Spanish chroniclers left precise information concerning the 'merchants' of Mexico and the customs they followed, customs that must have astonished the Spaniards. These 'merchants' led expeditions to unsafe territories. They often had to fight and they often prepared the way for a war, which explains the honour that attached to their profession. But the risk they assumed could not have been enough to make them the equals of the nobles. In the eyes of the Spaniards, business was demeaning, even if it led to adventure. The judgement of the Europeans derived from the principle of commerce based solely on interest. But the great 'merchants' of Mexico did not exactly follow the rule of profit; their trading was conducted without bargaining and it maintained the glorious character of the trader. The Aztec 'merchant' did not sell; he practised the *gift exchange*: he received riches as a *gift* from the 'chief of men' (from the sovereign, whom the Spanish called the *king*); *he made a present* of these riches to the lords of the lands he visited. 'In receiving these gifts, the great lords of that province hastened to give other presents in return . . . so that they might be offered to the king . . .' The sovereign gave cloaks, petticoats and precious blouses. The 'merchant' received as a gift for himself richly coloured feathers of various shapes, cut stones of all sorts, shells, fans, shell paddles for stirring cocoa, wild-animal skins worked and ornamented with designs.[3] As for the objects the 'merchants' brought back from their travels, they did not consider them to be mere commodities. On their return, they did not have them carried into their house in the daylight. 'They waited for nightfall and for a favourable time. One of the days called *ce calli* (a house) was regarded as propitious because they held that the objects of which they were the bearers, entering the house on that day, would enter as sacred things and, as such, would persevere there.'[4]

An article of exchange, in these practices, was not a *thing*; it was not reduced to the inertia, the lifelessness of the profane world. The *gift* that one made of it was a sign of glory, and the object itself had the radiance of glory. By giving, one exhibited one's wealth and one's good fortune (one's power). The 'merchant' was the man-who-gives, so much so that his first concern on returning from an expedition was with offering a banquet to which he invited his confrères, who went home laden with presents.

This was merely a feast celebrating a return. But if 'some merchant became rich and accounted himself rich, he would give a festival or a banquet for all the high-class merchants and for the lords, because it would have been considered base to die without having made some splendid expenditure that might add lustre to his person by displaying the favour of the gods who had given him everything'.[5] The festival began with the ingestion of an intoxicant giving visions which the guests would describe to each other once the narcosis had dissipated. For two days the master of the house would distribute food, drinks, reeds for smoking and flowers.

More rarely, a 'merchant' would give a banquet during a festival called *panquetzaliztli*. This was a type of sacred and ruinous ceremony. The 'merchant' who celebrated it sacrificed slaves for the occasion. He had to invite people from all around and assemble presents worth a fortune, including cloaks 'numbering eight hundred thousand', waistbands 'of which there were gathered four hundred of the richest and a great many others of ordinary quality'.[6] The most substantial gifts went to the captains and dignitaries; the men of lesser rank received less. The people danced countless *areitos*, into which entered splendidly dressed slaves, wearing necklaces, flower garlands and rondaches decorated with flowers. They danced, taking turns smoking and smelling their fragrant reeds. Then they were placed on a platform, 'so that the guests might see them better, and they were handed plates of food and drinks and attended to very graciously'. When the time came for the sacrifice, the 'merchant' who gave the festival dressed up like one of the slaves in order to go with them to the temple where the priests were waiting. These victims, armed for combat, had to defend themselves against the warriors who attacked them as they passed by. If one of the aggressors captured a slave, the 'merchant' had to pay him the price of the salve. The sovereign himself attended the solemn sacrifice, which was followed by the shared consumption of the flesh in the house of the 'merchant.'[7]

These customs, the *gift exchange* in particular, are far removed from present commercial practices. Their significance becomes apparent only when we compare them with an institution still in existence, the *potlatch* of the Indians of north-western America.

The 'Potlatch' of the Indians of the American North-West

Classical economy imagined the first exchanges in the form of barter. Why would it have thought that in the beginning a mode of acquisition such as exchange had not answered the need to acquire, but rather the contrary need to lose or squander? The classical conception is now questionable in a sense.

The 'merchants' of Mexico practised the paradoxical system of exchanges that I have described as a regular sequence of gifts; these customs, not barter, in fact constituted the archaic organization of exchange. Potlatch, still practised by the Indians of the north-west coast of America, is its typical form. Ethnographers now employ this term to designate institutions functioning on a similar principle; they find traces of it in all societies. Among the Tlingit, the Haida, the Tsimshian, the Kwakiutl, potlatch is of prime importance in social life. The least advanced of these small tribes give potlatches in ceremonies marking a person's change of condition, at the time of initiations, marriages, funerals. In the more civilized tribes a potlatch is still given in the course of a festival. One can choose a festival in which to give it, but it can itself be the occasion of a festival.

Potlatch is, like commerce, a means of circulating wealth, but it excludes bargaining. More often than not it is the solemn giving of considerable riches, offered by a chief to his rival for the purpose of humiliating, challenging and obligating him. The recipient has to erase the humiliation and take up the challenge; he must satisfy the *obligation* that was contracted by accepting. He can only reply, a short time later, by means of a new potlatch, more generous than the first: he must pay back with interest.

Gift-giving is not the only form of potlatch: a rival is challenged by a solemn destruction of riches. In principle, the destruction is offered to the mythical ancestors of the donee; it is little different from a sacrifice. As recently as the nineteenth century a Tlingit chieftain would sometimes go before a rival and cut the throats of slaves in his presence. At the proper time, the destruction was repaid by the killing of a large number of slaves. The Chukchee of the Siberian north-east have related institutions. They slaughter highly valuable dog teams, for it is necessary for them to startle, to stifle the rival group. The Indians of the north-west coast would set fire to their villages or break their canoes to pieces. They have emblazoned copper bars possessing a fictive value (depending on how famous or how old the coppers are): Sometimes these bars are worth a fortune. They throw them into the sea or shatter them.[8]

Theory of 'Potlatch'

1 The paradox of the 'gift' reduced to the 'acquisition' of a 'power'

Since the publication of Marcel Mauss's *The Gift*, the institution of potlatch has been the object of a sometimes dubious interest and curiosity. Potlatch enables one to perceive a connection between religious behaviours and economic ones. Nevertheless, one would not be able to find laws in common between these two types of behaviour – if by economy one understood a conventional set of human activities, and not the general economy in its irreducible movement. It would be futile, as a matter of fact, to consider the economic aspects of potlatch without first having formulated the viewpoint defined by *general economy*.[9] There would be no potlatch if, in a general sense, the ultimate problem concerned the acquisition and not the dissipation of useful wealth.

The study of this strange yet familiar institution (a good many of our behaviours are reducible to the laws of potlatch; they have the same significance as it does) has a privileged place in general economy. If there is within us, running through the space we inhabit, a movement of energy that we use, but that is not reducible to its utility (which we are impelled by reason to seek), we can disregard it, but we can also adapt our activity to its completion outside us. The solution of the problem thus posed calls for an action in two contrary directions: we need on the one hand to go beyond the narrow limits within which we ordinarily remain, and on the other hand somehow bring our going-beyond back within our limits. The problem posed is that of the expenditure of the surplus. We need to give away, lose or destroy. But the gift would be senseless (and so we would never decide to give) if it did not take on the meaning of an acquisition. Hence *giving* must become *acquiring a power*. Gift-giving has the virtue of a surpassing of the subject who gives, but in exchange for the object given, the subject appropriates the surpassing: he regards his virtue, that which he had the capacity for, as an asset, as a *power* that he now possesses. He enriches himself with a contempt for riches, and what he proves to be miserly of is in fact his generosity.

But he would not be able by himself to acquire a power constituted by a relinquishment of power: if he destroyed the object in solitude, in silence, no sort of *power* would result from the act; there would not be anything for the subject but a separation from power without any compensation. But if he destroys the object in front of another person or if he gives it away, the one who gives has actually acquired, in the other's eyes, the power of giving or destroying. He is now rich for having made use of wealth in the manner its essence would require: he is rich for having ostentatiously consumed what is wealth only if it is consumed. But the wealth that is actualized in the potlatch, *in consumption for others*, has no real existence except insofar as the other is changed by the consumption. In a sense, authentic consumption ought to be solitary, but then it would not have the completion that the action it has on the other confers on it. And this action that is brought to bear on others is precisely what constitutes the gift's power, which one acquires from the fact of *losing*. The exemplary virtue of the potlatch is given in this possibility for man to grasp what eludes him, to combine the limitless movements of the universe with the limit that belongs to him.

2 The apparent absurdity of gifts

But 'you can't have your cake and eat it too', the saying goes.

It is contradictory to try to be unlimited and limited at the same time, and the result is comedy: the gift does not mean anything from the standpoint of general economy; there is dissipation only for the giver.

Moreover, it turns out that the giver has only apparently lost. Not only does he have the power over the recipient that the gift has bestowed on him, but the recipient is obligated to nullify that power by repaying the gift. The rivalry even entails the return of a greater gift: in order to *get even* the giver must not only redeem himself, but he must also impose the 'power of the gift' on his rival in turn. In a sense the presents are repaid *with interest*. Thus the gift is the opposite of what it seemed to be: to give is obviously to lose, but the loss apparently brings a profit to the one who sustains it.

In reality, this absurdly contradictory aspect of potlatch is misleading. The first giver *suffers* the apparent gain resulting from the difference between his presents and those given to him in return. The one who repays only has the feeling of acquiring – a power – and of outdoing. Actually, as I have said, the ideal would be that a potlatch could not be repaid. The benefit in no way corresponds to the desire for gain. On the contrary, receiving prompts one – and obliges one – to give more, for it is necessary to remove the resulting obligation. .

3 The acquisition of rank

Doubtless potlatch is not reducible to the desire to lose, but what it brings to the giver is not the inevitable increase of return gifts; it is the rank *which it confers on the one who has the last word.*

Prestige, glory and rank should not be confused with *power*. Or if prestige is *power*, this is insofar as power itself escapes the considerations of force or right to which it is ordinarily reduced. It must be said, further, that the identity of the power and the ability to lose is fundamental. Numerous factors stand in the way, interfere and finally prevail, but, all things considered neither force nor right is the *human basis* of the differentiated value of individuals. As the surviving practices make clear, *rank* varies decisively according to an individual's capacity for giving. The animal factor (the capacity for defeating an adversary in a fight) is itself subordinated, by and large, to the value of giving. To be sure, this is the ability to appropriate a position or possessions, but it is also the fact of a man's having staked his whole being. Moreover, the gift's aspect of an appeal to animal force is brought out in fights for a common cause, to which the fighter gives himself. *Glory*, the consequence of a superiority, is itself something different from an ability to take another's place and seize his possessions: it expresses a movement of senseless frenzy, of measureless expenditure of energy, which the fervour of combat presupposes. Combat is glorious in that it is always beyond calculation at some moment. But the meaning of warfare and glory is poorly grasped if it is not related in part to the acquisition of *rank* through a reckless expenditure of vital resources, of which potlatch is the most legible form.

4 The first basic laws

But if it is true that potlatch remains the opposite of a rapine, of a profitable exchange or, generally speaking, of an appropriation of possessions, acquisition is nonetheless its ultimate purpose. Because the movement it structures differs from ours, it appears stranger to us, and so it is more capable of revealing what usually escapes our perception, and what it shows us is our basic ambiguity. One can deduce the following laws from it. Of course man is not definable once and for all and these laws operate differently – their effects are even neutralized – at different stages of history, but basically they never cease to reveal a decisive play of forces:

- a surplus of resources, which societies have constantly at their disposal at certain points, at certain times, cannot be the object of a complete appropriation (it cannot be usefully employed; it cannot be employed for the growth of the productive forces), but the squandering of this surplus itself becomes an object of appropriation;
- what is appropriated in the squander is the prestige it gives to the squanderer (whether an individual or a group), which is acquired by him as a possession and which determines his *rank*;
- conversely, rank in society (or the rank of one society among others) can be appropriated in the same way as a tool or a field; if it is ultimately a source of profit, the principle of it is nevertheless determined by a resolute squandering of resources that in theory could have been acquired.

5 Ambiguity and contradiction

While the resources he controls are reducible to quantities of energy, man is not always able to set them aside for a growth that cannot be endless or, above all, continual. He must waste the excess, but he remains eager to acquire even when he does the opposite, and so he makes waste itself an object of acquisition. Once the resources are dissipated, there remains the prestige *acquired* by the one who wastes. The waste is an ostentatious squandering to this end, with a view to a superiority over others that he attributes to himself by this means. But he misuses the negation he makes of the utility of the resources he wastes, bringing into contradiction not only himself but man's entire existence. The latter thus enters into an ambiguity where it remains: it places the value, the prestige and the truth of life in the negation of the servile use of possessions, but at the same time it makes a servile use of this negation. On the one hand, in the useful and graspable thing it discerns that which, being necessary to it, can be used for its growth (or its subsistence), but if strict necessity ceases to bind it, this 'useful thing' cannot entirely answer to its wishes. Consequently, it calls for that which cannot be grasped, for the useless employment of oneself, of one's possessions, for *play*, but it attempts to grasp that which it wished to be *ungraspable*, to *use* that whose *utility* it denied. It is not enough for our left hand not to know what the right hand gives: clumsily, it tries to take it back.

Rank is entirely the effect of this crooked will. In a sense, *rank* is the opposite of a thing: what founds it is sacred, and the general ordering of ranks is given the name of *hierarchy*. It is the stubborn determination to treat as a disposable and usable *thing* that whose essence is sacred, that which is completely removed from the profane utilitarian sphere, where the hand – unscrupulously and for servile ends – raises the hammer and nails the timber. But ambiguity encumbers the profane operation just as it empties desire's vehemence of its meaning and changes it into an apparent comedy.

This compromise given in our nature heralds those linked series of deceptions, exploitations and manias that give a temporal order to the apparent unreason of history. Man is necessarily in a mirage, his very reflection mystifies him, so intent is he on grasping the ungraspable, on using transports of lost hatred as tools. *Rank*, where loss is changed into acquisition, corresponds to the activity of the intellect, which reduces the objects of thought to *things*. In point of fact, the contradiction of potlatch is revealed not only throughout history, but more profoundly in the operations of thought. Generally, in sacrifice or in potlatch, in action (in history) or in contemplation (in thought), what we seek is always this semblance – which by definition we cannot grasp – that we vainly call the poetry, the depth or the intimacy of passion. We are necessarily deceived since we want to grasp this shadow.

We could not reach the final object of knowledge without the dissolution of knowledge, which aims to reduce its object to the condition of subordinated and managed things. The ultimate problem of knowledge is the same as that of consumption. No one can both know and not be destroyed; no one can both consume wealth and increase it.

6 Luxury and extreme poverty

But if the demands of the life of beings (or groups) detached from life's immensity define an interest to which every operation is referred, the *general* movement of life is nevertheless accomplished beyond the demands of individuals. Selfishness is finally disappointed. It seems to prevail and to lay down a definitive boundary, but it is surpassed in any case. No doubt the rivalries of individuals among themselves take away the multitude's ability to be overrun by the global exuberance of energy. The weak are fleeced, exploited by the strong, who pay them with flagrant lies. But this cannot change the overall results, where individual interest is mocked, and where *the lies of the rich are changed into truth.*

In the end, with the possibility of growth or of acquisition reaching its limit at a certain point, *energy*, the object of greed of every isolated individual, is necessarily liberated – truly liberated under the cover of lies. Definitively, men lie; they do their best to relate this liberation to interest, but this liberation carries them further. Consequently, in a sense they lie in any case. As a rule the individual accumulation of resources is doomed to destruction. The individuals who carry out this destruction do not truly possess this wealth, *this rank*. Under primitive conditions, wealth is always analogous to stocks of munitions, which so clearly express the annihilation, not the possession of wealth. But this image is just as accurate if it is a matter of expressing the equally ludicrous truth of *rank*: it is an explosive charge. The man of high rank is originally only an explosive individual (all men are explosive, but he is explosive in a privileged way). Doubtless he tries to prevent, or at least delay the explosion. Thus he lies to himself by derisively taking his wealth and his power for something that they are not. If he manages to enjoy them peacefully, it is at the cost of a misunderstanding of himself, of his real nature. He lies at the same time to all the others, before whom on the contrary he maintains the affirmation of a truth (his explosive nature), from which he tries to escape. Of course, he will be engulfed in these lies: *rank* will be reduced to a commodity of exploitation, a shameless source of profits. This poverty cannot in any way interrupt the movement of exuberance.

Indifferent to intentions, to reticences and lies, slowly or suddenly, the movement of wealth exudes and consumes the resources of energy. This often seems strange, but not only do these resources suffice; if they cannot be completely consumed productively a surplus usually remains, which must be annihilated. At first sight, potlatch appears to carry out this consumption badly. The destruction of riches is not its rule: they are ordinarily given away and the loss in the operation is reduced to that of the giver: the aggregate of riches is preserved. But this is only an appearance. If potlatch rarely results in acts similar in every respect to sacrifice, it is nonetheless *the complementary form of an institution whose meaning is in the fact that it withdraws wealth from productive consumption*. In general, sacrifice withdraws useful products from profane circulation; in principle the gifts of potlatch liberate objects that are useless from the start. The industry of archaic luxury is the basis of potlatch; obviously, this industry squanders resources represented by the quantities of available human labour. Among the Aztecs, they were 'cloaks, petticoats, precious blouses'; or 'richly coloured feathers . . . cut stones, shells, fans, shell paddles . . . wild-animal skins worked and ornamented with designs'. In the American north-west, canoes and houses are destroyed, and dogs or slaves are slaughtered: these are useful riches. Essentially the gifts are objects of luxury (elsewhere the gifts of food are pledged from the start to the useless consumption of feasts).

One might even say that potlatch is the specific manifestation, the meaningful form of luxury. Beyond the archaic forms, luxury has actually retained the functional value of potlatch, creative of *rank*. Luxury still determines the rank of the one who displays it, and there is no exalted rank that does not require a display. But the petty calculations of those who enjoy luxury are surpassed in every way. In wealth, what shines through the defects extends the brilliance of the sun and provokes passion. It is not what is imagined by those who have reduced it to their *poverty*; it is the return of life's immensity to the truth of exuberance. This truth destroys those who have taken it for what it is not; the least that one can say is that the present forms of wealth make a shambles and a human mockery of those who think they own it. In this respect, present-day society is a huge counterfeit, where this *truth* of wealth has underhandedly slipped into *extreme poverty*. The true luxury and the real potlatch of our times falls to the poverty-stricken, that is, to the individual who lies down and scoffs. A genuine luxury requires the complete contempt for riches, the sombre indifference of the individual who refuses work and makes his life on the one hand an infinitely ruined splendour, and on the other, a silent insult to the laborious lie of the rich. Beyond a military exploitation, a religious mystification and a capitalist misappropriation, henceforth no one can rediscover the meaning of wealth, the explosiveness that it heralds, unless it is in the splendour of rags and the sombre challenge of indifference. One might say, finally, that the lie destines life's exuberance to revolt.

Notes

1 Bernardino de Sahagún, *Historia general de las cosas de Nueva España* (Porrúa, Mexico City, 1956), book VII, ch. 20.
2 Ibid., book IX, ch. 4.
3 Ibid., book IX, ch. 5.
4 Ibid., book IX, ch. 6.
5 Ibid., book IX, ch. 10.
6 Ibid., book IX, ch. 7.
7 Ibid., book IX, chs 12 and 14.
8 These facts are drawn from the authoritative study by Marcel Mauss, *Essai sur le don: Forme et raison de l'échange dans les sociétés archaïques*, in the *Année sociologique*, 1923–4, pp. 30–186, translated as *The Gift: forms and functions of exchange in archaic societies* (Norton, New York, 1967).

9 Let me indicate here that the studies whose results I am publishing here came out of my reading of the *Essai sur le don*. To begin with, reflection on potlatch led me to formulate the laws of *general economy*. But it may be of interest to mention a special difficulty that I was hard put to resolve. The general principles that I introduced, which enable one to interpret a large number of facts, left irreducible elements in the potlatch, which in my mind remained the origin of those facts. Potlatch cannot be unilaterally interpreted as a consumption of riches. It is only recently that I have been able to reduce the difficulty, and give the principles of 'general economy' a rather ambiguous foundation. What it comes down to is that a squandering of energy is always the opposite of a thing, but it enters into consideration only once it has entered into the order of things, once it has been changed into a *thing*.

18

Sacrifice, the Festival and the Principles of the Sacred World

The Need that Is Met by Sacrifice and Its Principle

The first fruits of the harvest or a head of livestock are sacrificed in order to remove the plant and the animal, together with the farmer and the stock raiser, from the world of things.

The principle of sacrifice is destruction, but though it sometimes goes so far as to destroy completely (as in a holocaust), the destruction that sacrifice is intended to bring about is not annihilation. The thing – only the thing – is what sacrifice means to destroy in the victim. Sacrifice destroys an object's real ties of subordination; it draws the victim out of the world of utility and restores it to that of unintelligible caprice. When the offered animal enters the circle in which the priest will immolate it, it passes from the world of things which are closed to man and are *nothing* to him, which he knows from the outside – to the world that is immanent to it, *intimate*, known as the wife is known in sexual consumption [*consumation charnelle*]. This assumes that it has ceased to be separated from its own intimacy, as it is in the subordination of labour. The sacrificer's prior separation from the world of things is necessary for the return to *intimacy*, of immanence between man and the world, between the subject and the object. The sacrificer needs the sacrifice in order to separate himself from the world of things and the victim could not be separated from it in turn if the sacrificer was not already separated in advance. The sacrificer declares:

Intimately, I belong to the sovereign world of the gods and myths, to the world of violent and uncalculated generosity, just as my wife belongs to my desires. I withdraw you, victim, from the world in which you were and could only be reduced to the condition of a thing, having a meaning that was foreign to your intimate nature. I call you back to the *intimacy* of the divine world, of the profound immanence of all that is.

The text is from *Theory of Religion*, tr. Robert Hurley (Zone Books, New York, 1992), pp. 43–61. Appearing in France in 1974 through Editions Gallimard, the text was written in 1948. See *OC*, 7, pp. 307–18.

The Unreality of the Divine World

Of course this is a monologue and the victim can neither understand nor reply. Sacrifice essentially turns its back on real relations. If it took them into account, it would go against its own nature, which is precisely the opposite of that world of things on which distinct *reality* is founded. It could not destroy the animal as a thing without denying the animal's objective *reality*. This is what gives the world of sacrifice an appearance of puerile gratuitousness. But one cannot at the same time destroy the values that found reality and accept their limits. The return to immanent intimacy implies a beclouded consciousness: consciousness is tied to the positing of objects as such, grasped directly, apart from a vague perception, beyond the always unreal images of a thinking based on participation.

The Ordinary Association of Death and Sacrifice

The puerile unconsciousness of sacrifice even goes so far that killing appears as a way of redressing the wrong done to the animal, miserably reduced to the condition of a thing. As a matter of fact, killing in the literal sense is not necessary. But the greatest negation of the real order is the one most favourable to the appearance of the mythical order. Moreover, sacrificial killing resolves the painful antinomy of life and death by means of a reversal. In fact death is nothing in immanence, but because it is nothing, a being is never truly separated from it. Because death has no meaning, because there is no difference between it and life, and there is no fear of it or defence against it, it invades everything without giving rise to any resistance. Duration ceases to have any value, or it is there only in order to produce the morbid delectation of anguish. On the contrary, the objective and in a sense transcendent (relative to the subject) positing of the world of things has duration as its foundation: no *thing* in fact has a separate existence, has a meaning, unless a subsequent time is posited, in view of which it is constituted as an object. The object is defined as an operative power only if its duration is implicitly understood. If it is destroyed as food or fuel is, the eater or the manufactured object preserves its value in duration; it has a lasting purpose like coal or bread. Future time constitutes this real world to such a degree that death no longer has a place in it. But it is for this very reason that death means everything to it. The weakness (the contradiction) of the world of things is that it imparts an unreal character to death even though man's membership in this world is tied to the positing of the body as a thing insofar as it is mortal.

As a matter of fact, that is a superficial view. What has no place in the world of things, what is unreal in the real world is not exactly death. Death actually discloses the imposture of reality, not only in that the absence of duration gives the lie to it, but above all because death is the great affirmer, the wonder-struck cry of life. The real order does not so much reject the negation of life that is death as it rejects the affirmation of intimate life, whose measureless violence is a danger to the stability of things, an affirmation that is fully revealed only in death. The real order must annul – neutralize – that intimate life and replace it with the thing that the individual is in the society of labour. But it cannot prevent life's disappearance in death from revealing the *invisible* brilliance of life that is not a *thing*. The power of death signifies that this real world can only have a neutral image of life, that life's intimacy does not reveal its dazzling consumption until the moment it gives out. No one knew *it* was there when it was; it was overlooked in favour of real things: death was one real thing among others. But death suddenly shows that the real society was lying. Then it is not the loss of the thing, of the useful member, that is taken into consideration. What the real society has lost is not a member but rather its truth. That intimate life, which had lost the ability to fully reach me, which I regarded primarily as a thing, is fully restored to my sensibility through its absence. Death reveals life in its plenitude and dissolves the real order. Henceforth it matters very little that this real order is the need for the duration of that which no longer exists. When an element escapes its demands, what remains is not an entity that suffers bereavement; all at once that entity, the real order, has completely dissipated. There is no more question of it and what death brings in tears is the useless consumption of the intimate order.

It is a naive opinion that links death closely to sorrow. The tears of the living, which respond to its coming, are themselves far from having a meaning opposite to joy. Far from being sorrowful, the tears are the expression of a keen awareness of shared life grasped in its intimacy. It is true that this awareness is never keener than at the moment when absence suddenly replaces presence, as in death or mere separation. And in this case, the consolation (in the strong sense the word has in the 'consolations' of the mystics) is in a sense bitterly tied to the fact that it cannot last, but it is precisely the disappearance of duration, and of the neutral behaviours associated with it, that uncovers a ground of things that is dazzlingly bright (in other words, it is clear that the need for duration conceals life from us, and that, only in theory, the impossibility of duration frees us). In other cases the tears respond instead to unexpected triumph, to good fortune that makes us exult, but always madly, far beyond the concern for a future time.

The Consummation of Sacrifice

The power that death generally has illuminates the meaning of sacrifice, which functions like death in that it restores a lost value through a relinquishment of that value. But death is not necessarily linked to it, and the most solemn sacrifice may not be bloody. To sacrifice is not to kill but to relinquish and to give. Killing is only the exhibition of a deep meaning. What is important is to pass from a lasting order, in which all consumption of resources is subordinated to the need for duration, to the violence of an unconditional consumption; what is important is to leave a world of real things, whose reality derives from a long-term operation and never resides in the moment – a world that creates and preserves (that creates for the benefit of a lasting reality). Sacrifice is the antithesis of production, which is accomplished with a view to the future; it is consumption that is concerned only with the moment. This is the sense in which it is gift and relinquishment, but what is given cannot be an object of preservation for the receiver: the gift of an offering makes it pass precisely into the world of abrupt consumption.

This is the meaning of 'sacrificing to the deity', whose sacred essence is comparable to a fire. To sacrifice is to give as one gives coal to the furnace. But the furnace ordinarily has an undeniable utility, to which the coal is subordinated, whereas in sacrifice the offering is rescued from all utility.

This is so clearly the precise meaning of sacrifice, that one sacrifices *what is useful*; one does not sacrifice luxurious objects. There could be no sacrifice if the offering were destroyed beforehand. Now, depriving the labour of manufacture of its usefulness at the outset, luxury has already *destroyed* that labour; it has dissipated it in vainglory; in the very moment, it has lost it for good. To sacrifice a luxury object would be to sacrifice the same object twice.

But neither could one sacrifice that which was not first withdrawn from immanence, that which, never having belonged to immanence, would not have been secondarily subjugated, domesticated and reduced to being a thing. Sacrifice is made of objects that could have been spirits, such as animals or plant substances, but that have become things and that need to be restored to the immanence whence they come, to the vague sphere of lost intimacy.

The Individual, Anguish and Sacrifice

Intimacy cannot be expressed discursively.

The swelling to the bursting point, the malice that breaks out with clenched teeth and weeps; the sinking feeling that doesn't know where it comes from or what it's about; the fear that sings its head off in the dark; the white-eyed pallor, the sweet sadness, the rage and the vomiting . . . are so many evasions.

What is intimate, in the strong sense, is what has the passion of an absence of individuality, the imperceptible sonority of a river, the empty limpidity of the sky: this is still a negative definition, from which the essential is missing.

These statements have the vague quality of inaccessible distances, but on the other hand articulated definitions substitute the tree for the forest, the distinct articulation for that which is articulated.

I will resort to articulation nevertheless.

Paradoxically, intimacy is violence, and it is destruction, because it is not compatible with the positing of the separate individual. If one describes the individual in the operation of sacrifice, he is defined by anguish. But if sacrifice is distressing, the reason is that the individual takes part in it. The individual identifies with the victim in the sudden movement that restores it to immanence (to intimacy), but the assimilation that is linked to the return to immanence is nonetheless based on the fact that the victim is the thing, just as the sacrificer is the individual. The separate individual is of the same nature as the thing, or rather the anxiousness to remain personally alive that establishes the person's individuality is linked to the integration of existence into the world of things. To put it differently, work and the fear of dying are interdependent; the former implies the thing and vice versa. In fact it is not even necessary to work in order to be the *thing* of fear: man is an individual to the extent that his apprehension ties him to the results of labour. But man is not, as one might think, a thing because he is afraid. He would have no anguish if he were not the individual (the thing), and it is essentially the fact of being an individual that fuels his anguish. It is in order to satisfy the demands of the thing, it is insofar as the world of things has posited his duration as the basic condition of his worth, that he learns anguish. He is afraid of death as soon as he enters the system of projects that is the order of things. Death disturbs the order of things and the order of things holds us. Man is afraid of the intimate order that is not reconcilable with the order of things. Otherwise there would be no sacrifice, and there would be no mankind either. The intimate order would not reveal itself in the destruction and the sacred anguish of the individual. Because man is not squarely within that order, but only partakes of it through a thing that is threatened in its nature (in the projects that constitute it), intimacy, in the trembling of the individual, is holy, sacred and suffused with anguish.

The Festival

The sacred is that prodigious effervescence of life that, for the sake of duration, the order of things holds in check, and that this holding changes into a breaking-loose, that is, into violence. It constantly threatens to break the dikes, to confront productive activity with the precipitate and contagious movement of a purely glorious consumption. The sacred is exactly comparable to the flame that destroys the wood by consuming it. It is that opposite of a thing which an unlimited fire is; it spreads, it radiates heat and light, it suddenly inflames and blinds in turn. Sacrifice burns like the sun that slowly dies of the prodigious radiation whose brilliance our eyes cannot bear, but it is never isolated and, in a world of individuals, it calls for the general negation of individuals as such.

The divine world is contagious and its contagion is dangerous. In theory, what is started in the operation of sacrifice is like the action of lightning: in theory there is no limit to the conflagration. It favours human life and not animality; the resistance to immanence is what regulates its resurgence, so poignant in tears and so strong in the unavowable pleasure of anguish. But if man surrendered unreservedly to immanence, he would fall short of humanity; he would achieve it only to lose it and eventually life would return to the unconscious intimacy of animals. The constant problem posed by the impossibility of being human without being a thing and of escaping the limits of things without returning to animal slumber receives the limited solution of the festival.

The initial movement of the festival is given in elementary humanity, but it reaches the plenitude of an effusion only if the anguished concentration of sacrifice sets it loose. The festival assembles men whom the consumption of the contagious offering (communion) opens up to a conflagration, but one that is limited by a countervailing prudence: there is an aspiration for destruction that breaks out in the festival, but there is a conservative prudence that regulates and limits it. On the one hand, all the possibilities of consumption are brought together: dance and poetry, music and the different arts contribute to making the festival the place and the time of a spectacular letting-loose. But consciousness, awake in anguish, is disposed, in a reversal commanded by an inability to go along with the letting-loose, to subordinate it to the need that the order of things has – being fettered by nature and self-paralysed – to receive an impetus from the outside. Thus the letting-loose of the festival is finally, if not fettered, then at least confined to the limits of a reality of which it is the negation. The festival is tolerated to the extent that it reserves the necessities of the profane world.

Limitation, the Utilitarian Interpretation of the Festival and the Positing of the Group

The festival is the fusion of human life. For the thing and the individual, it is the crucible where distinctions melt in the intense heat of intimate life. But its intimacy is dissolved in the real and individualized positing of the ensemble that is at stake in the rituals. For the sake of a *real* community, of a social fact that is given as a thing – of a common operation in view of a future time – the festival is limited: it is itself integrated as a link in the concatenation of useful works. As drunkenness, chaos, sexual orgy, that which it tends to be, it drowns everything in immanence in a sense; it then even exceeds the limits of the hybrid world of spirits, but its ritual movements slip into the world of immanence only through the mediation of spirits. To the spirits borne by the festival, to whom the sacrifice is offered, and to whose intimacy the victims are restored, an operative power is attributed in the same way it is attributed to things. In the end the festival itself is viewed as an operation and its effectiveness is not questioned. The possibility of producing, of fecundating the fields and the herds is given to rites whose least servile operative forms are aimed, through a concession, at cutting the losses from the dreadful violence of the divine world. In any case, positively in fecundation, negatively in propitiation, the community first appears in the festival as a thing, a definite individualization and a shared project with a view to duration. The festival is not a true return to immanence but rather an amicable reconciliation, full of anguish, between the incompatible necessities.

Of course the community in the festival is not posited simply as an object, but more generally as a spirit (as a subject-object), but its positing has the value of a limit to the immanence of the festival and, for this reason, the thing aspect is accentuated. If the festival is not yet, or no longer, under way, the community link to the festival is given in operative forms, whose chief ends are the products of labour, the crops and the herds. There is no clear *consciousness* of what the festival *actually* is (of what it is at the moment of its letting-loose) and the festival is not situated distinctly in consciousness except as it is integrated into the duration of the community. This is what the festival (incendiary sacrifice and the outbreak of fire) is consciously (subordinated to that duration of the common thing, which prevents it from enduring), but this shows the festival's peculiar impossibility and man's limit, tied as he is to clear consciousness. So it is not humanity – insofar as clear consciousness rightly opposes it to animality – restored to immanence. The virtue of the festival is not integrated into its nature and conversely the letting loose of the festival has been possible only because of this powerlessness of consciousness to take it for what it is. The basic problem of religion is given in this fatal misunderstanding of sacrifice. Man is the being that has lost, and even rejected, that which he obscurely is, a vague intimacy. Consciousness could not have become clear in the course of time if it had not turned away from its awkward contents, but clear consciousness is itself looking for what it has itself lost, and what it must lose again as it draws near to it. Of course what it has lost is not outside it;

consciousness turns away from the obscure intimacy of consciousness itself. Religion, whose essence is the search for lost intimacy, comes down to the effort of clear consciousness which wants to be a complete self-consciousness: but this effort is futile, since consciousness of intimacy is possible only at a level where consciousness is no longer an operation whose outcome implies duration, that is, at the level where clarity, which is the effect of the operation, is no longer given.

War: The Illusions of the Unleashing of Violence to the Outside

A society's individuality, which the fusion of the festival dissolves, is defined first of all in terms of real works – of agrarian production – that integrate sacrifice into the world of things. But the unity of a group thus has the ability to direct destructive violence to the outside.

As a matter of fact, external violence is antithetical to sacrifice or the festival, whose violence works havoc within. Only religion ensures a consumption that destroys the very substance of those whom it moves. Armed action destroys others or the wealth of others. It can be exerted individually, within a group, but the constituted group can bring it to bear on the outside and it is then that it begins to develop its consequences.

In deadly battles, in massacres and pillages, it has a meaning akin to that of festivals, in that the enemy is not treated as a thing. But war is not limited to these explosive forces and, within these very limits, it is not a slow action as sacrifice is, conducted with a view to a return to lost intimacy. It is a disorderly eruption whose external direction robs the warrior of the intimacy he attains. And if it is true that warfare tends in its own way to dissolve the individual through a negative wagering of the value of his own life, it cannot help but enhance his value in the course of time by making the surviving individual the beneficiary of the wager.

War determines the development of the individual beyond the individual-as-thing in the glorious individuality of the warrior. The glorious individual introduces, through a first negation of individuality, the divine order into the category of the individual (which expresses the order of things in a basic way). He has the contradictory will to make the negation of duration durable. Thus his strength is in part a strength to lie. War represents a bold advance, but it is the crudest kind of advance: one needs as much naïveté – or stupidity – as strength to be indifferent to that which one overvalues and to take pride in having deemed oneself of no value.

From the Unfettered Violence of Wars to the Fettering of Man-as-Commodity

This false and superficial character has serious consequences. War is not limited to forms of uncalculated havoc. Although he remains dimly aware of a calling that rules out the self-seeking behaviour of work, the warrior reduces his fellow men to servitude. He thus subordinates violence to the most complete reduction of mankind to the order of things. Doubtless the warrior is not the initiator of the reduction. The operation that makes the slave a thing presupposed the prior institution of work. But the free worker was a thing voluntarily and for a given time. Only the slave, whom the military order has made a commodity, draws out the complete consequences of the reduction. (Indeed, it is necessary to specify that without slavery the world of things would not have achieved its plenitude.) Thus the crude unconsciousness of the warrior mainly works in favour of a predominance of the real order. The sacred prestige he arrogates to himself is the false pretence of a world brought down to the weight of utility. The warrior's nobility is like a prostitute's smile, the truth of which is self-interest.

Human Sacrifice

The sacrifices of slaves illustrate the principle according to which *what is useful* is destined for sacrifice. Sacrifice surrenders the slave, whose servitude accentuates the degradation of the human order, to the baleful intimacy of unfettered violence.

In general, human sacrifice is the acute stage of a dispute setting the movement of a measureless violence against the real order and duration. It is the most radical contestation of the primacy of utility. It is at the same time the highest degree of an unleashing of internal violence. The society in which this sacrifice rages mainly affirms the rejection of a disequilibrium of the two violences. He who unleashes his forces of destruction on the outside cannot be sparing of his resources. If he reduces the enemy to slavery, he must, in a spectacular fashion, make a glorious use of this new source of wealth. He must partly destroy these things that serve him, for there is nothing useful around him that can fail to satisfy, first of all, the mythical order's demand for consumption. Thus a continual surpassing toward destruction denies, at the same time that it affirms, the individual status of the group.

But this demand for consumption is brought to bear on the slave insofar as the latter is *his* property and *his* thing. It should not be confused with the movements of violence that have the outside, the enemy, as their object. In this respect the sacrifice of a slave is far from being pure. In a sense it is an extension of military combat, and internal violence, the essence of sacrifice, is not satisfied by it. Intense consumption requires victims at the top who are not only the useful wealth of a people, but this people itself; or at least, elements that signify it and that will be destined for sacrifice, this time not owing to an alienation from the sacred world – a fall – but, quite the contrary, owing to an exceptional proximity, such as the sovereign or the children (whose killing finally realizes the performance of a sacrifice twice over).

One could not go further in the desire to consume the life substance. Indeed, one could not go more recklessly than this. Such an intense movement of consumption responds to a movement of malaise by creating a greater malaise. It is not the apogee of a religious system, but rather the moment when it condemns itself: when the old forms have lost part of their virtue, it can maintain itself only through excesses, through innovations that are too onerous. Numerous signs indicate that these cruel demands were not easily tolerated. Trickery replaced the king with a slave on whom a temporary royalty was conferred. The primacy of consumption could not resist that of military force.

PART IV

Eroticism

19

Madame Edwarda

Preface

> Death is the most terrible of all things; and to maintain its works is what requires the greatest of all strength.
>
> Hegel

The author of this book has himself insisted upon the gravity of what he has to say. Nonetheless, it would seem advisable to underscore the seriousness of it, if only because of the widespread custom of making light of those writings that deal with the subject of sexual life. Not that I hope – or intend to try – to change anything in customs that prevail. But I invite the reader of this preface to turn his thoughts for a moment to the attitude traditionally observed towards pleasure (which, in sexual play, attains a wild intensity, an insanity) and towards pain (finally assuaged by death, of course, but which, before that, dying winds to the highest pitch). A combination of conditions leads us to entertain a picture of mankind as it ought to be, and in that picture man appears at no less great a remove from extreme pleasure as from extreme pain: the most ordinary social restrictions and prohibitions are, with equal force, aimed some against sexual life, some against death, with the result that each has come to comprise a sanctified domain, a sacred area which lies under religious jurisdiction. The greater difficulties began when the prohibitions connected with the circumstances attending the disappearance of a person's life were alone allowed a serious character, whilst those touching the circumstances which surround the coming into being of life – the entirety of genital activity – tended to be taken unseriously. It is not a protest against the profound general inclination that I have in mind: this inclination is another expression of the human destiny which would make man's reproductive organs the object of laughter. But

The Preface and *Madame Edwarda* were published in English translation in the collection *My Mother, Madame Edwarda, The Dead Man*, tr. Austryn Wainhouse, Marion Boyars, London, 1989), pp. 137–59. In French the text appeared pseudonymously in 1941 with Editions du Solitaire. 'Pierre Angélique' was the author, while Georges Bataille signed the Preface. In 1956 Bataille published an edition with his name attached. See *OC*, III, pp. 9–31.

this laughter, which accentuates the pleasure – pain opposition (pain and death merit respect, whereas pleasure is derisory, deserving of contempt), also underscores their fundamental kinship. Man's reaction has ceased to betoken respect: his laughter is the sign of aversion, of horror. Laughter is the compromise attitude man adopts when confronted by something whose appearance repels him, but which at the same time does not strike him as particularly grave. And thus when eroticism is considered with gravity, considered tragically, this represents a complete reversal of the ordinary situation.

I wish right away to make clear the total futility of those often-repeated statements to the effect that sexual prohibitions boil down to no more than prejudices which it is high time we got rid of. The shame, the modesty sensed in connection with the strong sensation of pleasure, would be, so the argument runs, mere proofs of backwardness and unintelligence. Which is the equivalent of saying that we ought to undertake a thorough housecleaning, set fire to our house and take to the woods, returning to the good old days of animalism, of devouring whoever we please and whatever ordures. Which is the equivalent of forgetting that what we call humanity, mankind, is the direct result of poignant, indeed violent impulses, alternately of revulsion and attraction, to which sensibility and intelligence are inseparably attached. But without wishing in any sense to gainsay the laughter that is roused by the idea or spectacle of indecency, we may legitimately return – partially return – to an attitude which came to be through the operation of laughter.

It is indeed in laughter that we find the justification for a form of castigation, of obloquy. Laughter launches us along the path that leads to the transforming of a prohibition's principle, of necessary and mandatory decencies, into an iron-clad hypocrisy, into a lack of understanding or an unwillingness to understand what is involved. Extreme licence wedded with a joking mood is accompanied by a refusal to take the underlying truth of eroticism seriously: by seriously I mean *tragically*.

I should like to make this preface the occasion of a pathetic appeal (in the strongest sense); for, in this little book, eroticism is plainly shown as opening directly out upon a certain vista of anguish, upon a certain lacerating consciousness of distress. Not that I think it surprising that, most often, the mind shuts itself off to this distress and to itself, and so to speak turning its back, in its stubbornness becomes a caricature of its own truth. If man needs lies . . . why, then let man lie. There are, after all, men enough who are proud to drown themselves in the indifference of the anonymous mass . . . But there is also a will, with its puissant and wonderful qualities, to open wide the eyes, to see forthrightly and fully *what is happening*, *what is*. And there would be no knowing what is happening if one were to know nothing of the extremest pleasure if one knew nothing of extremest pain.

Now let us be clear on this. Pierre Angélique is careful to say so: we know nothing, we are sunk in the depths of ignorance's darkness. But we can at least see what is deceiving us, what diverts us from knowledge of our distress, from knowing, more precisely, that joy is the same thing as suffering, the same thing as dying, as death.

What the hearty laugh screens from us, what fetches up the bawdy jest, is the identity that exists between the utmost in pleasure and the utmost in pain: the identity between being and non-being, between the living and the death-stricken being, between the knowledge which brings one before this dazzling realization and definitive, concluding darkness. To be sure, it is not impossible that this truth itself evokes a final laugh; but our laughter here is absolute, going far beyond scorning ridicule of something which may perhaps be repugnant, but disgust for which digs deep under our skin.

If we are to follow all the way through to its last the ecstasy in which we lose ourselves in love-play, we have got constantly to bear in mind what we set as ecstasy's immediate limit: horror. Nor only can the pain I or others feel, drawing me closer to the point where horror will force me to recoil, enable me to reach the state where joy slips into delirium; but when horror is unable to quell, to destroy the object that attracts, then horror *increases* the object's power to charm. Danger paralyses; but, when not overpoweringly strong, danger can arouse desire. We do not attain to ecstasy save when before the however remote prospect of death, of that which destroys us.

Man differs from animal in that he is able to experience certain sensations that wound and melt him to the core. These sensations vary in keeping with the individual and with his specific way of living. But, for example, the sight of blood, the odour of vomit, which arouse in us the dread of death, sometimes introduce us into a kind of nauseous state which hurts more cruelly than pain. Those sensations associated with the supreme giving-way, the final collapse, are unbearable. Are there not some persons who claim to prefer death to touching an even completely harmless snake? There seems to exist a domain where death signifies not only decease and disappearance, but the unbearable process by which we disappear *despite ourselves* and everything we can do, even though, *at all costs*, we *must not* disappear. It is precisely this *despite ourselves*, this *at all costs* which distinguishes the moment of extreme joy and of indescribable but miraculous ecstasy. If there is nothing that surpasses our powers and our understanding, if we do not acknowledge something greater than ourselves, greater than we are *despite ourselves*, something which *at all costs must* not be, then we do not reach the *insensate* moment towards which we strive with all that is in our power and which at the same time we exert all our power to stave off.

Pleasure would be a puny affair were it not to involve this leap, this staggering overshooting of the mark which common sense fixes – a leap that is not confined alone to sexual ecstasy, one that is known also to the mystics of various religions, one that above all Christian mystics experienced, and experienced in this same way. The act whereby being – existence – is bestowed upon us is an *unbearable* surpassing of being, an act no less unbearable than that of dying. And since, in death, being is taken away from us at the same time it is given us, we must seek for it in the feeling of dying, in those unbearable moments when it seems to us that we are dying because the existence in us, during these interludes, exists through nothing but a sustaining and ruinous excess, when the fullness of horror and that of joy coincide.

Our minds' operations as well never reach their final culmination save in excess. What, leaving aside the representation of excess, what does truth signify if we do not see that which exceeds sight's possibilities, that which it is unbearable to see as, in ecstasy, it is unbearable to know pleasure? what, if we do not think that which exceeds thought's possibilities? . . .[1]

At the further end of this pathetic meditation – which, with a cry, undoes itself, unravelling to drown in self-repudiation, for it is unbearable to its own self – we rediscover God. That is the meaning, that is the enormity of this *insensate* – this mad – book: a book which leads God upon the stage; God in the plenitude of His attributes; and this God, for all that, is what? A public whore, in no way different from any other public whore. But what mysticism could not say (at the moment it began to pronounce its message, it entered it – entered its trance), eroticism does say: God is nothing if He is not, in every sense, the surpassing of God: in the sense of common everyday being, in the sense of dread, horror and impurity, and, finally, in the sense of nothing . . . We cannot with impunity incorporate the very word into our speech which surpasses words, the word *God*; directly we do so, this word, surpassing itself, explodes past its defining, restrictive limits. That which this word is, stops nowhere, is checked by nothing, it is everything and, everywhere, is impossible to overtake anywhere. And he who so much as suspects this instantly falls silent. Or, hunting for a way out, and realizing that he seals himself all the more inextricably into the impasse, he searches within himself for that which, capable of annihilating him, renders him similar to God, similar to nothing.[2]

In the course of the indescribable journey upon which this most incongruous of books invites us to embark, we may perhaps make a few more discoveries.

For example, that, perchance, of happiness, of delight . . .

And here indeed joy does announce itself within the perspective of death (thus is joy made to wear the mask of its contrary, grief).

I am by no means predisposed to think that voluptuous pleasure is the essential thing in this world. Man is more than a creature limited to its genitals. But they, those inavowable parts of him, teach him his secret.[3] Since intense pleasure depends upon the presence of a deleterious vision before the mind's eye, it is likely that we will be tempted to try to slink in by some back way, doing our best to get at joy by a route that keeps us as far away as possible from horror. The images which quicken desire or provoke the critical spasm are usually equivocal, *louche*: if it be horror, if it be death these images present, they always present them guilefully. Even in Sade's universe, death's terrible edge is deflected away from the self and aimed at the partner, the victim, at the *other* – and, contradictorily, Sade shows the other as the most eminently delightful expression of life. The sphere of eroticism is inescapably plighted to duplicity and ruse. The object which causes Eros to stir comes guised as other than truly it is. And so it does appear that, in the question of eroticism, it is the ascetics who are right. Beauty they call a trap set by the Devil: and only beauty excuses and renders bearable the need for disorder, for violence and for unseemliness which is the hidden root of love. This would not be the place to enter into a detailed discussion of transports whose forms are numerous and of which pure love slyly causes us to experience the most violent, driving the blind excess of life to the very edge of death. The ascetic's sweeping condemnation, admittedly, is blunt, it is craven, it is cruel, but it is squarely in tune with the fear and trembling without which we stray farther and farther away from the truth darkness sequesters. There is no warrant for ascribing to sexual love a pre-eminence which only the whole of life actually has, but, again, if we were to fail to carry the light to the very point where night falls, how should we know ourselves to be, as we are, the offspring, the effect of being hurling itself into horror? of being leaping headlong into the sickening emptiness, into the very nothingness which *at all costs* being has got to avoid . . .

Nothing, certainly, is more dreadful than this fall. How ludicrous the scenes of hell above the portals of churches must seem to us! Hell is the paltry notion God involuntarily gives us of Himself. But it requires the scale of limitless doom for us to discover the triumph of *being* – whence there has never lacked anything save consent to the impulse which would have been perishable. The nature of our being invites us of our own accord to join in the terrible dance whose rhythm is the one that ends in collapse, and which we must accept as it is and for what it is, knowing only the horror it is in perfect harmony with. If courage deserts us, if we give way, then there is no greater torture. And never does the moment of torture fail to arrive: how, in its absence, would we withstand and overcome it? But the unreservedly open spirit – open to death, to torment, to joy – the open spirit, open and dying, suffering and dying and happy, stands in a certain veiled light: that light is divine. And the cry that breaks from a twisted mouth may perhaps twist him who utters it, but what he speaks is an immense *alleluia*, flung into endless silence, and lost there.

Madame Edwarda

> Anguish only is sovereign absolute. The sovereign is a king no more: it dwells low-hiding in big cities. It knits itself up in silence, obscuring its sorrow. Crouching thick-wrapped, there it waits, lies waiting for the advent of him who shall strike a general terror; but meanwhile and even so its sorrow scornfully mocks at all that comes to pass, at all there is.

There – I had come to a street corner – there a foul dizzying anguish got its nails into me (perhaps because I'd been staring at a pair of furtive whores sneaking down the stair of a urinal). A great urge to heave myself dry always comes over me at such moments. I feel I have got to make myself naked, or strip naked the whores I covet: it's in stale flesh's tepid warmth I always suppose I'll find relief. But this time I soothed my guts with the weaker remedy: I asked for a pernod at the counter, drank the glass in one gulp, and then went on and on, from zinc counter to zinc counter, drinking until . . . The night was done falling.

I began to wander among those streets – the propitious ones – which run between the boulevard Poisonnière and the rue Saint-Denis. Loneliness and the dark strung my drunken excitement tighter and tighter. I wanted to be laid as bare as was the night there in those empty streets: I slipped off my pants and moved on, carrying them draped over my arm. Numb, I coasted on a wave of overpowering freedom, I sensed that I'd got bigger. In my hand I held my straight-risen sex.

(The beginning is tough. My way of telling about these things is raw. I could have avoided that and still made it sound plausible. It would have seemed 'likely', detours would have been to my advantage. But this is how it has to be, there is no beginning by scuttling in sidewise. I continue . . . and it gets tougher.)

Not wanting trouble, I got back into my pants and headed toward the Mirrors. I entered the place and found myself in the light again. Amidst a swarm of girls, Madame Edwarda, naked, looked bored to death. Ravishing, she was the sort I had a taste for. So I picked her. She came and sat down beside me. I hardly took the time to reply when the waiter asked what it was to be, I clutched Edwarda, she surrendered herself: our two mouths met in a sickly kiss. The room was packed with men and women, and that was the wasteland where the game was played. Then, at a certain moment, her hand slid, I burst, suddenly, like a pane of glass shattering, flooding my clothes. My hands were holding Madame Edwarda's buttocks and I felt her break in two at the same instant: and in her starting, roving eyes, terror, and in her throat, a long-drawn whistled rasp.

Then I remembered my desire for infamy, or rather that it was infamous I had at all costs to be. I made out laughter filtering through the tumult of voices, of glare, of smoke. But nothing mattered any more. I squeezed Edwarda in my arms; immediately, icebound, I felt smitten within by a new shock. From very high above a kind of stillness swept down upon me and froze me. It was as though I were borne aloft in a flight of headless and unbodied angels shaped from the broad swooping of wings, but it was simpler than that. I became unhappy and felt painfully forsaken, as one is when in the presence of GOD. It was worse and more of a letdown than too much to drink. And right away I was filled with unbearable sadness to think that this very grandeur descending upon me was withering away the pleasure I hoped to have with Edwarda.

I told myself I was being ridiculous. Edwarda and I having exchanged not one word, I was assailed by a huge uneasiness. I couldn't breathe so much as a hint of the state I was in, a wintry night had locked round me. Struggling, I wanted to kick the table and send the glasses flying, to raise the bloody roof, but that table wouldn't budge, it must have been bolted to the floor. I don't suppose a drunk can ever have to face anything more comical. Everything swam out of sight. Madame Edwarda was gone, so was the room.

I was pulled out of my dazed confusion by an only too human voice. Madame Edwarda's thin voice, like her slender body, was obscene: 'I guess what you want is to see the old rag and ruin,' she said. Hanging on to the tabletop with both hands, I twisted around toward her. She was seated, she held one leg stuck up in the air, to open her crack yet wider she used fingers to draw the folds of skin apart. And so Madame Edwarda's 'old rag and ruin' loured at me, hairy and pink, just as full of life as some loathsome squid. 'Why,' I stammered in a subdued tone, 'why are you doing that?' 'You can see for yourself,' she said, 'I'm GOD.' 'I'm going crazy –' 'Oh, no you don't, you've got to see, look . . .' Her harsh, scraping voice mellowed, she became almost childlike in order to say, with a lassitude, with the infinite smile of abandon: 'Oh, listen, fellow! The fun I've had . . .'

She had not shifted from her position, her leg was still cocked in the air. And her tone was commanding: 'Come here.' 'Do you mean,' I protested, 'in front of all these people?' 'Sure,' she said, 'why not?' I was shaking, I looked at her: motionless, she smiled back so sweetly that I shook. At last, reeling, I sank down on my knees and feverishly pressed my lips to that running, teeming wound. Her bare thigh caressingly nudged my ear, I thought I heard a sound of roaring seasurge, it is the same sound you hear when you put your ear to a large conch shell. In the brothel's boisterous chaos and in the atmosphere of corroding absurdity I was breathing (it seemed to me that I was choking, I was flushed, I was sweating) I hung strangely suspended, quite as though at that same point we, Edwarda and I, were losing ourselves in a wind-freighted night, on the edge of the ocean.

I heard another voice, a woman's but mannish. She was a robust and handsome person, respectably got up. 'Well now, my children,' in an easy, deep tone, 'up you go.' The second in command of the house collected my money. I rose and followed Madame Edwarda whose tranquil nakedness was already traversing the room. But this so ordinary passage between the close-set tables, through the dense press of clients and girls, this vulgar ritual of 'the lady going up' with the man who wants her in tow, was, at that moment, nothing short of an hallucinating solemnity for me: Madame Edwarda's sharp heels clicking on the tiled floor, the smooth advance of her long obscene body, the acrid smell I drank in, the smell of a woman in the throes of joy, of that pale body . . . Madame Edwarda went on ahead of me, raised up unto the very clouds . . . The room's noisy unheeding of her happiness, of the measured gravity of her step, was royal consecration and triumphal holiday: death itself was guest at the feast, was there in what whorehouse nudity terms the pig-sticker's stab . . . .
. . . .
. . . .
. . . . the mirrors wherewith the room's walls were everywhere sheathed and the ceiling too, cast multiple reflections of an animal coupling, but, at each least movement, our bursting hearts would strain wide-open to welcome 'the emptiness of heaven'.

Making that love liberated us at last. On our feet, we stood gazing soberly at each other: Madame Edwarda held me spellbound, never had I seen a prettier girl – nor one more naked. Her eyes fastened steadily upon me, she removed a pair of white silk stockings from a bureau drawer, she sat on the edge of the bed and drew them on. The delirious joy of being naked possessed her: once again she parted her legs, opened her crack, the pungent odour of her flesh and mine commingled flung us both into the same heart's utter exhaustion. She put on a white bolero, beneath a domino cloak she disguised her nakedness. The domino's hood cowled her head, a black velvet mask, fitted with a beard of lace, hid her face. So arrayed, she sprang away from me, saying: 'Now let's go.'

'Go? Do they let you go out?' I asked. 'Hurry up, fifi,' she replied gaily, 'you can't go out undressed.' She tossed me my clothes and helped me climb into them, and as she did so, from her caprice, there now and then passed a sly exchange, a nasty little wink darting between her flesh and mine. We went down a narrow stairway, encountered nobody but the chambermaid. Brought to a halt by the abrupt darkness of the street, I was startled to discover Edwarda rushing away, swathed in black. She ran, eluded me, was off, the mask she wore was turning her into an animal. Though the air wasn't cold, I shivered. Edwarda, something alien; above our heads, a starry sky, mad and void. I thought I was going to stagger, to fall, but didn't, and kept walking.

At that hour of the night the street was deserted. Suddenly gone wild, mute, Edwarda raced on alone. The Porte Saint-Denis loomed before her, she stopped. I stopped too, she waited for me underneath the arch – unmoving, exactly under the arch. She was entirely black, simply there, as distressing as an emptiness, a hole. I realized she wasn't frolicking, wasn't joking, and indeed that, beneath the garment enfolding her, she was mindless: rapt, absent. Then all the drunken exhilaration drained out of me, then I knew that She had not lied, that She was GOD. Her presence had about it the unintelligible out-and-out simplicity of a stone – right in the middle of the city I had the feeling of being in the mountains at night time, lost in a lifeless, hollow solitude.

I felt that I was free of Her – I was alone, as if face to face with black rock. I trembled, seeing before me what in all this world is most barren, most bleak. In no way did the comic horror of my situation escape me: She, the sight of whom petrified me now, the instant before had . . . And the transformation had occurred in the way something glides. In Madame Edwarda, grief – a grief without tears or pain – had glided into a vacant silence. Nonetheless, I wanted to find out: this woman, so naked just a moment ago, who lightheartedly had called me 'fifi' . . . I crossed in her direction, anguish warned me to go no farther, but I didn't stop.

Unspeaking, she slipped away, retreating toward the pillar on the left. Two paces separated me from that monumental gate. When I passed under the stone overhead, the domino vanished soundlessly. I paused, listening, holding my breath. I was amazed that I could grasp it all so clearly: when she had run off I had known that, no matter what, she had had to run, to dash under the arch, and when she had stopped, that she had been hung in a sort of trance, an absence, far out of range and beyond the possibility of any laughter. I couldn't see her any longer: a deathly darkness sank down from the vault. Without having given it a second's thought, I 'knew' that a season of agony was beginning for me. I consented to suffer, I desired to suffer, to go farther, as far as the 'emptiness' itself, even were I to be stricken, destroyed, no matter. I knew, I wanted that knowing, for I lusted after her secret and did not for one instant doubt that it was death's kingdom.

I moaned underneath the stone roof, then, terrified, I laughed: 'Of all men, the sole to traverse the nothingness of this arch!' I trembled at the thought she might fly, vanish for ever. I trembled as I accepted that, but from imagining it I became crazed: I leaped to the pillar and spun round it. As quickly I circled the other pillar on the right: she was gone. But I couldn't believe it. I remained woestruck before the portal and I was sinking into the last despair when upon the far side of the avenue I spied the domino, immobile, just faintly visible in the shadow: she was standing upright, entranced still, planted in front of the ranged tables and chairs of a café shut up for the night. I drew near her: she seemed gone out of her mind, some foreign existence, the creature apparently of another world and, in the streets of this one, less than a phantom, less than a lingering mist. Softly she withdrew before me until in her retreat she touched against a table on the empty terrace. A little noise. As if I had waked her, in a lifeless voice she enquired: 'Where am I?'

Desperate, I pointed to the empty sky curved above us. She looked up and for a brief moment stood still, her eyes vague behind the mask, her gaze lost in the fields of stars. I supported her, it was in an unhealthy way she was clutching the domino, with both hands pulling it tight around her. She began to shake, to convulse. She was suffering. I though she was crying but it was as if the world and the distress in her, strangling her, were preventing her from giving way to sobs. She wrenched away from me, gripped by a shapeless disgust; suddenly lunatic, she darted forward, stopped short, whirled her cloak high, displayed her behind, snapped her rump up with a quick jerk of her spine, then came back and hurled herself at me. A gale of dark savagery blew up inside her, raging, she tore and hammered at my face, hit with clenched fists, swept away by a demented impulse to violence. I tottered and fell. She fled.

I was still getting to my feet – was actually still on my knees – when she returned. She shouted in a ravelled, impossible voice, she screamed at the sky and, horrified, her whirling arms flailing at vacant air: 'I can't stand any more,' she shrilled, 'but you, you fake priest. I shit on you –' That broken voice ended in a rattle, her outstretched hands groped blindly, then she collapsed.

Down, she writhed, shaken by respiratory spasms. I bent over her and had to rip the lace from the mask, for she was chewing and trying to swallow it. Her thrashings had left her naked, her breasts spilled through her bolero . . . I saw her flat, pallid belly, and above her stockings, her hairy crack yawned astart. This nakedness now had the absence of meaning and at the same time the overabundant meaning of death-shrouds. Strangest of all – and most disturbing – was the silence that ensnared Edwarda – owing to the pain she was in, further communication was impossible and I let myself be absorbed into this unutterable barrenness – into this black night hour of the being's core no less a desert nor less hostile than the empty skies. The way her body flopped like a fish, the ignoble rage expressed by the ill written on her features – cindered the life in me, dried it down to the lees of revulsion.

(Let me explain myself. No use laying it all up to irony when I say of Madame Edwarda that she is GOD. But GOD figured as a public whore and gone crazy – that, viewed through the optic of 'philosophy', makes no sense at all. I don't mind having my sorrow derided if derided it has to be, he only will grasp me aright whose heart holds a wound that is an incurable wound, who never, for anything, in any way, would be cured of it . . . And what man, if so wounded, would ever be willing to 'die' of any other hurt?)

The awareness of my irreparable doom whilst, in that night, I knelt next to Edwarda was not less clear and not less imposing than it is now, as I write. Edwarda's sufferings dwelt in me like the quick truth of an arrow: one knows it will pierce the heart, but death will ride in with it. As I waited for annihilation, all that subsisted in me seemed to me to be the dross over which man's life tarries. Squared against a silence so black, something leaped in my heavy despair's midst. Edwarda's convulsions snatched me away from my own self, they cast my life into a desert waste 'beyond', they cast it there carelessly, callously, the way one flings a living body to the hangman.

A man condemned to die, when after long hours of waiting he arrives in broad daylight at the exact spot the horror is to be wrought, observes the preparations, his too full heart beats as though to burst; upon the narrow horizon which is his, every object, every face is clad in weightiest meaning and helps tighten the vice whence there is no time left him to escape. When I saw Madame Edwarda writhing on the pavement, I entered a similar state of absorption, but I did not feel imprisoned by the change that occurred in me. The horizon before which Edwarda's sickness placed me was a fugitive one, fleeing like the object anguish seeks to attain. Torn apart, a certain power welled up in me, a power that would be mine upon condition I agree to hate myself. Ugliness was invading all of me. The vertiginous sliding which was tipping me into ruin had opened up a prospect of indifference, of concerns, of desires there was no longer any question: at this point, the fever's desiccating ecstasy was issuing out of my utter inability to check myself.

(If you have to lay yourself bare, then you cannot play with words, trifle with slow-marching sentences. Should no one unclothe what I have said, I shall have written in vain. Edwarda is no dream's airy invention, the real sweat of her body soaked my handkerchief, so real was she that, led on by her, I came to want to do the leading in my turn. This book has its secret, I may not disclose it. Now more words.)

Finally, the crisis subsided. Her convulsions continued a little longer, but with waning fury, she began to breathe again, her features relaxed, ceased to be hideous. Drained entirely of strength, I lay full length down on the roadway beside her. I covered her with my clothing. She was not heavy and I decided to pick her up and carry her. One of the boulevard taxi stands was not far away. She lay unstirring in my arms. I took time to get there, thrice I had to pause and rest. She came back to life as we moved along and when we reached the place she wanted to be set down. She took a step and swayed. I caught her, held her, held by me she got into the cab. Weakly, she said: '. . . not yet . . . tell him to wait.' I told the driver to wait. Half dead from weariness, I climbed in too and slumped down beside Edwarda.

For a long time we remained without saying anything. Madame Edwarda, the driver and I, not budging in our seats, as though the taxi were rolling ahead. At last Edwarda spoke to me. 'I want him to take us to Les Halles.' I repeated her instructions to the driver, and we started off. He took us through dimly lit streets. Calm and deliberate, Edwarda loosened the ties of her cloak, it fell away from her. She got rid of the mask too, she removed her bolero and, for her own hearing, murmured: 'Naked as a beast.' She rapped on the glass partition, had the cab stop, and got out. She walked round to the driver and when close enough to touch him, said: 'You see . . . I'm bare-arsed, Jack. Let's fuck.' Unmoving, the driver looked at that beast. Having backed off a short distance, she had raised her left leg, eager to show him her crack. Without a word and unhurriedly, the man stepped out of the car. He was thickset, solidly built. Edwarda twined herself around him, fastened her mouth upon his, and with one hand scouted about in his underwear. It was a long heavy member she dragged through his fly. She eased his trousers down to his ankles. 'Come into the back seat,' she told him. He sat down next to me. Stepping in after him, she mounted and straddled him. Carried away by voluptuousness, with her own hands she stuffed the hard stave into her hole. I sat there, lifeless and watching: her slithering movements were slow and cunning and plainly she gleaned a nerve-snapping pleasure from them. The driver retaliated, struggling with brute heaving vigour; bred of their naked bodies' intimacy, little by little that embrace strained to the final pitch of excess at which the heart fails. The driver fell back, spent and near to swooning. I switched on the overhead light in the taxi. Edwarda sat bolt upright astride the still stiff member, her head angled sharply back, her hair straying loose. Supporting her nape, I looked into her eyes: they gleamed white. She pressed against the hand that was holding her up, the tension thickened the wail in her throat. Her eyes swung to rights and then she seemed to grow easy. She saw me from her stare, then, at that moment, I knew she was drifting home from the 'impossible' and in her nether depths I could discern a dizzying fixity. The milky outpouring travelling through her, the jet spitting from the root, flooding her with joy, came spurting out again in her very tears: burning tears streamed from her wide-open eyes. Love was dead in those eyes, they contained a daybreak aureate chill, a transparence wherein I read death's letters. And everything swam drowned in that dreaming stare: a long member, stubby fingers prying open fragile flesh, my anguish, and the recollection of scum-flecked lips – there was nothing which didn't contribute to that blind dying into extinction.

Edwarda's pleasure – fountain of boiling water, heartbursting furious tideflow – went on and on, weirdly, unendingly; that stream of luxury, its strident inflexion, glorified her being unceasingly, made her nakedness unceasingly more naked, her lewdness ever more intimate. Her body, her face swept in ecstasy were abandoned to the unspeakable coursing and ebbing, in her sweetness there hovered a crooked smile: she saw me to the bottom of my dryness, from the bottom of my desolation I sensed her joy's torrent run free. My anguish resisted the pleasure I ought to have sought. Edwarda's pain-wrung pleasure filled me with an exhausting impression of bearing witness to a miracle. My own distress and fever seemed small things to me. But that was what I felt, those are the only great things in me which gave answer to the rapture of her whom in the deeps of an icy silence I called 'my heart'.

Some last shudders took slow hold of her, then her sweatbathed frame relaxed – and there in the darkness sprawled the driver, felled by his spasm. I still held Edwarda up, my hand still behind her head, the stave slipped out, I helped her lie down, wiped her wet body. Her eyes dead, she offered no resistance. I had switched off the light, she was half asleep, like a drowsy child. The same sleepiness must have borne down upon the three of us, Edwarda, the driver and me.

(Continue? I meant to. But I don't care now. I've lost interest. I put down what oppresses me at the moment of writing: Would it all be absurd? Or might it make some kind of sense? I've made myself sick wondering about it. I awake in the morning – just the way millions do, millions of boys and girls, infants and old men, their slumbers dissipated for ever . . . These millions, those slumbers have no meaning. A hidden meaning? Hidden, yes, 'obviously'! But if nothing has any meaning, there's no point in my doing anything. I'll beg off. I'll use any deceitful means to get out of it, in the end I'll have to let go and sell myself to meaninglessness, nonsense: that is man's killer, the one who tortures and kills, not a glimmer of hope left. But if there is a meaning? Today I don't know what it is. Tomorrow? Tomorrow, who can tell? Am I going then to find out what it is? No, I can't conceive of any 'meaning' other than 'my' anguish, and as for that, I know all about it. And for the time being: nonsense. Monsieur Nonsense is writing and understands that he is mad. It's atrocious. But his madness, this meaninglessness – how 'serious' it has become all of a sudden! – might that indeed be 'meaningful'? (No, Hegel has nothing to do with a maniac girl's 'apotheosis'.) My life only has a meaning insofar as I lack one: on, but let me be mad! Make something of all this he who is able to, understand it he who is dying, and there the living self is, knowing not why, its teeth chattering in the lashing wind: the immensity, the night engulfs it and, all on purpose, that living self is there just in order . . . 'not to know'. But as for GOD? What have you got to say, Monsieur Rhetorician? And you, Monsieur Godfearer? – GOD, if He knew, would be a swine.[4] O Thou my Lord (in my distress I call out unto my heart), O deliver me, make them blind! The story – how shall I go on with it?)

But I am done.

From out of the slumber which for so short a space kept us in the taxi, I awoke, the first to open his eyes . . . The rest is irony, long, weary waiting for death . . .

Notes

1 I regret having to add that this definition of being and of excess cannot repose upon a philosophical basis, excess surpassing any foundational basis: excess is no other than that whereby the being is firstly and above all else conveyed beyond all circumscribing restrictions. Being is also, doubtless, subject to certain other limits: were this not so, we should not be able to speak (I too speak, but as I speak I do not forget not only that speech will escape me, but that it is escaping me now). These methodically arranged sentences are possible (in a large measure possible since excess is rather the exception than the rule, since excess is the marvellous, the miraculous . . . ; and excess designates the attractive, if not the horrible, attraction, if not horror – designates everything which is *more than what is*, than what exists), but their impossibility is also fundamental. Thus: no tie ever binds me, never am I enslaved, subjugated, I always retain my sovereignty, a sovereignty only my death – which will demonstrate my inability to limit myself to being without excess – separates from me. I do not decline, I do not challenge consciousness, lacking which I cannot write, but this hand that writes is *dying* from the death promised unto it as its own, this hand escapes the limits it accepts in writing (limits accepted by the hand that writes, but refused by the hand dies).

2 Here then is the primary theological attitude which would be propounded by a man in whom laughter is illumination and who disdains to impose limits, or to accept them: he who knows not what a limit is. O mark the day when you read by a pebble of fire, you who have waxed pale over the texts of the philosophers! How may he express himself who bids these voices be still, unless it be in a way that is not conceivable to them?

3 I could also point our, moreover, that excess is the very principle and engine of sexual reproduction: indeed, *divine Providence* willed that in its works its secret remain impenetrable! Were it then possible to spare man nothing? The same day when he perceives that the ground he stands on has fallen out from under his feet, he is told that it has been *providentially* removed! But would he have issue of his blasphemy, it is with blasphemy, it is in spitting defiance upon his own limitations, it is with blasphemy in his mouth that he makes himself God.

4 I said 'GOD, if He knew would be a swine.' He (He would I suppose be, at that particular moment, somewhat in disorder, his peruke would sit all askew) would entirely grasp the idea . . . but what would there be of the human about him? Beyond, beyond everything . . . and yet farther, and even farther still . . . HIMSELF, in an ecstasy, above an emptiness . . . And now? I TREMBLE.

20

Preface to the History of Eroticism

... soon we'll be united for good. I'll lie down and take you in my arms.
I'll roll with you in the midst of great secrets. We'll lose ourselves, and
find ourselves again. Nothing will come between us any more. How
unfortunate that you won't be present for this happiness!

Maurice Blanchot

I

The lowliest and least cultured human beings have an experience of the
possible – the whole of it even – which approaches that of the great mystics
in its depth and intensity. It only takes a certain energy, which is not
infrequently available, at least in the first years of adulthood. But this
intensity and depth are equalled only by the stupidity, the vulgarity – and
even, it must be said, the cowardice – of the judgements they express
concerning the possible which they attained. These judgements contribute
to the ultimate failure of an operation whose meaning escapes them. Nothing is more widespread: by chance a human being finds himself in an
incomparably splendid place; he is not at all insensitive to it, but he can't
say anything about it. At the same time there occurs in his mind the
sequence of vague ideas that keeps conversations going at full tilt. If it is a
matter of erotic life, the majority are content with the most vulgar notions.
Its foul appearance is a trap into which it is rare for them not to fall. It
becomes a reason for placid contempt. Or they deny this awful appearance
and go from contempt to platitude: *there is nothing filthy in nature*, they
affirm. We manage in any case to substitute empty thinking for those
moments when it seemed to us, however, that the very heavens were
opening.

The text is from *The Accursed Share*, vol. II, The History of Eroticism; vol. III, Sovereignty, tr.
Robert Hurley (Zone Books, New York, 1991), pp. 13–18. 'L'histoire de l'érotisme' was
among the papers for *L'Erotisme* (Editions de Minuit, Paris, 1957). In 1953–4 Bataille began
to plan a three-volume edition of *La Part maudite*. The history of eroticism was to be the
second volume. It appeared posthumously in 1976. See *OC*, VIII, pp. 9–14.

I wanted in this book to lay out a way of thinking that would measure up to those moments – a thinking that was removed from the concepts of science (which would bind their object to a *way of being* that is incompatible with it), yet rigorous in the extreme, as the coherence of a *system* of thought exhausting the totality of the possible.

Human reflection cannot be casually separated from an object that concerns it in the highest degree; we need a thinking that does not fall apart in the face of horror, a self-consciousness that does not steal away when it is time to explore possibility to the limit.

II

My intention, moreover, goes beyond a desire to compensate for the humiliation resulting from the fact that men turn away from their intimate truth, that they flee from it. This second volume continues an effort whose object is a general critique of the ideas that *subordinate* men's activity to ends other than the useless consumption of their resources. It is a matter of discrediting those ways of looking at the world that are the basis of servile forms.

It has seemed to me that in the end the servility of thought, its submissiveness to useful ends, in a word its abdication, is infinitely dreadful. Indeed present-day political and technical thought, which is reaching a kind of hypertrophy, has gotten us ludicrous results in the very sphere of useful ends. Nothing must be concealed: what is involved, finally, is a failure of humanity. True, this failure does not concern humanity as a whole. Only SERVILE MAN, who averts his eyes from that which is not useful, which *serves* no purpose, is implicated.

But SERVILE MAN holds the power nowadays in all quarters. And if it is true that he has not yet reduced all of humanity to his principles, at least it is certain that no voice has denounced the servility and shown what made its failure inevitable . . . That may be difficult to do . . . All the same, two things are equally clear: no one has yet been able to contest the right of SERVILE MAN to be in power – and yet his failure is monstrous!

The impotence of those who are revolted by an otherwise tragic situation is less surprising than it seems. If the failure of SERVILE MAN is complete, if the consequences are terrifying, it is just as certain that the principles that utilitarian thought opposed have long been without vigour. To the extent that they survive their time, they are left with the empty prestige that is tied to the final defeat of those who vanquished them. But here there can only be the tedious rehashings of regret.

I feel quite alone in seeking, in the experience of the past, not the principles that were put forward but the unperceived laws that drove the world, laws the ignorance of which leaves us headed down the paths of our misfortune. The past, which did not accept servitude, lost itself on *devious* byways, constantly going astray and cheating. We lose ourselves in an opposite direction, in the fear we have of such senseless actions and such shameful trickery. But this humanity, seared by bad memories, has no other paths than those of a past that did not know how (and was not able) to follow them with enough consequence. Everything once *served* the interests of a *few*; we have finally decided that everything should serve the interest of *all*. We see that with use the most pernicious system is the second one, *in that it is less imperfect*. This is not a reason for returning to the first. But – if we do not make *consumption* the *sovereign* principle of activity, we cannot help but succumb to those monstrous disorders without which we do not know how *to consume* the energy we have at our disposal.

III

The paradox of my attitude requires that I show the absurdity of a system in which each thing *serves*, in which nothing is *sovereign*. I cannot do so without showing that a world in which nothing is sovereign is the most unfavourable one; but that is to say in sum that we need sovereign values, hence that it is *useful* to have useless values . . .

This made it extremely difficult to uphold the principle of the first volume of this work, where I analysed the relationship of production to consumption (to non-productive consumption).[1] I was showing, of course, that production mattered less than consumption, but I could not then prevent consumption from being seen as something useful (useful even, finally, to production! . . .).

This second volume is very different, describing as it does the effects in the human mind of a kind of consumption of energy generally considered base. No one therefore will be able to shift from the asserted sovereign character of eroticism to the usefulness it might have. Sexuality at least is good for something; but eroticism . . . We are clearly concerned, this time, with a sovereign form, *which cannot serve any purpose*.

Perhaps it will seem improper to have made activity that is disapproved, that is usually connected with shame, the key to sovereign behaviours.

I will have to excuse myself by saying that no one can act *usefully* without knowing that individuals committed to usefulness, which is his own object, all answer in the first instance to the demands of eroticism. Consequently, from whatever point of view we consider it, whether we see it as an unvarying form of man's wilful autonomy, or rather we insist on enquiring about the energy pressures that condition our decisions and activities at every stage, nothing interests us more than forcing out the *secrets* of eroticism.[2]

Moreover, this dual character of my studies is present in this book: I have tried, in an epilogue, to outline the consequences of the coherent system of human expenditures of energy, where eroticism's share is substantial. I do not think, as a matter of fact, that we can touch upon the underlying meaning of political problems, where horror is always in the background, unless we consider the connection between work and eroticism, eroticism and war. I will show that these opposed forms of human activity draw from the same fund of energy resources . . . Hence the necessity of giving economic, military and demographic questions a correct solution, if we are not to give up the hope of maintaining the present civilization . . .

IV

I am aware of the small chance I have of being understood. Not that volume I of *The Accursed Share* was not given a genuine reception, and precisely in the circles I wanted to reach. But my ideas are too new.

From the reactions of the most qualified persons, I saw at first that these ideas were appetizing, that they aroused interest, but I also very quickly saw that they took a long time to digest. Not that I saw in the objections that were made to me[3] anything other than misunderstandings to clear up. But the distance is considerable between the customary representations and those I offer instead.

Unfortunately, I fear that the present work may be entirely unsuitable for reassuring those whom my first book interested. My determination to question man's totality – the whole of *concrete* reality – will be unsettling once I begin to deal with the *accursed* domain *par excellence*.

I do not now wish to dispel a malaise that I have deliberately provoked; I believe this malaise is necessary. Let one consider the abyss that is open before humanity! Could minds ready to draw back from horror possibly measure up to the problems put in front of them by the present time, *the accursed time par excellence*?

I would like, however, to prevent a misunderstanding that might result from my attitude. My book might be seen as an apology for eroticism, whereas I only wanted to describe a set of reactions that are *incomparably* rich. But these reactions I have described are essentially contradictory. Follow me closely here, if you will: *human* existence commanded an abhorrence of all sexuality; this abhorrence itself commanded the attractive value of eroticism. If my perspective is apologetic, the object of this apology is not eroticism but rather, generally, *humanity*. That humanity does not cease to maintain a sum of stubborn and incompatible, *impossibly* rigorous reactions is something worthy of admiration; indeed, *nothing merits the same degree of admiration* . . . But on the contrary, the laxity and lack of tension, the slackness of a dissolute self-indulgence detract from *humanity's* vigour; for *humanity* would cease to exist the day it became something other than what it is, entirely made up of violent contrasts.

Notes

1 ['J'exposais le rapport de la production à la consumation (à la consommation improductive),' Bataille opposes *consumation* – a noun that doesn't exist in French – to *consommation*, or consumption proper. His neologism recalls the etymological sense of consuming, as in a fire that utterly destroys. It is his own concept of fire, sacrificial consumption, with a sense of nobility, as opposed to the bourgeois consumption of production and accumulation. Hereafter, Bataille consistently uses *consumation*, which will be translated here as non-productive (or useless) consumption, or simply as consumption. TR.]

2 This work will doubtless have a third volume (see *Sovereignty*, below). In a manner of speaking, the second presents the basis of the movement that animates humanity (the basis being the simplest form); the first describes its effects in human activities considered as an ensemble, in the economic and religious spheres; the third would set forth the solution to the problem of autonomy, of the independence of man relative to useful ends; it would be concerned directly with *sovereignty*. But I do not intend to write it for some time. For the moment, the first two books – each of which, moreover, constitutes a separate study – together have a coherence that suffices in itself.

3 In particular during a lecture ['The relations between the world and the sacred, and the growth of the forces of production'] that François Perroux had asked me to give at the Institute [of Applied Economic Sciences, on 8 June 1949].

21

Death

1 The Corpse and Decay

The natural domain of the prohibitions is not just that of sexuality and filth; it also includes death.

The prohibitions concerning death have two aspects: the first forbids murder and the second limits contact with corpses.

Like the prohibitions whose objects are dejecta, incestuous union, menstrual blood and obscenity, those applying to dead bodies and to murder have not ceased being generally observed (but the prohibition against murder is just about the only one to be sanctioned by laws, and, at least within well-defined limits, the demands of anatomy have ultimately opened up a margin of infraction in behaviour toward the dead).

Since it goes without saying, I will not linger over the possible anteriority of the horror of death. This horror is perhaps at the root of our repugnance (the loathing of nothingness would then be at the origin of the loathing of decay, which is not physical since it is not shared by animals). It is clear, in any event, that the nature of excrement is analogous to that of corpses and that the places of its emission are close to the sexual parts; more often than not, this complex of prohibitions appears inextricable. Death might seem to be the complete opposite of a function whose purpose is birth . . . , but we shall see further on that this opposition is reducible, and that the death of some is correlative with the birth of others, of which it is finally the precondition and the announcement. Moreover, life is a product of putrefaction, and it depends on both death and the dungheap.

In any case, the 'denial' of death is given in the original complex, not only as it relates to the horror of annihilation, but insofar as it restores us to the power of nature, of which the universal ferment of life is the *repulsive* sign.

The text is from *The Accursed Share* vol. II, The History of Eroticism; vol. III, Sovereignty, tr. Robert Hurley (Zone Books, New York, 1991), pp. 79–86. 'L'histoire de l'érotisme' was among the papers for *L'Erotisme* (Editions de Minuit, Paris, 1957). In 1953–4 Bataille began to plan a three-volume edition of *La Part maudite*. The history of eroticism was to be the second volume. It appeared posthumously in 1976. See *OC*, VIII, pp. 68–74.

Apparently, this aspect is not compatible with the noble and solemn representation of death. But the latter opposes, *through a secondary reaction*, the cruder representation which anguish, or rather terror, controls, and which is nonetheless primordial: death is that putrefaction, that stench . . . which is at once the source and the repulsive condition of *life*.

For primitives, the extreme dread of death – above all a dread of the distressing phenomenon for the survivor, more than of personal annihilation – is linked to the phase of decay: for them, whitened bones no longer have the intolerable look of decomposing flesh. In the confusion of their minds they attribute their loathing of putrefaction to the cruel rancour and hatred visited upon them by death, which the mourning rites are meant to appease. But they think that the whitened bones signify an appeasement: these bones are venerable for them; they finally have the look of death's solemn grandeur: it is to their form, still fearsome, dreadful, but without the excess of decay's active virulence, that the worship of ancestors, becoming guardians at last, is addressed.

2 Shamefully, We Get Life from Putrefaction, and Death, Which Reduces Us to Putrefaction, Is No Less Ignoble than Birth

At least those bleached bones no longer have that sticky movement that is the privileged object of our disgust. In that movement, nascent life is not distinct from the putrefaction of life which death is, and we are inclined to see in this unavoidable comparison a basic characteristic, if not of nature, at least of the notion we have been led to conceive of it. For Aristotle himself, these animals that formed spontaneously in the earth or in the water seemed to be born of corruption. The procreative power of decay is perhaps a naive idea expressing at the same time the insurmountable repugnance and the attraction it awakens in us. But it is undoubtedly the *source* of the idea that men are nature's offspring: as if decay finally summed up this world from which we emerge and into which we return, so that the shame – and the repugnance – is linked both to death and to birth.

We have no greater aversion than the aversion we feel toward those unstable, fetid and lukewarm substances where life ferments ignobly. Those substances where the eggs, germs and maggots swarm not only make our hearts sink, but also turn our stomachs. Death does not come down to the bitter annihilation of being – of all that I am, which expects to be once more, the very meaning of which, rather than to be, is to expect to be (as if we never received *being* authentically, but only the anticipation of being, which will be and is not, as if we were not the presence that we are, but the future that we will be and are not); it is also that shipwreck in the nauseous.

I will rejoin abject nature and the purulence of anonymous, infinite life, which stretches forth like the night, which is death. One day this living world will pullulate in my dead mouth. Thus, the inevitable disappointment of the expectation is itself, at the same time, the inevitable horror that I deny, that I should deny at all costs.

3 The Knowledge of Death

This vision coincides and is associated with our mortifying perceptions of obscenity, of sexual reproduction, of stench. And it has this effect: it holds in the background of every thought the anticipation of the outcome, which is the final disappointment of expectations, silence without appeal and that ignominious putrefaction whose shameful appearance our next of kin will take care to conceal from the survivors. What marks us so severely is the *knowledge* of death, which animals fear but do not *know*. Later I will show that in tandem with this prior *knowledge* of death there is the knowledge of sexuality, to which contribute, on the one hand, the abhorrence of sexuality or the sense that it is filthy, and on the other, the practice of *eroticism*, which is the consequence of such sentiments. But the two awarenesses differ profoundly in this respect: having a positive object, consciousness of the sexual domain cannot be manifested simply in repulsion, which in fact turns us away from sexuality; so it is necessary for eroticism, which is not immediate, to bring us back from repulsion to desire. However, the repulsion of death, having immediately a negative object, is first of all a consciousness of the positive counterpart of that object, that is, a consciousness of life, or more exactly, of self: it is easy to understand that consciousness of death is essentially self-consciousness – but that, reciprocally, consciousness of self required that of death.

This should be added at once: in that maze of reactions where humanity originated, it is natural to look for one decisive reaction of which the others would only be consequences. Thus, the consciousness of death – or self-consciousness – might appear primordial . . . But in my judgement it will always be possible to show that whichever primordial fact gets priority presupposes the existence of another one . . .

Might we not imagine – just as well – that work – and the anticipation of its result – are at the basis of the knowledge of death? The sequence is quite perceptible. It is in work that the expectation takes shape. How, if I had not begun a project, a task, unsatisfying in itself, perhaps arduous, but whose result I look forward to, how could I continue, as I do, to anticipate the authentic being which I never am in the present time and which I place in the time to come? But the fact is that death threatens to forestall me, and to steal away the object of my anticipation. In the immediacy of the animal impulse, the object of desire is already given: there is no voluntary patience or waiting; the waiting, the patience, are always unavoidable and the possession of the object is not separate from the vehement desire, which cannot be contained. Think of the voracity of animals, as against the composure of a cook. Animals lack an elementary operation of the intellect, which distinguishes between action and result, present and future, and which, subordinating the present to the result, tends to substitute the anticipation of something else for that which is given in the moment, without waiting. But the human intellect represents both the possibility of the operation and the precariousness of the one who reckons on its outcome: one may die too soon and so one's expectation will remain for ever disappointed.[1] Thus, work could well be the activity in which mankind's evolution originated, the source of the disgusts and prohibitions that determined its course.

4 On the Primary Meaning of a Complex of Movements

It is possible and yet it seems useless to isolate a particular aspect when a radical change involved every element of the system.

There wasn't so much a determining element as a coincidence of the various movements which the development of humanity composed. As we shall see, work goes against erotic freedom, hampers it; and, conversely, erotic excess develops to the detriment of work. But the lags on both sides do not prevent a reciprocal acceleration of movements. The consciousness of death is itself opposed to the return of eroticism, which is likely to reintroduce avidity, fever and violence that will not wait. But anguish, which lays us open to annihilation and death, is always linked to eroticism; our sexual activity finally rivets us to the distressing image of death, and the knowledge of death deepens the abyss of eroticism. The curse of decay constantly recoils on sexuality, which it tends to eroticize: in sexual anguish there is a sadness of death, an apprehension of death which is rather vague but which we will never be able to shake off.

If need be, it is possible to reduce the complexity of reactions to a constant pursuit of autonomy (or of sovereignty). But this way of looking at things results in an abstract view, where the immediate abhorrence of, and half-physical disgust for nature – that is, nature as putrefaction – are given arbitrarily as the consequence of a calculation, of a presumed politics of autonomy. As a matter of fact, nothing proves that the struggle for autonomy is not, materially, the consequence of the disgust.

5 Death Is Finally the Most Luxurious Form of Life

What is disconcerting about these movements where opposed forms are interdependent is due to the common misappreciation of death. It calls for us to despise the link associating death with eroticism, regarded as a promise of life. It is easy, but, all in all, it is dishonourable (a lack of intellectual virility) to turn away from the luxurious truth of death: there is no doubt that death is the youth of the world. We don't admit this, we don't want to admit it, for a rather sad reason: we are perhaps young at heart, but this doesn't mean we are more alert. Otherwise, how could we not be aware that death, and death alone, constantly ensures the renewal of life? The worst is that, in a sense, we know this very well, but we are just as quick to forget it. The law given in nature is so simple as to defy ignorance. According to this law, life is effusion; it is contrary to equilibrium, to stability. It is the tumultuous movement that bursts forth and consumes itself. Its perpetual explosion is possible on one condition: that the spent organisms give way to new ones, which enter the dance with new forces.[2]

We could really not imagine a more costly process. Life is possible at much less expense: compared to that of an infusorian, the individual organism of a mammal, especially a carnivore, is an abyss where enormous quantities of energy are swallowed up, are *destroyed*. The growth of plants presupposes the amassing of decayed substances. Plant-eaters consume tons of living (plant) substance before a small amount of meat allows a carnivore its great releases, its great nervous expenditures. It even appears that the more costly the life-generating processes are, the more squander the production of organisms has required, the more satisfactory the operation is. The principle of producing at the least expense is not so much a human idea as a narrowly capitalist one (it makes sense only from the viewpoint of the incorporated company). The movement of human life even tends toward anguish, as the sign of expenditures that are finally excessive, that go beyond what we can bear. Everything within us demands that death lay waste to us: we anticipate these multiple trials, these new beginnings, unproductive from the standpoint of reason, this wholesale destruction of effective force accomplished in the transfer of one individual's life to other, younger, individuals. Deep down, we even assent to the condition that results, that is almost intolerable, in this condition of individuals destined for suffering and inevitable annihilation. Or rather, were it not for this intolerable condition, so harsh that the will constantly wavers, we would not be satisfied. (How significant at present that a book[3] is entitled, ludicrously, *Afin que nul ne meure!* . . .) Today our judgements are formed in disappointing circumstances: those among us who best make themselves heard are unaware (and want *at all cost* to be unaware) that life is the luxury of which death is the highest degree, that of all the luxuries of life, human life is the most extravagantly expensive, that, finally, an increased apprehension of death, when life's security wears thin, is at the highest level of ruinous refinement . . . But oblivious of this, they only add to the anguish without which a life devoted entirely to luxury would be less boldly luxurious. For if it is human to be luxurious, what to say of a luxury of which anguish is the product and which anguish does not moderate?

Notes

1 Indeed, in the mind of a humanity living under the primacy of reason, it is as a disappointed anticipation that the death of a man is represented as being momentous and awful, in contrast with the insignificance of animal death. It is because he lives in anticipation of the future, to which his activity has committed him, that the death of a man is so important in our eyes.
2 See 'The three luxuries of nature: eating, death and sexual reproduction', in 'The laws of general economy', this volume, pp. 192–4.
3 On the life of doctors in the United States. The qualifying subtitle of [the French translation of] Frank Slaughter's novel is, however, *Sans le secours de la médecine* [that is, *Without the Aid of Medicine*. The novel's English title is *That None Should Die* (Doubleday, Doran, New York, 1941). TR.]

22

The Festival, or the Transgression
of Prohibitions

1 The Death of the King, the Festival and the Transgression
of Prohibitions

Sometimes, in the face of death, of the failure of human ambition, a
boundless despair takes hold. Then it seems that those heavy storms and
those rumblings of nature to which man is ordinarily ashamed to yield get
the upper hand. In this sense the death of a king is apt to produce the most
pronounced affects of horror and frenzy. The nature of the sovereign
demands that this sentiment of defeat, of humiliation, always provoked by
death, attain such a degree that nothing, it seems, can stand firm against the
fury of animality. No sooner is the event announced than men rush in from
all quarters, killing everything in front of them, raping and pillaging to beat
the devil. 'Ritual licence', says Roger Caillois, 'then assumes a character
corresponding strictly to the catastrophe that has occurred . . . Popular
frenzy is never resisted in the least way. In the Hawaiian islands, the
populace, upon learning of the king's death, commits every act ordinarily
regarded as criminal. It burns, pillages and kills, and the women are
required to prostitute themselves publicly . . .' The disorder 'ends only with
the complete elimination of the putrescent substance of the royal cadaver,
when nothing more is left of the royal remains but a hard, sound and
incorruptible skeleton'.[1]

2 The Festival Is Not Just a Return to One's Vomit

Looking at this second movement, we might imagine that, the first having
failed, man returns, without the least change, to the animality from which

The text is from *The Accursed Share*, vol. II, The History of Eroticism; vol. III, Sovereignty, tr.
Robert Hurley (Zone Books, New York, 1991), pp. 89–94. 'L'histoire de l'érotisme' was
among the papers for *L'Erotisme* (Editions de Minuit, Paris, 1957). In 1953–4 Bataille began
to plan a three-volume edition of *La Part maudite*. The history of eroticism was to be the
second volume. It appeared posthumously in 1976. See *OC*, VIII, pp. 77–82.

he started. But the explosion that follows death is in no way the abandonment of that world which the prohibitions *humanize*: it is the festival, it is of course, for a moment, the cessation of work, the unrestrained consumption of its products and the deliberate violation of the most hallowed laws, but the excess consecrates and completes an order of things based on rules; it goes against that order only temporarily.

Moreover, we should not be misled by the appearance of a return by man to nature. It is such a return, no doubt, but only in one sense. Since man has uprooted himself from nature, that being who returns to it is still uprooted, he is an uprooted being who suddenly goes back toward that from which he is uprooted, from which he has not ceased to uproot himself.[2] The first uprooting is not obliterated: when men, in the course of the festival, give free play to the impulses they refuse in profane times, these impulses have a meaning in the context of the human world: they are meaningful only in that context. In any case, these impulses cannot be mistaken for those of animals.

I can't give a better idea of the gulf separating the two kinds of free play than by drawing attention to the connection between laughter and the festival. Laughter is not the festival by itself, yet in its own way it indicates the festival's meaning – indeed, laughter is always the whole movement of the festival in a nutshell – but there is nothing more contrary to animality than laughter . . .[3]

I will go further: not only is the festival not, as one might think, a return by man to his vomit, but it *ultimately* has the opposite meaning. I said that the initial human negation, which created the *human* in contrast to the *animal*, had to do with the being's *dependence* on the natural given, on the body which it did not choose, but the break constituted by the festival is not at all a way of renouncing independence; it is rather the culmination of a movement toward autonomy, which is, for ever more, the same thing as man himself.

3 The Failure of the Denial of Animality

What then is the essential meaning of our horror of nature? Not wanting to depend on anything, abandoning the place of our carnal birth, revolting intimately against the fact of *dying*, generally mistrusting the body, that is, having a deep mistrust of what is accidental, natural, perishable – this appears to be *for each one of us* the sense of the movement that leads us *to represent* man independently of filth, of the sexual functions and of death. I have no objection, this clear and distinct way of looking at things is that of man in our time; it is assuredly not that of the first men. In fact, it assumes a discriminating consciousness and the articulated language on which that consciousness is founded. But I can start by envisaging the way of feeling and reacting that determined the first prohibitions. Everything suggests that these feelings and these early reactions respond obscurely to the fact that we now have the ability to think discursively. I won't labour this point: I am referring to the entire history of religions that I must only allude to, not wishing to review it in detail. The line of development from taboos on incest or menstrual blood to the religions of purity and of the soul's immortality is quite clear: it is always a matter of denying the human being's dependence on the natural given, of setting our dignity, our spiritual nature, our detachment, against animal avidity.

But obviously I cannot limit myself to this first perception. I know that that initial movement failed. If I look for the integral meaning of my will to act and of the earliest fears that I share, I cannot help but note the futility of an effort so wrongly placed. I can deny my dependence, denying sexuality, filth, death, and insisting that the world submit to my action. But this negation is fictitious. I finally have to tell myself that the carnal origin of which I am ashamed is my origin nonetheless. And however great my horror of death may be, how can I escape the fatal appointment? I know that I will die and that I will rot. Work, for its part, finally marks the limits of my means: so limited is the extent to which I can respond to the threats of misfortune.

4 What the Festival Liberates Is Not Merely Animality but also the Divine

Of course, in their own way men recognized long ago the failure of the negation of nature: it could not fail to appear inevitable from the beginning. But from the beginning there must have been two feelings about it. According to the second of these, it was neither possible nor desirable for man to be *truly* protected, to be so protected that the accursed element would permanently cease to matter. That element was denied, but this denial was the means of giving it a *different* value. Something unfamiliar and disconcerting came into being, something that was no longer simply nature, but nature transfigured, the *sacred*.

In a basic sense, what is *sacred* is precisely what is *prohibited*. But if the *sacred*, the *prohibited*, is cast out of the sphere of profane life (inasmuch as it denotes a disruption of that life), it nevertheless has a greater value than this profane that excludes it. It is no longer the despised bestiality; often it has retained an animal form, but the latter has become *divine*. As such, relative to profane life this *sacred* animality has *the same meaning* that the negation of nature (hence profane life) has relative to pure animality. What is denied in profane life (through prohibitions and through work) is a dependent state of the animal, subject to death and to utterly *blind* needs. What is denied by means of *divine* life is still *dependence*, but this time it is the profane world whose *lucid* and *voluntary* servility is contested. In a sense, the second contestation appeals to forces that the first had denied, but insofar as they cannot truly be confined within the limits of the first. Drawing on their input, the movement of the festival *liberates* these animal forces, but now their explosive liberation interrupts the course of an existence subordinated to ordinary ends. There is a breakdown – an interruption – of the rules; the regular course of things ceases: what originally had the meaning of limit has that of shattering limits. Thus, the *sacred* announces a new possibility: it is a leap into the unknown, with animality as its impetus.

What came to pass can be summed up in a simple statement: the force of a movement, which repression increased tenfold, projected life into a richer world.

5 The Negation of the Profane World and the Divine (or Sacred) World

I emphasized earlier[4] that 'the "nature" that is desired after being rejected is not desired in submission to the given . . . : it is nature transfigured by the *curse*, to which the spirit then accedes only through a new movement of refusal, of insubordination, of revolt'. This is the basic difference between ordinary and divine animality. Of course, it would not be possible to say that simple animality is analogous to the profane sphere. I only meant to point out that relative to profane life sacred animality had the same meaning that the horror of nature had relative to the first animality. For there was negation and overcoming each time. But now I will have to describe in detail, and discursively, a system of oppositions that is familiar to us, but unconsciously so, in an obscurity that favours confusion.

The negation of nature has two clearly and distinctly opposed aspects: that of horror or repugnance, which implies fever and passion, and that of profane life, which assumes the fever has subsided. I have already spoken[5] of those movements that we strive to make immutable, immobile, of those revolutions that we regard as a state, a lasting entity, that we naively preserve, as if their essence were not change. This is not necessarily the absurdity that one imagines it to be: we can neither preserve nor abolish change, yet we cannot always be changing. But we should not confuse change with the stable state that results from it, that ultimately resumes the course of the previous state, which the change had ended.

Profane life is easy to distinguish from mere animal life; it is very different from the latter. Taking it as a whole, animal life is nonetheless the model of life without history. And profane life is an extension of it in the sense that it knows nothing of destructive and violent changes: if such changes befall it, they befall it from the outside.[6]

If I return now to a characteristic thrust and counterthrust, ebb and flow of a twofold movement, the unity in the violent agitation of prohibition and transgression will be evident; it is the unity of the sacred world, contrasting with the calm regularity of the profane world.[7]

Notes

1 *L'Homme et le sacré*, 2nd edn (Editions Gallimard, Paris, 1950), pp. 152 and 153 [*Man and the Sacred*, tr. Meyer Barash (Free Press, Glencoe, IL, 1959), pp. 115 and 116].

2 If need be, one can still say that nature includes man, that the movement I speak of occurs within nature. This is true, but the human domain in nature is a new domain, which surpasses nature, which is not enclosed within its general laws. I will not address in the present book the problem that this raises.

3 That is, at any rate, laughter whose object is *comical*.

4 *The Accursed Share*, II, p. 77, part 3, ch. 2, sec. 5, 'Eroticism is essentially, from the first step, the scandal of "reversed alliances"'.

5 *The Accursed Share*, II, p. 78, part 3, ch. 2, sec. 5.

6 I don't deny that in its way profane life is itself capable of great changes. But I must first make it clear that war, love and political sovereignty cannot genuinely enter into profane life. The profane world does not change of itself except in terms of techniques and juridical modes of production, and then it is a question of *continuous* changes. One can even say that if there is *discontinuity* of change (revolution), it implies the intervention of elements heterogeneous to the profane order, such as armed mobs and so on.

7 We shall see further on that only animality viewed by scientific thought as a thing presents a real unity with profane life.

23

The Phaedra Complex

1 The Connection of Horror and Desire

It is obviously the combination of abhorrence and desire that gives the
sacred world a paradoxical character, holding the one who considers it
without cheating in a state of anxious fascination.

What is sacred undoubtedly corresponds to the object of horror I have
spoken of, a fetid, sticky object without boundaries, which teems with life
and yet is the sign of death. It is nature at the point where its effervescence
closely joins life and death, where it is death gorging life with decomposed
substance.

It is hard to imagine that a human individual would not withdraw from
such an object in disgust. But would he withdraw if he were not tempted?
Would the object nauseate if it offered him nothing desirable? Am I wrong,
then, to think the following: it often seems that, by overcoming a resistance,
desire becomes more meaningful; resistance is the test that assures us of
desire's authenticity and thus gives it a force that comes of the certainty of
its dominion. If our desire had not had so much difficulty overcoming our
undeniable repugnance we would not have thought it so strong, we would
not have seen in its object that which was capable of inciting desire to such
a degree. So it was that Phaedra's love increased in proportion to the fear
that arose from the possibility of a crime. But on the other hand, how would
the repugnance maintain itself, or more simply, to what would it respond if
its object did not present anything dangerous? Pure and simple danger
frightens one away, while only the horror of prohibition keeps one in the
anguish of temptation.

If I consider from this standpoint any repugnant object, a decomposing
corpse for instance, it is true that my argument seems no longer to hold.

The text is from *The Accursed Share*, vol. II, The History of Eroticism; vol. III, Sovereignty, tr.
Robert Hurley (Zone Books, New York, 1991), pp. 95–101. 'L'histoire de l'érotisme' was
among the papers for *L'Erotisme* (Editions de Minuit, Paris, 1957). In 1953–4 Bataille began
to plan a three-volume edition of *La Part maudite*. The history of eroticism was to be the
second volume. It appeared posthumously in 1976. See *OC*, VIII, pp. 83–8.

However, I can bring specific considerations to bear. I will take for granted the assertion that every horror conceals a possibility of enticement. I can then assume the operation of a relatively simple mechanism. An object that is repugnant presents a force of repulsion more or less great. I will add that, following my hypothesis, it should also present a force of attraction; like the force of repulsion, its opposite, the force of attraction will be more or less great. But I didn't say that the repulsion and the attraction were always directly proportional to one another. Things are far from being so simple. Indeed, instead of increasing desire, *excessive* horror paralyses it, shuts it off.

Of course, the *excessiveness* of the horror brings in the subjective element. Instead of the Hippolytus of the story, I imagine a parricide, who would not have just satisfied an incestuous desire but would have killed Theseus. I am free to picture a Phaedra overcome by the crime she would have unintentionally provoked, refusing to see her lover again. I might also, miles away from the classical theme, imagine her burning with renewed passion for the abominable Hippolytus. Or, finding another instance of the game that Racine delighted in, I can even see her overcome, lacerated, but all the more ardent despite – or because of – her horror of Hippolytus and of herself.

If the horror is in fact more or less great, this is not merely because of the object that gives rise to it; the individual who feels it is himself more or less inclined to feel it. This doesn't in any way alter the situation most favourable to desire: it is both the situation of Racine's Phaedra and the one that I proposed last, that I gave prominence to, placing it in the setting it requires – the situation that calls for the cries, the sighs and the silences of tragedy. The more difficult the horror is to bear, the more desirable it is – but one must be able to bear it!

But the Phaedra example relates to sexual desire, and to the incest prohibition that makes it criminal, but in a clearly defined case. A rotting carcass, it seems, still has nothing desirable about it; apparently, the prohibition on contact with decayed matter, dejecta, corpses, couldn't protect these objects from a non-existent desire!

2 The Allurement Linked to the Corpse's Putrefaction

Apparently and in principle, the prohibition concerning the dead is not designed to protect them from the *desire* of the living. The horror we have of them does not seem to correspond to any attraction. Freud, it is true, thought that their obvious defencelessness justified the forbidding of contact. But other subsidiary hypotheses of Freud's are groundless . . . It is not at all the same with corpses as with kinsmen who can't have sexual relations with us: the *forbidden*, criminal character may add an allurement to the horrible significance they have been given. But the horror of putrefaction, it would seem, will never be coupled with any desire. The value of what I said in reference to Phaedra would thus be limited to the narrow domain of objects of sexual desire. It would be wrong to suppose as I did that horror always conceals a possibility of desire.

Here I need to point out that, as concerns death, I spoke of the dead, with whom it is criminal to have contact; I only alluded briefly to the living, whom it is criminal to kill.

Now, while it is true that men seldom want *to have disrespectful contact with the dead* (which is after all only a venial crime), it is certain that sometimes they desire *to kill the living*. It may be, however, that the two prohibitions are connected. I have delayed speaking thus far of the universal law that forbids (in principle) the killing of human beings. Nevertheless, respect for the dead might be a corollary of respect for the living. Mightn't the prohibition on corpses turn out to be an extension of the prohibition on murder? Isn't a dead person, in the belief of primitives, the presumed victim of a murder? Primitives are inclined to tell themselves, in fact, that death cannot be natural: face to face with a dead person, one must suppose that a spell or some act of witchcraft is responsible for the death; one must set out in search of the culprit. We may suppose that, in a dead body, an attraction, a hidden response to our desire, doesn't relate to the very object that has filled us with horror, but rather to murder.

We shouldn't be surprised, if this is so, at our lack of consciousness of it. We don't much like to think that we might kill, and even less that we might enjoy killing.

Undoubtedly, if any desire is mixed with the horror of the dead, the lure of murder contributed to it. And yet this way of looking at things strikes me as being very incomplete; at most it gives us the beginning of an explanation. There is more in the horrible attraction of the dead than the desire to kill can bring into play. Going back to the festival I spoke of, which is rudimentary, shapeless, we can embrace the complex that combines death, eroticism and murder: perhaps that is the comprehensive view we must adhere to . . .

Sexual activity is ordinarily limited by rules, and murder is regarded as awful, unthinkable. This regular order of things means that the movement of life is restrained, controlled the way a horse is by a good rider. It is the prolonged life of old people that stabilizes the course of social activity. It is the stagnation, or at least the slowing down, that keeps this course under the sway of work. Conversely, the death of old people, and indeed death in general, accelerate the effusion and exuberance of life, with the best effect resulting from an alternation of arrest and sudden release of motion.

In the end, we don't know anything, or scarcely anything, if we isolate it from this movement that death liberates, from the immense seductive power that generally belongs to life and gives a response to the depressing look of corpses bearing no make-up. This passage from authority to impotence, from the uprightness of being to absence, from the negative, [word illegible] position of the living to the endless denial of limits heralds the return, the triumph even, of neglectful, reckless, capricious life, full of tender abandon and obscure disorder. Violence responds to decay, which calls it forth; the nothingness of decomposition, relative to the enormous abandon of disorderly passions, is analogous to that aura of sacred terror that tragedy radiates.

The crux of a convulsion as complete as this comes at the moment when life, assuming in death the look of impotence, appears, *at that cost*, in its endless breaking-loose. A power of annihilation, underlying a power of proliferation, of renewal, of freshness, is announced by a putrefaction inevitably full of life: would there be a young generation if the cemeteries did not fill up to make room for it?

3 The Secret of Desire

There is, however, a gulf between the decaying of flesh, given in nature, and the link associating youth with the dismal operations that the landscape of graves covers up. It is characteristic of man to obliterate or hide the traces of so black an alchemy; and, just as they are buried in the ground, so they are buried in the inaccessible parts of memory. Moreover, the most difficult job of recovery has to do with the *whole* of a vast movement. It may be possible to rediscover the connection between prescriptions of respect for the dead and the desire to kill. But, detached from the rest, this view is superficial. And however complete a picture the 'festival of the king' may be, linking the decay of the royal corpse to sexual licentiousness and the frenzy of murder, it is still only a schema whose meaning must be constructed.

What I have already shown enables us to grasp what links the horror of the dead and the desire that relates to the total movement of life. This is already an improvement over the theoretical connection exhibited in a festival tableau. But I must go further and show finally that, on the other hand, the sexual life of human beings, eroticism, would not be intelligible without this connection. It is possible no doubt to imagine eroticism independently of the horror of the dead. But actually this independence is not given. I can imagine passion independently of Phaedra's circumstances: nothing is more common than the *innocent* love a woman has for a man she is entitled to love (in our day, moreover, Phaedra's passion for Hippolytus ceases to appear criminal to us . . .). But leaving aside an extreme case, which is the efficient desire to kill, sexual desire – responsive to the pull of a movement that unceasingly casts a part of humanity into the grave – is stirred, as it were, by the horror we nonetheless have of this movement. Just as the crime, which horrifies her, secretly raises and fuels Phaedra's ardour, sexuality's fragrance of death ensures all its power. This is the meaning of anguish, without which sexuality would be only an animal activity, and would not be *erotic*. If we wish to clearly represent this extraordinary effect, we have to compare it to vertigo, where fear does not paralyse but increases an involuntary desire to fall; and to uncontrollable laughter, where the laughter increases in proportion to our anguish if some dangerous element supervenes and if we laugh even though at all costs we should stop laughing.

In each of these situations, a feeling of danger – yet not so pressing as to precluded any delay – places us before a nauseating void. A void in the face of which our being is a plenum, threatened with losing its plenitude, both desiring and fearing to lose it. As if the consciousness of plenitude demanded a state of uncertainty, of suspension. As if being itself were this exploration of all possibility, always going to the extreme and always hazardous. And so, to such a stubborn defiance of impossibility, to such a full desire for emptiness, there is no end but the definitive emptiness of death.

the vertigo of desire

24

Desire Horrified at Losing and at Losing Oneself

1 Joy Demands that We Consume Our Resources of Energy

Horror associated with desire and the poverty of a desire not enhanced by any horror cannot, however, prevent us from seeing that desire has the *desirable* as its object. Anguish, when desire opens on to the void – and, sometimes, on to death – is perhaps a reason for desiring more strongly and for finding the desired object more attractive, but in the last instance the object of desire always has the meaning of delight, and this object, whatever one might say of it, is not inaccessible. It would be inexcusable to speak of eroticism without saying essentially that it centres on joy. A joy, moreover, that is excessive. In speaking of their raptures, mystics wish to give the impression of a pleasure so great that the pleasure of human love does not compare. It is hard to assess the degree of intensity of states that may not be incommunicable, perhaps, but that can never be compared with any exactness, for lack of familiarity with other states than those we personally experience. But it does seem allowable to think that we may experience, in the related domains of eroticism and religious meditation, joys so great that we are led to consider them exceptional, unique, surpassing the bounds of any joy imaginable.

Be this as it may, there can be no doubt about the excessive, exorbitant character of the transports of joy that eroticism gives us. I believe that the scepticism shown by a small number of blasé individuals is a response either to the affectedness of statements, or to the awkwardness or bad conditions of an experience. It remains to be seen how the pursuit of such great joys must go via that of horrors and repugnant objects of every sort.

What I said earlier tended to show that horror was present and played a part in erotic attraction. I furnished what might be considered sufficient evidence of this paradoxical fact, but I still have not given a clear enough

The text is from *The Accursed Share*, vol. II, The History of Eroticism; vol. III, Sovereignty, tr. Robert Hurley (Zone Books, New York, 1991), pp. 103–10. 'L'histoire de l'érotisme' was among the papers for *L'Erotisme* (Editions de Minuit, Paris, 1957). In 1953–4 Bataille began to plan a three-volume edition of *La Part maudite*. The history of eroticism was to be the second volume. It appeared posthumously in 1976. See *OC*, VIII, pp. 89–95.

account of its peculiarities. To this end, I will put forward a hypothesis that is perhaps fundamental.

I think that the feeling of horror (I am not talking about fear) does not correspond, as most people believe, to what is bad for us, to what jeopardizes their interests. On the contrary, if they horrify us, objects that otherwise would have no meaning take on the highest present value in our eyes. Erotic activity can be disgusting; it can also be noble, ethereal, excluding sexual contact, but it illustrates a principle of human behaviour in the clearest way: what we want is what uses up our strength and our resources and, if necessary, places our life in danger.

Actually, we don't always have the means to want it; our resources run out and our desire fails us (it is quite simply inhibited) as soon as we are faced with a danger that is all too unavoidable. If, however, we are blessed with enough courage and luck, the object we desire most is in principle the one most likely to endanger or destroy us. Individuals differ in their ability to sustain great losses of energy or money – or serious threats of death. But insofar as they are able (once again it is a question of strength, a quantitative matter), men risk the greatest losses and go to meet the most serious threats. If we generally believe the contrary, this is because they generally have little strength; but within their personal limits they have nonetheless been willing to spend and to expose themselves to danger. In any event, whoever has the strength and of course the means for it indulges in continual spending and repeatedly exposes himself to danger. Through examples, and through detailed analysis of the operation of contrary factors, which is most clearly apparent in eroticism, I will attempt to show the significance and scope of this law; further, I will not neglect to come back to the theoretical aspect of the problem. I have presented its general lines in the first part of this work. What I first explained starting from the movement of production, I will now show at work in the individual fever, thus in a more concrete way contributing to a fuller view by way of a detour. What cannot change in any case is a way of looking at things that is radically opposed to the correct judgement of thought.

Everything that 'justifies' our behaviour needs to be re-examined *and overturned*: how to keep from saying simply that thought is an enterprise of enslavement; it is the subordination of the heart, of passion, to incomplete economic calculations. Humanity is letting itself be led the way a child submits to a professor; a feeling of poverty paralyses it. But those general interests that it alleges are valid to the extent that fear prevails, or energy is lacking. They make sense only in the short view that obtains in official discourse; but energy abounds and fear doesn't stop anything. Between an indolent thinking and a violent course of things, discord is sovereign; and our wars are the measure of those impotent and reasonable professors who lead us.

2 Literature and Anguish; Sacrifice and Horror

For the time being, in order to illustrate the law by which we seek the greatest loss or the greatest danger, I will limit myself to two references, the first being fictional literature. For the charm of a novel is linked to the misfortunes of a hero, to the threats that hang over him. Without troubles, without anguish, his life would have nothing that captivates us, nothing that excites us and compels us to live it with him. Yet the fictional nature of the novel helps us bear what, if it were real, might exceed our strength and depress us.[1] We do well to live vicariously what we don't dare live ourselves. Not that it is a question of bearing misfortune without weakening: on the contrary, enduring it without too much anguish, we should *take pleasure* in the feeling of loss or endangerment it gives us.

But literature only continues the game of religions, of which it is the principal heir. Above all, it has received sacrifice as a legacy: at the start, this longing to lose, to lose ourselves and to look death in the face, found in the ritual of sacrifice a satisfaction it still gets from the reading of novels. In a sense, sacrifice was a novel, a fictional tale illustrated in a bloody manner. A sacrifice is no less fictional than a novel; it is not a truly dangerous, or culpable, killing; it is not a crime but rather the enactment of one; it is a game. At its beginning it is the narrative of a crime whose final episode is *performed* for the spectators by the priest and the victim. Of course, the victim is the unnamed animal – or man – that *plays* the role of the god – in other cases, of the king – whom the priest is meant to kill: the ritual is connected with a myth of which it is the periodical re-enactment. Sacrifice is no less meaningful for that: as a rule, it even seems to have reached, in horror, the limit of anguish which the spectators could bear: otherwise, how to account for excesses that confound the imagination? And how many times was it required by softened conditions to adapt to a greater sensitivity?[2] That it was of a game's nature reduced its gravity, but it always involved plunging the spectators into anguish tied to a feeling of vertiginous, contagious destruction, which fascinated while it appalled.

What matters, in any case, is not the horror itself; nor does the anguish that is maintained in literature count purely as anguish. The fondness for literature is not a vice, where anguish would be morbidly sought after. An object fascinates in sacrifice – or in literature – which is not ordinarily present in horror or anguish. In the most common circumstances, horror may only have a putrescence as its object; or anguish, a kind of void. But the object that fascinates in sacrifice is not only horrible, it is *divine*, it is the god *who agrees* to the sacrifice – who exerts an attraction and yet has only one meaning: losing oneself in death. The horror is there only to accentuate an attraction that would seem less great if he did not offer himself up to a painful agony.

The novel seldom achieves the rigour of this movement. Yet it's the same with the basic narrative as with classical tragedy: it is most engaging when the character of the hero leads him, of his own accord, to his destruction. The closer the hero gets to divinity, the greater are the losses he incurs, and the greater are the dangers he willingly faces. Only divinity verifies, in an excessive way, the principle according to which desire has loss and danger as its object. But literature is closer to us, and what it loses in the way of excess is gained in the way of verisimilitude.

3 Life, 'on the Level of Death', Founded the Riches of Religion and Art

The kind of panic followed by a prolonged explosion that might respond to the death of a king shows the strength of a monstrous temptation that draws us to ruination. We are constantly tempted to abandon work, patience and the slow accumulation of resources for a contrary movement, where suddenly we squander the accumulated riches, where we waste and lose as much as we can. The enormous loss that the death of the sovereign constitutes does not necessarily give the idea of counterbalancing its effect: better, since the mischief is done, to plunge furiously into mischief. In a sense the death of a king is like looking into a void from which we are not separated by any guard rail: the view may cause us to step back, but the image of the possible fall, which is connected with it, may also suggest that we jump, in spite or because of the death that we will find there. This depends on the sum of available energy which remains in us, under pressure, but in a certain disequilibrium.

What is certain is that the lure of the void and of ruination does not in any way correspond to a diminished vitality, and that this vertigo, instead of bringing about our destruction, ordinarily is a prelude to the *happy* explosion which is the festival. Actually, trickery and failure are the rule of these movements: in the first instance, the prohibitions prepared for the transgression of the festival, and the measureless character of the festival observes the *happy* measure nonetheless, holding in store the return of life governed by the prohibitions. But when the prohibitions corresponded to the negation of nature and to the intention men had to do away with their dependence on the natural given, the failure was intentional. Men had to cheat to avoid recognizing the impossibility for them to reduce themselves to pure mind. Their failure was thus unintentional. If they brought measure into a movement that called for measurelessness, then, on the contrary, they intentionally failed. We generally don't consent to the definitive ruin and death where measurelessness would lead us. The festival is perhaps no less fictitious than the negation of nature, but whether it has the form of literature or of ritual this time, the fiction is purposely invented. It is intentional at least, even if it puts consciousness to sleep. The desire is perhaps fooled, but with the half-complicity of children who are deluded by the playthings we give them. Only the available resources are squandered. In principle, there is no collective festival that cuts into a basic wealth, without which the coming of the next festival – measureless and measured at the same time, like the first – could not be assured. And ultimately it is not ruination, let alone death, it is joy that the pursuit of ruination attains in the festival. We draw near to the void, but not in order to fall into it. We want to be intoxicated with vertigo, and the image of the fall suffices for this.

One might say rather precisely that true joy would require a movement to the point of death, but death would put an end to it! We will never know authentic joy . . . Moreover, death itself is not necessary. I believe that our strength fails us before life does: the moment death approaches it creates a void in us that incapacitates us in advance. So not only is trickery necessary in order not to die, we must avoid dying if we wish to attain joy. Thus, only the fictitious approach of death, through literature or sacrifice, points to the joy that would fully gratify us, if its object were real – that would gratify us at least in theory, since if we were dead we would no longer be in a condition to be gratified.

Further, why rebel too stubbornly against a definitive difficulty? Not that we should turn away from death, on the contrary: stare at it, look it straight in the face, that is the most we can do. Lasting gentleness, irony and cunning are worth more than that protest about which we can predict that if it's maintained it will turn, like all literature, to trickery. In fact, protest would soon be out of the question. Ought we not in a sense aim for a joy that involves the totality of being, setting ourselves against the interests of the egoist that, albeit in spite of ourselves, we never cease to be? In this connection, to the extent that they reflected, in the dazzling play of their facets, the changing multiplicity of life, didn't tragedy and comedy, and likewise the authentic novel, respond in the best way possible to the desire to lose ourselves – tragically, comically – in the vast movement where beings endlessly lose themselves? And if it is true that trickery presides over literature, that an excess of reality would break the momentum that carries us toward the point of resolution where literature aims us, it is also true that only a real daring has enabled us to find, in the anguish of figurative death or downfall, that singularly excessive joy that engages being in its destruction. *Without this daring we cannot oppose the riches of religion and art to the poverty of animal life.*

Notes

1 Think, for example, of the completely unsustainable daring of the characters of detective novels.
2 Animal sacrifice is the earliest type, but after a period in which human sacrifice developed, animals had to be substituted for human victims. See *The Accursed Share*, vol. I, pp. 55–6.

25

The Object of Desire and the Totality of the Real

1 The Object of Desire Is the Universe, or the Totality of Being

Rather strangely, I describe what is hardest to comprehend, but at the same time it is the most familiar thing. Spectators of tragedy and readers of novels get the meaning of it without fully understanding it; and in their own way those who attend mass religiously do nothing but contemplate its essence. But if from the world of passion, where without difficulty tragedy and the novel or the sacrifice of mass form recognizable signs, I pass to the world of thought, everything shuts off: in deciding to bring the movement of tragedy, that 'sacred horror' which fascinates, into the intelligible world, I am aware that, disconcerted, the reader will have some trouble in following me.

In reality, what fascinates in this way speaks to passion but has nothing to say to the intellect. Thus it appears, in many cases, that the latter is less lucid than a simpler reaction. In point of fact, the intellect cannot justify the power of passion, and yet it naively considers itself obliged to deny that power. But in choosing to hear no other reasons but its own, the intellect errs; for it can go into the reasons of the heart if it so chooses, provided it does not insist on reducing them first to the calculation of reason. Once it has made this concession it can define a domain in which it is no longer the sole rule of conduct: it does so if it speaks of the *sacred*, of what surpasses it by nature. The most remarkable thing is that it is quite capable of speaking of what surpasses it; indeed, it cannot conceive that it might finally be able to justify itself without abandoning its own calculations.

The intellect fails, in fact, in that with its first impulse it *abstracts*, separating the objects of reflection from the concrete totality of the real. It constructs, under the name of science, a world of abstract things, copied from the things of the profane world, a partial world dominated by utility.

The text is from *The Accursed Share*, vol. II, The History of Eroticism; vol. III, Sovereignty, tr. Robert Hurley (Zone Books, New York, 1991), pp. 111–19. 'L'histoire de l'érotisme' was among the papers for *L'Erotisme* (Editions de Minuit, Paris, 1957). In 1953–4 Bataille began to plan a three-volume edition of *La Part maudite*. The history of eroticism was to be the second volume. It appeared posthumously in 1976. See *OC*, VIII, pp. 96–103.

Nothing is stranger, once we have surpassed it, than this world of the intellect where each thing must answer the question 'What is the use of that?' We then realize that the mental process of abstraction never gets out of a cycle in which one thing is related to another, for which the first is useful; the other thing in turn must be useful . . . for something else. The scythe is there for the harvest, the harvest for food, the food for labour, the labour for the factory where scythes are made. If, beyond the labour necessary for the manufacture of as many new scythes as are needed to replace the old ones, there is a surplus, its utility is defined in advance: it will serve to improve the standard of living. Nowhere do we find a *totality* that is an end in itself, that is meaningful as such, that doesn't need to justify itself by pleading its usefulness for some other thing. We escape this empty and sterile movement, this sum of objects and abstract functions that is the world of the intellect, only by entering a very different world where objects are on the same plane as the subject, where they form, together with the subject, a sovereign totality which is not divided by any abstraction and is commensurate with the entire universe.

To make this radical difference between two worlds perceptible, there is no finer example than the domain of erotic life, where the object is rarely situated on another plane than the subject.

The object of sensual desire is by nature another desire. The desire of the senses is the desire, if not to destroy oneself, at least to be consumed and to lose oneself without reservation. Now, the object of my desire does not truly respond to it except on one condition: that I awaken in it a desire equal to mine. Love in its essence is so clearly the coincidence of two desires that there is nothing more meaningful in love, even in the purest love. But the other's desire is desirable insofar as it is not known as a profane object is, from the outside (as an analysed substance is known in a laboratory). The two desires fully respond to one another only when perceived in the transparence of an intimate comprehension.

Of course, a deep repulsion underlies this comprehension: without repulsion the desire would not be boundless, as it is when it does not give way to repulsion. If it were not so great, would it have that convincing force of the lover answering her lover, in darkness and silence, that nothing, absolutely nothing separates them now? But it doesn't matter: now the object is no longer anything but that immense and anguished desire for the other desire. Of course, the object is first known by the subject as *other*, as different from it, but at the moment it reduces itself to desire, the object, in a tremor that is no less anguished, is not distinct from it: the two desires meet, intermingle and merge into one. Without doubt, the intellect remains behind and, looking at things from the outside, distinguishes two solitary desires that are basically ignorant of one another. We only know our own sensations, not those of the other. Let us say that the distinction of the intellect is so clearly contrary to the operation that it would paralyse the latter's movement if it were compelled to fade from awareness. But the intellect is not wrong merely because the illusion denounced is efficacious, because it works and no purpose would be served by depriving the deluded partners of their contentment. It is wrong in that *this is not an illusion*.

To be sure, illusion is always possible in any domain whatever. We thus fool ourselves if some incomplete perception is interpreted by us as being that of a bottle: it is not a bottle; a simple reflection gave me the impression it was, and I thought I was going to touch it. But the example proves nothing. For an error of this kind is verifiable and other times it is indeed a bottle that my hand grasps. It is true that a bottle in the hand, a correct proof, is something certain, solid. Whereas, in the most favourable case, the possibility of attaining the desire or the existence of the other and not just its external signs is generally disputed. Yet an infant is not able, the first time at least, to deduce the presence of another, *internally* similar to it, from external signs. On the contrary, it can finally infer a presence on the basis of external signs only after having learned to associate the signs with that presence, which it must first have recognized in a *total* contact, without any prior analysis.

It is not easy to isolate this contact – an internal thing on both sides – when we are talking about the embrace of adults: it occurs under conditions in which the differentiated sensations and the complex associations can never be set aside (as they are for the very young child). We are always entitled to adopt the reasoning of science: this complex of definable sensations is associated by the subject with a belief in the desire of his partner. Possibly so. But it would be futile, in my opinion, to advance further on the path of isolation. This goes without saying: we will never find in this way an *isolable* moment in which it will be certain that these conventionally isolated elements are not sufficient. Better to take the opposite approach, focusing on the *total* appearance manifested in the embrace.

This is because in the embrace *everything* is revealed anew, everything appears in a new way, and we have every reason from the start for denying the interest, and even the possibility, of abstract mental operations that would follow this unfolding. Besides, no one has attempted these operations . . . Who would presume to delineate from ponderous analyses what appeared to him at that moment? This appearance might even be defined by showing that it cannot be grasped through treatises like those published in the journals of psychology.

What strikes one from the first is a 'recession' of discernible elements, a kind of drowning in which there is nothing drowned nor any depth of water that would drown. It would be easy to say to the contrary: not at all . . . and to cite distinct impressions. These impressions do in fact remain, despite the feeling of being drowned to which I refer.

This feeling is so strange that, as a rule, one gives up the idea of describing it. Actually, we have only one way to do so. When we describe a state we ordinarily do this by singling out aspects that distinguish it, whereas here we merely have to say:

> It seems to me that the totality of what is (the universe) swallows me (physically), and if it swallows me, or since it swallows me, I can't distinguish myself from it; nothing remains, except this or that, which are less meaningful than this nothing. In a sense it is unbearable and I seem to be dying. It is at this cost, no doubt, that I am no longer myself, but an infinity in which I am lost . . .
>
> No doubt this is not entirely true; in fact, on the contrary, never have I been closer to the one who . . . but it's like an aspiration followed by an expiration: suddenly the intensity of her desire, which destroys her, terrifies me; she succumbs to it, and then, as if she were returning from the underworld, I find her again, I embrace her . . .
>
> This too is quite strange: she is no longer the one who prepared meals, washed herself, or bought small articles. She is vast, she is distant like that darkness in which she has trouble breathing, and she is so truly the vastness of the universe in her cries, her silences are so truly the emptiness of death, that I embrace her inasmuch as anguish and fever throw me into a place of death, which is the absence of bounds to the universe. But between her and me there is a kind of appeasement which, denoting rebellion and apathy at the same time, eliminates the distance that separated us from each other, and the one that separated us both from the universe.

It is painful to dwell on the inadequacy of a description, necessarily awkward and literary, whose final meaning refers to the denial of any distinct meaning. We can keep this much in mind: that in the embrace the object of desire is always the totality of being, just as it is the object of religion or art, the totality in which we lose ourselves insofar as we take ourselves for a strictly separate entity (for the pure abstraction that the isolated individual is, or thinks he is). In a word, the object of desire is the *universe*, in the form of she who in the embrace is its mirror, where we ourselves are reflected. At the most intense moment of fusion, the pure blaze of light, like a sudden flash, illuminates the immense field of possibility, on which these lovers are subtilized, annihilated, submissive in their excitement to a rarefaction which they desired.

2 The Analytical Representation of Nature and the Vague Totality, Which Is Both Horrible and Desirable

In speaking of a totality, the problem is that we usually speak of it lightly, without being able to fix our attention on that total object we speak of (when in fact it would need to be considered with the exasperated attention of the lover . . .).

The totality is truly alien to ordinary reflection in that it includes at the same time objective reality and the subject who perceives the objective reality. Neither the object nor the subject can form by themselves a totality that involves the whole. In particular, what the totality, called 'nature', is for the scientific mind is a simple caricature; it is the complete opposite of a conception according to which, in the case of an unlimited sexual desire (a desire not hindered by any reservation, not contradicted by any plan, not curbed by any work), its object is precisely *the concrete totality of the real*; and this implies that fusion with the subject which I clumsily attempted to describe.

I am obliged to linger over the analytical representation of nature, as opposed to an accurate representation of the totality, since I myself have spoken of *nature*, in a very different sense of the word. Here I must look for a terminological exactness without which I will have spoken to no purpose.

Theistic philosophy contrasts nature with the totality: for it, there is God on the one hand, and nature on the other. (In this there is even an embryo of dualism, which theology prefers not to develop.) I don't mean to defend the theistic conception of the world; on the contrary, I would like to distance myself from a representation of nature that makes it, like the scientific spirit, a substitute for God. My intention is at all costs to protect the totality from the colorations that taint it; it is neither God nor nature; it is not anything that answers to the multiple meanings of these words, nor even to any one meaning among them. Insofar as such meanings do not deceive us, what they denote is in fact only an abstract part of it. And likewise, the nature of which I speak in this book, a part of the totality, cannot be envisaged in a concrete way except insofar as it is included in the totality. As I said, it is foul and repugnant: the object that I designate in this manner does not refer to anything abstract that one might isolate and stabilize, the way I isolate and stabilize in my thought some useful object – a piece of bread, for example. This detached piece of bread is an abstraction. But the moment I eat it, it re-enters the unstable totality, with which I connect it by eating, insofar as I connect myself with the concrete totality of the real. This becomes clearer if I come back to 'foul nature': it is the animality that I can grasp in the totality which the embrace constitutes.

The moment comes when my attention in the embrace has as its object the animality of the being I embrace. I am then gripped with horror. If the being that I embrace has taken on the meaning of the totality, in that fusion which takes the place of the subject and the object, of the lover and the beloved, I experience the horror without whose possibility I cannot experience the movement of the totality. There is horror in being: this horror is repugnant animality, whose presence I discover at the very point where the totality of being takes form. But the horror I experience does not repel me, the disgust I feel does not nauseate me. Were I more naive I might even imagine, and moreover I might even claim, that I did not experience this horror and this disgust. But I may, on the contrary, *thirst for it*; far from escaping, I may resolutely quench my thirst with this horror that makes me press closer, with this disgust that has become my delight. For this I have *filthy* words at my disposal, words that sharpen the feeling I have of touching on the *intolerable* secret of being. I may say these words in order to cry out the uncovered secret, wanting to be sure I am not the only one to know it; at this moment I no longer doubt that I am embracing the totality without which I was only *outside*: I reach orgasm.

Such moments require the growing intensity of sensations that inform us of the totality and braid together its objective and subjective elements inextricably: this is the complex of sensations that proclaims at the same time the other and oneself – that is not in any way reducible to an analysis where nothing ever appears but abstract elements, colours, sounds and so on, whose ground is always the totality . . . If the sensations do not have their greatest intensity, it is possible for us to isolate specific objects on the field of the totality; whereupon we no longer know anything but those objects; we know them clearly and distinctly, but the presence of the totality escapes us. The sense of the totality demands an extreme intensity of *the vaguest sensations, which reveal to us nothing clear or distinct*: these are essentially animal sensations, which are not merely rudimentary, which bring back our animality, effecting the reversal without which we could not reach the totality. Their high-pitched intensity overruns us, and they suffocate us at the very moment they overthrow us morally. The negation of nature (of animality) is what separates us from the concrete totality: it inserts us in the abstractions of a human order – where, like so many artful fairies, work, science and bureaucracy change us into abstract entities. But the embrace restores us, not to nature (which is itself, if it is not reintegrated, only a detached part), but rather to the totality in which man has his share by *losing himself*. For an embrace is not just a fall into the animal muck, but the anticipation of death, and of the putrefaction that follows it. Here eroticism is analogous to a tragedy, where the hecatomb at the end brings together all the characters. The point is that the totality reached (yet indefinitely out of reach) is reached only at the price of a sacrifice: eroticism reaches it precisely inasmuch as love is a kind of immolation.[1]

Note

1 We know that the ancients identified, at least in poetry, the possession of a woman with sacrifice. It seemed that except for the dying, women were treated in this instance like sacrificial animals. Here I must stress the fact that woman, more than man, is the centre of eroticism. She alone is able to devote herself to it, provided she doesn't have children in her care. Whereas man is nearly always a working or warring animal first of all. However, I have spoken of eroticism mainly in reference to man. I did not think it necessary to examine each of the situations I have spoken of from a woman's point of view. I was less anxious to fully describe the different aspects of eroticism than to grasp the movement whereby human existence encounters the totality in eroticism.

26

Epilogue to the History of Eroticism

In the universe as a whole, energy is available without limit, but *on the human scale* which is ours, we are led to take account of the quantity of energy we have at our disposal. We do this spontaneously, but in return we should recognize the need to consider another fact: *we have quantities of energy that we are obliged to spend in any case.* We can always dry up its source; we would only have to work less and be idle, at least in part. But then leisure is one way among others of squandering – of destroying – the surplus energy, or, to simplify, the surplus available resources. Twenty-four hours of leisure activities cost, in positive terms, the energy necessary for the production of a day's supply of necessary provisions; or negatively, if one prefers, a non-production of everything a worker would have produced in this lapse of time. Pure leisure (and of course labour strikes) is merely added to the outlets that the available energy has beyond what is required for basic necessities. These outlets are essentially eroticism, luxury products (whose energy value is calculable in labour time) and amusements, which are the small change of the holiday; then there is work, which in some way increases the amount of production we will have at our disposal; and lastly, wars . . .

Of course, what we spend in one category is in principle lost for the others. There are many possibilities of slippage: alcohol, war and holidays involve us in eroticism, but this means simply that the possible expenditures in one category are ultimately reduced by those we make in the others, so that only the profits found in war truly alter this principle; even so, in most cases these profits correspond to the losses of the vanquished . . . We need to make a principle of the fact that sooner or later the sum of excess energy that is managed for us by a labour so great that it limits the share available for erotic purposes will be spent in a catastrophic war.

The text is from *The Accursed Share*, vol. II, The History of Eroticism; vol. III, Sovereignty, tr. Robert Hurley (Zone Books, New York, 1991), pp. 187–91. 'L'histoire de l'érotisme' was among the papers for *L'Erotisme* (Editions de Minuit, Paris, 1957). In 1953–4 Bataille began to plan a three-volume edition of *La Part maudite*. The history of eroticism was to be the second volume. It appeared posthumously in 1976. See *OC*, VIII, pp. 161–5.

Of course, it would be childish to conclude right away that if we relaxed more and gave the erotic game a larger share of energy the danger of war would decrease. It would decrease only if the easing off occurred in such a way that the world did lose an already precarious equilibrium.

Indeed, this picture is so clear that we can immediately draw a different conclusion: we will not be able to decrease the risk of war before we have reduced, or begun to reduce, the general disparity of standards of living, that is, the general disequilibrium. This way of looking at things leads to a judgement that is clearly only theoretical at present: it is necessary to produce with a view to raising the global standard of living. So here I am reduced to repeating what every rational man already knows. To the common opinion I only need to add one particular: if nothing along such lines were to take place, war would soon be unavoidable.

Yet I don't wish to dwell on such a gloomy prospect. If the standard of living is prevented from rising, this is insofar as there exists in the world what is called a state of Cold War, accentuated at one point by actual war. We can say, consequently, that there exists for the time being a third solution, which is the present solution or Cold War. It is not very reassuring, but it affords us the time to think that barring war or extreme military tension a general raising of the standard of living might occur.

So there remains in the world a chance for peace connected with this resolve: to affirm, against all opposition, the unconditional value of a politics that would level individual resources, adding that such a politics can be pursued, exactly insofar as possible, without ceasing to respond to the immediate necessities imposed by the Cold War.

Once again, I cannot contribute anything here but these banalities, which will appear quite empty to most. It was not necessary to formulate a theory of eroticism for the purpose. Indeed, their relation with a theory of this kind ends up reducing the significance of these political considerations. In appearance at least, for the theory in question is essentially a historical exposition of the forms of eroticism, but an element is missing from the exposition.

Eroticism is in any case, even to the small extent that it has a history itself, on the fringe of history properly speaking, that is, military or political history. As it happens, this aspect of the matter carries a meaning that allows me to broach the conclusion of the historical account this book constitutes. For there remains, under the conditions I have laid out, the possibility of an episode of eroticism's history. We have known eroticism on the fringe of history, but if history finally came to a close, even if it drew near its close, eroticism would no longer be *on the fringe of history*. It would thus cease to be a minor truth, whose importance is overshadowed now, as it has been for a long time, by the factors that make up history. It might receive the full light of day and appear clearly to consciousness. True, the idea that history may end is shocking, but I can put it forward as a hypothesis. To my way of thinking, history would be ended if the disparity of rights and of living standards were reduced: this would be the precondition of an ahistorical mode of existence of which erotic activity is the expressive form. From this necessarily hypothetical point of view, consciousness of erotic truth anticipates the end of history; this consciousness brings profound indifference into the present time, the 'apathy' of an ahistorical judgement, of a judgement tied to perspectives that are very different from those of men totally engaged in struggle. This does not in any way mean that the perspectives of those who join battle are senseless from my point of view. But neither do they have the sense that the opposed parties ascribe to them. We know beforehand that the resolution of the combat lies beyond its internal perspectives: the two camps are both wrong in the sense that the defenders are protecting indefensible positions, and the attackers are attacking unassailable positions. We can't do anything, on the contrary, that goes against the levelling of living standards. Neither can we reduce the meaning of productive activity to its usefulness. The meaning of any activity is situated beyond its useful value, but we cannot grasp it so long as we insist on remaining confined to the perspective of the battle.

Actually, the circumstances we are experiencing open up precise possibilities in this regard. The battle cannot truly be decisive except on one condition, that it fail, that it not go to the limit. If the end of history is to emerge from these current convulsions, this is conditional on a *détente*, for nothing else is capable of bringing it about. A victory inevitably won on a heap of rubble would sanction the insensibility on which a victorious party would have based itself. If the vicissitudes of men come to an end, if the gross stupidity of a definitive victory is spared them, history might have the only end it can reach . . . in a fizzling-out [*en queue de poisson*].

We cannot by struggling find a truth on which to base anything: in struggling we never see more than a part of things, even if the movement opposing the will to remain where we are has its privileged value. On the contrary, it is by distancing ourselves from every reason for fighting, by achieving perfect moments, which we know we can't surpass, that we have the power to assign to the movement of history that end which can only be insofar as it escapes us.

This much that is clear might finally emerge from my book – and from the epilogue that follows it.

Men committed to political struggle will never be able to yield to the truth of eroticism. Erotic activity always takes place at the expense of the forces committed to their combat. But what is one to think of men so blinded as to be ignorant of the motives for the cruelty they unleash? At least we can be certain they are lying. But by no means can we try to replace their directives with our own. We don't expect anything from a *direction*.

We cannot base our hopes on anything but a *détente*, in which a wisdom coming from the outside might make itself heard. Of course this kind of wisdom is a challenge. But how could we not challenge the world by offering it the appeasement it needs? This can only be done rashly, in defiance of violent language, and far from prophetic agitation; it can only be done in defiance of politics.

Moreover, it is time in any case to oppose this mendacious world with the resources of an irony, a shrewdness, a serenity without illusions. For, supposing we were to lose, we would be able to lose cheerfully, without condemning, without prophesying. We are not looking for a rest. If the world insists on blowing up, we may be the only ones to grant it the right to do so, while giving ourselves the right to have spoken in vain.

PART V

Sovereignty

27

To Whom

The positing of a religious attitude that would result from clear consciousness, and would exclude, if not the ecstatic form of religion, then at least its mystical form, differs radically from the attempts at fusion that exercise minds anxious to remedy the weakness of current religious positions.

Those in the religious world who are alarmed about the lack of harmony, who look for the link between the different disciplines, who are determined to deny that which opposes the sannyasi to the Roman prelate, or the Sufi to the Kierkegaardian pastor, complete the emasculation – on both sides – of that which already originates in a compromise of the intimate order with the order of things. The spirit farthest removed from the virility necessary for joining *violence and consciousness* is the spirit of 'synthesis'. The endeavour to sum up that which separate religious possibilities have revealed, and to make their shared content the principle of a human life raised to universality, seems unassailable despite its insipid results, but for anyone *to whom human life is an experience to be carried as far as possible*, the *universal sum* is necessarily that of the religious sensibility in time. Synthesis is most clearly what reveals the need to firmly link this world to that which the religious sensibility is in its universal sum in time. This clear revelation of a decline of the whole living religious world (salient in these synthetic forms that abandon the narrowness of a tradition) was not given so long as the archaic manifestations of religious feeling appeared to us independently of their meaning, like hieroglyphs that could be deciphered only in a formal way; but if that meaning is now given, if, in particular, the behaviour of sacrifice, the least clear but the most divine and the most common, ceases to be closed to us, the whole of human experience is restored to us. And if we raise ourselves personally to the highest degree of clear consciousness, it is no longer the servile thing in us, but rather the *sovereign* whose presence in the world, from head to foot, from animality to science and from the archaic tool to the non-sense of poetry, is that of universal humanity. Sovereignty

The text is from *Theory of Religion*, tr. Robert Hurley (Zone Books, New York, 1992), pp. 109–11. Appearing in France in 1974 through Editions Gallimard, the text was written in 1948. See *OC*, VII, pp. 349–50.

designates the movement of free and internally wrenching violence that animates the whole, dissolves into tears, into ecstasy and into bursts of laughter, and reveals the impossible in laughter, ecstasy or tears. But the impossible thus revealed is not an equivocal position; it is the sovereign self-consciousness that, precisely, no longer turns away from itself.

28

Hegel, Death and Sacrifice[1]

The animal dies. But the death of the animal is the becoming of consciousness.

1 Death

Man's negativity

In the *Lectures* of 1805–6, at the moment of his thought's full maturity, during the period when he was writing *The Phenomenology of Spirit*, Hegel expressed in these terms the black character of humanity:

> Man is that night, that empty Nothingness, which contains everything in its undivided simplicity: the wealth of an infinite number of representations, of images, not one of which comes precisely to mind, or which [moreover] are not [there] insofar as they are really present. It is the night, the interiority – or – the intimacy of Nature which exists here: [the] pure personal-Ego. In phantasmagorical representations it is night on all sides: here suddenly surges up a blood-spattered head; there, another, white, apparition; and they disappear just as abruptly. That is the night that one perceives if one looks a man in the eyes; then one is delving into a night which becomes terrible; it is the night of the world which then presents itself to us.[2]

Of course, this 'beautiful text', where Hegel's Romanticism finds expression, is not to be understood loosely. If Hegel was a romantic, it was perhaps in a *fundamental* manner (he was at any rate a romantic at the beginning – in his youth – when he was a commonplace revolutionary), but he did not see in Romanticism the method by which a proud spirit deems itself capable of subordinating the real world to the arbitrariness of its own dreams. Alexander Kojève, in citing them, says of these lines that they

The text is from 'Hegel, death and sacrifice', tr. Jonathan Strauss, *Yale French Studies*, 78 (1990), pp. 9–28. The essay originally appeared in *Deucalion*, 5 (1955). See *OC*, XII, pp. 326–45.

express 'the central and final idea of Hegelian philosophy', which is 'the idea that the foundation and the source of human objective reality [*Wirklichkeit*] and empirical existence [*Dasein*] are the Nothingness which manifests itself as negative or creative Action, free and self-conscious'.

To permit access to Hegel's disconcerting world, I have felt obliged to mark, by a careful examination, both its violent contrasts and its ultimate unity.

For Kojève, 'the "dialectical" or anthropological philosophy of Hegel is in the final analysis a *philosophy of death* (or, which is the same thing, of atheism)' (K, 537; TEL, 539).

But if man is 'death living a human life' (K, 548; TEL, 550), man's negativity, given in death by virtue of the fact that man's death is essentially voluntary (resulting from risks assumed without necessity, without biological reasons), is nevertheless the principle of action. Indeed, for Hegel, action is negativity, and negativity action. On the one hand, the man who negates nature – by introducing into it, like a flip-side, the anomaly of a 'pure, personal ego' – is present within that nature's heart like a night within light, like an intimacy within the exteriority of those things which are *in themselves* – like a phantasmagoria in which nothing takes shape but to evanesce, nothing appears but to disappear, where nothing exists except absorbed without respite in the *annihilation* of time, from which it draws the beauty of a dream. But there is a complementary aspect: this negation of Nature is not merely given in consciousness – where that which exists *in itself* appears (but only to disappear) – this negation is exteriorized, and in being exteriorized, really (*in itself*) changes the reality of nature. Man works and fights; he transforms the given; he transforms nature and in destroying it he creates a world, a world which was not. On the one hand there is poetry, the destruction that has surged up and diluted itself, a *blood-spattered* head; on the other hand there is action, work, struggle. On the one hand, 'pure Nothingness', where man 'differs from Nothingness only *for a certain time*' (K, 573; TEL, 575). On the other, a historical world, where man's negativity, that nothingness that gnaws him from within, creates the whole of concrete reality (at once object and subject, real world changed or unchanged, man who thinks and changes the world).

Hegel's philosophy is a philosophy of death – or of atheism[3]

The essential – and the original – characteristic of Hegelian philosophy is to describe the totality of what is; and, consequently, at the same time that it accounts for everything which appears before our eyes, to give an integrated account of the thought and language which express – and reveal – that appearance.

'In my opinion,' says Hegel, 'everything depends on one's expressing and understanding Truth not (only) as substance, but also as subject.'[4]

In other words, natural knowledge is incomplete, it does not and cannot envisage any but abstract entities, isolated from a whole, from an indissoluble totality, which alone is concrete. Knowledge must at the same time be anthropological: 'in addition to the ontological bases of natural reality,' Kojève writes, '[knowledge] must find those of human reality, which alone is capable of being revealed through Discourse' (K, 528, TEL, 530). Of course, this anthropology does not envisage man as do the modern sciences but as a movement impossible to isolate from the heart of the totality. In a sense, it is actually a theology, where man has taken the place of God.

But for Hegel, the human reality which he places at the heart, and centre, of the totality is very different from that of Greek philosophy. His anthropology is that of the Judaeo-Christian tradition, which emphasizes man's *liberty*, *historicity* and *individuality*. Like Judaeo-Christian man, the Hegelian man is a spiritual (i.e., 'dialectical') being. Yet, for the Judaeo-Christian world, 'spirituality' is fully realized and manifest only in the hereafter, and Spirit properly speaking, truly 'objectively real' Spirit, is God: 'an infinite and eternal being'. According to Hegel, the 'spiritual' or 'dialectical' being is 'necessarily *temporal* and finite'. This means that death alone assures the existence of a 'spiritual' or 'dialectical' being, in the Hegelian sense. If the animal which constitutes man's natural being did not die, and – what is more – if death did not dwell in him as the source of his anguish – and all the more so in that he seeks it out, desires it and sometimes freely chooses it – there would be no man or liberty, no history or individual. In other words, if he revels in what nonetheless frightens him, if he is the being, identical with himself, who risks (identical) being itself, then man is truly a man: he separates himself from the animal. Henceforth he is no longer, like a stone, an immutable given, he bears within him *negativity*; and the force, the violence of negativity casts him into the incessant movement of history, which changes him and which alone realizes the totality of the concrete real through time. Only history has the power to finish what is, to finish it in the passage of time. And so the idea of an eternal and immutable God is in this perspective merely a provisional end, which survives while awaiting something better. Only completed history and the spirit of the Sage (of Hegel) – in whom history revealed, then revealed in full, the development of being and the totality of its becoming – occupy a sovereign position, which God only provisionally occupies, as a regent.

The tragi-comic aspect of man's divinity

This way of seeing things can with justice be considered comic. Besides, Hegel never expressed it explicitly. The texts where it is *implicitly* affirmed are ambiguous, and their extreme difficulty ultimately kept them from full consideration. Kojève himself is circumspect. He does not dwell on them

and avoids drawing precise conclusions. In order to express appropriately
the situation Hegel got himself into, no doubt involuntarily, one would
need the tone, or at least, in a restrained from, the horror of tragedy. But
things would quickly take on a comic appearance.

Be that as it may, to pass through death is so absent from the divine
figure that a myth situated in the tradition associated death, and the agony
of death, with the eternal and unique God of the Judaeo-Christian sphere.
The death of Jesus partakes of comedy to the extent that one cannot
unarbitrarily introduce the forgetting of his eternal divinity – which is his –
into the consciousness of an omnipotent and infinite God. Before Hegel's
'absolute knowledge', the Christian myth was already based precisely on
the fact that nothing divine is possible (in the pre-Christian sense of *sacred*)
which is finite. But the vague consciousness in which the (Christian) myth
of the death of God took form differed, nonetheless, from that of Hegel: in
order to misrepresent a figure of God that limited the infinite as the totality,
it was possible to add on, in contradiction with its basis, a movement
toward the finite.

Hegel was able – and it was necessary for him – to add up the sum (the
totality) of the movements which were produced in history. But humour, it
seems, is incompatible with work and its necessary assiduity. I shall return
to this subject; I have merely, for the moment, shuffled cards . . . It is
difficult to pass from a humanity humiliated by divine grandeur to
that . . . of the apotheosized and sovereign Sage, his pride swollen with
human vanity.

A fundamental text

In what I have written up to this point, only one necessity emerges in a
precise fashion: there can be authentic wisdom (absolute wisdom, or in
general anything approaching it) only if the Sage raises himself, if I can put
it this way, to the height of death, at whatever anguish to him.

A passage from the preface to the *Phenomenology of Spirit*[5] forcefully
expresses the necessity of such an attitude. There is no doubt from the start
of the 'capital importance' of this admirable text, not only for an understanding of Hegel, but in all regards.

'Death', writes Hegel,

– if we wish so to name that unreality – is the most terrible thing there
is and to uphold the work of death is the task which demands the
greatest strength. Impotent beauty hates this awareness, because understanding makes this demand of beauty, a requirement which
beauty cannot fulfil. Now, the life of Spirit is not that life which is
frightened of death, and spares itself destruction, but that life which

assumes death and lives with it. Spirit attains its truth only by finding itself in absolute dismemberment. It is not that (prodigious) power by being the Positive that turns away from the Negative, as when we say of something: this is nothing or (this is) false and, having (thus) disposed of it, pass from there to something else; no, Spirit is that power only to the degree in which it contemplates the Negative face to face (and) dwells with it. This prolonged sojourn is the magical force which transposes the negative into given-Being.

The human negation of nature and of the natural being of man

In principle, I ought to have started the passage just cited at an earlier point. I did not want to weigh this text down by giving the 'enigmatic' lines which precede it. But I shall sketch out the sense of the omitted lines by restating Kojève's interpretation, without which the consequences, in spite of an appearance of relative clarity, would remain closed to us.

For Hegel, it is both fundamental and altogether worthy of astonishment that human understanding (that is, language, discourse) should have had the force (an incomparable force) to separate its constitutive elements from the totality. These elements (this tree, this bird, this stone) are in fact inseparable from the whole. They are 'bound together by spatial and temporal, indeed material, bonds which are indissoluble'. Their separation implies the human negativity toward nature of which I spoke, without pointing out its decisive consequences. For the man who negates nature could not in any way live outside of it. He is not merely a man who negates nature, he is first of all an animal, that is to say the very thing he negates: he cannot therefore negate nature without negating himself. The intrinsic totality of man is reflected in Kojève's bizarre expression, that totality is first of all nature (natural being), it is 'the anthropomorphic animal' (nature, the animal indissolubly linked to the whole of nature, and which supports man). Thus human negativity, man's effective desire to negate nature in destroying it – in reducing it to his own ends, as when, for example, he makes a tool of it (and the tool will be the model of an object isolated from nature) – cannot stop at man himself; insofar as he is nature, man is exposed to his own negativity. To negate nature is to negate the animal which props up man's negativity. It is undoubtedly not the understanding, breaker of nature's unity, which seeks man's death, and yet the separating action of the understanding implies the monstrous energy of thought, of the 'pure abstract I', which is essentially opposed to fusion, to the inseparable character of the elements – constitutive of the whole – which firmly upholds their separation.

It is the very separation of man's being, it is his isolation from nature, and, consequently, his isolation in the midst of his own kind, which condemn him to disappear definitively. The animal, negating nothing, lost in a global animality to which it offers no opposition – just as that animality is itself lost in nature (and in the totality of all that is) – does not truly disappear . . . No doubt the individual fly dies, but today's flies are the same as those of last year. Last year's have died? . . . Perhaps, but *nothing* has disappeared. The flies remain, equal to themselves like the waves of the sea. This seems contrived: a biologist can separate a fly from the swarm, all it takes is a brushstroke. But he separates it *for himself*, he does not separate it for the flies. To separate itself from the others a fly would need the monstrous force of the understanding; then it would name itself and do what the understanding normally effects by means of language, which alone founds the separation of elements and by founding it founds itself on it, within a world formed of separated and denominated entities. But in this game the human animal finds death; it finds precisely human death, the only one which frightens, which freezes – but which only frightens and transfixes the man who is absorbed in his future disappearance, to the extent that he is a separated and irreplaceable being. The only true death supposes separation and, through the discourse which separates, the consciousness of being separated.

'Impotent beauty hates the understanding'

Up to this point, Hegel's text presents a *simple* and *common* truth, but one enunciated in a philosophical manner which is, properly speaking, sibylline. In the passage from the Preface cited above, Hegel, on the contrary, affirms and describes a *personal* moment of violence – Hegel, in other words the Sage, to whom an absolute knowledge has conferred definitive satisfaction. This is not an unbridled violence. What Hegel unleashes here is not the violence of nature, it is the energy, or the violence, of the understanding – the negativity of the understanding – opposing itself to the pure beauty of the dream, which cannot act, which is impotent.

Indeed, the beauty of the dream is on that side of the world where nothing is yet separated from what surrounds it, where each element, in contrast to the abstract objects of the understanding, is given concretely, in space and time. But beauty cannot *act*. It can only be and preserve itself. Through action it would no longer exist, since action would first destroy what beauty is: beauty, which seeks nothing, which is, which refuses to move itself but which is disturbed by the force of the understanding. Moreover, beauty does not have the power to respond to the request of the understanding, which asks it to uphold and preserve the work of *human* death. Beauty is incapable of it, in the sense that to uphold that work, it would be engaged in action. Beauty is sovereign, it is an end, or it is not: that is why it is not susceptible to acting, why it is, even in principle, powerless and why it cannot yield to the active negation of the understanding, which changes the world and itself becomes other than it is.[6]

This beauty without consciousness of itself *cannot therefore* really – but not for the same reason as life, which 'recoils in horror from death and wants to save itself from annihilation' – bear death and preserve itself in it. This impotent beauty at least suffers from feeling the break-up of the profoundly indissoluble totality of what is (of the concrete-real). Beauty would like to remain the sign of an accord of the real with itself. It cannot become conscious negativity, awakened in dismemberment, and the lucid gaze, absorbed in the negative. This latter attitude presupposes the violent and laborious struggle of man against nature and is its end. That is the historic struggle where man constitutes himself as 'subject' or as 'abstract I' of the 'understanding', as a separated and named being.

'That is to say', Kojève clarifies, 'that thought and the discourse which reveals the real are born of the negative Action which actualizes Nothingness by annihilating Being: the given being of Man (in the Struggle) and the given being of Nature (through Work – which results, moreover, from the real contact with death in the Struggle). That is to say, therefore, that the human being himself is none other than that Action: he is death which lives a human life' (K, 548; TEL, 550).

I want to insist on the continual connection between an abyssal aspect and a tough, down-to-earth aspect in this philosophy, the only one having the ambition to be complete. The divergent possibilities of opposed human figures confront each other and assemble in it: the figure of the dying man and of the proud one, who turns from death, the figure of the master and that of the man pinned to his work, the figure of the revolutionary and that of the sceptic, whose egotistical interest limits desire. This philosophy is not only a philosophy of death. It is also one of class struggle and work.

But within the limits of this study I do not intend to envisage this other side. I would like to compare that Hegelian doctrine of death with what we know about 'sacrifice'.

2 Sacrifice

Sacrifice, on the one hand, and on the other, the gaze of Hegel absorbed in death and sacrifice

I shall not speak of the interpretation of sacrifice which Hegel gives in the chapter of the *Phenomenology* devoted to religion.[7] It no doubt makes sense in the development of the chapter, but it strays from the essential and, from the point of view of the theory of sacrifice, it is, in my opinion, of less interest than the implicit representation which is given in the text of the Preface and which I shall continue to analyse.

Concerning sacrifice, I can essentially say that, on the level of Hegel's philosophy, man has, in a sense, revealed and founded human truth by sacrificing; in sacrifice he destroyed the animal[8] in himself, allowing himself and the animal to survive only as that non-corporeal truth which Hegel describes and which makes of man – in Heidegger's words – a being unto death (*Sein zum Tode*), or – in the words of Kojève himself – 'death which lives a human life'.

Actually, the problem of Hegel is given in the action of sacrifice. In sacrifice, death, on the one hand, essentially strikes the corporeal being; and on the other hand, it is precisely in sacrifice that 'death lives a *human* life'. It should even be said that sacrifice is the precise response to Hegel's requirement, the original formulation of which I repeat: 'Spirit attains its truth only by finding itself in absolute dismemberment. It does not attain that (prodigious) power by being the Positive that turns away from the Negative . . . no, Spirit is that power only in the degree to which it contemplates the Negative face to face [and] dwells with it . . .'

If one takes into account the fact that the institution of sacrifice is practically universal, it is clear that negativity, incarnated in man's death, not only is the arbitrary construction of Hegel, but also has played a role in the spirit of the simplest men, without any common grounds comparable to those which are regulated once and for all by the ceremonies of a church – but nonetheless in a univocal manner. It is striking to see that across the world a communal *negativity* has maintained a strict parallelism in the development of rather stable institutions, which have the same form and the same effects.

Whether he lives or dies, man cannot immediately know death

I shall speak later of the profound differences between the man of sacrifice, acting in ignorance (unconscious) of the full scope of what he is doing, and the Sage (Hegel) surrendering to the implications of a knowledge which, in his own eyes, is absolute.

Despite these differences, the question of manifesting the negative still remains (and still under a concrete form, i.e., at the heart of the totality, whose constitutive elements are inseparable). The privileged manifestation of negativity is death, but death, in fact, reveals nothing. In theory, it is his natural, animal being whose death reveals man to himself, but the revelation never takes place. For when the animal being supporting him dies, the human being himself ceases to be. In order for man to reveal himself ultimately to himself, he would have to die, but he would have to do it while living – watching himself ceasing to be. In other words, death itself would have to become (self-) consciousness at the very moment that it annihilates the conscious being. In a sense, this is what takes place (what at least is on the point of taking place, or which takes place in a fugitive, ungraspable manner) by means of a subterfuge. In the sacrifice, the sacrificer identifies himself with the animal that is struck down dead. And so he dies in seeing himself die, and even, in a certain way, by his own will, one in spirit with the sacrificial weapon. But it is a comedy!

At least it would be a comedy if some other method existed which could reveal to the living the invasion of death: that finishing off of the finite being, which *his* negativity – which kills him, *ends* him and definitively suppresses him – accomplishes alone and which it alone can accomplish. For Hegel, *satisfaction* can only take place, desire can be appeased only in the consciousness of death. If it were based on the exclusion of death, satisfaction would contradict that which death designates, if the satisfied being who is not conscious, not utterly conscious, of what in a constitutive manner he is, i.e., mortal, were eventually to be driven from satisfaction by death. That is why the consciousness that he has *of himself* must reflect (must mirror) the movement of negativity which creates him, which makes a man of him for the very reason that it will one day kill him.

He will be killed by his own negativity, but for him, thereafter, there will be nothing left; his is a creative death, but if the consciousness of death – of the marvellous magic of death – does not touch him before he dies, during his life it will seem that death is not destined to reach him, and so the death awaiting him will not give him a *human* character. Thus, at all costs, man must live at the moment that he really dies, or he must live with the impression of really dying.

Knowledge of death cannot do without a subterfuge: spectacle

This difficulty proclaims the necessity of *spectacle*, or of *representation* in general, without the practice of which it would be possible for us to remain alien and ignorant in respect to death, just as beasts apparently are. Indeed, nothing is less animal than fiction, which is more or less separated from the real, from death.

Man does not live by bread alone, but also by the comedies with which he willingly deceives himself. In man it is the animal, it is the natural being, which eats. But man takes part in rites and performances. Or else he can read: to the extent that it is sovereign – authentic – literature prolongs in him the haunting magic of performances, tragic or comic.

In tragedy,[9] at least, it is a question of our identifying with some character who dies, and of believing that we die, although we are alive. Furthermore, pure and simple imagination suffices, but it has the same meaning as the classic subterfuges, performances or books, to which the masses have recourse.

Agreement and disagreement between naive behaviours and
Hegel's lucid reaction

By associating it with sacrifice and, thereby, with the primary theme of *representation* (in art, in festivals, in performances), I have sought to demonstrate that Hegel's reaction is fundamental human behaviour. It is not a fantasy or a strange attitude, it is *par excellence* the expression endlessly repeated by tradition. It is not Hegel alone, it is all of humanity which everywhere always sought, obliquely, to seize what death both gave and took away from humanity.

Between Hegel and the man of sacrifice there nevertheless remains a profound difference. Hegel was *conscious* of his representation of the negative: he situated it, lucidly, in a definite point of the 'coherent discourse' which revealed him to himself. That totality included the discourse which reveals it. The man of sacrifice, who lacked a discursive consciousness of what he did, had only a 'sensual' awareness, i.e., an obscure one, reduced to an unintelligible emotion. It is true that Hegel himself, beyond discourse, and in spite of himself (in an 'absolute dismemberment'), received the shock of death even more violently. More violently, above all, for the primary reason that the broad movement of discourse extended its reach beyond limits, i.e., within the framework of the totality of the real. Beyond the slightest doubt, for Hegel, the fact that he was still alive was simply an aggravation. The man of sacrifice, on the other hand, maintains his life essentially. He maintains it not only in the sense that life is necessary for the representation of death, but [also in the sense that] he seeks to *enrich* it. But from an external perspective, the palpable and *intentional* excitement of sacrifice was of greater interest than the *involuntary* sensitivity of Hegel. The excitement of which I speak is well known, is definable; it is *sacred* horror: the richest and the most agonizing experience, which does not limit itself to dismemberment but which, on the contrary, opens itself, like a theatre curtain, on to a realm beyond this world, where the rising light of day transfigures all things and destroys their limited meaning.

Indeed, if Hegel's attitude opposes learned consciousness and the limitless organization of a discursive thinking to the naïveté of sacrifice, still that consciousness and that organization remain unclear on one point; one cannot say that Hegel was unaware of the 'moment' of sacrifice; this 'moment' is included, implicated in the whole movement of the *Phenomenology* – where it is the negativity of death, insofar as it is assumed, which makes a man of the human animal. But because he did not see that sacrifice in itself bore witness to the *entire* movement of death,[10] the final experience – the one peculiar to the Sage – described in the Preface to the *Phenomenology* was at first *initial and universal* – he did not know to what extent he was right – with what precision he described the intimate movement of negativity; he did not clearly separate death from the feeling of sadness to which naive experience opposes a sort of shunting yard of the emotions.

Pleasure and the sadness of death

It was precisely the univocal character of death for Hegel that inspired the following commentary from Kojève, which applies, again, to the passage from the Preface: (K, 549; TEL, 551). 'Certainly, the idea of death does not heighten the *well-being* of Man; it does not make him *happy* nor does it give him any pleasure.' Kojève wondered in what way satisfaction results from a familiarity with the negative, from a *tête-à-tête* with death. He believed it his duty, out of decency, to reject vulgar satisfaction. The fact that Hegel himself said, in this respect, that Spirit 'only attains it truth by finding itself in absolute dismemberment' goes together, in principle, with Kojève's negation. Consequently, it would even be superfluous to insist . . . Kojève simply states that the idea of death 'is alone capable if satisfying man's pride'. . . . Indeed, the desire to be 'recognized', which Hegel places at the origin of historical struggles, could be expressed in an intrepid attitude, of the sort that shows a character to its best advantage. 'It is only', says Kojève, 'in being or in becoming aware of one's mortality or finitude, in existing and in feeling one's existence in a universe without a beyond or without a God, that Man can affirm his liberty, his historicity and his individuality – "unique in all the world" – and have them be recognized.' (Ibid.). But if Kojève sets aside vulgar satisfaction – happiness – he now also sets aside Hegel's 'absolute dismemberment': indeed, such dismemberment is not easily reconciled with the desire for recognition.

Satisfaction and dismemberment coincide, however, in one point, but here they harmonize with *pleasure*. This coincidence takes place in 'sacrifice'; it is generally understood as the *naive form of life*, as every existence in present time, which manifests what man *is*: the novelty which he signifies in the world after he has become *man*, on the condition that he has satisfied his '*animal*' needs.

At any rate, *pleasure*, or at least sensual pleasure, is such that in respect to it Kojève's affirmation would be difficult to uphold: the idea of death helps, in a certain manner and in certain cases, to multiply the pleasures of the senses. I go so far as to believe that, under the form of defilement, the world (or rather the general imagery) of death is at the base of eroticism. The feeling of sin is connected in lucid consciousness to the idea of death, and *in the same manner* the feeling of sin is connected with pleasure.[11] There is in fact no *human* pleasure without some irregularity in its circumstances, without the breaking of an interdiction – the simplest, and the most powerful, of which is currently that of nudity.

Moreover, possession was associated in its time with the image of sacrifice; it was a sacrifice in which woman was the victim . . . That association from ancient poetry is very meaningful; it refers back to a precise state of sensibility in which the sacrificial element, the feeling of sacred horror itself, joined, in a weakened state, to a tempered pleasure; in which, too, the taste for sacrifice and the emotion which it released seemed in no way contrary to the ultimate uses of pleasure.

It must be said too that sacrifice, like tragedy, was an element of a celebration; it bespoke a blind, pernicious joy and all the danger of that joy, and yet this precisely the principle of *human joy*; it wears out and threatens with death all who get caught up in its movement.

Gay anguish, anguished gaiety

To the association of death and pleasure, which is not a given, at least is not an immediate given in consciousness, is obviously opposed the sadness of death, always in the background of consciousness. In principle, *consciously*, humanity 'recoils in horror before death'. In principle, the destructive effects of negativity have nature as their object. But for man's negativity to drive him into a confrontation with danger, for him to make of himself, or at least of the animal, of the natural being that he is, the object of his destructive negation, the banal prerequisite is his unconsciousness of the cause and the effects of his actions. Now, it was essential for Hegel to *gain consciousness* of negativity as such, to capture its horror – here the horror of death – by upholding and by looking the work of death right in the face.

Hegel, in this way, is less opposed to those who 'recoil' than to those who say: 'it is nothing'. He seems to distance himself most from those who react with gaiety.

I want to emphasize, as clearly as possible, after their similarity, the opposition between the naive attitude and that of the – *absolute* – wisdom of Hegel. I am not sure, in fact, that of the two attitudes the more naive is the less *absolute*.

I shall cite a paradoxical example of a gay reaction in the face of the work of death.

The Irish and Welsh custom of the 'wake' is little known but was still practised at the end of the last century. It is the subject of Joyce's last work,[12] *Finnegans Wake* – the deathwatch of Finnegan (however, the reading of this famous novel is difficult at best). In Wales, the coffin was placed *open*, standing at the place of honour of the house. The dead man would be dressed in his finest suit and top hat. His family would invite all of his

friends, who honoured the departed all the more the longer they danced ·
and the deeper they drank to his health. It is the death of an *other*, but
in such instances, the death of the other is always the image of one's
own death. Only under one condition could anyone so rejoice; with the
presumed agreement of the dead man – who is an other – the dead man
that the drinker in his turn will become shall have no other meaning than
his predecessor.

This paradoxical reaction could be considered a response to the desire to
deny *the existence of death*. A logical desire? Not in the least, I think. In
Mexico today, death is commonly envisaged on the same level as the
amusements that can be found at festivals: skeleton puppets, skeleton
candies, skeleton merry-go-rounds – but this custom is associated with an
intense cult of the dead, a visible obsession with death.[13]

If I envisage death gaily, it is not that I too say, in turning away from
what is frightening: 'it is nothing' or 'it is false'. On the contrary, gaiety,
connected with the work of death, causes me anguish, is accentuated by my
anguish, and in return exacerbates that anguish: ultimately, gay anguish,
anguished gaiety cause me, in a feverish chill,[14] 'absolute dismemberment',
where it is my joy that finally tears me apart, but where dejection would
follow joy were I not torn all the way to the end, immeasurably.

There is one precise opposition that I would like to bring out fully: on the
one hand Hegel's attitude is less whole than that of naive humanity, but this
is meaningless unless, reciprocally, one sees that the naive attitude is
powerless to maintain itself without subterfuge.

Discourse gives useful ends to sacrifice 'afterwards'

I have linked the meaning of sacrifice to man's behaviour once his animal
needs have been satisfied: man differs from the natural being which he also
is; the sacrificial gesture is what he humanly is, and the spectacle of sacrifice
then makes his humanity manifest. Freed from animal need, man is sovereign: he does what he pleases – his pleasure. Under these conditions he is
finally able to make a rigorously autonomous gesture. So long as he needed
to satisfy animal needs, he had to act with an end in view (he had to secure
food, protect himself from the cold). This supposes a servitude, a series of
acts subordinated to a final result: the natural, animal satisfaction without
which man properly speaking, sovereign man, could not subsist. But man's
intelligence, his *discursive thought*, developed as functions of servile labour.
Only sacred, poetic words, limited to the level of impotent beauty, have
retained the power to manifest full sovereignty. Sacrifice, consequently, is
a *sovereign, autonomous* manner of being only to the extent that it is unin-
formed by *meaningful* discourse. To the extent that discourse informs it,
what is *sovereign* is given in terms of *servitude*. Indeed by definition what is

sovereign does not *serve*. But simple discourse must respond to the question that discursive thought asks concerning the meaning that each thing must have on the level of utility. In principle, each thing is there to *serve* some purpose or other. Thus the simple manifestation of man's link to annihilation, the pure revelation of man to himself (at the moment when death transfixes his attention) passes from sovereignty to the primacy of servile ends. Myth, associated with ritual, had at first the impotent beauty of poetry, but discourse concerning sacrifice slipped into vulgar, self-serving interpretation. Starting with effects naively imagined on the level of poetry, such as the appeasing of a god or the purity of beings, the end of meaningful discourse became the abundance of rain or the city's well-being. The substantial work of Frazer, who recalls those forms of sovereignty that were the most *impotent* and, apparently, the least propitious for happiness, generally tends to reduce the meaning of the ritual act to the same purposes as labour in the fields, and to make of sacrifice an agrarian rite. Today that thesis of the *Golden Bough* is discredited, but it seemed reasonable insofar as the same people who sacrificed inscribed sovereign sacrifice within the frame of a language of ploughmen. It is true that in a very arbitrary manner, which never merited the credence of rigorous reason, these people attempted, and must have laboured to submit sacrifice to the laws of action, laws to which they themselves were submitted, or laboured to submit themselves.

Impotence of the Sage to attain sovereignty on the basis of discourse

Thus, the sovereignty of sacrifice is not absolute either. It is not absolute to the extent that the institution maintains within the world of efficacious activity a form whose meaning is, on the contrary, sovereign. A slippage cannot fail to occur, to the benefit of servitude.

If the attitude of the Sage (Hegel) is not, for its part, sovereign, at least things function in the opposite direction; Hegel did not distance himself and if he was unable to find authentic sovereignty, he came as near to it as he could. What separated him from it would even be imperceptible were we not able to glimpse a richer image through these alterations of meaning, which touch on sacrifice and which have reduced it from an *end* to a simple *means*. The key to a lesser rigorousness on the part of the Sage is the fact, not that discourse engages his sovereignty within a frame that cannot suit him and which atrophies it, but precisely the opposite: sovereignty in Hegel's attitude proceeds from a movement which *discourse* reveals and which, in the Sage's spirit, is never separated from its revelation. It can never, therefore, be fully *sovereign*; the Sage, in fact, cannot fail to subordinate it to the goal of a wisdom which supposes the completion of discourse. Wisdom alone *will be* full autonomy, the sovereignty of being . . . At least it *would be* if we could find sovereignty by searching for it: and, in fact, if I search for it, I am undertaking the project of being-sovereignly: but the *project* of being-sovereignly presupposes a servile being! What nonetheless assures the sovereignty of the moment described is the 'absolute dismemberment' of which Hegel speaks, the rupture, for a time, of discourse. But that rupture itself is not sovereign. In a sense it is an accident in the ascent. Although the two sovereignties, the naive and the sage ones, are both sovereignties of death, beyond the difference between a decline at birth (between a gradual alteration and an imperfect manife-station), they differ on yet another precise point: on Hegel's part, it is precisely a question of an accident. It is not a stroke of fate, a piece of bad luck, which would be forever deprived of sense. Dismemberment is, on the contrary, full of meaning. ('*Spirit only attains its truth*', writes Hegel (but it is my emphasis), 'by finding itself in absolute dismemberment.') But this meaning is unfortunate. It is what limited and impoverished the revelation which the Sage drew from lingering in the regions where death reigns. He welcomed sovereignty as a weight, which he let go . . .

Do I intend to minimize Hegel's attitude? But the contrary is true! I want to show the incomparable scope of his approach. To that end I cannot veil the very minimal (and even inevitable) part of failure.

To my mind, it is rather the exceptional certainty of that approach which is brought out in my associations. If he failed, one cannot say that it was the result of an error. The meaning of the failure itself differs from that of the failure which caused it: the error alone is perhaps fortuitous. In general, it is as an authentic movement, weighty with sense, that one must speak of the 'failure' of Hegel.

Indeed, man is always in pursuit of an authentic sovereignty. That sovereignty, apparently, was, in a certain sense, originally his, but doubtless that could not then have been in a *conscious* manner, and so in a sense it was not his, it escaped him. We shall see that in a number of ways he continued to pursue what forever eluded him. The essential thing is that one cannot attain it consciously and seek it, because seeking distances it. And yet I can believe that nothing is given us that is not given in that equivocal manner.

Notes

1 Excerpt from a study on the – fundamentally Hegelian – thought of Alexander Kojève. This thought seeks, so far as possible, to be Hegel's thought, such a contemporary spirit, knowing what Hegel did not know (knowing, for example, the events that have occurred since 1917 and, as well, the philosophy of Heidegger), could grasp it and develop it. Alexander Kojève's originality and courage, it must be said, is to have perceived the impossibility of going any further, the necessity, consequently, of renouncing the creation of an original philosophy and, thereby, the interminable starting-over which is the avowal of the vanity of thought.

2 G. W. F. Hegel, *Jenenser Philosophie des Geistes in Sämtliche Werke*, ed. Johannes

Hoffmeister (Felix Meiner, Leipzig, 1931), vol. 20, 180–1. Cited by Kojève in *Introduction to the Reading of Hegel* (Editions Gallimard, Paris, 1947), p. 573 (TEL edition (Editions Gallimard, Paris, 1980), p. 575). Henceforth cited in the text as K; TEL.

3 In this paragraph, and the following, I repeat in a different form what has been said by Alexander Kojève. But not only in a different form; essentially I have to develop the second part of that sentence, which is, at first glance, difficult to comprehend in its concrete aspect: 'The being or the annihilation of the "Subject" is the temporalizing annihilation of Being, which must be *before* the annihilated being: the being of the "Subject" necessarily has, therefore, a beginning. And being the (temporal) annihilation of the nothingness in Being, being nothingness which nihilates (insofar as Time), the "Subject" is essentially negation of itself: therefore it has an end.' In particular, I have followed for this (as I have already done in the preceding paragraph) the part of *Introduction to the Reading of Hegel* which concerns parts 2 and 3 of the present study, i.e., Appendix II, 'The idea of Death in the philosophy of Hegel', K, 527–73 (TEL, 529–75). [This appendix, from which all of Bataille's references to Kojève are taken, remains untranslated in English, it is not included in Allan Bloom's re-edition (and abridgment) of Kojève's *Introduction to the Reading of Hegel* (Basic Books, New York, 1969). TR.]

4 [Cf. G. W. F. Hegel, *The Phenomenology of Spirit*, tr. A. V. Miller (Oxford University Press, Oxford, 1977), pp. 9–10. In his footnotes, Bataille attributes the French versions he uses of Hegel to Jean Hyppolite's translation of *The Phenomenology of Spirit* and often also cites the pages from *Introduction à la lecture de Hegel* where Alexandre Kojève quotes the same passages. However, Kojève's version differs from that of Hyppolite and Bataille's from both. It is the latter that I have translated. Page references will hereafter be given to the English translation by A. V. Miller, which is often at significant variance with the quotations as I have rendered them. TR.]

5 [Cf. Hegel, *The Phenomenology of Spirit*, tr. A. V. Miller, p. 19. Cited by Kojève, pp. 538–9 (TEl, 540–1). Kojève, Hyppolite and Bataille all translate the German *Zerrissenheit* by *déchirement*, which I in turn have given as 'dismemberment', the same word which appears in Miller's translation of Hegel. It is important to note that the word *déchirement* has the meanings of 'shredding' and 'tearing' and, unlike 'dismemberment', does not imply a disarticulation into predetermined units. In *L'Expérience intérieure*, for example, Bataille speaks of himself as left in *lambeaux* (shreds, as of cloth or paper) which his 'inability to respond achevait de . . . déchirer' (Editions Gallimard, Paris, 1954), p. 19. TR.]

6 Here my interpretation differs slightly from Kojève's (p. 146 (TEL, 148)). [This passage too is missing from Bloom's abridgement of Kojève, which starts only with the lectures given in 1937–8. (The passage in question is from the 1936–7 lectures TR.] Kojève simply states that 'impotent beauty is incapable of bending to the requirements of the Understanding. The aesthete, the romantic, the mystic, flee the idea of death and speak of Nothingness itself as something which *is*.' In particular, he admirably describes the mystic in this way. But the same ambiguity is found in philosophers (in Hegel, in Heidegger), at least ultimately. In truth, Kojève seems to me wrong not to have envisaged, beyond classical mysticism, a 'conscious mysticism', conscious of making a being from Nothingness, and, in addition, defining that impasse as a negativity which would no longer have a field of action (at the end of history). The atheistic mystic, *self-conscious*, conscious of having to die and to disappear, would live, as Hegel *obviously said concerning himself*, 'in absolute dismemberment'; but, for him, it is only the matter of a certain period: unlike Hegel, he would never come out of it, 'contemplating the Negative right in the face', but never being able to transpose it into being, refusing to do it and maintaining himself in ambiguity.

7 *The Phenomenology of Spirit*, Chapter 8, 'Religion', B, 'Religion in the form of art', (a) 'The abstract work of art' (pp. 434–5). In these two pages, Hegel dwells on the dis-

appearance of *objective essence*, but without developing its consequences. On the second page Hegel limits himself to considerations proper to 'aesthetic religion' (the religion of the Greeks).

8 Still, although animal sacrifice seems to predate human sacrifice, there is nothing to prove that the choice of an animal signifies the unconscious desire to oppose the animal as such; man is only opposed to corporeal being, the being that is given. He is, furthermore, just as opposed to the plant.

9 I discuss comedy further on.

10 Perhaps for lack of a Catholic religious experience. I imagine Catholicism closer to pagan experience; I mean to a universal religious experience from which the Reformation distanced itself. Perhaps a profound Catholic piety could alone have introduced the inward sense without which the phenomenology of sacrifice would be impossible. Modern knowledge, much more extensive than that of Hegel's time, has assuredly contributed to the solution of that fundamental enigma (why, without any plausible reason, *has humanity in general* 'sacrificed'?), but I seriously believe that a correct phenomenological description could only be based on at least a Catholic *period*.

But at any rate, Hegel, hostile to *being* which does nothing – to what simply *is*, and is not *action* – was more interested in military death; it is through such death that he perceived the theme of sacrifice (but he himself uses the word in a moral sense): 'The state-of-the-soldier', he states in his *Lectures* of 1805–6, 'and war are the objectively real sacrifice of the personal-I, the danger of death for the particular – that contemplation of his abstract immediate Negativity . . .' (in Hegel, *Sämtliche Werke*, vol. 20, pp. 261–2. Cited by Kojève in *Introduction to the Reading of Hegel*, p. 558 (TEL, 560)). Nonetheless, religious sacrifice has, even from Hegel's point of view, an essential signification.

11 This is at least possible and, if it is a matter of the most common interdictions, banal.

12 On the subject of this obscure book, see E. Jolas, 'Elucidation du monomythe de James Joyce', *Critique* (July 1948), pp. 579–95.

13 This came out in the documentary which Eisenstein drew from his work for a long film: *¡Viva Mexico!* The crux of this film dealt with the bizarre practices which I have discussed.

14 Reading 'chaud et froid' for 'chaud-froid', which means a dish prepared hot but served cold.

29

Letter to X, Lecturer on Hegel

Paris, 6 December 1937

Dear X,

I am writing the following because it seems to me the only way to continue the conversation we have pursued in several forms. From the outset, I must say that your criticism of me helps me express myself more precisely.

I grant (as a likely supposition) that from now on history is ended (except for the denouement).[1] However, I picture things differently (I don't attribute much importance to the difference between fascism and communism; on the other hand, it certainly doesn't seem impossible that, in some very distant time, everything will begin again).

If action ('doing') is – as Hegel says – negativity, the question arises as to whether the negativity of one who has 'nothing more to do' disappears or remains in a state of 'unemployed negativity'. Personally, I can only decide in one way, being myself precisely this 'unemployed negativity' (I would not be able to define myself more precisely). I don't mind Hegel's having foreseen this possibility; at least he didn't situate it at the conclusion of the processes he described. I imagine that my life – or, better yet, its aborting, the open wound that is my life – constitutes all by itself the refutation of Hegel's closed system.

The question you ask about me comes down to knowing whether I am negligible. I have often asked myself that question; the negative answer haunts me. Furthermore, as the representation I make of myself to myself varies, and as it often happens that I forget, in comparing my life to that of more remarkable men, that mine might be mediocre, I have often said to myself that perhaps there is nothing at the summit of existence except what can be neglected; in effect, no one could 'recognize' a height that is as dark as night. A few facts – such as the exceptional difficulty experienced in

The text is the version published in *The College of Sociology*, ed. Denis Hollier, tr. Betsy Wing (University of Minnesota Press, Minneapolis, MN, 1988), pp. 89–93. The draft of this unfinished letter was sent to the addressee (Alexandre Kojève). A different version was appended to *Le Coupable*. See *OC*, V, pp. 369–71 The notes at the end of the text are written by Denis Hollier.

making myself be 'recognized' (on the simple level at which others are 'recognized') – have led me to assume the hypothesis of an irrevocable insignificance, seriously though cheerfully.

That doesn't bother me and I see no reason to take any pride in it. But I would be no longer human if I put up with it without a fight (by accepting I would seriously chance becoming not just comically insignificant but bitter and vindictive: then I would have to find my negativity again).

What I am saying about it encourages you to think that all that takes place is just some misfortune, and that's all. Confronted with you, my self-justification is no different from that of a howling animal with its foot in a trap.

Really, the question is no longer one of misfortune, or of life, but only of what becomes of 'unemployed negativity', if it is true that it becomes something. I am following it in the forms it engenders, though not in myself right at first but rather in others. Most often, negativity, being impotent, makes itself into a work of art. This metamorphosis, which has real consequences, usually is not a good answer to the situation left by the completion of history (or by the thought of its completion). A work of art answers by evading or, to the extent that it gives a lasting answer, it answers no specific situation. It answers worst of all to the end situation, when evading is no longer possible (when the *moment of truth* arrives). As far as I am concerned, my own negativity gave up on being used only when it no longer had any use; it is the negativity of a man with nothing left to do, and not that of a man who prefers to talk.[2]

But the fact – seemingly incontrovertible – that when negativity turns away from action it expresses itself in a work of art, is no less charged with meaning as far as the possibilities remaining for me are concerned. It is an indication that negativity can be objectified. This fact, moreover, does not just belong to art: religion, better than a tragedy, or than a painting, makes negativity an object of contemplation. But neither in the work of art, nor in the emotional elements of religion, is negativity 'recognized as such' at the moment when it enters the workings of existence as a stimulus to major vital reactions. To the contrary, it is introduced in a process of nullification[3] (here the interpretation of facts by a sociologist such as Mauss is extremely important for me). There is, then, a fundamental difference between the objectification of negativity as the past has known it and that which remains possible *at the end*. In effect, the man of 'unemployed negativity', not finding in the work of art an answer to the question that he himself is, can only become the man of 'recognized negativity'. He has recognized that his need to act no longer has any use. But since this need cannot follow art's false leads indefinitely, sooner or later it is recognized for what it is: a negativity empty of content. The temptation to reject this negativity as a sin resurfaces – such a convenient solution that we did not wait for the final

crisis to adopt it. But since this solution has already come up, its effectiveness has been previously exhausted. The man of 'unemployed negativity'
can hardly ever use it any more: to the extent that he is the consequence of
what has preceded him, the sentiment of sin no longer has any power for
him. He is confronted by his own negativity as if by a wall. No matter how
disquieted he is by it, he knows that henceforth nothing can be ruled out
since negativity no longer has any prospect.[4]

But the horror he feels looking at negativity within himself is no less
likely to end in satisfaction than in the case of a work of art (not to mention
religion). For it is precisely in needing to act that he has recognized
negativity; and this recognition is bound up with a conception that has it be
the condition of all human existence. Far from stopping in this investigation, he finds a total satisfaction in the fact of becoming the man of
'recognized negativity'. He will no longer rest as he begins the effort to
pursue this recognition to its very end. In this way science, to the extent that
its object is human negativity – especially the sacred left – becomes the
middle term of what is only a process of awareness. Thus it brings into play
representations extremely charged with emotive value (such as physical
destruction or erotic obscenity, an object of laughter, of physical excitation,
of fear and of tears). But at the same time these representations intoxicate
him, he strips off the straitjacket that has kept them from contemplation
and he sets them objectively within the eruption of time that nothing
changes. He understands then that it is his good, not his bad, luck that
brought him into a world where there was nothing left to do, and he offers
what he has become now, despite himself, to be recognized by others. For
he cannot be the man of 'recognized negativity' except to the extent that he
makes himself be recognized as such. Thus, once again, he discovers
something 'to do' in a world where, from the point of view of actions,
nothing is done any more. And what he has 'to do' is to satisfy the portion
of existence that is freed from doing: it is all about using free time.

For all that, moreover, he is not up against any less resistance than the
men of action who have preceded him. Not that this resistance is able to
manifest itself from the outset, but if he does not make a virtue of crime, he
generally makes *the* virtue of *the* crime (even if he objectifies crime, making
it thus neither more nor less destructive than it was before). It is true that
the first phase of resistance must be pure elusion, for no one can know
what he is after in confronting others as one who sees in a world of the
blind. All around him he encounters people who shy away and who prefer
to escape immediately to the side of the blind. And only when a sufficient
number achieve this recognition can it become the object of a positive
resistance because the blind will be unable to see that something must be
expelled until enough of it has been brought into play to make them
conscious of its presence.

Moreover, for the man of 'recognized negativity', at the moment in which he recognizes negativity in himself, what will then take place does not count (at least regarding the precise form that things are to take). For what is important to him is precisely the fact that he is doomed to conquer or to compel recognition. He knows that his destruction is certain if he does not win in the two possible phases of the struggle. First of all, in the phase of elusive resistance, in his isolation he risks being dedicated to a moral disintegration against which, at the outset, he has no recourse. (He can be one of those for whom losing face in his own eyes does not seem preferable to death.) It is only in the second phase that there can be a question of physical destruction, but in both cases, insofar as an individual becomes the man of 'recognized negativity', he disappears if the force he brings into play is not greater, first of all, than the force of elusion and, later, than the force of opposition.

I have spoken here of the man of 'recognized negativity' as if it were not solely a question of myself. I have to add, in fact, that I do not feel that I am absolutely isolated except insofar as I have become completely aware of what is happening to me. But if I want to complete the story of the owl,[5] I must also say that the man of 'unemployed negativity' is already represented by numerous dangers and that the recognition of negativity as a condition of existence has already been carried, in an uncoordinated state, very far. As for what is exclusively mine, I have only described my existence after it has reached a definite stance. When I speak of recognition of the 'man of recognized negativity', I speak of the state of my requirements now: description only comes afterward. It seems to me that until then Minerva can hear the owl.

Only from this precise point does extrapolation take place and it consists of representing everything as a fact, what must follow being produced as the arrival at a position of equilibrium in a well-defined play of forces. Hegel even permitted himself an extrapolation of the same order: moreover, his elusion of a possible later negativity seems to me harder to accept than the description I give of forms of existence that have already been produced – in myself in a very precise manner and independent of a description that frankly came later and in a rather vague way. I add this last thought: in order for phenomenology to have a meaning, Hegel would have to be recognized as its author (which perhaps only genuinely happens with you), and it is obvious that Hegel, as a result of not accepting the role of man of 'recognized negativity' to the end, risked nothing: he still belonged, therefore, to a certain extent, to the *Tierreich*.[6]

Notes

1 Wrongly perhaps, wrongly at the very least, as far as the next twenty years were concerned, X imagined the revolutionary solution of communism to be near.

2 It is not because it is afraid to act but because action fails it that negativity finds it has no use. Its situation is different from that of the 'beautiful soul': disinvolvement with historical and political action is not the result of an initial choice.

3 The version of this letter published in *Le Coupable* has at this point: 'It is introduced into a system that nullifies it and only affirmation is 'recognized.' The algebra of recognition prohibits negativity, in effect, from making itself recognized as such, as Bataille is to remind us on the following 5 February. Paradoxically, he will even go so far as to illustrate this law using Hegel himself as an example, saying that his work, 'insofar as it recognizes negativity, has itself not been recognized'.

4 What follows was not printed in *Le Coupable*. This censorship, like the addition mentioned in the preceding note, is indicative of the direction in which Bataille took his 'self-criticism' after the failure of the College of Sociology. At the time he writes this letter, he thinks that negativity must be able to make itself be recognized, that even without a historical use, it must, at least as a last resort, apply itself to making itself recognized. When he publishes it, he thinks that recognition focuses only on how negativity *betrays* itself, positively. In 1937 he sides with Hegel whom he wants to have recognized as the father of the negative. In 1944 he dissociates himself from Hegel because he is far too recognizable.

5 The owl is the bird of Minerva. Hegel said that it took fight only at nightfall: just like the philosopher who has the distinction of always arriving too late, when everything is over and done.

6 The *Tierreich*: Kojève translates this as 'bestiary', and Hyppolite translates it as 'the mind's animal kingdom'.

30

Knowledge of Sovereignty

1 The General and Immediate Aspect of Sovereignty

The sovereignty I speak of has little to do with the sovereignty of states, as international law defines it. I speak in general of an aspect that is opposed to the servile and the subordinate. In the past, sovereignty belonged to those who, bearing the names of chieftain, pharaoh, king, king of kings, played a leading role in the formation of that being with which we identify ourselves, the human being of today. But it also belonged to various divinities, of which the supreme god was one of the forms, as well as to the priests who served and incarnated them, and who were sometimes indistinguishable from the kings; it belonged, finally, to a whole feudal and priestly hierarchy that was different only in degree from those who occupied its pinnacle. But further, it belongs essentially to *all men* who possess and have never entirely lost the value that is attributed to gods and 'dignitaries'. I will speak at length about the latter because they *display* that value with an ostentation that sometimes goes with a profound baseness. I will also show that they *cheapen* it by displaying it. For I shall always be concerned, however it may seem, with the apparently lost sovereignty to which the beggar can sometimes be as close as the great nobleman, and from which, as a rule, the bourgeois is voluntarily the most far removed. Sometimes the bourgeois has resources at his disposal that would allow him to enjoy the possibilities of this world in a sovereign manner, but then it is in his nature to enjoy them in a furtive manner, to which he strives to give the appearance of servile utility.

The text is from *The Accursed Share*, vol. II, The History of Eroticism; vol. III, Sovereignty, tr. Robert Hurley (Zone Books, New York, 1991), pp. 197–211. *La Souveraineté* was planned, in 1953–4, as the third volume of *La Part maudite*. Though the final version was completed in 1953, Bataille decided not to publish it in 1956. Some chapters appeared in journals, but the volume was published posthumously in 1976. See *OC*, VIII, pp. 247–61.

2 The Basic Elements: Consumption beyond Utility, the Divine, the Miraculous, the Sacred

What distinguishes sovereignty is the consumption of wealth, as against labour and servitude, which produce wealth without consuming it. The sovereign individual consumes and doesn't labour, whereas at the antipodes of sovereignty the slave and the man without means labour and reduce their consumption to the necessities, to the products without which they could neither subsist nor labour.

In theory, a man compelled to work consumes the products without which production would not be possible, while the sovereign consumes rather the surplus of production. The sovereign, if he is not imaginary, truly enjoys the products of this world – beyond his needs. His sovereignty resides in this. Let us say that the sovereign (or the sovereign life) begins when, with the necessities ensured, the possibility of life opens up without limit.

Conversely, we may call sovereign the enjoyment of possibilities that utility doesn't justify (utility being that whose end is productive activity). Life *beyond utility* is the domain of sovereignty.

We many say, in other words, that it is *servile* to consider duration first, to employ the *present time* for the sake of the *future*, which is what we do when we work. The worker produces the machine bolt with a view to the moment when this bolt will itself be used to assemble the automobile, which another will enjoy in a sovereign fashion, in contemplative drives. The worker does not personally have in view the sovereign pleasure of the future car owner, but this pleasure will justify the payment that the factory owner anticipates, which authorizes him to give a wage to the worker without waiting. The worker turns the bolt in order to obtain this wage. In principle, the wage will enable him to meet his needs. Thus, in no way does he escape the circle of constraint. He works in order to eat, and he eats in order to work. We don't see the sovereign moment arrive, when nothing counts but the moment itself. What is sovereign in fact is to enjoy the present time without having anything else in view but this present time.

I know: these statements are theoretical; they account for the facts only vaguely. If I consider the real world, the worker's wage enables him to drink a glass of wine: he may do so, as he says, to give him strength, but he really drinks in the hope of escaping the necessity that is the principle of labour.

As I see it, if the worker treats himself to the drink, this is *essentially* because into the wine he swallows there enters a *miraculous* element of savour, which is precisely the essence of sovereignty. It's not much, but at least the glass of wine gives him, for *a brief moment*, the *miraculous* sensation of having the world at his disposal. The wine is downed mechanically (no sooner swallowed than the worker forgets it), and yet it is the source of intoxication, whose *miraculous* value no one can dispute. On the one hand, to freely take advantage of the world, of the world's resources, as does the worker drinking the wine, partakes in some degree of the *miraculous*. On the other, it is the substance of our aspirations. We must satisfy our needs, and we suffer if we fail, but where the necessities are at stake we are only obeying the animal injunction within us. Beyond need, the object of desire is, *humanly*, the *miracle*; it is sovereign life, beyond the necessary that suffering defines. This *miraculous* element *which delights us* may be simply the brilliance of the sun, which on a spring morning transfigures a desolate street. (Something that the poorest individual, hardened by necessity, sometimes feels.) It may be wine, from the first glass to the intoxication that drowns. More generally, this miracle to which the whole of humanity aspires is manifested among us in the form of beauty, of wealth – in the form, moreover, of violence, of funereal and sacred sadness; in the form of glory. What is the meaning of art, architecture, music, painting or poetry if not the anticipation of a suspended, wonder-struck moment, a miraculous moment? The Gospel says that 'man does not live by bread alone', that he lives by what is *divine*. This expression has such clear evidence in its favour that it must be seen as a first principle. 'Man does not live by bread alone' is a truth that sticks in the mind; if there is a truth that counts before the others, it has to be this one.[1]

The divine is doubtless but one aspect of the *miraculous*. There is nothing *miraculous* that is not in a sense *divine*. The question is difficult, moreover. The category of the *miraculous*, though not so narrow as that of the *divine*, is awkward nonetheless. I may say that the object of laughter is *divine*, but at first this is just my feeling; nowadays it is not that of everyone. If I am right, if my feeling is justified, I will still have to prove it. I may also say of this impure and repugnant thing that it is *divine*, but granting this assertion implies that one has understood the principle of the ambiguity of the divine, which is no different in principle from the ambiguity of the sacred.[2] The extreme aspects of eroticism, the obsessive desire in eroticism for a miraculous element, are doubtless more familiar, easier to grasp. (The difference, however, is not such that we would not also find in this domain the ludicrous and the repugnant in their murkiest form.) It is more than a little strange, certainly, that death and birth communicate to us the clearest sensation of the miracle of the sacred.

3 Considerations on Method

The domain that we shall survey fully, but only in its general lines, is so complex that one feels the need for a coherent description. If the sovereign partakes at once of the divine, of the sacred, of the ludicrous or the erotic, of the repugnant or the funereal, shouldn't I consider the general morphology of these aspects? It seems useless to go any further in our exploration of sovereignty without accounting for the underlying unity of aspects whose appearance is so varied. Nevertheless, it would seem to me untimely, at the outset, to pursue that course.[3] A morphology describing complex domains could only come after a posing of fundamental problems. It might be a final result, which would come at the end. I prefer to examine what is essential, without lingering over the question of method. I shall save for another volume the coherent exposition of the method I've followed. For the present I shall only make a few quick remarks about it. My 'labours', if I may speak in that way, only tend to continue the effort of 'researchers' who pursued various disciplines. I have not been overly concerned about the legitimacy of the results that I borrowed, as judiciously as I could, from the history of religions, from sociology, from political economy or from psychoanalysis . . . Moreover, my enquiries were made with shameful casualness (that of too long a patience, a bit wearily), but neither am I a stranger to the demands of phenomenology. On one point I contribute a new element.

I grant, in a fundamental way, that we know nothing beyond what is taught by action with a view to satisfying our needs. What action teaches undoubtedly goes beyond the purposes of the action: we may even say of science, acquired in practice, by means of practice, that it is, or at least can be, *disinterested*. But science is always subject to the primacy of the future over the present. To do science is to disregard the present time with a view to subsequent results. And the most surprising thing, no doubt, is that the situation doesn't change when, once the results are obtained, we have access to the knowledge itself, when, the science done, the knowledge is given us seemingly in the present time. Hegel saw very well that, were it acquired in a thorough and definitive way, knowledge is never given to us except by *unfolding in time*. It is not given in a sudden illumination of the mind but in a *discourse*, which is necessarily deployed in duration. Knowledge, and the most profound knowledge, never appears to us in full except, finally, as the result of a calculated effort, an operation useful to some end. Knowledge can't in any way be confused with the last moment or the *end* of the operation; it is the entire operation. The end of a useful operation may be an object devoid of utility, for example an automobile employed, as I said, for contemplative drives. By becoming useless, that automobile detaches itself rather clearly in thought (if not in mechanical reality) from the operation that produced it. This detachment is not in any way possible if one considers the operation of knowledge in its homogeneity. Knowledge is always comparable to what the enjoyment of an automobile would be if driving it were just that *and nothing more*, without any other essential and new aspect, a homogeneous extension of the work of the shop that made it.

To know is always to strive, to work; it is always a servile operation, indefinitely resumed, indefinitely repeated. Knowledge is never sovereign: to be *sovereign* it would have to occur in a moment. But the moment remains outside, short of or beyond, all knowledge. We know regular sequences in time, constants; we know nothing, absolutely, of what is not in the image of an operation, a servile modality of being, subordinate to the future, to its concatenation in time. We know nothing absolutely, of the moment. In short, we know nothing about what ultimately concerns us, what *is supremely* [*souverainement*] *important to us*. The operation leaves off as soon as sovereignty is its object.

Yet we are in fact conscious of the moment. (Indeed, we are conscious of nothing but the moment.) But this consciousness is at the same time a slipping-away of the moment, insofar as it might be clear and distinct, insofar as it is not a vague knowledge of oneself but knowledge of an object: knowledge of an object needs to apprehend that object caught up in duration, beyond the present moment. Consciousness of the moment is not truly such, is not sovereign, except in *unknowing*. Only by cancelling, or at least neutralizing, every operation of knowledge within ourselves are we in the moment, without fleeing it. This is possible in the grip of strong emotions that shut off, interrupt or override the flow of thought.

This is the case if we weep, if we sob, if we laugh till we gasp. It's not so much that the burst of laughter or tears stops thought. It's really the *object* of the laughter, or the *object* of the tears, that suppresses thought, that takes all knowledge away from us. The laughter or the tears break out in the vacuum of thought created by their object in the mind. But these moments, like the deeply rhythmed movements of poetry, of music, of love, of dance, have the power to capture and endlessly recapture the moment that counts, the moment of rupture, of fissure. As if we were trying to arrest the *moment* and freeze it in the constantly renewed gasps of our laughter or our sobs.[4] The miraculous moment when anticipation dissolves into NOTHING, detaching us from the ground on which we were grovelling, in the concatenation of useful activity.

So there are – at rare, privileged moments – objects of thought whose conditions can be known in the same way as the other objects of knowledge; thus the object of laughter, the object of tears . . . But what is peculiar to these objects is, at least hypothetically, that the thought that conceives them dissocates them, and thereby dissolves itself as thought. The content prior to this dissolution, even the conditions under which it dissolves, can be known: these conditions can be known, for example, if the object in question provokes a laughter that won't stop. Consequently, we shall stop speaking of the NOTHING into which the object dissolves; we shall speak rather of what the dissolved object was, and of what determined the dissolution. In this way it will be possible for us, perhaps, *to speak* of what is sovereign. The thought that comes to a halt in the face of what is sovereign rightfully pursues its operation to the point where its object dissolves into NOTHING, because, ceasing to be useful, or subordinate, it becomes *sovereign* in ceasing to be.

4 The Paradox of Happy Tears (Further Consideration on Method)

In principle there is no need, in an essay that considers the movement of sovereignty only in a general way, for us to linger over the specific aspect of laughter or tears to which the preceding suggestion refers in particular. I will merely remark that as concerns laughter this conception is classic. But I shall dwell longer on tears, for the reason that I derive from reflection on tears the general notion of *miraculous* that dominates this book.

It seems best to set out my thought here as it takes shape. Its final cohesion, I believe, would be less interesting (although achieving that cohesion would demand nothing more in sum than an enormous amount of time).

For many years, I was struck by the ambiguous aspect of tears, which a happy event provokes as readily as misfortune. But happy tears have not been the subject of innumerable and meticulous investigations as laughter has. This surprising lacuna, by itself, showed me the disappointing nature of the agglomeration that our psychological knowledge forms as a whole. I had observed that on occasion these tears would well up in my eyes in circumstances that left me disconcerted. I am not inclined to record these kinds of facts in succession, but one of them has stuck in my memory. One of my cousins by marriage is an officer in the British Navy; he served during the war on board the *Hood*. Just a few hours before the *Hood* was to sink, and the whole crew with it, my cousin was assigned a separate mission and sent on board a smaller boat. The admiralty officially reported his death to his mother. This was logical, since he was part of the crew of the *Hood*, which had perished almost to the last man. But some days alter, my mother received a letter from him relating the circumstances in which he had, 'by a miracle', escaped death. I didn't become acquainted with my cousin until much later, so these were events that had not affected me personally at first. But, without dwelling on it otherwise, I had the opportunity to tell the story to friends, and every time I did so, to my great surprise tears came to my eyes. I didn't see the reason for this, but I am in the habit of wondering, for this thing and that, what *is known about it* (even if I only have to tell myself, rather vaguely, that it must be found in some book . . .): finally, I began to suspect that no one knew anything about this. Apparently, no one had even advanced an absurd hypothesis, having at least the merit of initiating an inquiry; probably no one had even perceived the interest of these parado-xical tears (yet, in the case of laughter the most secondary questions have been the subject of numerous studies). I am no longer sure of this lack; I should look further, I know. But I spoke of the matter in a lecture attended by some eminent philosophers and no one seemed to know any more about it than I did.

This point is unimportant in itself, but I had to try to solve by myself a problem that astonished me. I reflected at first on the relationship between such tears and good fortune. Everyone knows that one weeps for joy. But I didn't feel any joy. The fortunate outcome appeared to me to correspond possibly to a set of circumstances about which I had, in spite of everything, a more general and more detailed picture than I now have. Then it dawned on me – while I was considering the problems of this work – that a *miracle*, that only a miracle, caused those happy tears to arise. A miracle, or, if not, something that seemed that, since in such circumstances we cannot expect a repetition of the same fact. In any case, we cannot expect it from our efforts. . . . This *miraculous* quality is conveyed rather exactly by the expression: *impossible and yet there it is*, which had once appeared to me to take on the meaning of the *sacred*. I imagined at the same time that art has no other meaning, that art is always a response to the supreme hope for the unanticipated, for a miracle. This is why the measure of art is genius, while talent relates to the rational, explicable means, whose result never has anything unanticipated about it.

I wanted to present the development of my thought, disclosing in the course of time, little by little, unexpected relations, rather than offer a drily theoretical statement of those relations or of the method I followed. From the beginning, this content, the *miraculous*, that I ultimately recognized where one would least expect it, in the object of tears, seemed to me to be in basic agreement with humanity's expectation. So I was able to say to myself with a feeling of certainty that 'man needed more than bread, that he was just as hungry for a miracle'. Above all, I understood this essential point: what I had found in happy tears was also found in unhappy ones. This *miraculous* element that, each time tears rose to my eyes, I recognized in amazement, was not lacking in unhappiness. The death that deprived me of my fellow man, of the very one in whom I had recognized being – what was it if not, in a negative form, the unanticipated, the miracle that takes one's breath away? *Impossible, yet there it is* – what better way to cry out the feeling that death inspires in men? May we not say of death that in it, in a sense, we discover the negative analogue of a miracle, something we find all the harder to believe as death strikes down the one we love, the one who is close to us, something we could not believe, *if it, if death were not there*.

5 The Equivalence of the Negative Miracle (Death) and the Positive Miracle (Final Considerations on Method)

The most remarkable thing is that this *negative miraculous*, manifested in death, corresponds quite clearly to the principle stated above, according to which the miraculous moment is the moment when *anticipation dissolves into* NOTHING. It is the moment when we are relieved of anticipation, man's customary misery, of the anticipation that enslaves, that subordinates the present moment to some anticipated result. Precisely in the miracle, we are thrust from our anticipation of the future into the presence of the moment, of the moment illuminated by a miraculous light, the light of the sovereignty of life delivered from its servitude.

But, as I said, the anticipation dissolves into NOTHING. So we must raise the two-part question: if this NOTHING is that of death, it is hard for us to see how the moment can be the sovereign illumination of life; if, on the other hand, what is involved is a miraculous appearance that captivates, like the extreme beauty of an authentic work of art, it is hard for us to see why the beauty would be NOTHING, why it would have no other meaning than NOTHING. I spoke of a *negative miraculous*, but in this negative the miraculous element is contrary to desire, and this manner of speaking implies the existence of a *positive miraculous*, which alone seems to justify the *value* that is ordinarily connected with the word 'miracle', and whose positive form corresponds with the anticipation of a blessing.

It is precisely on this point, in order to address this difficulty, that I bring out how the method I followed led me away from the usual paths of knowledge. I resolved long ago not to seek knowledge, as others do, but to seek its contrary, which is un-knowing. I no longer anticipated the moment when I would be rewarded for my effort, *when I would know at last*, but rather the moment when *I would no longer know, when my initial anticipation would dissolve into* NOTHING. This is perhaps a mysticism in the sense that my craving not to know one day ceased to be distinguishable from the experience that monks called mystical – but I had neither a presupposition nor a god.[5]

In any case, this way of going in the wrong direction on the paths of knowledge – to get off them, not to derive a result that others anticipate – leads to the principle of the *sovereignty* of being and of thought, which from the standpoint where I am placed at the moment has this meaning: that thought, subordinated to some anticipated result, completely enslaved, ceases to be in being *sovereign*, that only un-knowing is *sovereign*.

But the bias that I affirm, and, supreme result, the negation of future results, cannot by themselves give this thought that which engages one's attention. As I said, I will confine myself to the general lines, but at this point I must explain my basic position.

I reflected on un-knowing, and I saw that human life was full of moments – which I assign to knowledge – when the ceaseless operation of
cognition is dissolved. I referred to those moments in speaking of sobs,
of laughter that makes one gasp . . . saying that in them the train of thought
was broken off. I fastened on this aspect, if not of nature, of human life,
seeking in the experience a way out of my servitude. The object of tears or
of laughter – and of other effects such as ecstasy, eroticism or poetry –
seemed to me to correspond to the very point at which the object of thought
vanishes. Up to that point, that object might be an object of knowledge, but
only up to that point, so that the effect of knowledge would regularly fail.
(Every philosopher knows how exhausting is the impossibility of working
out the problem of laughter, but poetry, ecstasy, eroticism . . . doubtless
pose problems that are no less exhausting.) It was bound to fail insofar as
unknowing, that is, insofar as NOTHING, taken as the supreme object of
thought, which takes leave of itself, which quits itself and becomes the
dissolution of every object,[6] was not involved in the solution of the problem.

So it is easy to see, if I have been understood, how the 'paradox of tears',
which would hinder me did I not have this position, could appear to me,
quite on the contrary, at the apex of a thought whose *end* jumps the rails on
which it is travelling. What appeared to me was not the paradoxical aspect
of the equivalences: in my eyes the fact that a happy event might have the
same effect as death, usually thought of as the most unhappy event, was not
a revelation. I had long been aware of the *banal* character of these relationships, but it made a light that dazzled me a blinding one. A little phrase of
Goethe's on death,[7] 'an impossibility that suddenly changes into a reality',
had the merit of opening my eyes, unintentionally, to the *miraculous* character of the most dreaded event. But what was most striking was the
sameness of *uncalculated* reactions which, from a definite point of view, did
away with the difference between the positive and the negative, extreme
happiness and extreme unhappiness, situating both, indiscriminately, *at the
point of resolution of our processes.*

The clearest thing was that essentially *an unreasoned impulse gave a
sovereign value to the miraculous*, even if the miracle were an unhappy one.
What mattered, what the tears maintained, convulsively, in front of us and
for us, was the awful yet, in spite of ourselves, marvellous moment when
'the impossibility suddenly changed into a reality'. While determining our
unhappiness, no doubt, this moment nevertheless had the sense of a miracle, the power to dissolve in us that which up to then had been necessarily
subjugated, bound up. Moreover, there is no reason at all for thinking that
tears of happiness signify gratified expectations, because the object of these
tears is itself unanticipated; like death, it is only, all of a sudden, the
impossible coming true, becoming *that which is*. In this case the object of
anticipation is not that of desire: we anticipate, perhaps in anguish, what it

is reasonable to anticipate, the duration of a tiresome state of things, but we don't anticipate, we dare not, cannot anticipate the outcome that desire suggests. Or, if we anticipate it, this is without believing in it, and more truly, we don't anticipate it if we anticipate it *against all reason*. Thus, desire gives rise to unjustified hope, to hope that reason condemns, which is different from the anticipation of the desired object or of its duration. What I call anticipation, which dissolves into NOTHING, is always the unavoidable calculation of reason.

I insist on the fact that, from a point of view that is doubtless limited, but which we can adopt, it is only of secondary importance whether, in the anticipation that NOTHING follows, the surprise is sad or joyful. What matters most from this point of view is that an unanticipated, unhoped-for aspect, considered impossible, reveals itself. This is the place to recall a remarkable fact: in certain islands of Oceania, the death of the king would provoke an outburst of passion on the part of a whole people, where the rules ordinarily determining what was possible were overthrown, where all of a sudden the youngest men would try to outdo one another in killing and violating. When it struck the king, death would strike the whole population at its sore point and then the latent pressure would be directed toward a reckless dissipation, an enormous festival whose presiding theme was sorrow. Whenever it dissolves into NOTHING, disappointed anticipation suggests a sudden reversal of the course of life. Sometimes a fit of laughter or of tears exhausts the possibility of effervescence that opens up at this moment. But often the incipient transgression develops into an unbounded transgression: the disappointed anticipation heralds the reign of the moment, clearing the way for sexual disorder and violence, for revelry and frantic squander. In this way, sovereignty celebrates its marriage with death. A king is the creature *par excellence* of the miracle; in this person he concentrates the virtues of a miraculous presence. In keeping with a dynamic equilibrium, these virtues may help to maintain order and preserve the possible, but this is to the extent that the integrity of his power, so sacred that no one would dare imagine anything that might affect it, ensures the return of transgression and violence. The 'miracle' of death is understandable in terms of this sovereign exigency, which calls for the *impossible coming true*, in the *reign of the moment*.

That which counts is there each time that *anticipation*, that which binds one in activity, the meaning of which is manifested in the reasonable *anticipation* of the result, dissolves, in a staggering, unanticipated way, into NOTHING.

Notes

1 How childish it is to deny the force of the Gospel. There is no one who should not recognize Christianity for having made it the book of humanity *par excellence*. That resolution of

stinginess into indifference, irony and sympathy does not undermine the edifice of prudence so completely as it may have apappeared to; but how can one aspire to be sovereign without the vehemence that it opposes to the concern for self-interest, without the ingenuousness that it opposes to vehemence? The *evangelical* ethic is as it were, from beginning to end, an ethic of the sovereign moment. Narrow-mindedness did not originate with the Gospel, but that is what it kept, in its restraint, from the rules that it largely denied. True, its transparency allowed the rules to return, and even made their weight easier to bear. Apart from the use that fear and prudence made of it, this transparency has kept its virtue. In theory, transparency has never survived our practical *application* of the maxims on which it is based. Transparency is nonetheless the inaccessible object of a fundamental desire, which is the anticipation of a miraculous moment. Forgetting the Gospel's embeddedness in the world of its time, the concern for what was possible, linked to the acceptance of rules that have become odious in our day, and the masses' hatred – degrading in fact – of deviations that are inconsistent with the possible considered in a general way, ponderously, it has remained, for anyone capable of understanding it, the simplest, most human, 'manual of sovereignty'. Even the myth of the slaying of the king, which is its plot, contributes to this virtue, difficult to grasp perhaps, but raised to the level at which transparency and death are identical.

2 See Roger Caillois, *L'Homme et le sacré*, 2nd edn (Editions Gallimard, Paris, 1950), ch. 2, 'L'ambiguité du sacré', pp. 35–72 [*Man and the Sacred*, tr. Meyer Barash (Free Press, Glencoe, IL, 1959), 'The ambiguity of the sacred', pp. 33–59].

[*Crossed out in the author's manuscript*: In his preface (1939), Caillois says about the interest we both have in the subject of his study: 'It seems to me that with this subject there was established between us a kind of intellectual osmosis which, on my part, does not permit me to distinguish with certainty, after so many discussions, his contribution from mine, in the work that we pursued in common.' There is a good deal of exaggeration in this way of representing things. If it is that Caillois owes something to our discussions, whatever this is can only be quite secondary. At the very root I can say that if Caillois attaches an importance that was not attributed before him to the problem of the ambiguity of the sacred, I could not help but encourage him to do so. Along with 'The sacred as transgression: theory of the festival' (pp. 126–68), it is, I believe, one of the most personal parts of his book, to which I don't think I contributed in any way, but which the whole of my thinking constantly draws upon. I take this opportunity to express my indebtedness to the near perfect reformulation of the question of the sacred that Roger Caillois's little book constitutes. Moreover, it seems to me that it would be very hard, without having read it, to grasp the basic arguments of *The Accursed Share* in the context that justifies them. *Man and the Sacred* is not only an authoritative book but also an essential book for understanding all the problems to which the sacred is the key. Note that, in much the same form, but with the title *Le Pur et l'impur*, Roger Caillois's study constitutes one of the chapters of the *Introduction* to vol. 1 of the *Histoire générale des religions* (Quillet, Paris 1948), for which it was first written, in 1938.]

3 But I will go ahead and indicate the existence of a point where laughter that doesn't laugh and tears that don't cry, where the divine and the horrible, the poetic and the repugnant, the erotic and the funereal, extreme wealth and painful nudity coincide. This is not a fanciful notion. In fact, under the name of *theopathic state*, it has been the object of an implicit description. I don't mean to say that in the theopathic state this coincidence always appears in its full scope, but it *may appear*. The therapeutic state implies at the same time the coincidence of complete unknowing and unlimited knowledge. But only in this sense does absolute unknowing seem to respond, to be *the* response to the state of questioning that is brought about, beyond utility, by the search for knowledge. But this unlimited knowledge is *the knowledge* of NOTHING. Negative theology, which tries to carry the implication of the theopathic state over into the realm of knowledge, might merely take up the thought of Dionysius the Aeropagite. *God is nothingness*, but I prefer to say God is NOTHING, not without linking this negative truth to a perfect laughter: the laughter that doesn't laugh. What I said

about this state, a coincidence... of the poetic and the repugnant, etc., does seem contradictory with the negation of any content that seems to define it. But the principles put forward in Volume II prepare us for this and, as I will show further on, the object of laughter or tears, of horror or the feeling of the sacred, of repugnance, of the awareness of death... is always NOTHING, substituted for the anticipation of a given object. It is always NOTHING, but revealing itself suddenly as a supreme, *miraculous, sovereign* response. I define unalloyed sovereignty as *the miraculous reign of unknowing.*

4 I am aware that sobs in most cases signify unhappiness. I will return shortly to the scant difference that exists between unhappiness and happiness in the unfolding of some of our reactions. But at all events, in unhappiness sobs maintain the sacred moment of rift, and deliver us for a while from the *difficulty* in which the rift left us, so that in tears we find a strange comfort.

5 I have spoken of this experience in *L'Experience intérieure* (1943), *Le Coupable* (1944) and *Sur Nietzsche* (1945) [*Inner Experience*, tr. Leslie Anne Boldt (State University of New York Press, Albary NY, 1988), *Guilty*, tr. Bruce Boone The Lapis Press, Venice, CA, 1988]. These works will be brought together in a second edition under the general title of *Somme athéologique* (Editions Gallimard), and will be followed by a vol. IV, *Le Pur Bonheur*, and a vol. V, *Le Système inachevé du non-savoir*. Only the second edition of *L'Experience intérieure* has been published; that of *Le Coupable* is in preparation.

6 Needless to say, this NOTHING has little to do with *nothingness*. Nothingness is a metaphysical concept. The NOTHING I speak of is a datum of experience, and is considered here only insofar as experience implies it. No doubt the metaphysician may say that this NOTHING is what he has in mind when he speaks of *nothingness*. But the whole impetus of my thought demands that at the moment when this NOTHING becomes its object, it stops, it ceases to be, giving place to the unknowable of the moment. Of course, I admit that I valorize this NOTHING, but in valorizing it I make NOTHING of it. It's true that I confer on it – with an undeniable (but deeply comical) solemnity – the *sovereign* prerogative. But would *sovereign* be what the crowd imagines it to be? *Sovereign* is what you and I are – on one condition, that we forget, forget *everything*... To speak of NOTHING is really only to repudiate the enslavement, reducing it to what it is (it is useful); it is finally only to deny the non-practical value of thought, reducing it, beyond the useful, to insignificance, to the honest simplicity of imperfection, of that which dies and passes away.

7 Which I came across in Edgar Morin's book, *L'Homme et la mort dans l'histoire* (Corrêa, Paris, 1951). It had not struck me when I read the *Conversations with Eckermann*. 'Everyone', writes Morin, 'has been able to note, as Goethe did, that the death of someone close is always "incredible and paradoxical", "an impossibility that suddenly changes into a reality" (Eckermann).' Let it be said here that Morin's big book on death teems with truth and life.

31

The Schema of Sovereignty

1 The Sacred, the Profane, the Natural Given and Death

I must now go back over everything I've said concerning death and the link connecting it, in a fundamental way, to man's sovereign being.

I must take it up again from the beginnings, when the *object* became detached from an initial inner experience, which at first did not differ from the experience that animals apparently have.

The tool, the 'crude flint tool' used by primitive man was undoubtedly the first positing of the object as such. The objective world is given in the practice introduced by the tool. But in this practice man, who makes use of the tool, becomes a tool himself, he becomes himself an object just as the tool is an object. The world of practice is a world where man is himself a thing, which animals are not for themselves (which, moreover, in the beginning, animals were not for man). But man is not really a thing. A thing is identical in time, but man dies and decomposes and this man who is dead and decomposes is not the same thing as that man who lived. Death is not the only contradiction that enters into the edifice formed by man's activity, but it has a kind of pre-eminence.

Now, what appeared in the light of contradiction, in the world of practice, appeared by that very fact as something sacred, or in other terms, as something forbidden. Within the world of practice the sacred is essentially that which, although impossible, is nonetheless there,[1] which is at the same time removed from the world of practice (insofar as it might destroy it) and valorized as something that frees itself from the subordination characterizing the world. Its value is not, as it seems, essentially negative. The action that produces things is what negates that which is (the natural given), and the thing is the negation. The world of things or of practice is

---

The text is from *The Accursed Share*, vol. II, The History of Eroticism; vol. III, Sovereignty, tr. Robert Hurley (Zone Books, New York, 1991), pp. 213–23. *La Souveraineté* was planned, in 1953–4, as the third volume of *La Part maudite*. Though the final version was completed in 1953, Bataille decided against publishing it in 1956. Apart from some chapters appearing in journals, the text was not published until 1976. See *OC*, VIII, pp. 262–71.

the world in which man is subjugated, or simply in which he serves some purpose, whether or not he is the servant of another. Man is alienated therein, he is himself a thing, at least temporarily, to the extent that he serves: if his condition is that of a slave, he is entirely alienated; otherwise a relatively substantial part of himself is alienated, compared with the freedom of the wild animal. This relative alienation, and not slavery, defines from the first the sovereign man who, insofar as his sovereignty is genuine, alone enjoys a non-alienated condition. He alone has a condition comparable to that of the wild animal, and he is sacred, being above things, which he possesses and makes use of. But what is within him has, relative to things, a destructive violence, for example the violence of death.

It was the great preoccupation, if not of the first men, at least of archaic mankind, to define alongside the world of practice, that is, the profane world, a sacred world; alongside the man more or less constrained to serve, a sovereign man; alongside *profane* time, a *sacred* time. The divisions were always laid down with a morbid anxiety, but they were far from being sharply delineated. To say nothing of a degree of arbitrariness that inevitably enters into the constitution of the sacred domain, what was felt as a contradiction with respect to the world of things formed a bloodless domain, impossible by definition. What is sacred, not being based on a logical accord with itself, is not only contradictory with respect to things but, in an undefined way, is in contradiction with itself. This contradiction is not negative: inside the sacred domain there is, as in dreams, an endless contradiction that multiplies without destroying anything. What is not a thing (or, formed in the image of a thing, an object of science) is real but at the same time is not real, is impossible and yet is there. It is for example myself, or something that, presenting itself from the outside, partakes of me, something that, being me, is nevertheless not me (it is not me in the sense in which I take myself for an individual, a thing): it may be a god or a dead person, because, where it is concerned, *to be or not to be* is a question that can never be seriously (logically) raised. For that matter, it is not even impossible for me to represent it to myself as a thing. If it were a thing in the coherence of my thought, as is, in a fundamental way, the individual I take myself for, if I took this element for a thing at the moment when my thought organizes itself according to the laws of the world of practice, the negation peculiar to things would reduce this element to a thing, and that is all. But it is a thing that at the same time is not a thing. It is this paradox: a sacred thing, a basically defective and also, from a sovereign viewpoint, very badly made thing: for in spite of everything, the sacred thing ends up having a utility.

From the foregoing, it is evident that the sacred differs profoundly from the natural given, which the action that created things at first denied. The sacred *is*, in a sense, the natural given. But it is an aspect of the natural given that reveals itself after the fact, in the world of practice – where it is denied – through effects that have escaped the negating action of work, or that actively destroy the coherence established in work. Furthermore, it is an aspect perceived by minds that the order of *things* has shaped to meet the exacting demands of this world's coherence: even a person who rejects all those demands is well aware of them; only animals are oblivious of them.

Thus, death in the midst of things that are well ordered in their coherence is an effect that disturbs that order, and which by a kind of miracle escapes that coherence. Death destroys, it reduces to NOTHING the individual who took himself, and whom others took, for a thing identical to itself. Not only was this individual integrated into the order of things but the order of things had entered into him and, within him, had arranged everything according to its principles. Like other things he had a past, a present *and a future* – and an identity through that past, present and future. Death destroys what was to be, what has become a present in ceasing to be. The obliteration of what was supposed to continue being leads to the error that consists in believing that what no longer exists nonetheless *is*, in some other form (that of a ghost, a double, a soul . . .). No one believes in the pure and simple disappearance of the one who was there. But this error does not carry the conviction that prevails in the world of consistent things. The error is in fact always accompanied by the consciousness of death. It never completely obliterates the consciousness of death.

But what is certain is that the consciousness of death has moved far away from the natural given. Not only do animals not have this consciousness, they can't even recognize the difference between the fellow creature that is dead and the one that is alive. Death, in the disorder which, owing to its irruption, succeeds the idea of an individual regarded as part of the coherence of things, is the appearance that the whole natural given assumes insofar as it cannot be assimilated, cannot be incorporated into the coherent and clear world. Before our eyes, death embodied by a dead person partakes of a whole sticky horror; it is of the same nature as toads, as filth, as the most dreadful spiders. It is nature, not only the nature that we have not been able to conquer, but also the one we have not even managed to face, and against which we don't even have the chance to struggle. Something awful and bloodless attaches itself to the body that decomposes, in the *absence* of the one who spoke to us and whose silence revolts us.

2 The Fear of Death, the Prohibition of Murder and the Sovereign Transgression of that Prohibition

This return of the natural given in the guise of the definitive collapse goes against the plenitude of the world of efficacy. This collapse has not ceased to defeat us: it delivers us over to the event from which we remain sick in our inner being. We try to escape from this elementary horror but, in the darkness and the *dead* silence, it maintains the unpredictable and elusive movement of everything we have not been able to reduce to the reassuring order, a movement to which we know we shall later succumb. We tremble, we grow pale when it suddenly appears . . . From the very beginning, as a result of an immense confusion in which the consciousness of death takes hold, men have placed the beyond at a safe and distant remove from this undefinable menace, but their effort is futile. What they have perceived in the form of a 'ghost' or 'double' belongs to this world of trembling, which they cannot control. All the images of paradise, of glorious souls and bodies, or the commonplace representations of the dead reincarnated by metempsychosis, have never kept the true, immutable domain of death from remaining that of a chilling fear. All things considered, death only opposes the happy fecundity of practice with the pullulation of error – beyond a silence that gives us over to the worst. How can one withhold value from efficacious activity, reserving it for that which overwhelms us, for that which makes our powerlessness manifest?

The agreement seems unanimous, but the opposition is perhaps poorly situated.

In efficacious activity man becomes the equivalent of a tool, which produces; he is like the thing the tool is, being itself a product. The implication of these facts is quite clear: the tool's meaning is given by the future, in what the tool will produce, in the future utilization of the product; like the tool, he who serves – who works – has the value of that which will be later, not of that which is. What relates to death may be uniformly detestable, and may be only a pole of repulsion for us, situating all value on the opposite pole. But this cannot be all there is to the experience of death. The basic loss of value resides in the fact that man becomes a thing. Not entirely perhaps, but always. Without death, could we cease being a thing, destroying in us that which destroys us, and reducing that which was reducing us to less than nothing?

The fear of death appears linked from the start to the projection of oneself into a future time, which, being an effect of the positing of oneself as a thing, is at the same time the precondition for conscious individualization. The being that work made consciously individual is the anguished being. Man is always more or less in a state of anguish, because he is always in a state of anticipation, an anticipation that must be called anticipation of oneself. For he must apprehend himself in the future, through the anticipated results of his action. That is why he fully dies; for, in the perspective in which he constantly strives to attain himself, possible death is always there, and death prevents man from attaining himself. Death is what it is for us insofar as it may prevent us from attaining ourselves, insofar as it separates what we were, which is no longer, from the individual being that we cease to be. A being that would exist only in the moment would not be separated in this way from itself in a kind of 'traumatism'.[2] But subjectively this would not be an individual.

It is insofar as we are subordinate beings, accepting the subordination of the thing, that we die humanly. For to die humanly, in anguish, is to have the representation of death that enables the dividing of oneself into a present and a future: to die humanly is to have of the future being, of the one who matters most in our eyes, the senseless idea that he is not. If we live sovereignly, the representation of death is impossible, for the present is not subject to the demands of the future. That is why, in a fundamental sense, to live sovereignly is to escape, if not death, at least the anguish of death. Not that dying is hateful – but living servilely is hateful. The sovereign man escapes death in this sense: he cannot die *humanly*. He cannot live in an anguish likely to enslave him, to determine the flight from death that is the beginning of servitude. He cannot die fleeing. He cannot let the threat of death deliver him over to the horror of a desperate yet impossible flight. Thus, in a sense, he escapes death, in that he lives in the moment. The sovereign man lives and dies like an animal. But he is a man nevertheless.

Morin agrees with Hegel's conception, according to which the sovereign, the master, sets the risk of death against the horror of death.[3] But Morin thinks that the risk of death, which we take upon ourselves, is the 'affirmation of the individual'. With the risk of death, on the contrary, the human being in us slips away in the face of individual consciousness. The sovereign being is not an animal, but this is because, *familiar with death*, he resists individual consciousness, whose principle exists within him. To consciousness – and to the seriousness of death, which is its initial content – he opposes a *playful* impulse that proves stronger in him than the considerations that govern *work*. The individual affirmation is ponderous; it is the basis for reflection and the unhappy gravity of human life: it is essentially the negation of play. Sovereign affirmation is based only on the play of unconsidered sentiments, as are the impulses of rivalry, of prestige, the rebelliousness and intolerance toward the prohibition that has death and killing as its object. What the sovereign takes seriously is not the death of the *individual*, it is *others*: to the fact of surviving personally he prefers the prestige that will no longer add to his stature if he dies, and will continue to count only so long as others count.

On the other hand, in a fundamental way the impetus of the sovereign man makes a killer of him. Death is a negation brought into operation in the world of practice: the principle of that world is submerged in death like a city in a tidal wave. It is the world of the thing, of the tool, the world of identity in time and of the operation that disposes of future time. It is the world of limits, of laws and of the *prohibition*. It is basically a general subordination of human beings to works that satisfy the demands of a group. But not only does this world run up against unavoidable contradictions, not only is death its unavoidable stumbling block, but the man who has fully satisfied these demands – no sooner has he satisfied them then he calls *actively* for the negation of a servitude that he accepted, but accepted only insofar as it was imposed on him. The imperatives of the world of practice set many limits on the ravages of death; in addition to customs giving a precise and *limited* form to the moral disorder that results from its coming, civilization responds to it with the interdiction of killing. We find it hard to admit that it's the same with this prohibition as with the others, which are easily transgressed; we need to realize nonetheless that the limits set by civilization can dictate the conditions without which it could not exist. But it is enough for it to dictate them rather often. If the situation appears clear, it is as if the limits were there *to be transgressed*. The limits give passion the contracted movement that it did not have in animality. This properly human movement has forms regulated, relatively, by conventions that are often strange; it has a greater, perhaps less lasting, explosive intensity, but above all it leads to the refinements of pleasure and cruelty that civilization and prohibition alone made possible by contravention. The truth is that although man compels himself – or if he can, compels other men – to become a thing, this cannot go very far. To begin with, that temptation comes up against the fact that, passively, in spite of himself, if only because of death that decomposes him and suddenly makes it all look ghastly, it would be impossible for him to submit unreservedly to necessity (death received passively, and revealing him to be other than he is, by itself proclaims that man is not a thing). But beyond this passive negation, active rebellion is easy and is bound to occur in the end: he whom the world of utility tended to reduce to the state of a thing not subject to death, hence not subject to killing, ultimately demands the violation of the prohibition that he had accepted. Then, by killing, he escapes the subordination that he refuses, and he violently rids himself of the aspect of a tool or a thing, which he had assumed only for a time. At this price, sovereign existence is restored to him, the sovereign moment that *alone* finally justifies a conditional and temporary submission to necessity.

Sovereignty has many forms; it is only rarely condensed into a person and even then it is diffuse. The environment of the sovereign partakes of sovereignty, but sovereignty is essentially the refusal to accept the limits that the fear of death would have us respect in order to ensure, in a general way, the laboriously peaceful life of individuals. Killing is not the only way to regain sovereign life, but sovereignty is always linked to a denial of the sentiments that death controls. Sovereignty requires the strength to violate the prohibition against killing, although it's true this will be under the conditions that customs define. It also calls for the risk of death.

Sovereignty always demands the liquidation, through strength of character, of all the failings that are connected with death, and the control of one's deep tremors. If the sovereign, or sacred, world that stands against the world of practice is indeed the domain of death, it is not that of faintheartedness. From the viewpoint of the sovereign man, faintheartedness and the fearful representation of death belong to the world of practice, that is, of subordination. In fact, subordination is always rooted in necessity; subordination is always grounded in the alleged need to avoid death. The sovereign world does have an odour of death, but this is for the subordinate man; for the sovereign man, it is the world of practice that smells bad; if it does not smell of death, it smells of anguish; its crowds sweat from the anguish provoked by shadows; death exists in it in a contained state, but fills it up.

3 The Passage from the Negative Miracle of Death to the Positive Miracle of the Divine

The sovereign world is the world in which the limit of death is done away with. Death is present in it, its presence defines that world of violence, but while death is present it is always there only to be negated, never for anything but that. The sovereign is he who *is*, as if death were not. Indeed, he is the one who doesn't die, for he dies only to be reborn. He is not a man in the individual sense of the word, but rather a *god*; he is essentially the embodiment of the one he is but is not. He is the same as the one he replaces; the one who replaces him is the same as he. He has no more regard for the limits of identity than he does for limits of death, or rather these limits are the same; he is the transgression of all such limits. In the midst of all the others, he is not work that is performed but rather play. He is the perfect image of adult play, whereas we ordinarily only have an image of juvenile play (suited to children). As personified in the sovereign, play is what it would be as personified in God, if we had not imagined His Omnipotence within the limits of the subordinate world. The killing of the king is the greatest affirmation of sovereignty: the king cannot die, death is nothing to him, it is that which his presence denies, that which his presence annihilates even in death, that which his death itself annihilates. The pyramids were only a game giving its most costly form to the imperishable identity of man, but they were the 'works' of subordinate beings, *which a limitless sovereignty did not cease to make into a 'game'*.

In the eyes of the Egyptians, the pyramid was an image of solar radiation. In the person of the dead king, death was changed into a radiance, changed into an indefinite being. The pyramid is not only the most lasting monument, it is also the equivalency of the monument and the absence of a monument, of passage and obliterated traces, of being and the *absence* of being. There death is no longer anything but death's inability to maintain an icy little horror, which is the projected shadow of individual anguish. Horror is the limit of the individual. What it proclaims is man's reduction to thinghood. It announces the world of practice. The intent of the world of practice is always to banish, once and for all, the horror that cannot be separated from it by any means. But at the foot of the pyramid, the world of practice has disappeared; its limit is no longer perceptible.

Notes

1 It is, according to Goethe's phrase, 'an impossibility that suddenly changes into a reality'.
2 The term is from Morin, *L'Homme et la mort dans l'histoire* (Corrêa, Paris, 1951), p. 22.
3 Ibid., p. 63.

32

Un-knowing and its Consequences

At the end of yesterday's lecture ('The idea of truth and contemporary logic' by A. J. Ayer), Jean Wahl spoke of the subtle relationships which might be proposed between what Hegel said and what I have to say to you today. I am not certain that those relationships are very solid. I do think, however, that Jean Wahl has pointed to something with a precision of meaning which does justify emphasis on my part. It so happened that I met A. J. Ayer last night, and our reciprocal interest kept us talking until about three in the morning. Merleau-Ponty and Ambrosino also took part, and at the end of the conversation, I think, a compromise was reached.

It happened, nevertheless, that the conversation took a turn such that, despite our very pleasant surroundings, I began to feel as though I were beginning my lecture. I apologize for this distinction made between bar and lecture hall, but the outset does involve a certain confusion.

We finally fell to discussing the following very strange question. Ayer had uttered the very simple proposition: there was a sun before men existed. And he saw no reason to doubt it. Merleau-Ponty, Ambrosino and I disagreed with this proposition, and Ambrosino said that the sun had certainly not existed before the world. I, for my part, do not see how one can say so. This proposition is such as to indicate the total meaninglessness that can be taken on by a rational statement. Common meaning should be totally meaningful in the sense in which any proposition one utters theoretically implies both subject and object. In the proposition, there was the sun and there are no men, we have a subject and no object.

I should say that yesterday's conversation[1] produced an effect of shock. There exists between French and English philosophers a sort of abyss which we do not find between French and German philosophers.

I am not sure that I have sufficiently clarified the humanly unacceptable character of that proposition according to which there existed something prior to man. I really believe that so long as we remain within the discursive, we can always declare that prior to man there could be no sun. And yet one can also feel troubled, for here is a proposition which is logically

The text appeared in English in *October*, 36 (1986), pp. 81–5. Dated 12 January 1951, it is among the papers published in *OC*, VIII, pp. 190–8.

unassailable, but mentally disturbing, unbalancing – an object independent of any subject.

After leaving Ayer, Merleau-Ponty and Ambrosino, I ended by feeling regret.

It is impossible to consider the sun's existence without men. When we state this we think we know, but we know nothing. This proposition was not exceptional in this respect. I can talk of any object, whereas I confront the subject, I am positioned facing the object, as if confronting a foreign body which represents, somehow, something scandalous for me, because objects are useful. A given object enters into me insofar as I become dependent on objects. One thing that I cannot doubt is that I know myself. Finally, I wondered why I blamed that phrase of Ayer's. There are all sorts of facts of existence which would not have seemed quite as debatable to me. Which means that this un-knowing, whose consequences I seek out by talking to you, is to be found everywhere.

Let me clarify what I mean by this un-knowing; the effect of any proposition the penetration of whose content we find disturbing.

I shall begin with an antithetical proposition, not from a review of knowledge which may appear systematic, but rather from the concern with the attainment of maximum knowledge. It is, indeed, quite evident that insofar as I have a satisfiable curiosity of an unknown realm reducible to a known one, I am unable to say what it is that Hegel called absolute knowledge. It is only if I knew all, that I might claim to know nothing, only possession of this discursive knowledge would give me an ineradicable claim to have attained un-knowing. As long as I misunderstand things, my claim to un-knowing is an empty one. Were I to know nothing, I should have nothing to say, and would therefore keep silent. The fact remains that while recognizing that I cannot attain absolute knowledge, I can imagine knowing everything, that is, I bracket my remaining curiosity. I may consider that continued investigation would not teach me much more. I might thereby expect a major personal change in knowledge, but it would stop there. Assuming better knowledge of everything than I now have, I should still not be free of that disturbance of which I speak. Whatever proposition I may utter, it will resemble the first one. I find myself confronting that question, that question raised, we may say, by Heidegger.

Speaking for myself, the question has long seemed to me unsatisfactory, and I have tried to frame another: why is there what I know? Ultimately, this can be perfectly expressed in a turn of phrase. It still seems to me that the fundamental question is posed only when no phrase is possible, when in silence we understand the world's absurdity.

I have tried my best to learn what can be known, and that which I have sought is inexpressibly deep within me. I am myself in a world which I recognize as deeply inaccessible to me, since in all the relations I have sought to establish with it, there remains something I cannot conquer, so that I remain in a kind of despair. I have realized that this feeling is rather rare. I was quite surprised that someone like Sartre shared no such feeling at all. He has said approximately the following: if you know nothing, you've no need to repeat it.

This is the position of one ignorant of the contents of a locked trunk he is unable to open. At a moment like this, one uses a literary language which contains more than need strictly be said. Only silence can express what one has to say, in a language therefore of disquiet, and in a state of perfect despair which, in at least one sense, is not comparable to that of one in search of something he does not have. This is a much deeper despair, one which we have always known, for, essentially bent on objects, we have projects in mind which cannot be realized, and we are on the point of frustration. This despair is equivalent to that of death. As foreign to death as it is ignorant of the contents of this coffer of which I have just spoken.

We can imagine death. We can, at the same time, know that this conception is erroneous. Our proposition concerning death is always tainted with some error. Un-knowing in regard to death is like un-knowing in general. It would seem quite natural to me that, in all that I have just said, each of you has seen a wholly special position (involving an exceptional individual placed outside the norm). As a matter of fact, this judgement of me is entirely consistent with present-day man. I do think, nevertheless, that we may say that this was not ever so – a view which may appear to you somewhat lightly framed.

This is a rather debatable hypothesis, the position of people whose object is precisely that of knowledge. Knowing that you know nothing helps considerably; you have to persevere in thought so as to discover the world of those who know they know nothing. It is a very different world from that of people who possess confidence (children), from that of those who have extended intellectual knowledge. It is a profound difference. These residues may even involve un-knowing in sometimes disconcerting syntheses, since they are, it must be said, no more satisfactory than the first position.

I think it well to refer to an experience as widespread as sacrifice (and in a context different from that offered in my other lectures): the difference and similarities between un-knowing and sacrifice. In sacrifice, one destroys an object, but not completely. A residue remains, and from the scientific point of view, on the whole, nothing of any account has taken place. And yet, if we consider symbolic values, we can conceive this destruction as altering the notion with which we started. The immediate satisfaction provided by a slaughtered cow may be either that of the peasant, or that of the biologist, but it is not what is expressed in sacrifice. The slaughtered cow has nothing to do with these practical notions. In all this, there was a limited, but solid knowledge. By engaging in the ritual destruction of the cow, one destroyed all the notions to which mere life had accustomed us.

Man has need of inventing a prospect of un-knowing in the form of death. These are not regular intellectual operations. There is always some cheating. We all have the feeling of death, and we can assume that this feeling played a strong part in sacrifice. There is a profound difference between Catholics and Protestants; Catholics still experience sacrifice, reduced to a symbolic thinness. Nevertheless, the difference should not be exaggerated: traditional sacrifice and Catholic sacrifice are sacrifice of the soma and of the mass. The act of saying certain words over a bit of bread is quite as satisfying to the spirit as the slaughter of a cow. There is, ultimately, in sacrifice a rather frequent desire for horror. It seems to me that in this respect the spirit will assume as much horror as it can stand. An atmosphere of death, knowing's disappearance, the birth of that world we call sacred. We can say of the sacred that it is sacred, but at that moment language must at least submit to a pause. It is in fact the leitmotiv of this exposition that such operations are ill-conducted, debatable. It is all beside the point. And for a very simple reason: the only way of expressing myself would be for me to be silent; thence the flaw of which I have spoken. It is diametrically opposed to that which troubles us in the first proposition, in the phrase which set off the discussion with Ayer. A trouble felt, as well, in those who seek knowledge. That which I feel in confronting un-knowing comes from the feeling of playing a comedy, and in a position of weakness. I stand before you, challenging, while at the same time offering all the reasons for silence; I may consider, too, that perhaps I have no right to keep silent – a still more difficult position to maintain.

There remains simply the following: un-knowing does not eliminate sympathy, which can be reconciled with psychological knowledge.

When one knows that the hope of salvation must really disappear, the situation of someone wholly rejected (the difference between a lecturer and a servant dismissed in humiliation) – it is a painful situation because there is no project one can form which is not tainted by a kind of death. When one reaches this sort of despair but continues to exist in the world with the same hopes and the same instincts (human and bestial aspects), one realizes suddenly that one's possession of the world has greater depth than that of others. These possibilities are, in effect, more open to him who has relinquished knowledge (the walk through fields with a botanical textbook). Each time we relinquish the will to knowledge, we have the possibility of a far more intense contact with the world.

With a woman, insofar as one knows her, one knows her badly, that is, one's knowing is a kind of knowledge. Insofar as one tries to know a woman psychologically, untransported by passion, one distances oneself from her. It is only when we try to know her in relation to death that we draw near.

By a series of contradictions, it is when someone fails that we draw close, but we are asked to deny this feeling of the 'perishable'. In love, the will to project the loved one within the imperishable is a wish that goes contrary to this. It is insofar as an individual is not a thing that he can be loved. It is insofar as he bears some resemblance to the sacred. Just as the loved one cannot be perceived unless projected into death, thereby resulting in the imagination of death.

Still, we can, of course, through a conception of aspects of ordinary life, which provides a basis of un-knowing, endow them with extreme splendour. We have put a great distance between ourselves and un-knowing. Love cannot be successful. That attempt at magnification of the human being reduces such magnification to this world of practical knowledge.

Now that I have set forth the first consequence of un-knowing, I have again lost the right to speak of it. I have, in assuming the posture of un-knowing, returned to the categories of knowledge.

One can move indefinitely between both positions; neither one has greater validity than the other. I should be saved only by attaining the impossible.

There is, however, a perspective within which we can discern a true triumph for un-knowing – that of the end of history. Hegel's position in this respect is strongly subject to criticism. History must come to an end before it can be discussed; Hegel was mistaken in announcing the end of history; from 1830 on it accelerated. We can, however, without assuming responsibility, speak of the end of history. The position I have set forth would tend toward closure. The last man would find himself in a situation that would be wholly meaningless. If we consider our death as that of the last man, we can say that history has come full circle. He who would be last would have to continue the enterprise. Surely within him night would fall, overwhelming, burying him. This, one might almost say, would be his last spasm.

I think that I have also given the impression of having, in all these matters, a bias toward destruction. The world situation does not, in my view, imply that one is bound to the impossible. The relinquishing of investigation in that direction is true freedom.

There is no reason to adapt narrowly moral views but rather those which are moral in their intensity.

This situation does contain a sort of resolution. In relinquishing all, we can be rich. We are, as it happens, in the situation of the gospels, in that state of grace whose criterion is intensity.

The elements of cheating become a matter of indifference. There is no meaning in death, no project-related meaning. In this negation of means, in which salvation lies beyond everything, all is opened up within the limits of the instant, were I the last of men, and dying.

If I succeed in living within the instant, I break free of all difficulty, but I am no longer a man (to be a man means living in view of the future); and there is no recourse to animality in this situation, which requires a considerable energy available to few.

I pass no value judgement. I cannot manage the slightest condemnation of those who know, who live in the world in which I myself live, in which I can no longer live.

Note

1 [*D'hier, d'Ayer*: Bataille is punning on the resemblance between the word 'yesterday' and the name of the philosopher. TR.]

33

Un-knowing and Rebellion

I have, in several talks given in this hall, tried to communicate my experience of un-knowing. Although it is in certain respects a personal one, I nonetheless consider it to be communicable in that it does not seem a priori to differ from that of others, except in a kind of defect which is my own: the consciousness that this experience is that of un-knowing.

It is, of course, obvious that whenever I speak of un-knowing, I must incur the same difficulty, and must each time, therefore, invoke it. But I do, nevertheless, proceed, promptly acknowledging it, for what I shall now develop before you will be, as on other occasions, that paradox, the knowledge of un-knowing, a knowledge of the absence of knowledge.

I intend, as indicated by the title of my talk, to speak of rebellion. I consider that we are enslaved by knowledge, that there is a servility fundamental to all knowledge, an acceptance of a mode of life such that each moment has meaning only in terms of another, or of others to follow. For clarity's sake, I shall present things thus. Naturally I shall fail, as I have done heretofore. But I should like, first of all, to state the measure of my failure. I can, in fact, say that had I succeeded, the contact between us would have perceptibly been of the sort that exists not in work, but in play. I should have made you understand something that is decisive for me: that my thought has but one object, play, in which my thinking, the working of my thought, dissolves.

Those who have followed my thinking as set forth have realized that it was, in a way that is fundamental, in perpetual rebellion against itself. I shall try today to offer an example of this rebellion on a point which is of prime importance relative to those philosophical considerations which form my point of departure.

I shall, in brief, start with the utterance of a general philosophy which I can offer as my own. I must begin with this statement. It's a very crude philosophy, one which must really seem far too simple, as though a philosopher capable of stating commonplaces of this sort bears no relation to the subtle sort of character now known as a philosopher. For this sort of

The text appeared in English in *October*, 36 (1986), pp. 86–8. Dated 24 November 1952, it is among the papers collected in *OC*, VIII, pp. 210–13.

idea might really be anyone's. I do mean that this thought which appears common to me is my thought. I recall meeting, a long time ago, a young medical intern who held a philosophy of this sort. He never stopped repeating, with an extraordinarily cool self-assurance, one explanatory idea; everything, in his view, came down to the instinct of self-preservation. That was thirty years ago. One is less likely to hear this refrain today. My conception is surely less out of date, and may, despite all, correspond more closely, or somewhat less badly, to the idea of philosophy. It consists in saying that all is play, that being is play, that the idea of God is unwelcome and, furthermore, intolerable, in that God, being situated outside time, can be only play, but is harnessed by human thought to creation and to all the implications of creation, which go contrary to play (to the game).

We find, moreover, in this respect, a blunting of that most ancient register of human thought which remains largely within the idea of play in its consideration of the totality of things. This blunting is, however, by no means peculiar to Christian thought. Plato still considered the sacred action, that very action which religion offers man as a possibility of sharing in the essence of things, as a game. Nevertheless, Christianity, Christian thinking remains the screen separating us from what I shall call the beatific vision of the game.

It seems to me to be our characteristically Christian conception of the world and of man in the world which resists, from the very outset, this thought that all is play.

The possibility of a philosophy of play – this presupposes Christianity. But Christianity is only the spokesman of pain and death. From this point of departure, and given the conditions of space and duration within which being exists, one could see a series of problems arising. To these I shall give no further consideration. Another question arises; if one sets play against the expediency of action, the game in question can be termed a lesser one. The problem: if this is a lesser game, it cannot be made the end of serious action. We cannot, on the other hand, attribute to useful action any end other than that of the game. There is something amiss here.

Let us say that we can take some edge off the game. It is then no longer a game.

The philosophy of play appears, in a manner that is fundamental, to be truth itself, common and indisputable; it is, nevertheless, out of kilter in that we suffer and we die.

The other solution: we can think and be the game, make of the world and of ourselves a game on condition that we look suffering and death in the face. The greater game – more difficult than we think – the dialectic of the master who confronts death. Now, according to Hegel, the master is in error, it is the slave who vanquishes him, but the slave is nonetheless vanquished, and once he has vanquished the master, he is made to conquer himself. He must act not as master, but as rebel. The rebel first wants to eliminate the master, expel him from the world, while he, at the same time, acts as master, since he braves death. The rebel's situation is thus highly equivocal.

Rebellion's essential problem lies in extricating man from the obligation of the slave.

For the master, the game was neither greater nor lesser. The rebel, however, revolting against the game which is neither lesser nor greater, who must reduce the game to the state of a lesser one, must see the necessity of the greater one, which is essentially rebellion against the lesser, the game's limit. Otherwise, it is the lesser man who prevails over reason.

The rebel is thus constrained, because he has had to accept death. He must go to the limit of his revolt; he has certainly not rebelled in order to complete his submission. From this follows the awareness that the worst is a game, a negation of the power of suffering and death – cowardice in the face of this sort of prospect.

I think, though, that this time I have found my way out of the first proposition of a philosophy of play by passing to the game itself [*crossed out*: and no one will be surprised if] I've set a trap.

It thus appears that we extricate ourselves from the philosophy of play, that we reach the point at which knowledge gives way, and that un-knowing then appears as the greater game – the indefinable, that which thought cannot conceive. This is a thought which exists only timidly within me, one which I do not feel apt to sustain. I do think this way, it is true, but in the manner of a coward, like someone who is inwardly raving mad with terror. Still, what can so cowardly a reaction . . .

34

On Nietzsche: The Will to Chance

Enter Giovanni with a heart upon his dagger.
Giovanni: Be not amazed. If you misgiving hearts
Shrink at an idle sight, what bloodless fear
Of coward passion would have seized your senses,
Had you beheld the rape of life and beauty which I have acted! – O,
    my sister!
Florio: Ha! What of her?
Giovanni: The glory of my deed
Darkened the mid-day sun, made noon as night.

John Ford, 'Tis Pity She's a Whore

Do you want to warm yourself near me? I advise you not to come too close; you may singe your hands. For I am much too fiery, you see. I can hardly prevent my body from erupting into flames.

Nietzsche

I

I write, I suppose, out of fear of going mad.

I suffer from a fiery, painful yearning, which persists, like desire unslaked, within me.

My tension is, in a sense, like that of a mad impulse to laughter; it differs little from the passions that inflamed Sade's heroes, and yet it approaches that of the martyrs or of saints . . .

I am certain that what is human in my nature is accentuated by this transport. But it does, I must admit, lead to imbalance and a painful restlessness. I burn, I lose my bearings, and in the end I remain empty. I can set myself large, necessary tasks, but none is commensurate with my fever.

The text is from *October*, 36 (1986), pp. 47–57. This version, dated 1949, is the Preface to *Sur Nietzsche: volonté de chance*, the third volume of the *Somme athéologique*. See *OC*, VI, pp. 7–24.

I am speaking of a moral concern, of the search for an object surpassing all others in value.

This object is, in my eyes, incommensurable with the moral ends usually proposed; those ends seem dull and false. But they are precisely those that might be achieved (are they not determined as requirement of definite acts?). True, the concern with a limited good can sometimes lead to the summit toward which I tend. By a detour, however. The moral end is then distinct from the excess of which it is the occasion. The states of glory, the sacred moments which disclose the incommensurable, exceed the desired results. Common morality places these results on the same plane as the aims of sacrifice. Sacrifice explores the depths within worlds, and its requisite destruction reveals its laceration. But the purpose of celebration is banal. Morality is always concerned with well-being.

(This seemingly changed on that day when God was presented as the sole true end. I am certain that the incommensurable of which I speak will be described, when all is said and done, as merely God's transcendence. In my view, however, this transcendence is a flight from my object. When we replace consideration of the satisfaction of human beings with that of the heavenly Being, nothing is fundamentally changed! The person of God shifts the problem, but does not eliminate it. It merely makes for confusion; being as God can claim at will an incommensurable essence. No matter; one serves God, one acts in his behalf; he is thus reducible to ordinary purpose. Were he to be situated in the beyond, we could not serve his gain.)

II

Man's extreme, unconditional yearning was first expressed independently of a moral end or of service to God by Nietzsche.

Nietzsche is unable precisely to define it, but he is driven by it, he assumes it utterly. This burning with no relation to a dramatically expressed moral obligation is surely paradoxical. It cannot serve as a point of departure for preaching or for action. Its consequences are disconcerting. If we cease to make burning the condition of another, further state, one that is distinguished as good, it appears as a pure state, one of empty consumption. Unless related to some enrichment such as the strength and influence of a community (or of a God, a church, a party), this consumption is not even intelligible. *The positive value of loss can seemingly be conveyed only in terms of profit.*

Of this difficulty, Nietzsche was not clearly aware. He must have realized that he had failed; he knew, in the end, that he had been preaching in the desert. In destroying duty, the good, in denouncing the emptiness and

the life of morality, he destroyed the effective value of language. Fame
came late, and when it came, he had to shut up shop. No one came up to
his expectations. It appears that now we must say: those who read or admire
him flout him (he knew it, he says so). *Except myself?* (I simplify.) But to try,
as he demanded, to follow him is to give oneself up to the same trial, to the
same derangement.

This total liberation, as he defined it, of human possibility, of all possibility, is surely the only one not yet attempted (I repeat: in simplification,
except by myself [?]). At this present point of history, I suppose that out
of all the conceivable doctrines that have been preached, his teaching has,
in some measure, had consequences. Nietzsche, in turn, conceived and
preached a new doctrine; he went in search of disciples, he dreamed of
founding an order; he hated what he got . . . common praise!

I now think it well to declare my confusion; I have tried to draw from
within myself the consequences of a doctrine of clarity, attractive to me
as light; my reward was anguish and the repeated impression of being
overpowered.

III

I could not, at the point of death, in the least ever abandon the aspiration
of which I have spoken. Or rather, this aspiration should not quit me; in
dying I should not keep silence any the more (at least, I think not); I would
wish for those dear to me that they persist or be stricken in turn.

There is in man's essence a violent movement, a will to autonomy, to
freedom. Freedom can surely be understood in several ways, but who,
nowadays, is going to be surprised that one might die for it? The difficulties
Nietzsche encountered – casting off God and the good while fired, nonetheless, with the ardour of those who have died for God and the good –
those difficulties I have, in turn, encountered. The disspiriting solitude he
described has disheartened me. But the break with morality gives to the air
we breathe a truth so great that I should prefer to live as a cripple rather
than relapse into slavery.

IV

I admit that now, at this time of writing, a moral quest which takes as its
object that which is beyond good will, to begin with, miscarries. One has
no assurance of passing the test. This admission, founded in painful experience, justifies my laughter at those who, whether by attacking or by
adopting it, confuse Nietzsche's position with that of Hitler. 'How high is

my abode? Never have I counted the steps while climbing there: where all steps end, there is my roof and my abode.'

Such is the expression of a demand focused on no distinguishable *good*, and which consumes him who lives that demand.

I wish to put an end to this vulgar misunderstanding. To see that thought which has remained ludicrously neglected, and which, for those inspired by it, opens only upon the void, now reduced to the level of propaganda – to see this is horrendous. Nietzsche, according to some, has exerted the greatest influence on our time. This is doubtful; trifling with the laws of morality had begun well before he arrived. He had, above all, no political position. Irritated at being considered as belonging either on the Right or the Left, he refused, when solicited, to choose any party whatsoever. He loathed the idea of subordination to any cause.

His firm opinions on politics date from his break with Wagner, from his disillusionment with Wagner's display of German vulgarity; Wagner the socialist, francophobe, anti-Semite.... The spirit of the second Reich, above all in its pre-Hitlerian tendencies, epitomized in anti-Semitism, is what he despised most. Pan-German propaganda was revolting to him.

And why should I not go all the way? I like to make a clean sweep of things. It is part of my ambition to be considered a despiser of the Germans *par excellence*. My mistrust of the German character I expressed even when I was twenty-six (in the third Untimely One, section 6) – the Germans seem impossible to me. When I imagine a type of man that antagonizes all my instincts, it always turns into a German.[1]

On the political level Nietzsche was, if the truth were known, the prophet, the harbinger of Germany's glaring misadventure. He was the first to denounce it. He loathed the closed, smug, hateful folly which, after 1870, took hold of Germany's mind, and which now exhausts itself in the Hitlerian madness. Never has an entire people been so led astray in mortal error, never so cruelly destined for the abyss. From this mass, doomed in advance, he detached himself, however, refusing to take part in the orgy of 'self-satisfaction'. His inflexibility had consequences. Germany decided to ignore a genius who would not flatter her. Only his reputation abroad belatedly attracted the attention of his countrymen. I know of no finer example of disregard between a man and his country: an entire nation remaining deaf to this voice for fifteen years – isn't that serious? Today, as we witness Germany's ruin, we must wonder that just as she was entering upon the path to disaster, the wisest and most ardent of Germans turned from her in a horror he was unable to restrain. We must, however, recognize on both sides, in both the attempt to flee and in aberration, the dead ends – disarming, is it not?

Nietzsche and Germany, mutually antagonistic, will, in the end, have had the same fate; they were both driven by mad hope, but in vain. Apart from this tragically vain drive, all between them is hatred and destruction. The resemblances are insignificant. Were it not for the habitual jeering at Nietzsche, the transforming of Nietzsche into what most depressed him (a rapid reading, a facile use, made without even rejecting positions inimical to him), his doctrine would be grasped for what it is: the fiercest of solvents. To make him the collaborator in causes devalorized by his thought is to trample upon it, to prove one's ignorance even as one pretends to care for that thought. He who would attempt, as I have done, to go to the limit of the possibility addressed by that doctrine becomes in turn the field of infinite contradiction. He sees, insofar as he would follow this teaching of paradox, that he can no longer embrace an already existent cause, that his solitude is entire.

V

In this hastily written book, I have not developed this point of view theoretically. An effort of that kind might even be vitiated in pedantry. Nietzsche wrote 'with his blood'; to criticize or, better still, to test him, one must bleed in turn.

I wrote in the hope that my book would, if possible, appear on the occasion of the centenary of his birth (15 October 1944). I wrote it between February and August, hoping that the Germans' flight would make publication possible. I began it by theoretically posing the problem (this is the second part), but this short exposition is merely a narrative of life experience: an experience of twenty years, finally full of fear. I find it necessary to clear up a misunderstanding on this subject. Nietzsche is supposedly the philosopher of the 'will to power'; he presented himself as such, and was received as such. I believe him to be rather the philosopher of evil. It is the charm, the *value* of evil in which, I think, he saw the sense of his intention in speaking of power. If this is not so, how else are we to explain this passage?

Spoiling the taste
A: 'You keep spoiling the taste; that is what everybody says.'
B: 'Certainly. I spoil the taste of his party for everyone – and no party forgives that.'[2]

This reflection, one of many, is wholly irreconcilable with the practical, political conduct derived from the principle of the 'will to power'. Nietzsche had an aversion toward that which, in his lifetime, was disposed towards that will; without the taste, or the sense of the necessity for trampling accepted morality, he would no doubt have surrendered to the disgust inspired by the oppressive methods of the police. He justified his hatred of well-being as the very condition of freedom. Personally, although under no illusions as to the consequence of my attitude, I feel myself to be opposed, I *do* oppose, all forms of constraint. For evil is the opposite of constraint, which is exercised, theoretically, for good.

Evil is certainly not what hypocritical misunderstanding has tried to make of it; is it not really concrete freedom, the troubling break with taboo?

I find anarchism irritating, especially the vulgar doctrine which provides apology for the common criminal. The practices of the Gestapo, as clearly revealed, demonstrate the deep affinity between the police and the criminal mob: no one is more apt to torture, to serve the cruel apparatus of constraint than faithless, lawless men. I hate even those weak and confused minds for whom all rights are the privilege of the individual. The individual is limited not only by the rights of other individuals, but, more strictly, by those of the people. All men are bound to the people, all share their conquests or sufferings; all are of the fibre of the living mass (and no less alone in moments of gravity).

I believe that we freely overcome the major difficulties involved in the individual's opposition to the collective, of good and evil, and, in general, of those mad contradictions ordinarily escaped only by denial, by a stroke of chance, obtained in the boldness of play. The depression felt by life lived at the limits of the possible cannot exclude the passing of chance. What cannot be resolved by the wisdom of logic may perhaps be accomplished by a recklessness unbounded. unhesitating, which does not look back. That is why it is only *with my life* than I could write this projected book on Nietzsche in which I wanted if possible to solve the inner problem of morality.

Thus it is only in my life and through its paltry resources that I have found myself able to pursue that quest of that Grail which is chance. And chance has proved to correspond more closely than does power to Nietzsche's intentions. Only in 'play' could possibility be deeply explored, with no prejudging of results, with the future alone enjoying the fullness of time, the power usually invested in the firm decision which is merely a form of the past. My book is partly the day-to-day account of the casting of dice, performed, really, with very modest resources. I offer my apology for what is, in this present year, the really comic aspect of private life brought into play by these pages of my diary. I do not suffer through them; I willingly laugh at myself and know of no better way to lose myself in immanence.

VI

Although to be laughable and knowing myself to be so is to my taste. I cannot carry this to the point of misleading my reader. The problem essential to this (necessarily) disorderly book is that experienced by Nietzsche, the problem he aimed to solve in his work: that of the whole man.

'Most men', he wrote,

> represent pieces and fragments of man: one has to add them up for a complete man to appear. Whole ages, whole peoples are in this sense somewhat fragmentary; it is perhaps part of the economy of human evolution that man should evolve piece by piece. But that should not make one forget for a moment that the real issue is the production of the synthetic man, that lower men, the tremendous majority, are merely preludes and rehearsals out of whose medley the whole man appears here and there, the milestone man who indicates how humanity has advanced so far.[3]

But what does this fragmentation mean, or, better still, what is its cause, if not this need to act which specializes and limits the horizon to a given activity? Even if performed in the general interest (and this is rarely the case), activity which subordinates each instant of our lives to some precise result effaces the individual's total character. Whoever acts substitutes for that reason-for-being which he himself is as totality a given purpose of, a particular sort in the least specious of cases, the greatness of a state, the triumph of a party. All action is specializing in that all action is limited. A plant is not usually active, is not specialized; it is specialized when swallowing flies!

I can exist totally only by transcending in some way the stage of action. Otherwise I become soldier, professional revolutionary, scholar – not 'the whole man'. Man's fragmentary state is, essentially, the same thing as the choice of an object. When a man limits his desires, for example, to the possession of power within the state, he acts, he knows what has to be done. It matters little if he fails; he profits from the outset. He inserts himself advantageously within time. Each of his moments becomes *useful*. It becomes possible for him to advance, with each passing instant, toward his chosen goal. His time becomes a progression toward this goal (that is what we usually call living). Similarly, if his object is his own salvation. Every action makes of man a fragmentary being. Only by refusing to act, or at least by denying the pre-eminence of the time reserved for action, can I maintain the quality of wholeness within myself.

Life remains whole only when not subordinated to a precise object which transcends it. Totality in this sense is essentially freedom. I cannot try to attain a wholeness simply by fighting for freedom. Even though that battle is preferable above all other action, I must not confuse my struggle with inner wholeness. It is the positive exercise of freedom, not the negative struggle against a particular form of oppression which has raised me above a mutilated existence. Each of us learns the bitter lesson that to fight for his freedom means, first of all, to alienate it.

As I have stated, the exercise of freedom has its place on the side of evil, while the fight for freedom is the conquest of *good*. Insofar as life is whole within me, I cannot, without dividing it, engage it in the service of a good, whether that of someone else, of God, or of my own. I cannot acquire, but only give, and give without reckoning, without a gift ever having, as its object, another's *interest*. (I see the good of another as a kind of decoy, for if I wish the good of another, it is in order to find my own, unless I identify it with my own. Totality within myself is this exuberance: it is only an empty yearning, the unhappy desire to be consumed for no reason other than desire itself – which it wholly is – to burn. Thus it is that desire for laughter of which I have spoken, that itch for pleasure, for saintliness, for death . . . It has no further task to fulfil.)

VII

A problem this strange can be understood only through experience. Its sense is easily contested; we can say that we're faced with an infinity of tasks. Precisely now, at the present time. No one dreams of denying the facts. It is still true that the question of man's totality – as inevitable end – now arises, and for two reasons. The first is negative: specialization is emphasized on all sides to an alarming degree. As to the second, tasks of an overwhelming nature are nevertheless in our time seen within their exact limits.

The horizon was once dark. The object of grave import was first the city's well-being, but the city was one with the gods. The next object was the soul's salvaton. Action was aimed, on the one hand, at a limited, understandable goal and, on the other hand, at a totality defined as inaccessible down here (transcendent). Action under modern conditions has precise goals, entirely adequate to possibility; man's totality no longer has a mythical character. Clearly accessible, it is consigned to the accomplishment of tasks materially set and defined. It is distant (these tasks, in dominating the mind, fragment consciousness) but it is, nonetheless, discernible.

This totality, aborted within us by the need to work, is nonetheless provided in this work. Not as a goal (the goal is to change the world, to adjust it to man's measure) but as an ineluctable result. At the end of this change, the man-attached-to-the-task-of-changing-the-world, who is but a fragment of man, will himself be changed into whole-man. This result seems distant for humanity, but it is specified in the *defined* task; it is not transcendent, like the gods (the sacred city), or the soul's survival; it is immanent to the attached-man . . . We can put off thinking of it; it is close nevertheless. Although men cannot be clearly aware of it in common existence, they are separated from this notion neither by being men (and not gods) nor by not being dead; it is a temporary necessity.

So must a man in battle 'temporarily' think only of reducing the enemy. There is surely no fierce combat which does not allow for the introduction, during moments of calm, of peaceful concerns. But immediately, these preoccupations seem minor. The tough-minded allow for these moments of relaxation and see to it that their gravity is dispelled. They are in one sense mistaken; is not gravity really the cause of bloodshed? But it makes no difference; it is necessary that the blood be serious, it is necessary that the free life, without struggle, unfragmented and detached from the necessity of action, appear in the guise of frivolity. In a world delivered from gods, from the concern with salvation, 'tragedy' is a mere distraction – relaxation dominated by goals directed only toward activity.

This mode of entry – by the back door – into man's reason-for-being does have several advantages. The whole man is, in this way, revealed first in immanence, on the level of a frivolous life. We must laugh at him, even though he be tragic, deeply so. This perspective is liberating; the utmost simplicity, nudity are his. I feel sincere gratitude toward those whose posture of gravity and whose life, near to death, define me as a man of emptiness, a dreamer. (I sometimes take their part.) Essentially, man is only a being in whom transcendence is cancelled, no longer separate from anything: part puppet, part god, part madman . . . this is transparency.

VIII

The accomplishment of my totality in consciousness requires my relation to the immense, comic, painful convulsion which is that of all men. This is a movement in all directions and all senses.[4] This incoherence is surely traversed by meaningful action in a definite direction, but it is precisely this that is responsible for humanity's fragmentary character in my own time (as in the past). Forgetting for a moment this defined sense, I see rather the Shakespearean, tragi-comic sum of vagaries, madness, lies, pain and laughter; I begin to understand totality, but as a rending movement; all existence is now beyond sense; it is man's conscious presence in the world insofar as he is nonsense, with nothing to do but be what he is, unable to transcend himself to take on sense or direction in action.

This awareness of totality is related to two antithetical uses of a single expression. *Non-sense* is usually a simple negation, it is what we say of an object that is to be eliminated. The intent which rejects that which is lacking in sense (or direction) is really the rejection of being whole; it is insofar as we reject it that we remain unaware of the totality of being with ourselves. But if I say *non-sense* while searching, on the contrary, for an object free of sense, I deny nothing, I utter the affirmation in which *all of life* is finally revealed in consciousness.

The tending toward this consciousness of a totality, toward this total amity of man with himself is quite correctly held to be fundamentally lacking in gravity. In following this path, I become absurd. I take on the inconsistency of all men, considered generally, bracketing that which leads to major changes. I would not account in this way for Nietzsche's sickness (insofar as it seems to have been of somatic origin); nevertheless it is true that the movement toward wholeness begins as madness. I cast off good, I cast off reason (sense), I open beneath my feet the abyss from which action and its consequent judgements have separated me. At the very least the consciousness of totality begins in despair and inner crisis. When I abandon the framework of action, my perfect nakedness is revealed to me. I am without recourse in the world, without support, I collapse. There is no possible outcome other than an endless incoherence in which chance is my only guide.

IX

An experience so disarming is obviously to be made only when all others have been tried and completed, when all possibilities have been exhausted. It is, consequently, only in extremis that it can become the action of humanity as a whole. It is, in our time, accessible to only a very isolated individual, through mental disorder conjoined with unquestionable vigour. He can, if chance is with him, discern in incoherence an unforeseen balance. Since this divine state of balance expresses in the bold simplicity of its ceaseless play the discordance, the imbalance of the dancing equilibrist, I take it to be inaccessible to the 'will to power'. In my understanding, the 'will to power', considered as a goal, means a return to the past. In following it, I should be returning to the bondage of fragmentation, accepting once again duty and the good, be dominated by power. Divine exuberance, the lightness expressed in Zarathustra's laughter and his dance, would be lost; in place of the joy in suspension over the abyss,

I should be inseparably bound by gravity, by the servility of strength through joy.

If we set aside the 'will to power', the destiny conferred by Nietzsche upon man places him beyond anguish; no return to the past is possible, and that is the source of the doctrine's deep inviability. In the notes to *The Will to Power*, projected action, the temptation of formulation of goals and politics merely end in a labyrinth. The last completed text, *Ecce Homo*, declares the absence of goal, the author's insubordination to a plan of any kind. Nietzsche's work, seen from the perspective of action, is an abortion – a strongly defensible one; his life is a failed life, like that which attempts to put his writing into action.

X

Let no one doubt for an instant! One has truly not heard a single world of Nietzsche's unless one has lived this signal dissolution in totality; without it, this philosophy is a mere labyrinth of contradictions, and worse; the pretext for lying by omission (if, like the fascists, one isolates passages for purposes which negate the rest of the work). I wish at this point to be particularly attended to. The foregoing criticism is the masked form of approval. It is a justification of that definition of the whole man: 'the man whose life is an unmotivated feast'; it celebrates, in every sense of the word, a laughter, a dance, an orgy which knows no subordination, a sacrifice heedless of purpose, material or moral.

The foregoing introduces the necessity of dissociation. Extreme states of being, whether individual or collective, were once purposefully motivated. Some of those purposes no longer have meaning (expiation, salvation). The well-being of communities is no longer sought through means of doubtful effectiveness, but directly, through action. Under these conditions, extreme states of being fell into the domain of the arts, and not without a certain disadvantage. Literature (fiction) took the place of what had formerly been the spiritual life; poetry (the disorder of words) that of real states of trance. Art constituted a small free domain, outside action: to gain freedom it had to renounce the real world. This is a heavy price to pay, and most writers dream of recovering that lost reality. They must then pay in another sense, by renouncing freedom in the service of propaganda. The artist who restricts himself to fiction knows that he is not a whole man, but the same is true of the writer of propaganda. The domain of the arts does, in a sense, embrace totality, which nevertheless escapes it.

Nietzsche is far from having resolved the difficulty. Zarathustra is also a poet, and a literary fiction at that! Only he refused ever to accept. Praise exasperated him. He thrashed about in all directions, seeking a way out. He never lost that Ariadne's thread which means *having no goal* to serve, no cause; he knew that a cause clips one's *wings*. But, on the other hand, lack of a cause casts one out into solitude; it means the sickness of the desert, a cry dying away in a vast silence . . .

The understanding which I solicit leads surely to the same point of no exit; it implies the same fervent torture. I believe that we must, in this sense, reverse the idea of the Eternal Return. Our anguish derives, not from the promise of infinite repetition, but from the following: the moments grasped within the immanence of return suddenly appear as ends. Remember that *in all systems* those instants are considered and assigned as means: morality always says: 'let every instant of your life be *motivated*'. The Return *de-motivates* the instant, frees life from purpose and is thereby, first of all, its downfall. The Return is the whole man's dramatic mode and his mask; it is the desert of a man whose every instant is henceforward unmotivated.

There is no point in seeking an expedient; one must choose at last between the desert and a mutilation. Affliction cannot be disposed of like a package. Suspended in a void, my extreme moments are followed by depression wholly unrelieved by hope. When I nevertheless arrive at a clear awareness of what is thus lived, I cannot look for an exit where none exists. (I have therefore insisted on my criticism.) How can we not draw the consequences of the purposelessness inherent in Nietzsche's desire? Chance – and the quest of chance – represents inexorably the sole remaining recourse (whose vicissitudes are described in this book).

If it is true that the man of action cannot, in the generally understood sense, be a whole man, the whole man does retain a possibility of action. On condition that action is reduced to principles and to goals which are his own (in a word, to reason). The whole man cannot be transcended (dominated) by action; he would lose his totality. He cannot, on the other hand, transcend action (subordinate it to his purpose); he thereby defines himself as a motive, entering and being annihilated in the machinery of motivation. We must distinguish between the world of motives, in which each thing has sense (rational) and the world of non-sense (free of all sense). Each of us belongs partly to one, partly to the other. We can distinguish clearly and consciously that which is bound only in ignorance. Reason can, in my view, be limited only by herself. If we act, we wander beyond the motives of equity and the rational action. Between these two domains, there is only one acceptable relation: action must be rationally limited by a principle of freedom.[5]

The rest is silence.

Notes

1 Friedrich Nietzsche, *Ecce Homo*, ed. and tr. Walter Kaufmann (Vintage, New York, 1967), pp. 322–3.

2 Friedrich Nietzsche, *The Gay Science*, tr. Walter Kaufmann (Random House, New York, 1974), p. 201.
3 Friedrich Nietzsche, *The Will to Power*, tr. Walter Kaufmann and R. J. Hollingdale (Vintage, New York, 1968), pp. 470–1.
4 [Bataille's use of the word *sens*, as meaning both 'direction' and 'sense', establishes the basis for discourse on sense and non-sense. TR].
5 The share of fire, of madness, of the whole man – the rejected share – accorded (conceded from without) by reason, in line with liberal and reasonable norms. This means the condemnation of capitalism as an irrational mode of activity. As soon as the whole man (his irrationality) sees himself as outside of action, when he recognizes all possibilities of transcendence as traps and as loss of his totality, we give up irrational domination (feudal, capitalist) in the sphere of action. Nietzsche no doubt foresaw the necessity of its abandon without discerning the cause. The whole man becomes possible only if he refrains from positing himself as the end or object of others; he enslaves himself if he goes past those limits, restricting himself to the limits of feudalism or of the bourgeoisie, short of freedom. Nietzsche, it is true, still insisted on social transcendence, on hierarchy. To say that there is nothing sacred in immanence means the following; that which was sacred must no longer serve. The advent of freedom means the advent of laughter: 'To witness the fall of tragic natures and to be able to laugh . . .' (Would we dare to apply this proposition to current events? instead of committing ourselves to new moral transcendences . . .) In freedom, abandon, the immanence of laughter, Nietzsche did away in advance with that which still linked him (his youthful immoralism) to vulgar forms of transcendence – which are forms of enslaved freedom. The bias in favour of evil is that of freedom, 'the freedom from all constraint'.

Bibliography

Georges Bataille in English Translation

Books

Literature and Evil [1957], tr. Alastair Hamilton (Calder and Boyars, London, 1973).

Blue of Noon [c.1935; pub. 1957], tr. Harry Matthews (Marion Boyars, London, 1979).

Story of the Eye [1928], tr. Joachim Neugroschal (Penguin, Harmondsworth, 1982).

L'Abbé C [1950], tr. Philip A. Facey (Marion Boyars, London, 1983).

Visions of Excess: selected writings, 1927–1939, ed. Allan Stoekl, tr. Allan Stoekl with Carl R. Lovitt and Donald M. Leslie, Jr (University of Minnesota Press, Minneapolis, MN 1985).

Erotism: death and sensuality [1957], tr. Mary Dalwood (City Lights, San Fransisco, CA, 1986).

The Accursed Share, vol. I, Consumption [1967], tr. Robert Hurley (Zone Books, New York, 1988).

Inner Experience [1954], tr. Leslie Anne Boldt (SUNY Press, New York, 1988).

Guilty [1961], tr. Bruce Boone (The Lapis Press, San Francisco, CA, 1988).

My Mother [1966], *Madame Edwarda* [1956], *The Dead Man* [1967], tr. Austryn Wainhouse (Marion Boyars, London, 1989).

The Tears of Eros [1961], tr. Peter, Connor (City Lights, San Francisco, CA, 1989).

The Impossible [1962], tr. Robert Hurley (City Lights, San Francisco, CA, 1991).

The Trial of Gilles de Rais [1965], tr. Richard Robinson (Amok, Los Angeles, CA, 1991).

The Accursed Share, vol. II, The History of Eroticism; vol. III, Sovereignty [1976], tr. Robert Hurley (Zone Books, New York, 1991).

On Nietzsche [1945], tr. Bruce Boone (Paragon House, New York, 1992).

Theory of Religion [1973], tr. Robert Hurley (Zone Books, New York, 1992).

The Absence of Myth: writings on surrealism, ed. and tr. Michael Richardson (Verso, London, 1994).

Encyclopaedia Acephalica ed. Georges Bataille [*Documents*, 1929, 1930], assembled and introduced by Alastair Brotchie, biographies by Dominique Lecoq, tr. Iain White (Atlas Press, London, 1995).

Articles

'On Hiroshima', tr. R. Raziel, *Politics*, 4 (1947), pp. 147–50.

'The psychological structure of fascism', tr. Carl R. Lovitt, *New German Critique*, 16 (1979), pp. 64–87.

'Extinct America' [1928], 'Slaughterhouse' [1929], 'Smokestack' [1929], 'Human face' [1929], 'Metamorphosis' [1929], 'Museum' [1930], 'Counterattack: call to action' [1936], 'The threat of war', 'Additional notes on the war', 'Toward real revolution' [1936], 'Nietzsche's madness' [1939], 'On Nietzsche: the will to chance' [1949], 'Van Gogh as Prometheus' [1937], 'Sacrifice' [1939–40], 'Celestial bodies' [1938], 'Programme (relative to *Acéphale*)' [1936], 'Un-knowing and its consequences' [1951], 'Un-knowing and rebellion' [1952], 'Un-knowning: laughter and tears' [1953], 'The ascent of Mount Aetna' [1939], 'Autobiographical note' [1958], *October*, 36 (1986), pp. 1–110.

'Hegel, death and sacrifice' [1955], tr. Jonathan Strauss, *Yale French Studies*, 78 (1990), pp. 9–28.

'Letter to René Char on the incompatibilities of the writer' [1950], tr. Christopher Carsen, *Yale French Studies*, 78 (1990), pp. 31–43.

'The reasons for writing a book . . .', tr. Elizabeth Rottenberg, *Yale French Studies*, 79 (1991), p. 11.

'Reflections on the executioner and the victim' [1947], tr. Elizabeth Rottenberg, *Yale French Studies*, 79 (1991), pp. 15–19.

Critical Writing on Bataille in English

Roland Barthes, 'The metaphor of the eye', in Georges Bataille, *The Story of the Eye* (Penguin, Harmondsworth, 1982), pp. 119–27.

Jean Baudrillard, 'When Bataille attacked the metaphysical principle of economy', tr. David James Miller, *Canadian Journal of Political and Social Theory*, 15 (1991), pp. 63–6. Reprinted in *Bataille: a critical reader*, eds Fred Botting and Scott Wilson (Blackwell, Oxford, 1997).

——, 'Death in Bataille', in *Symbolic Exchange and Death*, tr. Iain Hamilton Grant with an Introduction by Mike Gane (Sage, London, 1993), pp. 154–8. Reprinted in *Bataille: a critical reader*, eds Fred Botting and Scott Wilson (Blackwell, Oxford, 1997).

Jean-Michel Besnier, 'Georges Bataille in the 1930s: a politics of the impossible', *Yale French Studies*, 78 (1990), pp. 169–80.

Maurice Blanchot, 'The negative community', in *The Unavowable Community*, tr. Pierre Joris (Station Hill Press, Barrytown, NY, 1988), pp. 1–26.

Leslie Anne Boldt-Irons (ed.), *Bataille: critical essays* (SUNY Press, Albany, NY, 1995).

Mikkel Borch-Jacobsen, 'The laughter of being', *Modern Language Notes*, 102 (1987), pp. 737–60. Reprinted in *Bataille: a critical reader*, eds Fred Botting and Scott Wilson (Blackwell, Oxford, 1997).

Fred Botting, 'Relations of the real in Lacan, Bataille and Blanchot', *Substance*, 73 (1994), pp. 24–40.

——, 'Signs of evil: Bataille, Baudrillard and postmodern Gothic', *Southern*

Review, 27 (1994), pp. 493–510.
—— and Scott Wilson, 'Literature as heterological practice: Georges Bataille, writing and inner experience', *Textual Practice*, 7 (1993), pp. 195–207.

David Carroll, 'Disruptive discourse and critical power: the conditions of archaeology and genealogy', *Humanities in Society*, 5 (1982), pp. 175–200.

Rebecca Comay, 'Gifts without presents: economies of "experience" in Bataille and Heidegger', *Yale French Studies*, 78 (1990), pp. 66–89.

Carolyn J. Dean, *The Self and its Pleasures: Bataille, Lacan, and the history of the decentered subject* (Cornell University Press, Ithaca, NY, and London, 1992).

Jacques Derrida, 'From restricted and general economy: a Hegelianism without reserve', in *Writing and Difference*, tr. Alan Bass (Routledge and Kegan Paul, London, 1985). Reprinted in *Bataille: a critical reader*, eds Fred Botting and Scott Wilson (Blackwell, Oxford, 1997).

Joseph C. Flay, 'Hegel, Derrida and Bataille's laughter', in *Hegel and his Critics*, ed. William Desmond (SUNY Press, Albany, NY, 1989), pp. 163–73.

Michel Foucault, 'Preface to transgression', in *Language, Counter-Memory, Practice*, ed. Donald F. Bouchard, tr. Donald F. Bouchard and Sherry Simon, (Cornell University Press, Ithaca, NY, 1977). Reprinted in *Bataille: a critical reader*, eds Fred Botting and Scott Wilson (Blackwell, Oxford, 1997).

Marina Galletti, '*Masses*: A Failed *College?*', *Stanford French Review*, 12 (1988), pp. 49–73.

Jane Gallop, *Intersections: a reading of Sade with Bataille, Blanchot and Klossowski* (University of Nebraska Press, Lincoln, NB, and London, 1981).

Carolyn Bailey Gill (ed.), *Bataille: writing the sacred* (Routledge, London, 1994).

Jean-Joseph Goux, 'General economics and postmodern capitalism', tr. Kathryn Ascheim and Rhonda Garelick, *Yale French Studies*, 78 (1990), pp. 206–24. Reprinted in *Bataille: a critical reader*, eds Fred Botting and Scott Wilson (Blackwell, Oxford, 1997).

Suzanne Guerlac, '"Recognition" by a woman!: a reading of Bataille's *L'Erotisme*', *Yale French Studies*, 78 (1990), pp. 90–105.

Jürgen Habermas, 'The French path to postmodernity: Bataille between eroticism and general economics', tr. Frederic Lawrence, *New German Critique*, 33 (1984), pp. 79–102. Reprinted in *Bataille: a critical reader*, eds Fred Botting and Scott Wilson (Blackwell, Oxford, 1997).

Jean-Michel Heimonet, 'From Bataille to Derrida: *Différance* and Heterology', tr. A. Engstrom, *Stanford French Review*, 12 (1988), pp. 129–47.

——, 'Recoil in order to leap forward: two values of Sade in Bataille's text', tr. Joanicho Kohchi, *Yale French Studies*, 78 (1990), pp. 227–36.

Denis Hollier, 'Bataille's tomb: a Halloween story', tr. Richard Miller, *October*, 33 (1985), pp. 73–102.

—— (ed.), *The College of Sociology*, tr. Betsy Wing (University of Minnesota Press, Minneapolis, MN, 1988).

——, 'January 21st', tr. Mark W. Andrews, *Stamford French Review*, 12 (1988), pp. 31–47.

——, *Against Architecture: the writings of Georges Bataille*, tr. Betsy Wing (MIT Press, London, 1989).

——, 'Bloody Sundays', tr. Betsy Wing, *Representations*, 28 (1989), pp. 77–89.

——, 'The dualist materialism of Georges Bataille', tr. A. Hilari, *Yale French Studies*, 78 (1990), pp. 124–39. Reprinted in *Bataille: a critical reader*, eds Fred Botting and Scott Wilson (Blackwell, Oxford, 1997).

——, 'On equivocation (between literature and politics)', tr. Roslaind Krauss, *October*, 55 (1990), pp. 3–22.

——, 'The use-value of the impossible', *October*, 60 (1992), pp. 1–25.

Rosalind Krauss, 'Antivision', *October*, 36 (1986), pp. 147–54.

Marie-Christine Lala, 'The conversions of writing in Georges Bataille's *L'Impossible*', tr. Robert Livingston, *Yale French Studies*, 78 (1990), pp. 237–45.

Nick Land, *The Thirst for Annihilation* (Routledge, London, 1992).

Charles Larmore, 'Bataille's heterology', *Semiotext(e)*, 2 (1976), pp. 87–104.

John Lechte, 'An introduction to Bataille: the impossible as (a practice of) writing', *Textual Practice*, 7 (1993), pp. 173–94.

Michel Leiris, 'From the impossible Bataille to the impossible *Documents*', in *Brisées*, tr. Lydia Davis (North Point Press, San Francisco, 1989), pp. 237–47.

Joseph Libertson, 'Bataille and communication: from heterogeneity to continuity', *Modern Language Notes*, 89 (1974), pp. 669–98.

Jean-François Lyotard, *Libidinal Economy*, tr. Iain Hamilton Grant (Athlone Press, London, 1993).

Pierre Macherey, 'Georges Bataille: materialism inverted', in *The Object of Literature* (Cambridge University Press, Cambridge, 1995), pp. 112–31.

Annette Michelson, 'Heterology and the critique of instrumental reason', *October*, 36 (1986), pp. 111–27.

Jean-Luc Nancy, *The Inoperative Community*, tr. Peter Connor, Lisa Garbus, Michael Holland and Simona Sawhney (University of Minnesota Press, Minneapolis, MN, 1991).

——, 'The unsacrificable', *Yale French Studies*, 79 (1991), pp. 20–38.

——, 'Exscription', in *The Birth to Presence* (Stanford University Press, Stanford, CA, 1993), pp. 47–65.

Julian Pefanis, 'The issue of Bataille', in *Postmodern Conditions*, eds Andrew Milner, Philip Thomson and Chris Worth (Berg, New York, Oxford, Munich, 1990), pp. 133–55.

——, *Heterology and the Postmodern: Bataille, Baudrillard and Lyotard* (Duke University Press, Durham, NC, 1991).

Arkady Plotnitsky, *Reconfigurations: critical theory and general economy* (University of Florida Press, Gainsville, FL, 1993).

——, *Complementarity* (Duke University Press, Durham, NC, 1994).

Franco Rella, *The Myth of the Other: Lacan, Deleuze, Foucault, Bataille* (Maisonneuve Press, Washington, DC, 1993).

Michèle Richman, *Beyond the Gift: reading Georges Bataille* (The Johns Hopkins University Press, Baltimore, MD, 1982).

——, 'Introduction to the Collège de sociologie: poststructuralism before its time?', *Stanford French Review*, 12 (1988), pp. 79–95.

——, 'Bataille moralist? *Critique* and the postwar writings', *Yale French Studies*,

78 (1990), pp. 143–68.

Lawrence R. Schehr, 'Bataille and philosophical catachresis', *Stanford French Review* 12 (1988), pp. 97–117.

Steven Shapiro, *Passion and Excess: Blanchot, Bataille and literary theory*, (Florida State University Press, Tallahassee, FL, 1990).

Philippe Sollers, 'The roof from *Writing and the Experience of Limits* (Columbia University Press, New York, 1983). Reprinted in *Bataille: a critical reader*, eds Fred Botting and Scott Wilson (Oxford, Blackwell, 1997).

Allan Stoekl, 'The death of *Acéphale* and the will to chance: Nietzsche in the text of Bataille', *Glyph*, 6, Johns Hopkins Textual Studies (Johns Hopkins University Press, Baltimore, MD, and London, 1979), pp. 42–67.

——, *Politics, Writing, Mutilation: the cases of Bataille, Blanchot, Roussel, Leiris and Ponge* (University of Minnesota Press, Minneapolis, MN, 1985).

——, 'Hegel's return', *Stanford French Review*, 12 (1988), pp. 119–28.

——, 'Truman's apotheosis: Bataille, "planisme", headlessness', *Yale French Studies*, 78 (1990), pp. 181–205.

Susan Rubin Suleiman, 'Pornography, transgression and the avant-garde: Bataille's story of the eye', in *The Poetics of Gender*, ed. Nancy K. Miller (Columbia University Press, NY, 1986), pp. 117–38.

Steven Ungar, 'Phantom Lascaux: origin of the work of art', *Yale French Studies*, 78 (1990), pp. 246–62.

Allen S. Weiss, 'Impossible sovereignty: between *The Will to Chance* and *The Will to Power*', *October*, 36 (1986), pp. 129–46.

Scott Wilson, 'Heterology', in *The Merchant of Venice*, ed. Nigel Wood (Open University Press, Buckingham, 1996), pp. 124–68.

Index

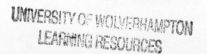